The Eucharistic Vision of *Laudato Si'*

The Eucharistic Vision of *Laudato Si'*
Praise, Conversion, and Integral Ecology

Lucas Briola

The Catholic University of America Press
Washington, D.C.

Copyright © 2023
The Catholic University of America Press
All rights reserved

Cataloging in Publication data available from the Library of Congress ISBN: 9780813235813
eISBN: 9780813235820

Contents

Acknowledgments vii

Introduction 1

Part 1: Toward a Eucharistic Vision of Care for Our Common Home 19

    Chapter 1. The Unfulfilled Potential of a Eucharistic Turn 21

    Chapter 2. The Integral Ecology of *Laudato Si'* 63

Part 2: Toward a Eucharistic Theology of History 105

    Chapter 3. A Theory of Redemptive Agency for the Church's Mission 107

    Chapter 4. The Integral Scale of Values and the Eucharist 155

Part 3: A Eucharistic Vision of Care for Our Common Home within a Eucharistic Theology of History 189

    Chapter 5. A Eucharistic Integral Ecology 191

Conclusion: Receiving the Eucharistic Vision of *Laudato Si'* 237

Bibliography 243

Index 273

Acknowledgments

> What do you have that you did not receive? And if you received it, why do you boast as if it were not a gift? (1 Cor 4:7)

The Eucharistic vision of *Laudato Si'* invites its readers to receive the gift of all creation in praise. This book is itself the product of many gifts that I have received from others. I thank Drs. William Loewe, Christopher Ruddy, and David Cloutier, who helped me lay the foundation for this study in my dissertation research. I hope this book mirrors the charity, intelligence, and holiness with which they have gifted me in their work and their lives. I also thank Msgr. Paul McPartlan as well as Drs. Eric Mabry and Brian Bajzek, for having invited me to present portions of this project in academic settings. So too am I grateful to *Theological Studies* and Marquette University Press for allowing revised portions of previous writings to appear here.[1]

I have been gifted with wonderful support from priests throughout my life, including in this project. I thank Fr. Robert Doran for his generous support throughout the project. It was he who helped me find my Lonergan voice, granting me the confidence to apply Lonergan's pastoral vision to contemporary ecclesiological questions. I am saddened that his recent passing will not allow him to read this book; at the very least, I hope this book helps further his theological legacy. I also thank Fr. Dave Poecking, whose pastoral example and academic brilliance—and willingness to employ me in graduate school—has helped me weave together the pastoral and theological in a way that I hope is captured in this book. Conversations with Msgr. Kevin Irwin have greatly enriched my understanding of *Laudato Si'*, and I am grateful for his time. Finally, I thank Fr. Nathan Munsch, OSB, whose spiritual support, friendship, and holy witness to my family have provided grace upon grace.

---

[1] Lucas Briola, "Praise Rather Than Solving Problems: Understanding the Doxological Turn of *Laudato Si'* through Lonergan," *Theological Studies* 81, no. 3 (September 2020): 693–716; and Lucas Briola, "Responding to the One Cry of Earth and Poor: An Integral Ecology, the Scale of Values, and Eucharistic Healing," in *Everything Is Interconnected: Toward a Globalization with a Human Face and an Integral Ecology*, ed. Joseph Ogbonnaya and Lucas Briola, 119–35 (Milwaukee, Wis.: Marquette University Press, 2019).

I have also been gifted with insightful conversation partners—both teachers and peers—throughout my theological journey, conversations that cannot but shape the words of this book. I especially thank Ben Hohman who agreed to read an earlier draft of this book, offering most thoughtful feedback and encouragement. I also thank my faithful friend Justin Petrovich for reading through drafts of this project, ensuring its writing remain accessible. Departmental work-study Elizabeth Elin helped catch typos through her meticulous proofreading of the entire manuscript; for that laborious task, I thank her profusely. I am grateful to John Martino, The Catholic University of America Press staff, and the two anonymous reviewers for encouraging me in this project and improving its final form. I also thank Michele Callaghan for her expert copy editing of the manuscript.

Saint Vincent College first instilled my love of theology and has gifted me with a sense of home for a long time. I am grateful for the unfailing support of my colleagues in the theology department, especially Patty Sharbaugh and Jason King. I am especially thankful to the chair of my department, Chris McMahon, who has mentored me since my freshman year in college and continues to do so throughout today with patience. I also thank the Saint Vincent College administration for their support, especially Fr. Paul Taylor, OSB, and Br. Norman Hipps, OSB. So too am I eternally grateful for the spiritual support of Saint Vincent Archabbey and the many holy friendships that I have discovered there.

I thank my shoulder companion in graduate studies, Rob Ryan, whose sudden death continues to shock the many people who loved him. This project crystallizes the many gifts he provided me: our heated arguments, mutual moments of discovery, and, most importantly, our worship and prayer together. The gift of his never-forgotten presence pervades these pages.

My wife, Catherine, remains the greatest gift of my life. Her patience with, attentiveness to, and support of me has been truly paschal. Her brilliance and love of biblical wisdom has been truly inspiring. Her deep love of God has been truly holy. I pray every day that I can at least begin to gift her with the same love that she has shown me. It has been my life's greatest joy to welcome our gift, Nathan, with her; perhaps one day he will read this book.

Finally, my parents serve as daily reminders that my life is itself a gift. They have gifted me with bottomless love. They have gifted me with a love of learning and, by extension, a love of God. Above all, they have gifted me with their trust in having allowed me to study theology, even when they did not understand why. To them I dedicate this book, a fruit of this gift.

that God may be glorified in all things through Jesus Christ (1 Pt 4:11)

June 16, 2022
Feast of Corpus Christi

Introduction

In the summer of 2015, I served as a pastoral assistant for my home Catholic parish in a blue-collar, former mill town outside of Pittsburgh. At that time, Pope Francis promulgated his highly anticipated social encyclical, *Laudato Si': On Care for Our Common Home*, in which he urged the church to promote an "integral ecology."[1] The encyclical impressed upon me the profound connections between care for our common home and themes that I easily recognized as distinctive markers of Catholic identity, whether it be the protection of all human life (especially the unborn) or eucharistic worship. It precipitated a veritable conversion for me, one that Pope Francis would qualify as "ecological."[2] I was so enthralled by the urgency, profundity, and veracity of the encyclical that, with the urging of my pastor, I promptly organized a class on *Laudato Si'* at the parish. I hoped to establish for my friends that, as Francis echoed Pope John Paul II, "Living our vocation to be protectors of God's handiwork is *essential* to a life of virtue" and "is *not* an optional or a secondary aspect of our Christian experience."[3]

To my surprise, the presentation provoked considerable resistance. While some parishioners embraced the encyclical's message with enthusiasm, others contested the pope's affirmation that the acceleration of global warming is indeed partly the work of human hands.[4] Some worried that the reforms proposed by Francis would endanger the jobs in coal mining and the steel industry that have sustained the region and its families for generations (my own maternal grandfather mined coal and died of black lung in the 1970s, while my father and paternal grandfather each spent time working in steel factories). For others, in an area where being a Catholic often presumes a certain partisan persuasion, the ostensibly progressive proposals of *Laudato Si'* simply did not cohere with preexisting patterns of thought. The

---

[1] Francis, Encyclical Letter *Laudato Si'* (May 24, 2015), chap. 4.

[2] *Laudato Si'*, 217. As the encyclical also notes, John Paul II first employed the term *ecological conversion*. *Laudato Si'*, 5.

[3] *Laudato Si'*, 217. Emphasis added. In 1990, John Paul II urged Christians to "realize that their responsibility within creation and their duty toward nature and the Creator are an essential part of their faith." See his *Peace with God the Creator, Peace with All of Creation* (January 1, 1990), 15.

[4] *Laudato Si'*, 23.

ubiquitous reductions of *Laudato Si'* to sound bites in the news—religious and secular, liberal and conservative—only exacerbated the problem.

My experience furnishes anecdotal evidence for larger trends throughout the U.S. Catholic Church in its reception of *Laudato Si'*. At the encyclical's fifth anniversary, Archbishop Paul Coakley, chair of the United States Conference of Catholic Bishops' Committee on Domestic Justice and Human Development, confessed that the reception of *Laudato Si'* remains "uneven. I think in some quarters, [*Laudato Si'*] has been received with great enthusiasm and in other quarters with great suspicion."[5] The data support Coakley's appraisal. One sociological study published shortly after the encyclical's release ascertains that *Laudato Si'* has only marginally increased U.S. Catholic concern for the current ecological crisis.[6] In fact, as another poll demonstrates, more than half of U.S. Catholics had not heard of *Laudato Si'* one year after its release, and only slightly over a third of U.S. Catholics at the time indicated agreement with Francis's assessment of the ecological crisis.[7] From the same year, yet another poll discerns that Catholics in the United States were more likely to be influenced by their political party than by *Laudato Si'* regarding their stance on the environment.[8] A more recent 2019 poll echoes these findings.[9] Specifically, the study finds that 80 percent of Catholic Democrats believe that the Earth is warming because of human activity, while only 22 percent of Catholic Republicans believe the same. The study likewise reports that 55 percent of Catholic Republicans believe that abortion should be illegal in all or most cases, while only 31 percent of

---

[5] United States Catholic Conference of Bishops, "*Laudato Si'* Roundtable," May 26, 2020, video, at 6:20, https://www.youtube.com/watch?v=2wF4AnOn7OI.

[6] Edward Maibach et al., *The Francis Effect: How Pope Francis Changed the Conversation about Global Warming*, (Fairfax, Va.: George Mason University Center for Climate Change Communication, 2015). See also Associated Press–NORC Center for Public Affairs Research, "Speaking Out on Global Warming: Public Attitudes toward the Papal Encyclical on Climate Change," August 2015, http://www.apnorc.org/PDFs/PopeGlobalWarming/Speaking%20Out%20on%20Global%20Warming%20Issue%20Brief.pdf, which concluded that "Catholics are no more likely than the rest of the population to say they have heard of the encyclical" (3).

[7] Center for Applied Research in the Apostolate, "CARA Catholic Poll (CCP) 2016: Attitudes about Climate Change," 2016, https://cara.georgetown.edu/climate%20summary.pdf, 3, 5.

[8] See Nan Li et al., "Cross-pressuring Conservative Catholics? Effects of Pope Francis' Encyclical on the U.S. Public Opinion on Climate Change," *Climatic Change* 139, no. 3 (December 2016): 367–80.

[9] Michael Lipka and Gregory A. Smith, "Like Americans Overall, U.S. Catholics Are Sharply Divided by Party," Pew Research Center, January 24, 2019, https://www.pewresearch.org/fact-tank/2019/01/24/like-americans-overall-u-s-catholics-are-sharply-divided-by-party/.

Catholic Democrats believe the same. In both cases, despite the importance Francis gives to both issues in *Laudato Si'*, Catholics mirror the polarized divisions of the United States.[10]

The shallowing effects of polarization in the U.S. Catholic Church itself in part account for the encyclical's uneven reception.[11] Soon after the release of the encyclical, a number of conservative Catholic commentators in the United States publicly dismissed substantial amounts of the encyclical.[12] A number of more progressive Catholic commentators downplayed or ignored portions of the encyclical that discussed causes conventionally associated with conservative wishes, like care for the unborn.[13] These phenomena present classic cases in which one's political preferences and group belongings shape one's Christian identity, rather than vice-versa.

Such data point to a key ecclesiological question of the twentieth and twenty-first centuries, namely how "to come to grips with the death of Christendom without simply acquiescing in the privatization of the church."[14] Read through this light, the cases above anticipate the larger question of how to envision the church's mission in a way that navigates between the Scylla of a nostalgia for a Christendom no longer tenable and the Charybdis of a relegation of the church to a mere "special interest group" and

---

[10] See *Laudato Si'*, 120: "Since everything is interrelated, concern for the protection of nature is also incompatible with the justification of abortion. How can we genuinely teach the importance of concern for other vulnerable beings, however troublesome or inconvenient they may be, if we fail to protect a human embryo, even when its presence is uncomfortable and creates difficulties?" This passage and ones like it receive much deeper attention in later chapters.

[11] See Annie Selak, "Inheriting Climate Controversies: Reception in a Polarized Church," presentation for the Catholic Theological Society of America, June 9, 2017. See also Michael Agliardo, "The Reception of *Laudato Si'* in the United States in Secular and Sacred Arenas," in *All Creation Is Created: Voices in Response to Pope Francis's Encyclical on Ecology*, ed. Daniel R. DiLeo (Winona, Minn.: Anselm Academic, 2018), 53–56.

[12] See, e.g. Maureen Mullarkey, "Where Did Pope Francis's Extravagant Rant Come From?," *The Federalist*, June 24, 2015, http://thefederalist.com/2015/06/24/where-did-pope-franciss-extravagant-rant-come-from/, who characterizes *Laudato Si'* as "a malignant jumble of dubious science, policy prescriptions, doomsday rhetoric, and what students of Wordsworthian poetics call, in Keats' derisive phrase, 'the egotistical sublime.'" For an overview of other, similarly negative reactions, see Michael Sean Winters, "*Laudato Si—Magistra No*," *National Catholic Reporter*, June 19, 2015, https://www.ncronline.org/blogs/distinctly-catholic/laudato-si-magistra-no.

[13] See Brian Fraga, "Political Role Reversal: Democrats Praise Encyclical, While GOP Remains Cautious," *National Catholic Register*, June 26, 2015, https://www.ncregister.com/daily-news/political-role-reversal-democrats-praise-encyclical-while-gop-remains-cauti.

[14] William T. Cavanaugh, *Migrations of the Holy: God, State, and the Political Meaning of the Church* (Grand Rapids, Mich.: Eerdmans, 2011), 123.

"one more negotiator with the government."[15] With regard to the latter, the more prevalent tendency today, the cost of admission to be yet another negotiator within a pluralistic society frequently entails a watering down of the church's mission to a set of eclectic policy positions translatable to public discourse. As a result, the partisanship determining that discourse distorts ecclesial mission and the salt of the church's redemptive message loses its flavor.[16] Those fears came to fruition both in my experience with *Laudato Si'* at my parish and, more broadly, as the encyclical was filtered through partisan lenses. The mixed reception of *Laudato Si'* in the broader U.S. Catholic Church highlights how default understandings of ecclesial mission still fail to grapple with the post-Christendom existence in which the church finds itself today.

This book proposes two resources for resolving these timely questions: Bernard Lonergan's theology of history, read ecclesiologically, and the centrality of the Eucharist in the life of the church. Lonergan, a Jesuit priest like Pope Francis, is widely acknowledged to be one of the most precise Catholic thinkers of the twentieth century, and his theology and philosophy remains a key resource for many aspects of twenty-first century Catholic thought. Although ecology was not a major focus of Lonergan's work, the need to overcome the kind of polarization and superficial solutions that have hampered the reception of *Laudato Si'* certainly was. Lonergan scholars have begun to demonstrate this promise. In his *Re-Visioning the Church*, Neil Ormerod uses Lonergan's presentation of the "scale of values" to sketch an alternative to both a Christendom ideal and a reduction of the church to simply another special interest group.[17] Lonergan's scale of values can thus resolve one of the issues-under-the-issues represented in the mixed reception of *Laudato Si'* in the United States. Another point of connection justifying this book's focus on Lonergan is the close similarity between

---

15 Ian Linden, *Global Catholicism: Diversity and Change since Vatican II* (New York: Columbia University Press, 2009), 263.

16 See Michael J. Baxter, "Murray's Mistake," *America* (September 23, 2013): 13–18. See also David L. Schindler, *Heart of the World, Center of the Church:* Communio *Ecclesiology, Liberalism, and Liberation* (Grand Rapids, Mich.: Eerdmans, 1996), 1–142.

17 Neil Ormerod, *Re-Visioning the Church: An Experiment in Systematic-Historical Ecclesiology* (Minneapolis, Minn.: Fortress Press, 2014), 75, 111, 114–17, 356–57. Ormerod invites further development of his project, admitting that he "cannot fulfill all the expectations such an account demands" (365). As is explored at length later, Ormerod offers an ecclesiological distillation of Robert Doran's systematic study of Lonergan's scale of values. See Robert M. Doran, *Theology and the Dialectics of History* (Toronto: University of Toronto Press, 1990).

Lonergan's diagnosis of "general bias" and Francis's critique of the "technocratic paradigm" in *Laudato Si'*, as is explored at much greater length later in the book. If Francis and Lonergan share a similar cultural diagnosis, then Lonergan's scale of values can illuminate the shape of the prognosis—the contours of the care that our common home requires—in such a way that defends against the polarizing forces that distort it.

Recovering the inextricable relationship between eucharistic praise and the church's social mission can afford a second means of resolving the precarious reception of *Laudato Si'*. The Second Vatican Council asserts that the liturgy is "the source and summit of the Christian life" and presents the church as essentially doxological.[18] The Eucharist necessarily shapes the church's mission, including as articulated in Catholic social teaching, since that mission simultaneously flows from and culminates in its work of praise. In a discussion of Catholic parish life, the United States Conference of Catholic Bishops posits:

> The most important setting for the Church's social teaching is not in a food pantry or in a legislative committee room, but in prayer and worship, especially gathered around the altar for the Eucharist. It is in the liturgy that we find the fundamental direction, motivation, and strength for social ministry. Social ministry not genuinely rooted in prayer can easily burn itself out. On the other hand, worship that does not reflect the Lord's call to conversion, service, and justice can become pious ritual and empty of the gospel.[19]

The eucharistic celebration and the church's social mission interpenetrate. Each brings the other to fruition.

Applied to *Laudato Si'*, this eucharistic focus can embed the calls of *Laudato Si'* firmly within Catholic identity. In their *American Catholics in Transition*, William D'Antonio, Michelle Dillon, and Mary Gautier find that 63 percent of U.S. Catholics see sacraments, especially the Eucharist, as central to their faith and, on a different question, discover that "very large

---

18 See, e.g., Vatican Council II, *Lumen Gentium* (November 21, 1964), 11; and Vatican Council II, *Ad Gentes* (December 7, 1965), 7. See also Christopher Ruddy, "'In My End Is My Beginning': *Lumen Gentium* and the Priority of Doxology," *Irish Theological Quarterly* 79, no. 2 (2014): 144–64.

19 United States Catholic Conference of Bishops, *Communities of Salt and Light: Reflections on the Social Mission of the Parish* (Washington, D.C.: United States Catholic Conference of Bishops, 1994), 7–8.

majorities indicated that the Mass (84 percent) and the grace of the other sacraments (80 percent) are personally meaningful to them."[20] Such sociological data follow the theological assertions above: the Eucharist serves as the primary source of Catholic identity and ecclesial belonging. So too does it serve as a common source of identity that subverts partisan belongings, an insight articulated as early as the time of Saint Paul (1 Cor 11:17-34). Whereas *Laudato Si'* risks being subsumed by political polarization, eucharistic worship can instantiate a common setting for appropriating the encyclical in its fullness. Responding to concerns over how to link ecological concerns to Catholic life, Walter Grazer submits that "[p]rayer [and] liturgy . . . are primary experiential vehicles for Catholic engagement. Worship of our Creator, our life in Christ, and creating a spiritual underpinning for ecological and environmental concerns are the entry points and foundation for any effort to engage lay Catholics in addressing this concern."[21] Indeed, I am confident that my friends in the parish would have more wholeheartedly embraced my class on *Laudato Si'* had I begun with an extended reflection on the Eucharist and how it grounds the integral ecology presented in the encyclical. In fact, framing the encyclical in this eucharistic way has yielded much fruit, as I have presented *Laudato Si'* to parishes and ecclesial ministers since. Coupling care for our common home with eucharistic praise best shows how that care is "*essential* to a life of Christian virtue," integrating ecological conversion with conversion to Christ and his enduring, eucharistic presence.

THE ARGUMENT

With the uneven reception of *Laudato Si'* in mind, this book substantiates these tentative solutions in a systematic fashion. While it does not answer the above pastoral questions directly, it provides the systematic scaffolding from which a pastoral approach can be built. I focus specifically on integral ecology, as this term best names the overarching intentions of *Laudato Si'*

---

[20] William V. D'Antonio, Michelle Dillon, and Mary L. Gautier, *American Catholics in Transition* (Lanham, Md.: Rowman & Littlefield Publishers, 2013), 53–54, 57.

[21] William Somplatsky-Jarman, Walter Grazer, and Stan L. LeQuire, "Partnership for the Environment among U.S. Christians: Report from National Partnership for the Environment," in *Christianity and Ecology: Seeking the Well-Being of Earth and Humans*, ed. Dieter T. Hessel and Rosemary Radford Reuther (Cambridge, Mass.: Harvard University Press, 2000), 581. Grazer similarly stresses the need to embed care for creation "within the spiritual and sacramental context of Catholic theology" (574).

and the sources of Catholic social teaching that predate and undergird it.[22] Given that focus, I employ the thought of Lonergan—particularly his theology of history understood through the scale of values—to determine the doxological and eucharistic contours of the church's mission as understood through an integral ecology. Against those forces that would domesticate the church's mission within the terms and conditions of our current political situation in the West, this book advances a radically Catholic exposition of an integral ecology that reclaims the eucharistic vision of *Laudato Si'*.

I pursue this argument in three parts that span five chapters. Part 1 examines the tensions between the capacious reach of the church's social approach to the ecological crisis and the place of eucharistic praise within that approach. Two chapters comprise the section. In chapter 1, I examine popes John Paul II and Benedict XVI's development of the church's distinctively comprehensive approach to the environment: how they read the ecological crisis within a matrix of other interconnected social crises. I suggest that the way they name this social approach, through human ecology, raises several issues that risk undermining the comprehensive approach they intend to take. Without a proper means of integrating human ecology with natural ecology, the two ecologies can be read competitively and, thus, recalling the questions raised at the beginning of this introduction, the reception of the church's social teaching remains susceptible to ideological colonization. At the same time, both popes intimate that doxology, especially in its eucharistic form, can provide an integrating context and safeguard a more seamless understanding of these two ecologies. However, neither pope makes this connection clear, as neither inserts his rich eucharistic reflections into the sources where he pursues his comprehensive approach to the ecological crisis. Both popes do, however, provide indispensable and fecund foundations for future development.

In chapter 2, I survey how Pope Francis assembles the insights bequeathed by John Paul II and Benedict XVI, weaving together a comprehensive approach to the ecological crisis with a decisively Catholic emphasis on eucharistic praise. The integral ecology of *Laudato Si'* represents this achievement. In using this term, Francis synthesizes the concerns of both

---

22 Kevin Irwin calls the term "the most distinctive contribution of the encyclical" and "the most important theological insight about ecology in the document" in his *A Commentary on* Laudato Si': *Examining the Background, Contributions, Implementation, and Future of Pope Francis's Encyclical* (New York: Paulist Press, 2016), 102, 117, although the term is not defined precisely in the encyclical and remains to be explored by subsequent theological reflection.

human and natural ecologies, securing the earlier papal insight that the ecological crisis cannot be grasped apart from other social concerns. At the same time, the term definitively precludes any possibility that the concerns of either ecology can be separated or set against the other. The chapter suggests that Francis achieves this integration precisely by turning to doxology, especially in its eucharistic form. That is, the integral ecology of *Laudato Si'* achieves its truly integrated approach to the ecological crisis—and the concerns of human and natural ecologies that constitute it—through its radically doxological and eucharistic character. In this way, Francis crystallizes the intimations of John Paul II and Benedict XVI and so achieves the integrated approach latent in their work. Still, the achievement of *Laudato Si'* raises questions concerning the precise place of the Eucharist within an integral ecology—namely, how exactly the Eucharist provides this integrating role and how it might shape the care that our common home needs. The eucharistic vision of *Laudato Si'* remains inchoate as long as it lacks the systematic, ecclesiological reflection that can capture the dynamics incipiently named by the encyclical. The relative inattention to the liturgical emphases of *Laudato Si'* indicates the lack of a systematic, liturgically centered account of the church's social mission. The integral ecology of *Laudato Si'* calls for a vision of ecclesial mission that reflects its doxologically and eucharistically shaped vision of integral conversion.

Part 2 accordingly aims to develop an explanatory, ecclesiological framework that can more clearly discern the role of the Eucharist within an integral ecology. That is, it seeks a schema that can relate eucharistic praise to the other components that constitute the church's comprehensive approach to the ecological crisis. It turns to the thought of Bernard Lonergan for this need, as he himself hoped to provide for Catholic social teaching precisely a framework for understanding its mission, even if he and his commentators leave the liturgical component of this edifice largely unstated. Lonergan's theology of history, as developed through the scale of values, affords a set of coordinates that can relate elements of Catholic social teaching to each other. Two chapters comprise this section, each of which centers around the responsiveness of Lonergan's theology to the demands set forth by the integral ecology of *Laudato Si'*. The result of this dialogue, in a way left uncaptured by Lonergan and his commentators, is a liturgically centered account of the church's social mission and the integral conversion it leavens.

Specifically, in chapter 3, I focus on Lonergan's work itself and the pastoral intentions that animated it. Lonergan aspired to formulate a theology of history able to frame the church's redemptive mission, especially as expressed in Catholic social teaching. Selective in approach, this chapter sketches the central pillars of this attempt: emergent probability, progress, decline, and redemption. While Lonergan valued the need for a theology of history, the need to pursue other questions and the limitations of personal circumstances meant that he left the work incomplete. Still, his fundamental insights remain a sound foundation upon which to build a fully adequate theology of ecclesial mission that is theological, social, cultural, and ecological in scope. Lonergan is exceedingly helpful in naming the social and cultural dimensions of decline, but he never identifies at length the analogous social and cultural dimensions of redemption that the integral ecology of *Laudato Si'* demands be named. Before proceeding to elaborate that fuller account of redemption, the chapter concludes with two seminal themes that Lonergan discussed in the waning years of his career: the scale of values and the processes of healing and creating in history. These sources furnish the foundation for a fuller explanatory account able to capture the precise place and role of the Eucharist within an integral ecology.

In chapter 4, I develop Lonergan's thought with the help of commentator Robert Doran to complete this framework, showing how the scale of values can capture the eucharistic mission of the church within his theology of history. Doran, through an account of social grace, defines more precisely the social and cultural character of redemption within Lonergan's theology of history and so unearths the ecclesiological dimensions of Lonergan's thought. The chapter spells out Doran's development of Lonergan's theology of history, showing how he captures the dynamics of healing and creating for the sake of what he calls an "integral scale of values." Neither Doran nor many other readers of Lonergan discuss the role of eucharistic praise within this approach, however, despite its rich potential for unearthing the relationship between the Eucharist and social transformation. Using but going beyond Doran's reading, the chapter interprets Lonergan's theology of history eucharistically, schematizing how eucharistic praise ultimately heals distortions throughout the scale of values. In supplying the eucharistic vision of ecclesial mission demanded by *Laudato Si'*, this chapter offers a unique, liturgically cast reading of Lonergan's theology of history and recovers the radically theological and ecclesial character of his work in general. This theology of history generates a systematic justification for the central place of the Eucharist within the integral scale of values, indeed within an integral ecology. So too does it supply an explanatory framework that allows one to understand the way that the Eucharist shapes an integral conversion and reverses the forces that endanger that ecology.

Part 3 develops both the integral ecology of *Laudato Si'* and Lonergan's theology of history by bringing together the framework of Part 2 with the conclusions and questions of Part 1. In chapter 5, I demonstrate how Lonergan's theology of history, as read through the scale of values, organizes the data of an integral ecology. This exhibits how, generally, the components of an integral ecology relate to each other and how, specifically, the Eucharist functions within that ecology. At the same time, this chapter goes beyond mere application. Not only does it continue to excavate the deeply doxological and eucharistic dimensions implicit in Lonergan's theology of history, so too does it enlarge this theology of history to incorporate the novel demands set forth by an integral ecology, such as an option for the earth alongside that of the poor. The chapter employs the scale of values to grasp the multifaceted nature of decline in our common home and—guided by the teachings of John Paul II, Benedict XVI, and Francis—how eucharistic praise catalyzes the personal, cultural, and social transformations that an integral ecology demands. Likewise, the chapter explains more fully why rooting an integral ecology in eucharistic praise resolves the tensions in previous papal approaches to the ecological crisis. Following the ecclesiology modeled in *Laudato Si'*, the chapter also address how, rather than jeopardizing the broad intentions of *Laudato Si'*, turning to the decisively Catholic secures the dialogical impetus of the encyclical most fully. The chapter caps the book's overall argument that reading an integral ecology through the scale of values displays the enduring relevance of Lonergan's theology of history for the life of the church and confirms the centrality of eucharistic praise in the church's social mission.

Throughout this book, I presume a close relationship between doxology and the Eucharist. I derive this relationship from Thomas Aquinas's distinction between "interior" and "exterior" worship, respectively. He writes:

> since we are composed of a twofold nature, intellectual and sensible, we offer God a twofold adoration; namely, a spiritual adoration, consisting in the internal devotion of the mind; and a bodily adoration, which consists in an exterior humbling of the body. And since in all acts of *latria* that which is without is referred to that which is within as being of greater import, it follows that exterior adoration is offered on account of interior adoration, in other words we exhibit signs of humility in our bodies in

order to incite our affections to submit to God, since it is connatural to us to proceed from the sensible to the intelligible.[23]

Chapters 3 and 4 of this book intimate that "interior" and "exterior" worship correspond to Lonergan's distinction between the "inner" and "outer" word.[24] By "Eucharist," I refer in particular to the Mass, to which "[t]he other sacraments, as well as with every ministry of the Church and every work of the apostolate, are tied together . . . and are directed toward."[25] The Eucharist is the unsurpassable, concrete shape of the church's doxological essence. At various times, to stress this close relationship, this book refers to eucharistic praise. As *Lumen Gentium*'s description of the baptismal priesthood makes clear, eucharistic praise is a way of life embodied not only (though centrally so) in explicit worship but also "in the witness of a holy life, and by self-denial and active charity."[26]

THE CONTEXT OF THE PROJECT

The pastoral exigencies described at this introduction's beginning arise in part from the lack of an ecclesiological framework that can adequately resolve them. Stated more positively, this book makes a distinctive contribution both to the study of Lonergan's work and to the theological study of an integral ecology. Several book-length studies consider the ways that Lonergan's theology of history, understood primarily through the scale of values, can explain components of Catholic social teaching.[27] Still, none engages the most recent emphasis of Catholic social teaching on an integral ecology. While unsurprising given the term's novelty, the need for work in this area remains acute, especially if one considers its potential significance within the tradition. As Donal Dorr surmises, "I

---

[23] Thomas Aquinas, *Summa theologiae* 2–2, q. 84, a. 2.
[24] See Bernard J. F. Lonergan, *Method in Theology* (New York: Herder and Herder, 1972), 113.
[25] Vatican Council II, *Presbyterorum Ordinis* (December 7, 1965), 5.
[26] *Lumen Gentium*, 10.
[27] See Joseph Ogbonnaya, *Lonergan, Social Transformation, and Sustainable Human Development* (Eugene, Ore.: Pickwick Publications, 2013); Rohan Michael Curnow, *The Preferential Option for the Poor: A Short History and a Reading Based on the Thought of Bernard Lonergan* (Milwaukee, Wis.: Marquette University Press, 2012); Neil Ormerod and Shane Clifton, *Globalization and the Mission of the Church* (New York: Bloomsbury T & T Clark, 2009); and Stephen L. Martin, *Healing and Creativity in Economic Ethics: The Contribution of Bernard Lonergan's Economic Thought to Catholic Social Teaching* (Lanham, Md.: University Press of America, 2007).

am inclined to say that what [Pope Francis] offers us is not just an integral ecology but a framework for an *integral Catholic social teaching*, which includes not just the items that Francis emphasizes but also all the other significant elements in the Catholic social tradition."[28] Indeed, integral ecology served as the leitmotif for the 2019 Synod of Bishops that delineated the church's mission in the Pan-Amazon region.[29] Since then, in the disorienting wake of the COVID-19 pandemic, Pope Francis has asserted that "the future we are called to build has to begin with an integral ecology."[30] Both instances confirm Dorr's prescience. Assuming then that integral ecology does represent a new synthetic, foundational category for Catholic social teaching, the church's promotion of an integral ecology accordingly deserves an analysis through Lonergan's theology of history as well.

As this book argues, eucharistic praise plays a central role in the integral ecology promoted by Catholic social teaching. Reading an integral ecology in this way better protects it from the partisan colonization described above. However—and this omission cannot but have pastoral implications—treatment of the eucharistic and doxological depths of *Laudato Si'* has been sporadic and ad hoc.[31] This book, after all, maintains that Lonergan's theology of history, read through the scale of values, affords the conceptual clarity to recognize this centrality. Those studies that associate the Eucharist with an integral ecology are primarily descriptive and so invite further constructive work; they fail to explain precisely how the Eucharist shapes and heals an integral ecology, something that a detailed theology of history can explain. So too do the eucharistic emphases of this project distinguish it from other Lonergan-based studies of *Laudato Si'*, including those that employ the scale

---

28 Donal Dorr, *Option for the Poor and for the Earth: From Leo XIII to Pope Francis*, rev. ed. (Maryknoll, N.Y.: Orbis Books, 2016), 467.

29 See Synod of Bishops, *The Amazon: New Paths for the Church and for an Integral Ecology* (October 28, 2019); and Francis, Post-Synodal Apostolic Exhortation *Querida Amazonia* (February 12, 2020).

30 Francis, with Austen Ivereigh, *Let Us Dream: The Path to a Better Future* (New York: Simon & Schuster, 2020), 35.

31 No book-length study has devoted itself to exploring this centrality in a sustained, let alone ecclesiological, way. For several sources that do treat this theme, albeit briefly, see Anthony J. Kelly, Laudato Si': *An Integral Ecology and the Catholic Vision* (Adelaide, Australia: ATF Theology, 2016), 111–38; Sandra Yocum, "Liturgy: The Exaltation of Creation," in *The Theological and Ecological Vision of* Laudato Si', ed. Vincent J. Miller, 127–44 (New York: Bloomsbury T & T Clark, 2017); and Kevin W. Irwin, *Pope Francis and the Liturgy: The Call to Holiness and Mission* (New York: Paulist Press, 2020), 102–25.

of values.³² In fact, as will become clear, my eucharistic interpretation of the scale of values in chapter 4 distinguishes it from other studies of Lonergan's theology of history. Treatments of the ecclesiological relevance of Lonergan's work have tended to neglect the eucharistic contours of the church's mission.³³ The Lonergan-grounded doxological ecclesiology and eucharistic social ethic developed in the book represents a unique contribution of this book that can be applied to a range of questions.

This book also implicitly addresses three questions that transcend both Lonergan studies and commentary on *Laudato Si'*. As my opening anecdote about the reception of *Laudato Si'* in my home church highlights, the first of these questions concerns the polarization that beleaguers the contemporary ecclesial situation. Both Lonergan and the spirit behind an integral ecology offer an alternative catholic vision of both/and. For his part, convinced that "the world lies in pieces before man and pleads to be put together again," Lonergan aims to "to seek a common ground on which men of intelligence might meet."³⁴ Elsewhere, Lonergan beckons his readers to inhabit what he terms a "not numerous center," a creative minority caught between "a solid right that is determined to live in a world that no longer exists" and "a scattered left, captivated by now this, now that new development, exploring now this and now that new possibility."³⁵ A similarly synthetic, challenging vision marks Catholic social teaching, especially in its comprehensive approach to

---

32 See Neil Ormerod and Cristina Vanin, "Ecological Conversion: What Does It Mean?" *Theological Studies* 77, no. 2 (2016): 328–52; and Eugene R. Schlesinger, "Ecological Conversion, Social Grace, and the Four-Point Hypothesis," in *Intellect, Affect, and God: The Trinity, History, and the Life of Grace*, ed. Joseph Ogbonnaya and Gerard Whelan, 19–33 (Milwaukee, Wis.: Marquette University Press, 2021). While Ormerod and Vanin's article focuses on "ecological conversion" (appearing first with John Paul II), this book focuses on the new (for Catholic social teaching) concept of integral ecology. Moreover, because of this focus, Ormerod and Vanin do not include a genetic account of the church's approach to the ecological crisis that this book does in its first two chapters. As a result, Ormerod and Vanin do not use the scale of values to address tensions within that tradition, as this book does.

33 For a critique of Ormerod's ecclesiology in this general direction, see Ligita Ryliškytė, "Non-*Communio* Trinitarian Ecclesiology: Furthering Neil Ormerod's Account," *Irish Theological Quarterly* 83, no. 2 (2018): 107–27, at 113–19. A notable exception includes Joseph C. Mudd, *Eucharist as Meaning: Critical Metaphysics and Contemporary Sacramental Theology* (Collegeville, Minn.: Liturgical Press, 2014). However, Mudd does not link his study of the Eucharist to Lonergan's theology of history, which would make it more explicitly an ecclesiological project.

34 Bernard J. F. Lonergan, *Insight: A Study of Human Understanding*, vol. 3 of *Collected Works of Bernard Lonergan* (hereafter CWL), ed. Frederick E. Crowe and Robert M. Doran (Toronto: University of Toronto Press, 2005), 552, 7.

35 Bernard J. F. Lonergan, "Dimensions of Meaning," in *Collection*, vol. 4 of CWL (Toronto: University of Toronto Press, 1993), 245.

the ecological crisis. As chapter 2 makes clear, that vision culminates in the integral ecology of Francis, in his incessant refrain that "everything is interconnected," and in his ability to seamlessly weave together issues that commonly divide U.S. Catholics.[36] This book hopes to promote the synthesizing vision of both Lonergan and an integral ecology, reattaching poles too often estranged from each other, whether it be systematic theology and pastoral activity, concern for human life and concern for the environment, or liturgy and social ethics. By so doing, it hopes to broaden the "not numerous center" to which all Catholics are called.

Second, in this same spirit and by examining the theological heart of *Laudato Si'*, my book proffers an "evangelically Catholic" approach to environmental ethics, social ethics, and ecclesiology, albeit from an unlikely source in Lonergan.[37] In taking this approach, this project contributes to a methodological debate concerning the role of a specifically Catholic approach to social ethics and public theology. As Michael Baxter has identified, at least two strains of social-ethical reflection exist in U.S. Catholicism, epitomized most influentially by the priest-architect of the New Deal, John A. Ryan, and the Benedictine pioneer of the American Liturgical Movement, Virgil Michel.[38] As evidenced in something like the 1919 Bishops' Program for Social Reconstruction, Ryan extracted general moral principles from Catholic social teaching to formulate policy recommendations that would enable the church to speak and remain relevant to a pluralistic American public.[39] That modus operandi, as Baxter observes, has dominated contemporary Catholic social ethics through today. The unintended result of such a methodology, however, is "a social ethic evacuated of specifically Christian content" and thus one evacuated of its prophetic power.[40] As suggested at

---

[36] See *Laudato Si'*, 70, 91, 92, 117, 120, 137, 138, 142, 240. For a popular presentation of the consistent ethic of life promoted by Pope Francis in general, see Charles C. Camosy, *Resisting Throwaway Culture: How a Consistent Life Ethic Can Unite a Fractured People* (Hyde Park, N.Y.: New City Press, 2019). As Camosy writes in the book's introduction, "I will leave it to others to elaborate these issues in a purely academic fashion" (23); this book takes up that charge.

[37] See William L. Portier, "Here Come the Evangelical Catholics," *Communio: International Catholic Review* 31, no. 1 (Spring 2004): 35–66.

[38] Michael J. Baxter, "Reintroducing Virgil Michel: Toward a Counter-Tradition of Catholic Social Ethics in the United States, *Communio: International Catholic Review* 24 (Fall 1997): 499–528, at 519–23.

[39] See Charles Curran, *American Catholic Social Ethics* (South Bend, Ind.: University of Notre Dame Press, 1982), 85–86.

[40] Baxter, "Reintroducing Virgil Michel," 521–22.

the beginning of this introduction, that prospect at least partially explains the lukewarm reception of *Laudato Si'* and its colonization by partisan forces. Against the integrating vision described above, this tactic divides the church's social teaching from cornerstones of Catholic ecclesial identity.

Given that possibility, this book's evangelically Catholic approach follows Baxter's call for a recovery of the approach taken by Michel, in many ways a foil to Ryan. Baxter, in the spirit of Michel, calls specifically for a "liturgically-cast social theory" that both recognizes the indispensability of the Eucharist for social transformation and the liturgy as the primary locus of the church's social ethic.[41] Presentations of Catholic social ethics largely neglect this starting point today, and the dominant narrative presents Michel as a liturgist rather than a social ethicist (with the assumption that these fields are hermetically distinct). As Christopher Ruddy remarks, contemporary presentations of the church and pastoral practice too often presume that "what is truly real is what is 'out there' in the 'real world,' not 'in here' in the liturgy," that "worship and prayer are somehow 'churchy' and 'introverted,' and at best a fueling up for the 'real' work of service and mission."[42] I hope to remedy this distortion by reading the church's presentation of an integral ecology through the lens of eucharistic worship. As becomes apparent in chapter 2, the unique structure and framing of *Laudato Si'* offers a fecund opportunity to retrieve Michel's radical approach and read the encyclical's proposal of an integral ecology through that lens. In the spirit of *Laudato Si'*, the book follows Ruddy's call for a "doxological ecclesiology" that positions right praise at the center of the church's mission.[43] The eucharistic vision of *Laudato Si'* very much invites "a eucharistic politics that redefines and broadens the concept of the political away from its narrow focus on electoral processes and the bureaucratic apparatus of

---

[41] Baxter, 525–26. Writes Portier "most forms of Catholic social teaching in the U.S. today are designed to be detachable from Catholic theology as a whole so they can be put to "nonsectarian" use in public policy debate. The claim here is that this body of thought will remain impotent to inspire people to evangelize culture in the name of Jesus until it receives an infusion of theological energy"; "Here Come the Evangelical Catholics," 65.

[42] Ruddy, "'In My End Is My Beginning,'" 163.

[43] Ruddy, 161. This work, while sharing Ruddy's ecclesiological focus, also follows other recent theological retrievals of the centrality of doxology. For a doxologically shaped fundamental theology, see Andrew Prevot, *Thinking Prayer: Theology and Spirituality Amid the Crises of Modernity* (Notre Dame, Ind.: University of Notre Dame Press, 2015). For a doxologically shaped soteriology, see Khaled Anatolios, *Deification through the Cross: An Eastern Christian Theology of Salvation* (Grand Rapids, Mich.: Eerdmans, 2020).

governance."⁴⁴ Moreover, as Baxter recognizes, grounding Catholic social teaching eucharistically can foster a "parish-centered social ethic."⁴⁵ In other words, underscoring the eucharistic character of an integral ecology can make it more practical and more concrete for parishioners in, for example, Western Pennsylvania. Supporting the recommendations of people like Baxter and Ruddy thus also serves a pastoral purpose. This evangelically Catholic approach ultimately hopes to overcome the increasingly tiresome divides between the left and the right that impede the full richness of the church's redemptive mission.

Third, at the same time, developing this eucharistic primacy through Lonergan's theology of history can afford explanatory heft to the approach taken by theologians like Baxter and Ruddy. Such liturgically grounded approaches commonly beg the question of exactly how eucharistic praise catalyzes social transformation.⁴⁶ Neglecting such an account can lead to a tacit dismissal of the church's social mission, much to the opposite effect that these theologians intend.⁴⁷ Lonergan's theology of history, especially as read through the scale of values and as interpreted doxologically, furnishes the explanatory power to understand the doxological and eucharistic contours of an integral ecology and, more generally, of the church's social mission into the future. Recent efforts have made clear the desire of social ethicists for a theoretical underpinning of their work, one that establishes both "more confidence in a true and accurate account of 'social reality'" and "a better way to connect such an account of structure with more precise responsibilities for moral agency."⁴⁸ The sensitivities and intricacies of

---

44 Larry Chapp, "Liberalism, the Church, and the Unreality of God," *Communio: International Catholic Review* 48, no. 3 (Fall 2021): 518–35, at 533.

45 Baxter, "Reintroducing Virgil Michel," 528.

46 See, e.g., Massimo Faggioli, "A View from Abroad," *America* (February 24, 2014): 20–23.

47 See Michael J. Baxter and William T. Cavanaugh, "Reply to 'A View from Abroad' by Massimo Faggioli," *America* (April 21, 2014): 8. As Khaled Anatolios adds, "An integral account of Christian salvation must prioritize this properly transcendent and doxological dimension [of Christian discipleship] without abstracting from concrete historical existence and the dimension of interhuman relations" (Anatolios, *Deification through the Cross*, 394). Lonergan's theology of history, as will become clear, can concretize the redemptive effects of praise on those interhuman relations.

48 David Cloutier, "Cavanaugh and Grimes on Structural Evils of Violence and Race: Overcoming Conflicts in Contemporary Social Ethics," *Journal of the Society of Christian Ethics* 37, no. 2 (2017): 59–78, at 60. Cloutier concludes:

> Without these, I fear that Christian ethics remains a kind of elite theoretical game, able to offer some unique and prophetic challenges to the world but without the resources to help actual agents engage in real action for the Kingdom. As important as a powerful and

INTRODUCTION

Lonergan's theology of history provide precisely that. At the same time, the thoroughly doxological and eucharistic character of the integral ecology of *Laudato Si'* occasions a recovery of the radically ecclesial dimensions implied in Lonergan's theology of history. While some social ethicists highlight the need for explanatory theory, others have worried that Catholic social theory "is remarkably bereft of references to Christ, the sacraments, scripture, the saints, and other tradition-specific theological terms and categories that do not easily conform to the discursive protocols of the modern liberal state."[49] What follows hopes to show how Lonergan can furnish a thoroughly theological, though methodologically responsible, reading of history for an evangelically Catholic articulation of the church's redemptive mission.[50] As the American Catholic radical sociologist Paul Hanly Furfey once dared Catholic social theorists, "Let's be extremely Catholic and extremely scientific at once!"[51] The theological depth of an integral ecology invites such an undertaking.

Lonergan's theology of history can facilitate the appropriation of the thoroughly Catholic contours of an integral ecology, albeit from a thoroughly scientific perspective. The integral ecology of *Laudato Si'* invites theologians to develop an "integral doxology" that ties together the church's social mission and its doxological essence.[52] This effort can help remove the lamentable "wedge driven between street and sanctuary in the

---

    imaginative critique is for confronting structural evil, ethics remains a discipline that is ultimately about practical reason. Identifying and choosing the good amid structures should lead us to articulate more carefully how practical reason of agents is shaped by and shapes the structures we inhabit. (75)

Cloutier has joined others in turning to the critical realist social theory of Margaret Archer to fill this need. Lonergan, himself a critical realist, offers a most apt dialogue partner in this effort.

49 Michael J. Baxter, "'Blowing the Dynamite of the Church': Catholic Radicalism from a Catholic Radicalist Perspective," in *The Church as Counterculture*, ed. Michael L. Budde and Robert W. Brimlow (Albany: State University of New York Press, 2000), 199. Cf. Doran, *Theology and the Dialectics of History*, 6: "The structure of history cannot be understood correctly if one prescinds from the realities affirmed in the Christian doctrines of grace and sin, in the theological doctrines of the natural and the supernatural, and in the religious doctrines of radical evil and gratuitous redemption."

50 This holds true despite someone like Michael Baxter's stated fears that Lonergan's project undermines such an attempt. See Kristen Heyer, *Prophetic and Public: The Social Witness of U.S. Catholicism* (Washington, D.C.: Georgetown University Press, 2006), 106n98.

51 As quoted in Nicholas K. Rademacher, *Paul Hanly Furfey: Priest, Scientist, Social Reformer* (New York: Fordham University Press, 2017), 162.

52 Prevot, *Thinking Prayer*, 220.

years after the Second Vatican Council," both in the parish and in the academy.⁵³ As Ruddy tenders, the acknowledgment that "we are saved precisely by and precisely for the praise and worship of God" will allow both "mission and soteriology to flourish."⁵⁴ Lonergan's theology of history, as read through the scale of values, illustrates how such a claim is true and, in so doing, fashions a liturgically cast social theory on a firm foundation. In the catholic spirit of Lonergan and of an integral ecology, this book thus shows how the church's "work" of conversion, whether in liturgy or justice, remains one in our common home. The eucharistic vision of *Laudato Si'* demands nothing less.

---

53 Robert Barron, "Evangelizing the American Culture," *Bridging the Great Divide: Musings of a Post-Liberal, Post-Conservative Evangelical Catholic* (Lanham, Md.: Rowman & Littlefield Publishers, 2004), 271.

54 Ruddy, "'In My End Is My Beginning,'" 145. As he writes later, "If the Church gets the primacy of worship right, the rest will follow" (155), a tantalizing claim upon which this book hopes to expand.

Part 1

Toward a Eucharistic Vision of Care for Our Common Home

Chapter 1

The Unfulfilled Potential of a Eucharistic Turn

Popes John Paul II and Benedict XVI garner more citations than do any other figures in *Laudato Si'*.[1] This fact supports those theological commentators who have challenged narratives that pit Pope Francis against his two papal predecessors.[2] The present chapter showcases those earlier foundations laid by John Paul II and Benedict XVI for Francis's doxologically and eucharistically centered presentation of an integral ecology in *Laudato Si'*. At the same time, the chapter also highlights areas for development within that earlier tradition. Some areas for development lay dormant in the thought of John Paul II and Benedict XVI. Other areas for development lay in the differing contexts and theological emphases of the persons who happen to hold the papal office. These spaces for development ground the achievement of *Laudato Si'*.

This chapter outlines the distinctively integral approach that John Paul II and Benedict XVI take on the ecological crisis. Both name this approach through the category of *human ecology*, a term, as will become clear, that can undermine this aim. On occasion, John Paul II and Benedict XVI highlight the doxological and eucharistic character of all creation. This feature raises questions of how these profoundly Catholic themes might facilitate the two popes' integral approaches to the ecological crisis and how well both of them combine eucharistic praise with their articulations of an integrated approach. The chapter concludes that the potential of a doxological, eucharistic turn to ecological concern remains unrealized in both pontificates. Grasping that lacunae allows

---

1 Seventy of the encyclical's 172 footnotes refer to those two.

2 See, e.g., Robert P. Imbelli, "Benedict and Francis," in *Go into the Streets! The Welcoming Church of Pope Francis*, ed. Thomas P. Rausch and Richard Gaillardetz, 11–27 (New York: Paulist Press, 2016); and Kevin W. Irwin, "Background to and Contributions of *Laudato Si'*: On Care for Our Common Home," in *All Creation Is Connected: Voices in Response to Pope Francis's Encyclical on Ecology*, ed. Daniel R. DiLeo, 15–30 (Winona, Minn.: Anselm Academic, 2018).

one to recognize the organic, yet significant, developments of the Catholic social tradition that *Laudato Si'* introduces in its eucharistic vision of an integral conversion.

POPE JOHN PAUL II

While previous popes referenced ecological questions sporadically, John Paul II offered the first sustained papal attempt to address the ecological crisis. With his unique celebrity status, geopolitical influence, and far-ranging missionary outreach, John Paul II stands as the first pope for a global age.[3] His travels and personality positioned him well for highlighting the global dimensions of the ecological crisis. Not only did John Paul II's worldwide stage raise his awareness of the crisis, so too did it furnish him with a platform to contribute to a solution.[4] Such a solution aimed to mirror the global, interconnected breadth of the problem.

An Integrated Approach to the Environment

It is a key premise of this book that Catholic social teaching takes a distinctively comprehensive, integral approach to the environmental crisis. Catholic social teaching views and understands the environmental crisis within a broader matrix of social problems; thus, for Catholic social teaching, the challenges of the present day pose a breakdown in an ecology of both natural and human relationships. Celia Deane-Drummond captures the significance of this emphasis in writing that "[e]cology perceived as an aspect of other social injustices perhaps marks out *the distinctive* contribution of [Catholic social teaching] to ecotheology."[5] While traditional environmental ethics and Christian ecotheologies tend to isolate subjects like biodiversity and climate change from other social questions, Catholic social teaching

---

[3] See James Corkery, "John Paul II: Universal Pastor in a Global Age," in *The Papacy since 1500: From Italian Prince to Universal Pastor*, ed. James Corkery and Thomas Worcester, 223–42 (New York: Cambridge University Press, 2010).

[4] For instance, Marybeth Lorbiecki views John Paul II's 1980 visit to the Sahel region in Africa—an intersection of drought, homelessness, famine, and extreme poverty—as a turning point that allowed him to encounter the intimate connections between underdevelopment and environmental devastation. See her *Following St. Francis: John Paul II's Call for Ecological Action* (New York: Rizzoli Ex Libris, 2014), 89–94.

[5] Celia Deane-Drummond, "Joining in the Dance: Catholic Social Teaching and Ecology," *New Blackfriars* 93, no. 1044 (2012): 193–212, at 197. Emphasis added. See also Marjorie Keenan, *From Stockholm to Johannesburg: An Historical Overview of the Concern of the Holy See for the Environment: 1972–2002* (Vatican City: Vatican Press, 2002), 16.

offers a more integrated perspective.[6] Though conventional narratives of the left and the right often pit protection of human life and protection of natural resources and economic flourishing and environmental conscientiousness against each other, this tradition can enumerate some form of a catholic alternative.[7] Part of the success of Catholic social tradition can accordingly be judged on how well it preserves this integration.

John Paul II developed this comprehensive approach at length, setting a key precedent for his papal successors. From his very first encyclical, *Redemptor Hominis*, he discusses the environmental crisis alongside other contemporary social concerns. There, he writes:

> Are we of the twentieth century not convinced of the overpoweringly eloquent words of the Apostle of the Gentiles concerning the "creation (that) has been groaning in travail together until now" (Rom 8:22) and "waits with eager longing for the revelation of the sons of God" (Rom 8:19), the creation that "was subjected to futility"? Does not the previously unknown immense progress—which has taken place especially in the course of this century—in the field of man's dominion over the world itself reveal—to a previously unknown degree—that manifold subjection "to futility"? It is enough to recall certain phenomena, such as the threat of pollution of the natural environment in areas of rapid industrialization, or the armed conflicts continually breaking out over and over again, or the prospectives of self-destruction through the use of atomic, hydrogen, neutron and similar weapons, or the lack of respect for the life of the unborn.[8]

Here, John Paul II associates the "groanings of creation" with other social exigencies, whether industrialization, war, nuclear proliferation, or abortion. From the beginning of his pontificate, John Paul II intimates that the environmental crisis cannot be solved apart from a comprehensive solution that mitigates environmental and social crises alike.

This insight endured and matured throughout his pontificate. Eventually, John Paul II began to treat the environmental crisis under the cate-

---

[6] For calls from the field to broaden the scope of environmental ethics in this manner, see Willis Jenkins, *Ecologies of Grace: Environmental Ethics and Christian Theology* (New York: Oxford University Press, 2008), 10–18; and his "After Lynn White: Religious Ethics and Environmental Problems," *Journal of Religious Ethics* 37 no. 2 (2009): 283–309.

[7] See Benjamin Wiker, *In Defense of Nature: The Catholic Unity of Environmental, Economic, and Moral Ecology* (Steubenville, Ohio: Emmaus Road Publishing, 2017).

[8] John Paul II, Encyclical Letter *Redemptor Hominis* (March 4, 1979), 8.

gory of development.⁹ First, in his 1987 social encyclical *Sollicitudo Rei Socialis*, he stresses "the need to respect the integrity and the cycles of nature and to take them into account when planning for development, rather than sacrificing them to certain demagogic ideas about the latter" and encourages ongoing international efforts for a more humane development, particularly in Third World countries.¹⁰ He details this more holistic understanding of development later in the encyclical, adding that development cannot use any beings (animals, plants, natural elements) purely according to economic needs and must respect the limits of natural resources.¹¹ John Paul II repeats these claims in his 1988 post-synodal apostolic exhortation, *Christifideles Laici*, where he notes that "in an ever-increasingly acute way, the so-called 'ecological' question poses itself in relation to socio-economic life and work."¹² For the pope, development supplied a helpful category to capture the close relationship between the environmental crisis and socioeconomic questions.

The 1990s provoked a subtle, yet significant, shift in the way that John Paul II presented this relationship. In the wake of the Cold War, the global effervescence of the decade reinvigorated collective attempts to resolve the environmental crisis; in 1992, world leaders famously met in Rio de Janeiro and produced several binding agreements to mitigate the crisis.¹³ The globe's renewed commitment to the environment also shaped the church's understanding of its social mission, especially in the new postcommunist era. In 1990, John Paul II used his annual World Day of Peace message to serve as the first Vatican document devoted specifically to environmental concerns. It too continues a social approach, while also hinting at a different manner of articulating that approach. The pope opens the message by recognizing that world peace is threatened not only by arms races and injustice but also "by a lack of *due respect for nature*, by the plundering of natural resources and by a progressive decline in the quality of life."¹⁴ John Paul II connects

---

[9] See Lucia A. Silecchia, "Environmental Ethics from the Perspectives of NEPA and Catholic Social Teaching: Ecological Guidance for the 21st Century," *William & Mary Environmental Law and Policy Review* 28, no. 3 (2004): 659–798, at 696.

[10] John Paul II, Encyclical Letter *Sollictudo Rei Socialis* (December 30, 1987), 26.

[11] *Sollictudo Rei Socialis*, 34.

[12] John Paul II, Post-Synodal Apostolic Exhortation *Christifideles Laici* (December 30, 1988), 43.

[13] See Ranee K. L. Panjabi, *The Earth Summit at Rio: Politics, Economics, and the Environment* (Boston: Northeastern University Press, 1997).

[14] John Paul II, *Peace with God the Creator* (January 1, 1990), 1.

the environmental crisis to the "indiscriminate application of advances in science and technology," as it has caused climate change, the misdistribution of the world's resources, structural forms of poverty, war, and consumeristic lifestyles alike.[15] Within this web of crises, however, the "most profound and serious indication of the moral implications underlying the ecological crisis is the lack of respect for life evident in many of the patterns of environmental pollution."[16] Referencing genetic manipulation and the "unacceptable experimentation regarding the origins of human life itself," John Paul II insists that "[r]*espect for life, and above all the dignity of the human person, is the ultimate guiding norm for any sound economic, industrial or scientific progress.*"[17] This passage prefigures a key shift, particularly as John Paul II incorporated this more focused ecological awareness into his humanistically shaped theological and pastoral horizon.

That new approach ripened the following year. In *Centesimus Annus*, the pope again treats environmental degradation within a larger social context—in a chapter entitled "Private Property and the Universal Destination of Material Goods." He associates "the ecological question" with consumerism and attributes the ecological crisis to an "anthropological error" in which one "thinks he can make arbitrary use of the earth, subjecting it without restraint to his will, as though it did not have its own requisites and a prior God-given purpose."[18] He then introduces a new term in papal vocabulary, *human ecology*, which represents a shift in his ecological writing:

> In addition to the irrational destruction of the natural environment, we must also mention the more serious destruction of the human environment, something which is by no means receiving the attention it deserves. Although people are rightly worried—though much less than they should be—about preserving the natural habitats of the various animal species threatened with extinction, because they realize that each of these species makes its particular contribution to the balance of nature in general, too little effort is made to safeguard the moral conditions for an authentic "human ecology." Not only has God given the earth to man, who must use it with respect for the original good purpose for which it was given to him,

---

15 *Peace with God the Creator*, 6, 8, 11, 12, 13.
16 *Peace with God the Creator*, 7.
17 *Peace with God the Creator*, 7.
18 John Paul II, Encyclical Letter *Centesimus Annus* (May 1, 1991), 37.

but man too is God's gift to man. He must therefore respect the natural and moral structure with which he has been endowed.[19]

Within the field of sociology, human ecology denotes how humans too belong to a sensitive ecology of life.[20] Notably, John Paul II interprets this reality in a distinctive way; for him, the moral conditions that secure an authentic human ecology include the protection of family structures—"the heart of the culture of life"—and the denunciation of abortive practices and mentalities, the "culture of death."[21] Prior to *Centesimus Annus*, John Paul II tended to discuss the environmental crisis under the auspices of development; after *Centesimus Annus*, he does so primarily under the auspices of human ecology. John Paul II's perception of the strong ties between environmental concerns and threats against human life blossomed naturally from the comprehensive, social approach that he took on the ecological crisis. After the fall of communism, he began to devote energies that had been occupied with overcoming communism to reinforcing his proclamation of a "culture of life" against a "culture of death," especially in the form of urgent bioethical questions.[22] Human ecology expresses this new linking, and so Kevin Irwin rightly senses that reference to the term "marks an important terminological development in the way the magisterium speaks about ecological issues."[23] The shift in vocabulary proved to be a lasting one for John Paul II's discussion of environmental concern thereafter.

In his 1995 encyclical on the value and inviolability of human life, *Evangelium Vitae*, John Paul II continues this humanistic approach to the environment. This encyclical most develops his juxtaposition of a culture of life against a culture of death.[24] At one point, he refers to "the ecological question—ranging from the preservation of the natural habitats of the different species of animals and of other forms of life to 'human ecology' properly speaking—which finds in the Bible clear and strong ethical direction, leading

---

19 *Centesimus Annus*, 38.

20 See, e.g., Amos Hawley, *Human Ecology: A Theory of Community Structure* (New York: Ronald Press, 1950); and William R. Catton, "Foundations of Human Ecology," *Sociological Perspectives* 37, no. 1 (1994): 75–95.

21 *Centesimus Annus*, 39.

22 On this shift, see George Weigel, *The End and the Beginning: Pope John Paul II—The Victory of Freedom, the Last Years, the Legacy* (New York: Image Books, 2010), 464–66.

23 Irwin, "Background to and Contributions of *Laudato Si'*," 22.

24 John Paul II, Encyclical Letter *Evangelium Vitae* (March 25, 1991), 21, 28, 50, 77, 82, 86, 87, 92, 95, 98, 100.

to a solution which respects the great good of life, of every life."²⁵ One of the pope's last major documents, his 2003 post-synodal apostolic exhortation on the episcopacy, *Pastores Gregis*, reiterates this approach. Besides calling for an "ecological conversion," John Paul II asserts that "what is called for is not simply a physical ecology, concerned with protecting the habitat of the various living beings, but a *human ecology*, capable of protecting the radical good of life in all its manifestations and of leaving behind for future generations an environment which conforms as closely as possible to the Creator's plan."²⁶ By the end of his pontificate, John Paul II had enshrined human ecology as the primary means by which the Vatican spoke about the environment and linked it to other social concerns, especially those regarding the inviolability of human life. The category of human ecology permitted him to incorporate ecological concern into his broader pastoral and theological horizon.

The Limits of Human Ecology

A personalistic and humanistic thrust governed this horizon. "The form of John Paul II's scholarly work, the dominant concern of his pastoral life, the chief interest of his personal life," avers one commentator, "all is centered on the mysterious richness of the *person*."²⁷ Influences from minds like Thomas Aquinas, Max Scheler, Emmanuel Mounier, and Jacques Maritain produced what some have labeled John Paul II's "Thomistic Personalism."²⁸ Prior to his election as pope, his book *The Acting Person* established a philosophical personalism resistant to the "pulverization of the fundamental uniqueness of each human person" displayed by Hitler's fascist Germany and Stalin's communist Russia alike.²⁹ As Karol Wojtyla proclaimed boldly

---

25 *Evangelium Vitae*, 42.

26 John Paul II, Post-Synodal Apostolic Exhortation *Pastores Gregis* (October 16, 2003), 70.

27 Ronald Lawler, "Personalism in the Thought of John Paul II," in *Catholic Social Thought and the Teaching of John Paul II*, Proceedings of the Fifth Convention (1982) of the Fellowship of Catholic Scholars, ed. Paul L. Williams (Scranton, Penn.: Northeast Books, 1983), 3. Emphasis added.

28 See Ronald Modras, "The Thomistic Personalism of Pope John Paul II," *The Modern Schoolman* 59, no. 1 (January 1982): 117–26.

29 Karol Wojtyla, *The Acting Person*, trans. Andrzej Potocki (Boston: D. Reidel Publishing Company, 1979). The full quotation comes from a 1968 letter Wojtyla wrote to Henri de Lubac:

> I devote my very rare free moments to a work that is close to my heart and devoted to the metaphysical significance and the mystery of the PERSON. It seems to me that the debate today is being played on that level. The evil of our times consists in the first place in a kind of degradation, indeed in a pulverization, of the fundamental uniqueness of each human person. This evil is even much more of the metaphysical than of the moral order. To this

in another writing, "The central value, upon which other values in love depend, is the value of the human person."[30] The emphases of personalism proved especially valuable in Wojtyla's mid-twentieth century Poland, as it afforded a dialogue point with non-Catholics in Eastern Europe and supplied a third way between the equally dehumanizing forces of communism and liberal individualism. This framework and the concerns that emerged from it proved powerfully prophetic.[31]

Indeed, the human person occupied a central place in John Paul II's ministry as pope. Many view *Redemptor Hominis* as his papal vision statement because it sounds many of his humanistic, personalist themes. John Paul II writes that, through Christ's redemption, "Man finds again the greatness, dignity, and value that belong to his humanity."[32] "In reality," he continues, "the name for that deep amazement at man's worth and dignity is the Gospel, that is to say: the Good News. It is also called Christianity."[33] This amazement consequently "vivifies every aspect of authentic humanism" and "fixes Christ's place" as the focal point of human history.[34] And thus, the human person "is the primary route that the Church must travel in fulfilling her mission."[35] *Redemptor Hominis* urges that this humanistic and personalist thrust should direct the church's mission in all its forms. For the Polish pope, it did. In the words of one of his biographers, "John Paul II's pontificate has been a series of variations on the one great theme he announced . . . in his 1979 inaugural encyclical, *Redemptor Hominis*: Christian humanism as the Church's response to the crisis of world civilization at the end of the twentieth century."[36] These humanistic variations took many forms: ranging from his preaching of a culture of life over a culture

---

disintegration, planned at times by atheistic ideologies, we must oppose, rather than sterile polemics, a kind of "recapitulation" of the mystery of the person. (Cited in Henri de Lubac, *At the Service of the Church: Henri de Lubac Reflects on the Circumstances That Occasioned His Writings*, trans. Anne Elizabeth Englund [San Francisco: Ignatius Press, 1989], 171–72)

30 Karol Wojtyla, *Fruitful and Responsible Love* (New York: Seabury Press, 1979), 20.

31 See, e.g., Avery Dulles, "The Prophetic Humanism of John Paul II," in *Church and Society: The Laurence J. McGinley Lectures, 1988–2007*, 142–56 (New York: Fordham University Press, 2008).

32 *Redemptor Hominis*, 10.

33 *Redemptor Hominis*, 10.

34 *Redemptor Hominis*, 10.

35 *Redemptor Hominis*, 14.

36 George Weigel, *Witness to Hope: The Biography of Pope John Paul II* (New York: Cliff Street Books, 2001), 845.

of death to his enduring concern for the dignity of human labor and to his formulation of a human ecology.

And, yet, an agenda centered so intensely on the human person complicates a full, seamless integration of ecological concern into John Paul II's pastoral-theological horizon. While humanistic concerns dominated the pope's entire career, ecological concerns became central for him only in the 1990s. That is, his overarching philosophical and theological framework formed much earlier than and independently of his explicit concern for the integrity of creation.[37] Incorporating ecological concern into this framework accordingly proved awkward at times. On occasion, for example, John Paul II employs language that risks driving an excessively anthropocentric wedge between humans and the rest of creation: words like "master," "subdue," "exploit" (*usus*), and "dominate."[38] As a counter to "the development of a one-sidedly materialistic civilization, which gives prime importance to the objective dimension of work," John Paul II's influential presentation of labor in *Laborem Exercens* focuses on the subjective, human dimension of work to the practical exclusion of the larger context of creation in which labor takes place.[39] Rather than environmental concerns, at the forefront of the encyclical's attention are the corrosive effects on human work of both an increasingly consumeristic culture in the West and the presence of communism in Eastern Europe—specifically, labor tensions in Poland between the Solidarity trade union movement and the Polish communist government.[40] Even in places where John Paul II lent environmental questions central attention, such as his 1990 World Day of Peace message, questions remained regarding whether harm against creation was sinful in itself (or merely a consequence of sin) and whether creation contained value apart

---

[37] Daniel M. Cowdin, "John Paul II and Environmental Concern: Problems and Possibilities," *Living Light* 28 (1991): 44–52, at 44.

[38] See, e.g., *Redemptor Hominis*, 15; Encyclical Letter *Laborem Exercens* (September 14, 1981), 4, 5, 6, 15, 25; and *Sollicitudo Rei Socialis*, 30. The official Vatican translation renders the more neutral Latin *usus* as *exploit* in English; even *usus*, however, connotes a relatively extrinsic relationship between human beings and the rest of creation (see, e.g., *Sollicitudo Rei Socialis*, 34). The fact that translators rendered the word as *exploit* shows the potential pitfalls of employing utilitarian language like this. In fact, at the same time, John Paul II rejects an image of the human person as a "heedless exploiter" from the onset of his pontificate (see *Redemptor Hominis*, 15).

[39] *Laborem Exercens*, 7. See Deane-Drummond, "Joining in the Dance," 198.

[40] Patricia A. Lamoureux, "Commentary on *Laborem Exercens* (On Human Work)," in *Modern Catholic Social Teaching: Commentaries and Interpretations*, ed. Kenneth R. Himes (Washington, D.C.: Georgetown University Press, 2005), 390–91.

from its usefulness to humans.⁴¹ All these examples reveal an incomplete maturation in John Paul II's writings on the environment. Moreover, this incompleteness resulted directly from his humanistic thrust, albeit an emphasis necessary and prophetic given the time.⁴²

The most important consequence of this incomplete integration regards John Paul II's introduction of human ecology in *Centesimus Annus*.⁴³ As the previous section suggested, Catholic social teaching offers an invaluable contribution to discussions of environmental questions insofar as it preserves the interconnectedness of environmental and social crises. Nevertheless, the way that John Paul II speaks of human ecology in *Centesimus Annus* stands in tension with that integration.⁴⁴ While the pope rues the paltry attention environmental degradation receives and again insightfully connects environmental concern to other social issues, the passage that introduces the term—particularly in John Paul II's use of a phrase like "the *more serious* destruction"—implies a contrastive, if not competitive, relationship between human and natural ecologies. Similarly, in the next sentence, the passage appears to juxtapose attention to the environmental issues with attention to human life issues. As Donal Dorr comments:

---

41 See Peter C. Phan, "Pope John Paul II and the Ecological Crisis," *Irish Theological Quarterly* 60, no. 1 (1994): 59–69, at 64–66; and Donal Dorr, *Option for the Poor and for the Earth: From Leo XIII to Pope Francis*, rev. ed. (Maryknoll, N.Y.: Orbis Books, 2016), 373. For the passages under question, see *Peace with God the Creator*, 3–5, 7.

42 This is a point also made by John Carmody, *Ecology and Religion: Toward a New Christian Theology of Nature* (New York: Paulist Press, 1983), 5–6; Michael Northcott, *The Environment and Christian Ethics* (New York: Cambridge University Press, 1996), 136; and Dorr, *Option for the Poor and for the Earth*, 373–74, 389.

43 The encyclical also continues to use language of domination to refer to the human person's relationship to nature as well as hailing the human person as "the only creature on earth which God willed for its own sake" (*Centesimus Annus*, 31, 53).

44 Again, the passage reads:

> In addition to the irrational destruction of the natural environment, we must also mention the more serious destruction of the human environment, something which is by no means receiving the attention it deserves. Although people are rightly worried—though much less than they should be—about preserving the natural habitats of the various animal species threatened with extinction, because they realize that each of these species makes its particular contribution to the balance of nature in general, too little effort is made to safeguard the moral conditions for an authentic "human ecology". Not only has God given the earth to man, who must use it with respect for the original good purpose for which it was given to him, but man too is God's gift to man. He must therefore respect the natural and moral structure with which he has been endowed. (*Centesimus Annus*, 38)

The difficulty here is the unduly sharp contrast [John Paul II] makes between "human ecology" and "natural" ecology. The term "human ecology" is one that has been used in the social sciences since the early 1920s. It is a global term that refers to the relationship between humans and their natural, social, and cultural environments. So, it includes our relationship to nature. For this reason, it seems inappropriate to contrast it with "natural ecology," except when the latter term is wrongly taken in a restricted sense that fails to include humans in the natural order.[45]

The social-scientific meaning of human ecology implies a more comprehensive vision than the tenor of the encyclical suggests. However, John Paul II's overriding personalist concern seemingly narrows this vision in a way that, along with the lacunae in his environmental writings listed above, can lead to and justify lending a greater importance to matters of human ecology than to matters of natural ecology in ecclesial mission. This division risks undermining the integrated approach to environmental concern that John Paul II's use of human ecology points toward in his other writings.

John Paul II's concept of human ecology, therefore, deserves a critical assessment. As the previous section showed, human ecology encapsulates the final stage of John Paul II's understanding of the church's broad approach to the environment. However, as concern for the environment progressively became intertwined with John Paul II's humanistic program, it risked being eclipsed, if not subsumed, precisely by that program. In the ecclesial imagination, ecological concerns could fade amid a dramatic battle between the cultures of life and death. It is for this reason that, in the year after John Paul II's death, Denis Edwards could opine, "Commitment to ecology has not yet taken its central place in Christian self-understanding. It is far from central in terms of structure, personnel, and money."[46] While John Paul II's connecting of environmental concern with other pressing social concerns delivered a visionary, indispensable first step in the church's response to the ecological crisis, a more fundamental question emerges concerning the performance of this connection: does human ecology seamlessly integrate concern for the environment with these other social issues? The contrastive language used above suggests that it does not and risks taming this prophetic linking as a result.

---

45 Dorr, *Option for the Poor and for the Earth*, 375.
46 Denis Edwards, *Ecology at the Heart of Faith: The Change of Heart That Leads to a New Way of Living on Earth* (Maryknoll, N.Y.: Orbis Books, 2006), 3.

Presenting human ecology in contrast to natural ecology unnecessarily divides and sets in tension concern for the environment from concern for other social issues, particularly the protection of human life. Ecclesial discourse accordingly risks downplaying concern for the environment for the sake of promoting other, seemingly more important social concerns. The omission of any mention of the environment in *Veritatis Splendor* (published two years after *Centesimus Annus*), despite deeming it *"necessary to reflect on the whole of the Church's moral teaching,"* only confirms this fear.[47] Such a distortion obscures the distinctive contribution that Catholic social teaching can offer to the ecological crisis: Its balanced integration of care for creation with a range of social issues, one of which is unmistakably the preservation of human life. Without sustained reflection on the relationship between the two ecologies, natural ecology risks becoming untethered from human ecology and vice-versa. The unduly narrow horizon of human ecology indicates the need for a more capacious, integrative vision.

The Promise of a Doxological, Eucharistic Turn

Numerous biblical texts describe the teleology of all creation as doxological. Fourteen Psalms contain almost fifty references to creation's praise of God.[48] For example, from the "shining stars" to the "sea monsters and all deeps"—and everything between, from "fire and hail" to "creeping things and flying birds"—Psalm 148 exalts all to "praise the name of the Lord."[49] In response to God's saving work, the prophetic voice of Deutero-Isaiah declares, "Sing, O heavens, for the Lord has done it; shout, O depths of the earth; break forth into singing, O mountains, O forest, and every tree in it!" (Is 44:23).[50] The author of Revelation recalls triumphantly, "Then I heard every creature in heaven and on earth and under the earth and on the sea, and all that is in them, saying: 'To him who sits on the throne and

---

[47] John Paul II, Encyclical Letter *Veritatis Splendor* (August 6, 1993), 4. See Sean McDonagh, *Passion for the Earth: The Christian Vocation to Promote Justice, Peace, and the Integrity of Creation* (Maryknoll, N.Y.: Orbis Books, 1994), 135.

[48] Terence E. Fretheim, *God and World in the Old Testament: A Relational Theology of Creation* (Nashville, Tenn.: Abingdon Press, 2005), 249, 267–68.

[49] For an overview of this theme within the Psalms, see William P. Brown, *Seeing the Psalms: A Theology of Metaphor* (Louisville, Ky.: Westminster John Knox Press, 2002), 164–65.

[50] For other instances of this theme in prophetic literature, see Isa 43:20, Hab 3:3, and Dan 3:57–90.

to the Lamb be praise and honor and glory and power, for ever and ever!'" (Rv 5:13).[51] This biblical material suggests that salvation history interpenetrates both the human and the natural world, finding its climax when the entire created order raises its praise to and through Christ (Col 1:15–20). "This reality," Terence Fretheim proffers, "suggests a symbiosis in praise; every element in all of God's creation is called to praise together, and given the depth of their interrelatedness, the response of one will affect the response of the other."[52] In this chorus of praise, the human and the nonhuman, though distinct, cannot be separated. Oriented together toward God, each enables the praise of the other.

Many classical sources within the Christian tradition develop this ecology of doxology.[53] In homilies, Basil of Caesarea describes the "general chorus of creation" as one of praise.[54] In battles against the world-denying tendencies of the Manicheans, Augustine maintains that "the very forms of created things are as it were the voices with which they praise their Creator."[55] In prayer, Francis of Assisi urges all creation "in heaven, on earth, in the sea and in the depths" to give "praise, glory, honor, and blessing" to God.[56] In the silence of his cell, John of the Cross meditates on the silent praise of creation, that though each creature "sings His praises differently," together, "[a]ll these voices form one voice of music praising the grandeur, wisdom, and wonderful knowledge of God."[57] While some have accused

---

[51] See also Rev 12:12 and 18:20. For this theme, see Craig R. Koester, *Revelation and the End of All Things* (Grand Rapids, Mich.: Eerdmans, 2001), 71–74, 80, 192.

[52] Fretheim, *God and World in the Old Testament*, 264.

[53] See Jame Schaefer, *Theological Foundations for Environmental Ethics: Reconstructing Patristic and Medieval Concepts* (Washington, D.C.: Georgetown University Press, 2009), 103–20. This paragraph is especially indebted to Schaefer's work here.

[54] Basil, *On the Hexameron, in Exegetic Homilies*, trans. Agnes Clare Way (Washington, D.C.: The Catholic University of America Press, 1963), 52–53.

[55] Augustine, *On the Psalms*, vol. 29, *Ancient Christian Writers*, trans. Scholastica Hebgin and Felicitas Corrigan (New York: Newman Press, 1960), 272. See also "On Free Will," in *Augustine: Earlier Writings*, trans. John H. S. Burleigh (Philadelphia: Westminster Press, 1953), 3.15.42 (196); and *The Confessions of St. Augustine*, trans. John K. Ryan (Garden City, N.Y.: Image Books, 1960), 7.13.19 (172–73), 13.33.48 (367).

[56] Francis of Assisi, "The Second Version of the Letter to the Faithful," in *Francis and Clare: The Complete Works*, trans. Regis J. Armstrong and Ignatius C. Brady (New York: Paulist Press, 1982), 71. See also his "The Canticle of Brother Sun," in *Francis and Clare*, 37–38.

[57] John of the Cross, "The Spiritual Canticle," in *The Collected Works of St. John of the Cross*, trans. Kieran Kavanaugh and Otilio Rodriguez (Washington, D.C.: ICS Publications, 1973), 473.

Christianity and its foundations as excessively anthropocentric,[58] these sources sketch an inclusive vision of salvific concern.

Many years later, John Paul II (who wrote his doctoral dissertation on John of the Cross) became the first modern pope to employ these doxological themes for understanding humans' place and role within creation. The conclusion of his 1990 World Day of Peace message first introduces this approach in formal papal teaching. The pope highlights the "aesthetic value of creation" that "has a deep restorative power; contemplation of its magnificence imparts peace and serenity." Scripture warrants this truth, as it "speaks again and again of the goodness of creation, which is called to *glorify God.*"[59] A few paragraphs later, directly before invoking Francis of Assisi's "The Canticle of the Sun," John Paul II places human beings within this cosmic vocation to glorify God: "Respect for life and for the dignity of the human person extends also to the rest of creation, *which is called to join man in praising God* (cf. Ps 148:96)."[60] All creation shares this common doxological end.

The pope returns to this theme a year later in *Centesimus Annus*. There, he develops his aesthetic valuing of creation in the 1990 message that, at first glance, risks rendering creation as merely an object to be enjoyed. After detailing the rejection of human limits at the heart of ecological devastation and immediately before introducing human ecology, John Paul II writes in *Centesimus Annus*: "In all this, one notes first the poverty or narrowness of man's outlook, motivated as he is by a desire to possess things rather than to relate them to the truth, and lacking that disinterested, unselfish and aesthetic attitude that is born of *wonder* in the presence of being and of the beauty which enables one to *see in visible things the message of the invisible God who created them.*"[61]

Rather than meriting value simply because it imparts peace and serenity, creation is first and foremost sacramental. Made evident in the Incarnation, creation can reveal something about God, inasmuch as it magnifies God by glorifying God. Conversely, by revealing something about God,

---

[58] An argument made famous by Lynn White in his "The Historical Roots of Our Ecologic Crisis," *Science* 155 (1967): 1203–7.

[59] *Peace with God the Creator*, 14. Emphasis added.

[60] *Peace with God the Creator*, 16. Emphasis added. In 1979, Pope John Paul II named Francis of Assisi the patron saint of ecology.

[61] *Centesimus Annus*, 37. Emphasis added.

creation praises God.⁶² Thus, this section "breaks new ground. By introducing an explicitly sacramental reading of nature, John Paul profoundly deepens his category of aesthetic value. Nature is not merely to be enjoyed, nor is it merely spiritually soothing in some rather vague way; it is a vehicle for knowledge of God and self."⁶³ The revelatory quality of creation inspires the human wonder that roots a right relationship with creation, inspiring humans to hear and join its chorus of praise. As *Centesimus Annus* indicates, wonder represents an alternative posture to the unchecked "desire to possess things" that pillages creation and positions the human person as an unmoored center of the universe. Wonder, as a basis of praise, places humans within an ecosystem that has God, not themselves, at the center.

The pope intimates the eucharistic and, by extension, Christological nature of these doxological and sacramental themes in the years following *Centesimus Annus*. His 1995 apostolic letter, *Orientale Lumen*, employs these themes to describe the ecological significance of the Eucharist.⁶⁴ John Paul II observes how the Eucharist reveals the sacramental, incarnational quality of creation, that "the Word who became flesh imbues matter with a saving potential which is fully manifest in the sacraments."⁶⁵ In actualizing this potential, the Eucharist concretizes the cosmic vocation to glorify God through Christ; in the Eucharist, "[c]osmic reality . . . is summoned to give thanks because the whole universe is called to recapitulation in Christ the Lord."⁶⁶ These claims ground the ethical implications of the Eucharist. As

---

62 This point also enjoys biblical precedent. See Fretheim, *God and World in the Old Testament*, 257. For the patristic, medieval, and early modern theological roots of this claim, see Schaefer, *Theological Foundations for Environmental Ethics*, 65–102.

63 Cowdin, "John Paul II and Environmental Concern," 50.

64 This eucharistic approach to ecological questions characterizes Eastern Christianity. See, e.g., John D. Zizioulas, *The Eucharistic Communion and the World*, ed. Luke Ben Tallon, 113–73 (New York: Bloomsbury T & T Clark, 2011); and John Chryssavgis, *Creation as Sacrament: Reflections on Ecology and Spirituality* (New York: Bloomsbury T & T Clark, 2019).

65 John Paul II, Apostolic Letter *Orientale Lumen* (May 2, 1995), 11. This sacramental claim extends John Paul II's cosmic Christology. As he writes elsewhere:

> The Incarnation of God the Son signifies the taking up into unity with God not only of human nature, but in this human nature, in a sense, of everything that is "flesh": the whole of humanity, the entire visible and material world. The Incarnation, then, also has a cosmic significance, a cosmic dimension. The "first-born of all creation" (Col 1:15), becoming incarnate in the individual humanity of Christ, unites himself in some way with the entire reality of man, which is also "flesh"—and in this reality with all "flesh," with the whole of creation. (Encyclical Letter *Dominum et Vivificantem* [May 18, 1986], 50)

66 *Orientale Lumen*, 11.

the pope writes: "To those who seek a truly meaningful relationship with themselves and with the cosmos, so often disfigured by selfishness and greed, the liturgy reveals the way to the harmony of the new man, and invites him to respect the eucharistic potential of the created world. That world is destined to be assumed in the Eucharist of the Lord, in his Passover, present in the sacrifice of the altar."[67]

In its reliance on Christology, this passage develops the sacramental approach of *Centesimus Annus* in a more explicitly eucharistic way. The recognition that creation has "eucharistic potential," that it can make God present and culminates in the glorification of God, challenges a reductionistic and restrictive attitude of "selfishness and greed." In the Eucharist, the destiny of creation lies not in human grasping but in God, who is always greater. The eucharistic vocation of the human person thus lies in the task of allowing, if not enabling, creation to move toward God in praise. In this way, the Eucharist guides genuine care for creation.

In his 1998 apostolic letter "On Keeping the Lord's Day," *Dies Domini*, the pope sounds similar themes. Identifying the eucharistic assembly as the "very heart of Sunday," he remarks how "Sunday becomes a moment when people can look anew upon the wonders of nature, allowing themselves to be caught up in that marvelous and mysterious harmony."[68] Sunday worship situates human beings within a more inclusive cosmic context. It thaws any attempt to pit the good of the human person against the good of nonhuman creation, as the "marvelous and mysterious harmony" of the cosmos depends on both. The pope adds that the Sabbath enables people to "come to a deeper sense, as the Apostle says, that 'everything created by God is good and nothing is to be rejected if it is received with thanksgiving, for then it is consecrated by the word of God and prayer' (1 Tm 4:4-5)."[69] John Paul II submits that the Eucharist, especially the sacramental worldview in which it forms congregants, demands a new way of life that receives the world in glad thanksgiving rather than possesses it ravenously.[70]

---

67 *Orientale Lumen*, 11.

68 John Paul II, Apostolic Letter *Dies Domini* (May 31, 1998), 46.

69 *Dies Domini*, 67.

70 John Paul II briefly reiterated this theme in his post-synodal apostolic exhortation, *Ecclesia in Oceania* (November 22, 2001), 31, which exhorts "the people of Oceania to rejoice always in the glory of creation in a spirit of thanksgiving to the Creator."

In his final encyclical, the 2003 *Ecclesia de Eucharistia*, John Paul II also gestures toward the ecological significance of the Eucharist. Speaking from his own experience as traveler, pastor, and priest, he writes:

> I have been able to celebrate Holy Mass in chapels built along mountain paths, on lakeshores and seacoasts; I have celebrated it on altars built in stadiums and in city squares. . . . This varied scenario of celebrations of the Eucharist has given me a powerful experience of its universal and, so to speak, cosmic character. Yes, cosmic! Because even when it is celebrated on the humble altar of a country church, the Eucharist is always in some way celebrated *on the altar of the world*. It unites heaven and earth. It embraces and permeates all creation. The Son of God became man in order to restore all creation, in one supreme act of praise, to the One who made it from nothing.[71]

Just as Christian redemption has cosmic dimensions, so too does the Eucharist. All creation comes together in "one supreme act of praise" through Christ. Far from competing for glory, in the Eucharist, humans and the rest of creation participate together in this one vocation to glorify God. This encyclical was the last John Paul II wrote, yet the first encyclical to make an explicit—even if brief—reference to the ecological significance of the Eucharist. Indeed, the passage tantalizes with its brevity.

After all, John Paul II's turn to praise and, specifically, eucharistic praise, is promising in the integrative vision it presumes. Because praise orients human and nonhuman creation alike toward their common source in God, doxology can dissolve competitive understandings of the relationship between humans and the rest of creation. Thomas Nairn labels this strain in John Paul II's thought as "contemplative." Assessing its relevance for ecological questions, Nairn writes:

> The contemplative dimension of a religious ecological ethic, such as proposed by Pope John Paul, may indeed extricate the tradition from [a] "people vs. nature" impasse. In any such system, contemplation becomes the basis for an ethics of appreciation. . . . This creation and we in relation to creation are indeed gifts from God. Such a point of view brings with it an implicit framework from which to evaluate one's conduct in this world. A contemporary ethic . . . would challenge Christians to move from a

---

[71] John Paul II, Encyclical Letter *Ecclesia de Eucharistia* (April 17, 2003), 8.

point of view in which nature has little or no value apart from human choices to one which sees humanity itself as part of the larger ecosystem.[72]

Counter to tendencies that set humans and the rest of creation against each other, this emphasis unites all creation in a common chorus and vocation of praise set within a theocentric ecosystem.

In other words, a doxological, eucharistic vision can ensure that John Paul II's introduction of human ecology remains appropriately broad. That all creation shares a common vocation of praise, a calling that climaxes and is concretized through the Eucharist, provides a broader vision that can more seamlessly link human and natural ecologies alike. So too, as the documents above suggest, might eucharistic praise form habits that safeguard both ecologies by demanding that humans approach all creation with wonder, appreciation, and thanksgiving, rather than with possession, manipulation, and self-centeredness. These attitudes can counterbalance the manner that John Paul II sometimes described humans' relationship to creation (e.g., "dominate," "master," and even "use"). Affirming the sacramentality of creation—that it gives praise to God through its very existence—offers a way to affirm the intrinsic value of creation apart from its usefulness to humans, a lingering question throughout John Paul II's pontificate.

Nevertheless, the potential issues that arise from John Paul II's approach to the environment still exist. Given its importance for the church's overall approach to the ecological crisis, the competitive connotation that came to characterize human ecology in relation to natural ecology especially deserves critical assessment. These lacunae stand in tension with the doxological, eucharistic themes that also emerge in John Paul II's environmental writings. Those themes never receive fuller integration into his broader approach to the environmental crisis. Out of those documents most representative of this comprehensive approach—social encyclicals and World Day of Peace messages—John Paul II refers to the theme of praise only briefly in his 1990 World Day of Peace message and the closely related theme of sacramentality in only one of his social encyclicals, *Centesimus Annus*. The Eucharist appears in neither, despite its promise to overcome competitive understandings of both the human and the nonhuman good. References to the ecological significance of the Eucharist occur only in doc-

---

[72] Thomas A. Nairn, "The Roman Catholic Social Tradition and the Question of Ecology," in *The Ecological Challenge: Ethical, Liturgical, and Spiritual Responses*, ed. Richard N. Fragomeni and John T. Pawlikowski (Collegeville, Minn.: Liturgical Press, 1994), 37.

uments concerned with other subjects, whether Eastern Christianity, the Sabbath, or eucharistic theology.

Even in those documents, John Paul II treats this theme only briefly, as he leaves vague exactly how the Eucharist might heal ecological crises. He mentions only how the Eucharist brings about a renewed attitude toward creation in individuals without an explanation of how it responds to the many social, political, and cultural crises that constitute the ecological crisis. It is noteworthy that, though it refers to the ecological significance of the Eucharist most explicitly and most authoritatively, *Ecclesia de Eucharistia* arrived only in the last stage of John Paul II's pontificate. While John Paul II supplies a crucial first step in introducing these doxological and eucharistic themes into magisterial reflections on the environment, further theological elaboration is needed to better integrate his reflections on eucharistic praise into the comprehensive approach he takes to ecological breakdown. If "the Eucharist builds the Church and the Church makes the Eucharist," then the Eucharist necessarily informs the church's integrated approach to the ecological crisis.[73] Understanding how it does so demands a deeper explanation.

This question serves as a fitting conclusion to assess John Paul II's environmental writings. On the one hand, he deepened the distinctive contribution that Catholic social teaching makes to environmental reflection by connecting harm against creation to a panoply of social crises. On the other hand, his introduction of human ecology, the way that John Paul II names this connection, warrants further development. While including concern for human life and dignity—issues dear to his humanistic and personalist vision—ostensibly sustains that integral approach, John Paul II's initial presentation of human ecology as somehow different from, if not at odds with, natural ecology poses a potential problem. A particular type of emphasis on matters of human ecology (abortion, contraception, family structures, etc.) can end up excluding concern for natural ecology in the church's imagination, even if, as John Paul II also suggests, these two ecologies remain intimately related.

An alternative, if not complementary, strain in John Paul II's environmental thought can provide a more integrating context. The pope's turn to praise and the Eucharist can situate the human person within a broader horizon of creation's praise of God in which human and nonhuman creation are inseparably interdependent. So too, by describing the alternative attitudes

---

73 *Ecclesia de Eucharistia*, 26; see also 3, 31.

that eucharistic praise requires, can this turn begin to chart a radically, evangelically Catholic way of responding to the environmental crisis. However, despite its potential to resolve the concerns outlined above, these connections remained undeveloped observations rather than integrated reflections. The need for a fuller integration persisted for the next two pontificates; the remainder of this chapter and the next ask whether it was finally resolved.

POPE BENEDICT XVI

Following in the footsteps of his predecessor, Pope Benedict XVI also delineated a broad-angled Catholic response to the environmental crisis. In his first papal homily, he struck an ecological note in observing that "[t]he external deserts in the world are growing, because the internal deserts have become so vast."[74] Many subsequent speeches and writings from him repeated such themes. This steady concern for creation once earned him the title as "the 'greenest' Pope in history."[75] For instance, in the early days of his pontificate, he made Vatican City the first fully carbon-neutral country. He also replaced the cement roof tiles of the Paul VI auditorium with 2,400 solar panels. Most significantly, Benedict XVI deepened the intellectual foundations of the reflections of John Paul II.

Deepening Human Ecology

After clamorous shouts of "*Santo sùbito!*" at John Paul II's funeral Mass, Joseph Ratzinger was an appealing candidate for the papacy precisely as an affirmation and perpetuation of John Paul II's contagious, worldwide popularity.[76] Thus it is no surprise that, when Benedict XVI spoke on the environment, he employed his predecessor's notion of human ecology to connect environmental concern with other social concerns. Likewise, the term supported Benedict XVI's own distinct pastoral concerns. Throughout his pontificate, Benedict XVI preoccupied himself with identifying and healing the contradictions that surfaced on the political landscape of Western Europe. Whereas John Paul II decried a "culture of death," before he became pope, Benedict XVI decried a "dictatorship of relativism" that had

---

[74] Benedict XVI, *Homily for the Solemn Inauguration of the Petrine Ministry*, April 24, 2005.

[75] Woodeene Koenig-Bricker, *Ten Commandments for the Environment: Pope Benedict XVI Speaks Out for Creation and Justice* (Notre Dame, Ind.: Ave Maria Press, 2009), 8.

[76] John L. Allen, Jr., *The Rise of Benedict XVI: The Inside Story of How the Pope Was Elected and Where He Will Take the Catholic Church* (New York: Doubleday, 2005), 69–73.

come to rule the West.⁷⁷ Such relativistic contradictions, he believed, arose from Europe's forgetfulness of its Christian roots and so the Logos of its political foundations.⁷⁸ Human ecology served as a helpful category for Benedict XVI in this context, as he believed that Europe's growing ecological concern could serve as an apt toothing-stone for recovering a fuller concern for human dignity and a more consistent concern for life in general. As one example, in a 2011 speech to the German Bundestag seemingly aimed at the excesses of the German Green Party, Benedict XVI proposed that efforts to preserve the environment should logically spur, rather than oppose, similar attempts to preserve a human ecology.⁷⁹ Because of the category's importance for the aims of his pontificate, he deepened the meaning of human ecology on several occasions.

Given that John Paul II's 1990 World Day of Peace message marked the first major papal document devoted to environmental matters, Benedict XVI regularly used World Day of Peace messages to discuss the environmental crisis. Entitled *The Human Person, the Heart of Peace*, his 2007 World Day of Peace message introduces what Benedict XVI labels a "transcendent 'grammar'— . . . the body of rules for individual action and the reciprocal relationships of persons in accordance with justice and solidarity."⁸⁰ Both violations of life (including war, terrorism, maldistribution of food, abortion, experimentation on human embryos, and euthanasia) and violations of the natural equality of all persons (ranging from excessive social inequality to the discrimination and exploitation of women) violate this grammar and solidarity.⁸¹ The pope then turns to environmental degradation as an additional crisis and urges the need to preserve both a natural ecology and a human ecology. As Benedict XVI explains this dual need, "All

---

77 See, e.g., Joseph Ratzinger, *Homily at the Mass Pro Eligendo Romano Pontifice*, February 24, 2007.

78 See Jeffrey Morris, "Pope Benedict XVI on Faith and Reason in Western Europe," *Pro Ecclesia* 17, no. 3 (2008): 326–42. For some of his own reflections on this question, see Joseph Ratzinger, *A Turning Point for Europe? The Church in the Modern World—Assessment and Forecast*, trans. Brian McNeil (San Francisco: Ignatius Press, 1994); and *Europe: Today and Tomorrow*, trans. Michael J. Miller (San Francisco: Ignatius Press, 2007).

79 See Benedict XVI, *Address to the German Bundestag*, September 22, 2011. The contorted faces of Green Party members sitting in the front row during this part of the speech only confirms how prophetic holding these two ecologies together is. I thank Dr. Christopher Ruddy for drawing my attention to this speech.

80 Benedict XVI, *The Human Person* (January 1, 2007), 3.

81 *The Human Person*, 4–7.

this means that humanity, if it truly desires peace, must be increasingly conscious of the links between natural ecology, or respect for nature, and human ecology. Experience shows that *disregard for the environment always harms human coexistence*, and vice-versa."[82] To support this claim, he highlights how an insatiable desire for energy supplies and an inhumane, reductive concept of development harm both the environment and people.[83] Like it did for John Paul II, for Benedict XVI, human ecology bridges concern for natural ecology with other social concerns.

In his 2008 World Day of Peace message, "The Human Family, A Community of Peace," Benedict XVI continues to make these connections. As in the previous year, he stresses the importance of respecting a grammar, in this case the grammar of peace taught by the family.[84] After denouncing all forces that undermine the structure of the family—which, as John Paul II proposed in *Centesimus Annus*, threaten human ecology—he employs this familial language to observe how the earth serves as "our common home."[85] He accordingly exhorts men and women to care for this home, which "means not selfishly considering nature to be at the complete disposal of our own interests."[86] Specifically, people must consider future generations, remember the poor, and promote "a model of sustainable development capable of ensuring the well-being of all while respecting environmental balances."[87] Discussions of economics, law, armed conflict, and nuclear disarmament follow.[88] Once again, Benedict XVI interprets the environmental crisis within a spectrum of urgent and interrelated social concerns. While he does not explicitly employ the phrase *human ecology*, he does so implicitly by locating environmental questions within the context of the human family.

In the following year, Benedict XVI published his only social encyclical, *Caritas in Veritate*, devoting it to the question of integral human development. As John Paul II had exhibited early in his pontificate, discussions of development naturally raise questions about care for creation. Benedict

---

82 *The Human Person*, 8.
83 *The Human Person*, 9–10.
84 Benedict XVI, *The Human Family* (January 1, 2008), 3.
85 *The Human Family*, 8.
86 *The Human Family*, 7.
87 *The Human Family*, 7.
88 *The Human Family*, 9–14.

XVI writes in the encyclical that "the subject of development is . . . closely related to the duties arising from *our relationship to the natural environment.*"[89] Reiterating and developing many of the themes found in his previous writings, he urges that, since the environment is God's gift to everyone, caring for it involves responsibility toward current and future generations, especially the poor. In short, as he writes, "projects for integral human development . . . need to be *marked by solidarity and inter-generational justice.*"[90] Benedict XVI couples this stress on solidarity to his notion of the grammar of creation. Precisely because nature is a gift prior to the human person and "*expresses a design of love and truth . . . an inbuilt order,*" people must see it not as "raw material to be manipulated at our pleasure" but instead as "a wondrous work of the Creator containing a 'grammar' which sets forth ends and criteria for its wise use, not its reckless exploitation."[91] Whereas Benedict XVI alluded to a "grammar" of relationships and responsibilities in his previous World Day of Peace messages, here he begins to apply this language explicitly to the environment.

The twin themes of solidarity and the grammar of creation contextualize Benedict XVI's treatment of human ecology in the encyclical. Echoing his 2007 World Day of Peace message, the pope begins, "*The way humanity treats the environment influences the way it treats itself, and vice-versa.*"[92] Thus, he continues, the church's responsibility toward creation requires safeguarding both human and natural ecologies. "The deterioration of nature is in fact closely connected to the culture that shapes human coexistence: *when 'human ecology' is respected within society, environmental ecology also benefits.*"[93] This bond illustrates that the environmental crisis marks something more than simply an economic crisis; it is a moral crisis. He writes:

> If there is a lack of respect for the right to life and to a natural death, if human conception, gestation and birth are made artificial, if human embryos are sacrificed to research, the conscience of society ends up

---

[89] Benedict XVI, Encyclical Letter *Caritas in Veritate* (June 29, 2009), 48. For an especially helpful commentary on the encyclical, see David L. Schindler, "The Anthropological Vision of *Caritas in Veritate* in Light of Economic and Cultural Life in the United States," *Communio: International Catholic Review* 37, no. 4 (Winter 2010): 558–79.

[90] *Caritas in Veritate*, 48.

[91] *Caritas in Veritate*, 48.

[92] *Caritas in Veritate*, 51.

[93] *Caritas in Veritate*, 51.

losing the concept of human ecology and, along with it, that of environmental ecology. . . . The book of nature is one and indivisible: it takes in not only the environment but also life, sexuality, marriage, the family, social relations: in a word, integral human development. Our duties towards the environment are linked to our duties towards the human person, considered in himself and in relation to others. It would be wrong to uphold one set of duties while trampling on the other. Herein lies a grave contradiction in our mentality and practice today: one which demeans the person, disrupts the environment and damages society.[94]

Here, Benedict XVI completes the trajectory begun in *Centesimus Annus*: human ecology links the environment to other urgent social issues. The pope integrates environmental concern with threats to human ecology, such as artificial contraception, stem cell research, euthanasia, and shifting family structures. The relativistic, "grave contradictions" of Western politics, where factions such as the German Green Party support environmental sustainability while also supporting abortion, likely foreground Benedict XVI's admonitions here. Though political platforms throughout the West seemingly assume otherwise, Benedict XVI maintains that neglecting one ecology jeopardizes the other ecology, as both comprise the one and indivisible book of nature. A genuinely integral development demands promoting both ecologies.

His 2010 World Day of Peace message, "If You Want to Cultivate Peace, Protect Creation," also advances this integrated approach. After decrying pollution, climate change, loss of biodiversity, the emergence of environmental refugees, and conflicts over access to natural resources, Benedict XVI concludes, "It should be evident that the ecological crisis cannot be viewed in isolation from other related questions, since it is closely linked to the notion of development itself and our understanding of man in his relationship to others and to the rest of creation."[95] The opening chapters of Genesis, he submits, clarify the nature of these relationships by indicating that humans' exploitative and dominative relationship to creation is the result of sin. The true meaning of God's original command is "not a simple conferral of authority, but rather a summons to responsibility."[96] Applied to the environment, this responsibility includes a greater sense of intergen-

---

94 *Caritas in Veritate*, 51.

95 Benedict XVI, *If You Want to Cultivate Peace* (January 1, 2010), 5. He adds in the same section, "our present crises—be they economic, food-related, environmental or social—are ultimately moral crises, and all of them are interrelated."

96 *If You Want to Cultivate Peace*, 6.

erational and intragenerational solidarity, more sober lifestyles, and "a model of development based on the centrality of the human person."[97] Since the "degradation of nature is closely linked to the cultural models shaping human coexistence," Benedict adds, this responsibility must be anchored in a human ecology.[98]

In all these writings, Benedict XVI continues to develop the integral approach to the environmental crisis that characterizes Catholic social teaching. Most significantly, he cements human ecology as the primary way to name that approach. While John Paul II developed the concept only in the latter half of his pontificate as he came to incorporate the environmental crisis into his broader pastoral-theological framework, Benedict XVI's pontificate afforded ampler opportunity to reflect more deeply on the meaning of human ecology and its precise relationship to natural ecology.

Relating Human and Natural Ecologies

Given the competitive connotations that the term came to carry, however, Benedict XVI's development of John Paul II's notion of human ecology once again raises questions. The theological reception of Benedict XVI's writings confirms as much. Several commentators fear that his continued use of the term collapses matters of natural ecology into matters of human ecology, violating the integrity of natural ecology.[99] If matters of human ecology are assumed to hold a more pressing place within Catholic social teaching, then continued use of the term risks obscuring environmental concern in the church's life and mission.

Still, Benedict XVI ushers in a deeper maturation of the tradition regarding care for creation. Whereas John Paul II sometimes uses language like "dominate" and "subdue" to describe humans' relationship to creation, Benedict XVI avoids such language, opting for words like "care" and "cultivate" instead. Likewise, though John Paul II seemingly implies a competitive relationship between human and natural ecologies in *Centesimus Annus*, Benedict XVI balances these ecologies with more circumspection, insisting on the

---

97 *If You Want to Cultivate Peace*, 8, 9.

98 *If You Want to Cultivate Peace*, 11–12.

99 See Daniel P. Scheid, "Common Good: Human, or Cosmic?" *Journal of Religion & Society Supplement* 9 (2013): 5–15, at 7; Jame Schaefer, "Solidarity, Subsidiarity, and Preference for the Poor: Extending Catholic Social Teaching in Response to the Climate Crisis," in *Confronting the Climate Crisis: Catholic Theological Perspectives*, ed. Jame Schaefer (Milwaukee, Wis.: Marquette University Press, 2012), 409–10; and Dorr, *Option for the Poor and for the Earth*, 377, 384.

mutual interpenetration between caring for the environment and caring for the human person. As he says in his 2007 World Day of Peace message, "*disregard for the environment always harms human coexistence,* and vice-versa,"[100] and, as he states in *Caritas in Veritate,* "*The way humanity treats the environment influences the way it treats itself, and vice-versa.*"[101] These words show that while human and natural ecologies are inextricable, each does retain its own integrity and validity. Far from being at odds with or competing against each other, human and natural ecologies inform each other.[102]

Precisely how the two ecologies relate to each other remains unclear, nevertheless. Again, the reception of Benedict XVI's writings illustrates this point. For instance, while appreciative of Benedict XVI's effort to conduct an integral approach, Maura Ryan finds his "'whole cloth environmentalism' . . . ultimately unconvincing," noting that, as the U.S. political landscape has exposed, "it is not obvious that believing in the immorality of abortion or same-sex marriage leads to respect for creation or to a commitment to environmental sustainability."[103] In the words of another commentator, the main reason for this quandary is that "Benedict does not . . . provide a straightforward explanation of precisely how human ecology generates environmental ecology."[104] The absence of a straightforward explanation feeds the fears of the commentators referenced at the beginning of this section. An insufficient account of how human and natural ecologies sustain each other can allow concerns of human ecology to supersede concerns of natural ecology in the reception of church teaching.

At least two distinct, though related, themes in Benedict XVI's environmental writings can help explain this connection and thus strengthen it: the grammar of creation and solidarity.[105] As he did in many other cases, here,

---

[100] Benedict XVI, *The Human Person,* 8.

[101] Benedict XVI, *Caritas in Veritate,* 51.

[102] See Stratford Caldecott, "At Home in the Cosmos: The Revealing of the Sons of God," *Nova et Vetera,* English ed., 10, no. 1 (2012): 105–20, at 108–9.

[103] Maura A. Ryan, "A New Shade of Green? Nature, Freedom, and Sexual Difference in *Caritas in Veritate,*" *Theological Studies* 71, no. 2 (June 2010): 335–49, at 345.

[104] Mary Ashley, "If You Want Responsibility, Build Relationship: A Personalist Approach to Benedict XVI's Environmental Vision," in *Environmental Justice and Climate Change: Assessing Pope Benedict XVI's Ecological Vision for the Catholic Church in the United States,* ed. Jame Schaefer and Tobias Winright (Lanham, Md.: Lexington Books, 2013), 30.

[105] David Cloutier, "Working with the Grammar of Creation: Benedict XVI, Wendell Berry, and the Unity of the Catholic Moral Vision," *Communio: International Catholic Review* 37 (Winter 2010): 606–33.

Benedict XVI can provide the intellectual scaffolding for a claim made initially by John Paul II. Ratzinger's consistent emphasis on the priority of gift and receptivity over the "makeable" and "doable" (*Machbarkeit*) grounds the first possible link: the grammar of creation.[106] This distinct emphasis, he believes, permits Christianity to challenge modernity's instrumentalist, Marxist assumptions and its creeping cult of technology—encapsulated in Karl Marx's phrase, "*verum quia faciendum*."[107] Ratzinger frequently contrasts this stance of modernity with the stance of Christian faith: "For in fact man does not live on the bread of practiceability (*Machbarkeit*) alone... Meaning, that is, the ground on which our existence as a totality can stand and live, cannot be made (*machen*) but only received."[108] The theme resurfaces throughout his writings, whether in his defining "the very heart of sin" as "human beings' denial of their creatureliness, inasmuch as they refuse to accept the standard and the limitations that are implicit in it,"[109] describing "making liturgy" as idolatrous,[110] deploring a "merely human church" that "is reduced to the level of the makeable, of the obvious, of opinion,"[111] fearing the "neo-chiliasm" of certain liberation theologies in their expectations of "an intra-historical perfectibility of the world,"[112] or coining a "grammar of creation" in *Caritas in Veritate*.

---

[106] For an overview of this theme, see James Corkery, *Joseph Ratzinger's Theological Ideas: Wise Cautions and Legitimate Hopes* (New York: Paulist Press, 2009), 31–33, 40–41, 52–56.

[107] See Joseph Ratzinger, "The Christian and the Modern World: Reflections on the Pastoral Constitution of the Second Vatican Council," in *Dogma and Preaching: Applying Christian Doctrine to Daily Life*, ed. Michael J. Miller, trans. Michael J. Miller and Matthew J. O'Connell (San Francisco: Ignatius Press, 2011), 173–76; and "Neuheidentum," in *Lexikon für Theologie und Kirche* VII, ed. Josef Höfer and Karl Rahner (Freiburg: Verlag Herder, 1962), 907–9.

[108] Joseph Ratzinger, *Introduction to Christianity*, trans. J. R. Foster and Michael J. Miller (San Francisco: Ignatius Press, 2004), 72–73, also see 63–70, 266–69; and Ratzinger, "Sühne: V. Systematisch," in *Lexikon für Theologie und Kirche* IX, ed. Josef Höfer and Karl Rahner (Freiburg: Verlag Herder, 1964), 1157: "Das Beschenktsein bestimmt die ganze Struktur der christlichen Existenz."

[109] Joseph Ratzinger, *"In the Beginning...": A Catholic Understanding of the Story of Creation and the Fall*, trans. Boniface Ramsey (Grand Rapids, Mich.: Eerdmans, 1995), 70.

[110] Joseph Ratzinger, "The Spirit of the Liturgy," in *Theology of the Liturgy*, vol. 11, *Joseph Ratzinger Collected Works*, ed. Michael J. Miller (San Francisco: Ignatius Press, 2014), 11. See also Joseph Ratzinger, *Milestones, Memoirs: 1927–1977*, trans. Erasmo Leiva-Merikakis (San Francisco: Ignatius Press, 1998), 148–49.

[111] Joseph Ratzinger, *Called to Communion: Understanding the Church Today*, trans. Adrian Walker (San Francisco: Ignatius Press, 1996), 139. See also Joseph Ratzinger, with Vittorio Messori, *The Ratzinger Report: An Exclusive Interview on the State of the Church*, trans. Salvator Attanasio and Graham Harrison (San Francisco: Ignatius Press, 1985), 46.

[112] Joseph Ratzinger, *Eschatology: Death and Eternal Life*, 2nd ed., trans. Michael Waldstein and Aidan Nichols (Washington, D.C.: The Catholic University of America Press, 1988), 213.

This grammar imparts an ontological claim that comprehensively prioritizes gift and instills a stance of receptivity in human living. Lauding Benedict XVI's ability to integrate matters of natural ecology with matters of human ecology in *Caritas in Veritate*, David Cloutier writes:

> the pope here suggests that a presumptuous refusal to recognize and respect the given order of nature is what connects these issues. Respect for the dignity of persons and the integrity of the environment are one, because creation is one. We threaten it by our presumptions to make such an order ourselves, by our wills, rather than receive it and work with the natural order as a gift that is "prior to us."[113]

Neglecting the gift character of either the environment or the human person violates the common grammar of creation in which both participate. The undue manipulation of this grammar, in its human or nonhuman form, reveals the quasi-idolatrous, "promethean presumption" of modernity.[114] Conversely, the flourishing of both ecologies demands from oneself a consistent stance of humble receptivity toward the sacred irreducibility of both the human and the nonhuman other. Rather than imposing one's will on creation, the grammar of creation demands that one be attentive to and cooperate patiently with its inner logic. Care for human and nonhuman creation thus forms a single vocation; the grammar of creation yokes together natural and human ecologies.

The "dialogical" or "pro-existent" character of Ratzinger's theology provides a second way to tie the ecologies together.[115] Like gift, this emphasis buttresses Ratzinger's critical stance toward modernity. Against the Cartesian *Cogito*, Ratzinger asserts that the human person "is a being that can only 'be' by virtue of others."[116] In the same work, he states, "Being a Christian means

---

[113] Cloutier, "Working with the Grammar of Creation," 609. See also "Working with the Grammar of Creation," 611–12, where Cloutier remarks on the "schizophrenia" of those who apply this logic of gift to the human person but not to the environment, and vice-versa.

[114] See Matthew Philipp Whelan, "The Grammar of Creation: Agriculture in the Thought of Pope Benedict XVI," in *Environmental Justice and Climate Change*, 113–18. See also Benedict XVI, Encyclical Letter *Spe Salvi* (November 30, 2007), 16–17.

[115] For overviews of this theme, see, e.g., Christopher Ruddy, "'For the Many': The Vicarious-Representative Heart of Joseph Ratzinger's Theology," *Theological Studies* 75 (September 2014): 564–84; Christopher S. Collins, *The Word Made Love: The Dialogical Theology of Joseph Ratzinger* (Collegeville, Minn.: Liturgical Press, 2013); and Corkery, *Joseph Ratzinger's Theological Ideas*, 38–43.

[116] Ratzinger, *Introduction to Christianity*, 246. See also *Caritas in Veritate*, 53: "As a spiritual being, the human creature is defined through interpersonal relations. The more authentically

essentially changing over from being for oneself to being for one another."[117] The theme spans the entirety of Ratzinger's thought, whether in recalling that the doctrine of the Trinity means that "the dialogue, the *relatio*, stands beside the substance as an equally primordial form of being,"[118] in presenting the Son as totally "from" the Father and "for" others,[119] in understanding true active participation in liturgy "as a *logike latreia*, the 'logicizing' of my existence, my interior contemporaneity with the self-giving of Christ,"[120] or in underscoring the "new 'we'" that ecclesial existence forges.[121] Even eternal life takes on a "dialogical character"—with both God and others (the "Body of Christ")—since "relation makes immortal; openness, not closure, is the end in which we find our beginning."[122] Hell is the final rejection of this dialogical character of authentic human existence, of conforming oneself to Christ's own pro-existence, and of sharing in God's triune relationship.[123] Ratzinger believes that the reduction of salvation to the individual betrays the relational essence of Christianity and presents one of the greatest challenges to the church today.[124] As pope, in outlining Catholic social teaching, he continually urged Christians to take a counterclutural stance of solidarity to anticipate this communal scope of salvation.

---

he or she lives these relations, the more his or her own personal identity matures. It is not by isolation that man establishes his worth, but by placing himself in relation with others and with God."

117 Ratzinger, *Introduction to Christianity*, 252. See also Ratzinger, "On the Understanding of 'Person' in Theology," in *Dogma and Preaching*, 181–96.

118 Ratzinger, *Introduction to Christianity*, 183.

119 Joseph Ratzinger, *From the Baptism in the Jordan to the Transfiguration*, pt. 1, *Jesus of Nazareth*, trans. Adrian Walker (New York: Doubleday, 2007), 7; and Ratzinger, *Holy Week: From the Entrance into Jerusalem to the Resurrection*, pt. 1, *Jesus of Nazareth*, trans. Philip J. Whitmore (San Francisco: Ignatius Press, 2011), 134: "[Jesus'] entire being is expressed by the word 'pro-existence'—he is there, not for himself but for others. This is not merely a dimension of his existence, but its innermost essence and its entirety. His very being is a 'being-for'. If we are able to grasp this, then we have truly come close to the mystery of Jesus, and we have understood what discipleship is."

120 Ratzinger, "The Spirit of the Liturgy," 34; see also, "The Spirit of the Liturgy," 54–55.

121 Joseph Ratzinger, *Pilgrim Fellowship of Faith: The Church as Communion*, trans. Henry Taylor (San Francisco: Ignatius Press, 2005), 78.

122 Ratzinger, *Eschatology*, 157–58, 236.

123 Ratzinger, *Introduction to Christianity*, 300.

124 See, e.g., Joseph Ratzinger, foreword to *Catholicism: Christ and the Common Destiny of Man*, by Henri de Lubac, trans. Lancelot C. Sheppard and Elizabeth Englund (San Francisco: Ignatius Press, 1998), 11–12; Ratzinger, *Principles of Catholic Theology* (San Francisco: Ignatius Press, 1987), 44–55; Ratzinger, *Eschatology*, 13–14; and Benedict XVI, *Spe Salvi*, 13–15, 25.

In this worldview, humans can never be defined entirely in themselves but always in relation to others, whether with God, with other persons, or with creation. All creation, human and nonhuman alike, is inextricably tied together as it shares a common end (and beginning) in the God who is loving relationship.[125] What Cloutier labels Benedict XVI's "teleology of universal solidarity" challenges an "anemic individualism [that] allows social solidarity to atrophy," which promotes "purely secular narratives of earthly progress" corrosive to both ecologies.[126] Without this cosmic vision of solidarity, humans can envision themselves apart from creation, and human progress can devolve into a nihilistic consumption of creation that knows no limits. To truncate, whether vertically or horizontally, the world's eschatological end fragments the relational character of all existence. So too does it undermine the openness to relationship, including with creation, that constitutes the human vocation, instead leaving one to suffocate in the confines of one's own existence. A broader, genuinely theological conception of progress, meanwhile, orients human and natural ecologies together toward God, breaking open the human person to the ecstatic "being-for" that defines Christian existence. In this communal framework, Benedict XVI's understanding of the human person (human ecology) within the natural world (natural ecology) is thoroughly noncompetitive. In view of their common end, each implies the other.

These themes of gift and relationality supply two principal connections between human and natural ecologies in Benedict XVI's thought. Avoiding the potential pitfalls found in John Paul II's initial presentation of human ecology, Benedict XVI presents an unequivocally noncompetitive understanding of human and natural ecologies. Nevertheless, the presence of at least two distinct ways to connect these two ecologies, as well as the large amount of commentary that attempts to account for their connection, suggests that this seamlessness remains only an implication.[127] This ambiguity

---

[125] See Ratzinger, *Eschatology*, 238.

[126] Cloutier, "Working with the Grammar of Creation," 612–13.

[127] Along with secondary literature referenced already in this section, for additional treatments of the connection between human and natural ecologies in Benedict XVI's thought, see Damien Marie Savino, "Nature, Soil, and God: Soils and the 'Grammar of Nature,'" in *Jesus Christ: The New Face of Social Progress*, ed. Peter Casarella (Grand Rapids, Mich.: Eerdmans, 2015), 322–23; Scott G. Hefelfinger, "Human, Social, and Natural Ecology: Three Ecologies, One Cosmology, and the Common Good," in *Environmental Justice and Climate Change*, 71–72; and Michael Baur, "Natural Law and the Natural Environment: Pope Benedict XVI's Vision beyond Utilitarianism and Deontology," in *Environmental Justice and Climate Change*, 53–54.

poses a problem, since human ecology had become freighted with contrastive connotations under John Paul II.

It is precisely this ambiguity that enables continuing contrastive interpretations of human ecology as it relates to natural ecology. For instance, in a study of Benedict XVI's environmental teaching, Liju Porathur states that "[f]or him natural ecology is important, but human ecology is first" and, despite acknowledging the interdependency Benedict XVI establishes between the two ecologies, concludes, "The Pope gives, however, preference to human ecology over natural ecology."[128] In a polarized landscape, the ambiguity poses a particular risk for receiving Catholic social teaching in a U.S. context. Intending to define "human ecology" for the Institute for Human Ecology formed at The Catholic University of America in 2016, Jay Richards—a leading fellow of the Institute—writes:

> There's a paradox for those of us who live in the United States and Western Europe. In the last fifty years, we've become more concerned about natural ecosystems. And despite problem areas, the air we breathe and water we drink are cleaner than ever. Almost no one dies from the air and water borne diseases that beset our ancestors for millennia. Most of the industrial pollutants of the last century, from lead to sulfur dioxide, are gone. . . . And still, leading voices in our culture push the cause of natural ecology with life-and-death urgency. In contrast, our culture has grown detrimental to genuine human flourishing. In the last fifty years, institutions most vital to human flourishing have been under assault. The first environment in which we enter the world—our mother's womb—is now a high-risk zone. Roughly one in four American children are raised by only one parent. . . . About half of marriages end in divorce. Governments around the world now deign to redefine marriage, an institution that predates every state and society. And fast on the heels of that assault is the attack on human nature itself. Even the existence of men and women, of male and female, father and mother, is up for grabs. Any defense of human ecology, then, must seek to protect and preserve not just our natural environment, but our moral and cultural environment as well. Man cannot, and should not, live by clean food, water, and air alone; an ecology is needed that cultivates the mind, the will, and freedom.[129]

---

[128] Liju Porathur, "Ecology vis-à-vis Human Ecology after Pope Benedict XVI," *Journal of Dharma* 39, no. 2 (April–June 2014): 405–22, at 422, 411.

[129] Jay W. Richards, "What Exactly Is Human Ecology?" *The Spotlight—A Monthly Digest from The Institute for Human Ecology at The Catholic University of America* (September 2017), https://ihe.catholic.edu/exactly-human-ecology/. For a less contrastive presentation of human ecology from the Institute that more closely approximates John Paul II and Benedict XVI's

In downplaying environmental exigencies like industrial pollution and contaminated water to focus instead on questions like abortion, gay marriage, and gender identity—as central as those issues are to the church's moral teaching—Richards typifies here the concrete consequences of competitive interpretations of the relationship between natural and human ecologies. Natural ecology is presented as a threat to a full concern for human ecology. Conversely, as the beginning of this section showed, others risk seeing concern for human ecology as a threat to concern for natural ecology. Both presume a competitive relationship between the two ecologies, to the detriment of each. This zero-sum logic jeopardizes the whole cloth environmentalism of Catholic social teaching. In a place like the United States, partisan politics easily co-opts this division of concern between natural and human ecologies, as it correlates roughly to the polarized concerns of progressives and conservatives, respectively.

Such interpretations set human ecology and natural ecology in tension, despite Benedict XVI's insistence on their interdependent integrity. Each ecology necessarily implies the other. Asking which one deserves precedence obscures the common ground that allows each ecology to build up the other and flourish. Ironically, this distortion perpetuates the internal contradictions of the West that Benedict XVI critiqued. Thus, these competitive interpretations impoverish the valuable integral approach to the environment that distinguishes Catholic social teaching by domesticating this prophetic linking through the artificial divisions of Western politics. As was the case with John Paul II, the work of Benedict XVI raises the question of how to integrate the two ecologies in a more seamless framework.

The Promise of a Doxological, Eucharistic Turn

Throughout his theological and ministerial career, Benedict XVI stressed the vital place of the liturgy in the life and mission of the church. In the spirit of his papal namesake, he hoped to highlight the centrality of the *opus Dei*, how the church's *ora* suffuses its *labora*.[130] In his words,

---

synthetic intentions, see Reinhard Hütter, "The Ecological Crisis: A Common Responsibility," The Institute for Human Ecology (October 22, 2019), https://ihe.catholic.edu/the-ecological-crisis-a-common-responsibility/.

130 See Benedict, *RB 1980: The Rule of St. Benedict*, trans. Timothy Fry (Collegeville, Minn.: Liturgical Press, 1981), chap. 43. On the Benedictine influences on Benedict XVI, see Elio Guerriero, *Benedict XVI: His Life and Thought*, trans. William J. Melcher (San Francisco: Ignatius Press, 2018), 440–44.

> The Church becomes visible for people in many ways, in charitable activity or in missionary projects, but the place where the Church is actually experienced most of all as Church is the liturgy. And that is also as it should be. At the end of the day, the point of the Church is to turn us toward God and to enable God to enter into the world. The liturgy is the act in which we believe that *he* enters our lives and that we touch him. It is the act in which what is really essential takes place: We come into contact with God. He comes to us—and we are illumined by him.[131]

Whether in his writings on ecclesiology, anthropology, Christology, social ethics, or environmental concern, Benedict XVI prioritized worship as the unsurpassable locus of the Christian life.

Indeed, prior to his election as pope, Ratzinger educed the doxological and eucharistic character of creation as well as the cosmic quality of worship. At the heart of this recurring theme lies his insistence that the "historical liturgy of Christendom is and always will be cosmic, without separation and without confusion, and only as such does it stand erect in its full grandeur."[132] Believing that "we are in the midst of a crisis in the anthropocentric view of the world," Ratzinger recommends that "we ... need to be reminded that liturgy involves the cosmos—that Christian worship is cosmic worship. In it we pray and sing in concert with everything 'in heaven, on earth, and under the earth'; we join in with the praise rendered by the sun and the stars."[133] "Creation exists for the sake of worship,"[134] since, as the authors of Genesis indicate, "Creation moves to the Sabbath, to the day on which man and the whole created order participates in God's rest, in his freedom."[135] The doxological dynamism of creation grounds its sacramentality. The Eucharist enacts this upward dynamism in a unique way, carrying created reality into this chorus of praise: "The elements of the earth are transubstantiated, pulled, so to speak from their

---

[131] Benedict XVI, with Peter Seewald, *Light of the World: The Pope, the Church, and the Signs of the Times*, trans. Michael J. Miller and Adrian J. Walker (San Francisco: Ignatius Press, 2010), 155. See Christopher Ruddy, "*Deus Adorans, Homo Adorans*: Joseph Ratzinger's Liturgical Christology and Anthropology," in *The Center Is Jesus Christ Himself: Essays on Revelation, Salvation, and Evangelization in Honor of Robert P. Imbelli*, ed. Andrew Meszaros, 173–88 (Washington, D.C.: The Catholic University of America Press, 2021).

[132] Ratzinger, "The Spirit of the Liturgy," 19.

[133] Joseph Ratzinger, "Eastward- or Westward-Facing Position? A Correction," in *Theology of the Liturgy*, 391. See also Ratzinger, "The Spirit of the Liturgy," 42.

[134] Ratzinger, "*In the Beginning ...*," 27.

[135] Ratzinger, "The Spirit of the Liturgy," 13.

creaturely anchorage, grasped at the deepest ground of their being, and changed into the Body and Blood of the Lord. The New Heaven and the New Earth are anticipated."[136] This cosmic understanding of praise, Ratzinger insists, must be remembered since "man's own being is insufficient for what he has to express, and so he invites the whole of creation to become a song with himself."[137] These passages intimate how Ratzinger's liturgical vision overcomes competitive understandings of the relationship between the human person and the rest of creation. Together, both form a common song of praise; one without the other makes that hymn incomplete.

At the same time, Ratzinger employs this liturgical framework to safeguard the human person's unique dignity and to outline a responsible exercise of this dignity. At one point, he designates the human person as a priestly "kind of bridge" charged with "sharing the responsibility for the unity of creation, incarnating spirit in himself and, conversely, lifting material being up to God—and, thereby, all in all, making a contribution to the great symphony of creation."[138] This worshipful vocation also directs its participants toward the humble, receptive shape of this responsibility for creation. As Ratzinger writes, "Thanksgiving for creation could . . . become a reflection on creation, a reflection on behavior appropriate to our being part of creation," particularly since "[t]he problems of our time are attributable in good measure to the fact that we have regarded the world as mere matter, and matter as mere raw material for the production line."[139] Rejecting the doxological end and sacramental character of creation, Ratzinger suggests, traps oneself and all of creation under the "slavery of activity (*Knechtschaft des Machens*)," triggering ecological catastrophe.[140] Recovering this doxological posture thus has ethical implications.

---

[136] Ratzinger, "The Spirit of the Liturgy," 107.

[137] Ratzinger, "The Spirit of the Liturgy," 84.

[138] Joseph Ratzinger, *God and the World: A Conversation with Peter Seewald*, trans. Henry Taylor (San Francisco: Ignatius Press, 2002), 89. Ratzinger proposes elsewhere that this is how one can read Gen 1:28 in a nonexploitative way: "The Creator's directive to humankind means that it is supposed to look after the world as God's creation, and to do so in accordance with the rhythm and the logic of creation." "*In the Beginning . . .*," 34.

[139] Joseph Ratzinger, "Think of Acting According to the Spirit," in *Seek That Which Is Above: Meditations through the Year*, 2nd ed., trans. Graham Harrison (San Francisco: Ignatius Press, 2007), 112.

[140] Ratzinger, "*In the Beginning . . .*," 32. "The inner rhythm that we infer from the scriptural account—the rhythm of worship, which is the rhythm of the history of God's love for humankind—is stilled. Today we can see without any difficulty the horrible consequences of this

Ratzinger's liturgical writings disclose an integral understanding of human and natural ecologies. Admitting that "too much reliance on the 'human' half of the phrase [human ecology] derogates from ensuring that the fullness of our belief in the goodness, beauty and value of all created things might be sustained," Kevin Irwin accordingly perceives that Ratzinger's "own appreciation for the liturgy does provide a way to remind ourselves of the wide angle lens which Catholicism puts on the world and *all* that dwell on it, humans and all of God's creatures."[141] For Ratzinger, worship holds together both the themes of solidarity and the grammar of creation undergirding human and natural ecologies. Worship patterns the theological teleology of the cosmos that joins all creation in solidarity. All of creation participates in this common praise of and orientation toward God, even as humans play a unique mediatory role in realizing this end. Befitting the receptive stance demanded by the grammar of creation, worship likewise promotes a human attitude of humble thanksgiving for the gift of creation. This posture challenges an attitude that reduces all creation, including humans, to mere matter manipulated at will. The priestly vocation of humans requires that they conduct, rather than force, this common grammar of praise. Ratzinger's liturgical theology intimates that worship concretizes a noncompetitive relationship between human and natural ecologies and frames an ethics that serves both simultaneously.

Ratzinger continued to sound many of these themes after his election as Benedict XVI. In his first post-synodal apostolic exhortation, the 2007 *Sacramentum Caritatis*, he locates these themes explicitly in a eucharistic context. Highlighting the ecological significance of the presentation of the gifts, he states, "in the bread and wine that we bring to the altar, all creation is taken up by Christ the Redeemer to be transformed and presented to the Father."[142] The Eucharist, while offered uniquely by the human person through Christ, unites all creation in a doxological solidarity. Under the heading of how the Eucharist is "a mystery to be offered to the world," Bene-

---

attitude. We sense a threat that does not lie in the distant future but that encounters us in the immediate present. The humility of faith has disappeared, shattered on the arrogance of activity (*Hochmut des Machens*)." *"In the Beginning . . . ,"* 37–38.

[141] Kevin W. Irwin, "The World as God's Icon: Creation, Sacramentality, Liturgy," in *Environmental Justice and Climate Change*, 155.

[142] Benedict XVI, Post-Synodal Apostolic Exhortation *Sacramentum Caritatis* (February 22, 2007), 47.

dict XVI discusses how eucharistic participation demands care for creation. The passage deserves quotation at length:

> Finally, to develop a profound eucharistic spirituality that is also capable of significantly affecting the fabric of society, the Christian people, in giving thanks to God through the Eucharist, should be conscious that they do so in the name of all creation, aspiring to the sanctification of the world and working intensely to that end. The Eucharist itself powerfully illuminates human history and the whole cosmos. In this sacramental perspective we learn, day by day, that every ecclesial event is a kind of sign by which God makes himself known and challenges us. The eucharistic form of life can thus help foster a real change in the way we approach history and the world. The liturgy itself teaches us this, when, during the presentation of the gifts, the priest raises to God a prayer of blessing and petition over the bread and wine, "fruit of the earth," "fruit of the vine" and "work of human hands." With these words, the rite not only includes in our offering to God all human efforts and activity, but also leads us to see the world as God's creation, which brings forth everything we need for our sustenance. The world is not something indifferent, raw material to be utilized simply as we see fit. Rather, it is part of God's good plan, in which all of us are called to be sons and daughters in the one Son of God, Jesus Christ (cf. Eph 1:4–12).[143]

Here, the pope continues to present eucharistic worship in a cosmically solidaristic, nondualistic way, namely as something performed "in the name of all creation." He also locates his previous insistence on fostering a humble stance of receptive thanksgiving toward creation over a reductive, exploitative lens (characteristic of *Machbarkeit*) explicitly in a "sacramental perspective." That is, the eucharistic celebration gives flesh to the grammar of creation and the cosmic solidarity that both link human and natural ecologies. Finally, Benedict XVI notes the ethical implications of the Eucharist, as it "fosters a real change in the way we approach history and the world." It forms and "teaches us" to live in relationship with and in humble thanksgiving toward the wondrous gift of God's creation, such that it becomes a "form of life." *Sacramentum Caritatis* sketches the most developed and richest reflection on the ecological relevance of the Eucharist in papal teaching to this point.

Caritas in Veritate, Benedict XVI's most extensive treatment of the environment in a major Vatican document, refers to these eucharistic themes

---

[143] *Sacramentum Caritatis*, 92.

only implicitly, however. In the encyclical, Benedict stresses the importance of seeing creation, including the human person, as a "*wondrous* work" and "the *wonderful* result of God's creative activity." To see creation otherwise misconstrues it as either an "untouchable taboo" or "the result of mere chance or evolutionary determinism." The latter, Benedict believes, leads either to a "waning" of human responsibility toward creation or, even worse, to a "reckless exploitation" of creation.[144] As he proposed in *Sacramentum Caritatis*, the "sacramental perspective" that characterizes the Eucharist allows one to see creation as revelatory of God, as God's wondrous work. Nevertheless, this section in *Caritas in Veritate* refers to neither sacramentality, doxology, nor Eucharist explicitly. As Michael Budde laments, the encyclical in general "has relatively little on the Church as a material, institutional reality."[145] The Eucharist, a specific and concrete Christian practice, plays no overt role in the encyclical.

Benedict XVI refers to these themes in only one of his World Day of Peace messages: his 2010 message. As opposed to seeing creatures "merely as products of chance or an evolutionary determinism," he again calls humanity to see "creation as God's gift" so that, "[w]ith the Psalmist, we can exclaim with wonder: 'When I look at your heavens, the work of your hands, the moon and the stars which you have established; what is man that you are mindful of him, and the son of man that you care for him?' (Ps 8:4–5)."[146] The pope implies that wonder, the basis of praise, mediates between two opposite views. It can avoid an "ecocentrism and biocentrism" that "eliminate[s] the difference of identity and worth between the human person and other living beings" and "open[s] the way to a new pantheism tinged with neo-paganism, which would see the source of man's salvation in nature alone." Conversely, wonder can also avoid "absolutizing technology and human power," which "results in a grave assault not only on nature, but also on human dignity itself."[147] Interestingly, Benedict XVI does not use the word *anthropocentrism* here. He does, however, implicitly reiterate his earlier claim that the human person serves as a priestly mediator, a "kind of bridge" between God and the rest of creation. In this way, viewing the

---

[144] *Caritas in Veritate*, 48. Emphasis added.
[145] Michael Budde, "The Alice's Restaurant of Catholic Social Teaching: Global Order in *Caritas in Veritate*," in *Jesus Christ: The New Face of Social Progress*, 143.
[146] *If You Want to Cultivate Peace*, 2.
[147] *If You Want to Cultivate Peace*, 13.

human person as channeling the hymn of the universe transcends both biocentric and anthropocentric excesses. The solution, Benedict XVI intimates, lies not in rejecting the unique dignity of the human person *tout court* but in orienting him or her in a less contrastive manner. Nevertheless, this promising line of reflection remains unstated. He mentions the Eucharist in neither document.

Thus, though emphasizing the centrality of worship throughout his career, Benedict XVI fails to integrate fully this eucharistic vision into his comprehensive approach to the environment. Despite his rich reflections on the ecological relevance of the Eucharist in *Sacramentum Caritatis*, this vision disappears when elsewhere he treats the ecological crisis as a social issue connected to many others. This oversight has at least three consequences. First, as was the case with John Paul II, the doxological, eucharistic tenor of Benedict XVI's environmental writings can overcome competitive understandings of human and natural ecologies. Explicitly incorporating this perspective could thus recover the integrated approach with which he attempts to address that crisis. Since he did not employ his eucharistic vision in this way, however, that potential remains unfulfilled.

Second, while John Paul II hinted vaguely about the new attitudes that the Eucharist brings to humans' relationship to creation, *Sacramentum Caritatis* underscores more directly the formative dimensions of the Eucharist in caring for creation. In this way the Eucharist can become missiological, "a mystery to be offered to the world."[148] Neglecting the Eucharist in papal documents that take an integral approach to the environmental crisis, however, subverts this wish and isolates the Eucharist from a social issue that Benedict XVI values so highly. Furthermore, like John Paul II, he fails to indicate how exactly eucharistic praise resolves the many social and cultural components that constitute the ecological crisis. Such an account can answer Benedict XVI's plea that the "relationship between the eucharistic mystery and social commitment . . . be made explicit."[149]

Third, Benedict XVI affirms that the Eucharist plays a unique role in countering patterns of thought and action that devastate creation. Failing to apply this eucharistic vision in trying to address the environmental crisis

---

[148] See Benedict XVI, Encyclical Letter *Deus Caritas Est* (December 25, 2005), 13: "A Eucharist which does not pass over into the concrete practice of love is intrinsically fragmented" (13). See also *Sacramentum Caritatis*, 82–83, 91.

[149] See *Sacramentum Caritatis*, 89.

thus belies his enduring belief that worship plays an indispensable role in social transformation and integral conversion.[150] Such an omission, against these intentions, risks keeping the social and environmental dynamite of the Eucharist under a bushel, privatizing its transformative power in a way that he consistently rejects.[151] Benedict XVI's eucharistic treatment of environmental questions teems with promise and yet is left underdeveloped and unintegrated within his social-ethical approach.

These unresolved questions serve as a fitting conclusion. Benedict XVI deepened Catholic social teaching's integrated approach to the environmental crisis by amplifying the human ecology of John Paul II. More specifically, Benedict XVI contended that matters of human ecology and natural ecology, rather than competing against each other, relate profoundly to each other. At the same time, in the reception of Benedict XVI's teaching, confusion emerged over how to ensure the interdependency of these two ecologies, whether it be through his understanding of the "grammar of creation" or through his emphasis on the relational nature of reality. This lack of development continued to allow for competitive understandings of the two ecologies and so undercut Benedict XVI's insistence on their seamless connection. His rich understanding of the doxological end of creation and the ecological significance of Eucharist provides an especially promising, concrete way to recover this seamlessness and hold the two ecologies together, precisely by instantiating both the grammar of creation (sacramentality) and cosmic solidarity (doxology). While the publication of *Sacramentum Caritatis* anticipated a papacy poised to make this promising eucharistic vision central to environmental concern, Benedict XVI's subsequent treatments of the ecological crisis as a social issue left it largely unstated. This lacuna frustrates the integral approach he sought in *Caritas in Veritate* and elsewhere, indicating the need for still further development and integration.

[150] As Ratzinger once wrote, "Faced with the political and social crises of the present time and the moral challenge they offer to Christians, the problems of liturgy and prayer could easily seem to be of second importance. But the question of the moral standards and spiritual resources that we need if we are to acquit ourselves in this situation cannot be separated from the question of worship." Preface to *The Feast of Faith: Approaches to a Theology of the Liturgy*, trans. Graham Harrison (San Francisco: Ignatius Press, 2006), 7.

[151] As Benedict XVI avers in *Sacramentum Caritatis*:
> Here we can see the full human import of the radical newness brought by Christ in the Eucharist: the worship of God in our lives cannot be relegated to something private and individual, but tends by its nature to permeate every aspect of our existence. Worship pleasing to God thus becomes a new way of living our whole life, each particular moment of which is lifted up, since it is lived as part of a relationship with Christ and as an offering to God. (71)

CONCLUSION

"By their fruits will you know them" applies equally well to the life of holiness as it does to assessing texts. Ormond Rush writes that, in any process of ecclesial reception:

> the receiver is a co-creator of the meaning of what is communicated. Hence that appropriated meaning could legitimately go beyond original authorial intention. Ricoeur speaks of a text's "surplus of meaning." With multiple contexts from which a text may be interpreted, the original authors "need" future readers to make sense of a text whose authors may not have had those future contexts in mind.[152]

This dynamic applies to the function of human ecology within Catholic social teaching. John Paul II and Benedict XVI employed human ecology to achieve a key goal: to express the way that the environmental crisis intersects with other social crises. At the same time, John Paul II's initially competitive presentation of natural and human ecologies stood in tension with this hope, even if, as his extensive reflection on creation suggests, he did not intend to devalue Catholic concern for creation. While Benedict XVI at times asserted that the category preserved the importance of environmental concerns, the reception of the category likewise undermined this aim. In a polarized United States, commentators could use human ecology to downplay Catholic responsibilities toward creation or play natural and human ecologies against each other. The result disintegrates the church's integrated approach to the environmental crisis. While this reception does not necessarily reflect the original authorial intentions of John Paul II and Benedict XVI, nevertheless, as Rush makes clear, this distortion still comprises part of the meaning that they generated with the category. Human ecology thus fails to capture the church's integrated approach to the ecological crisis. Needed is an organic development that can fulfill the original authorial intentions of John Paul II and Benedict XVI and make it impossible to set care for creation and care for human life against each other.

Those two popes' emphasis on the doxological orientation of creation, concretized in the Eucharist, showed much promise for overcoming some

---

[152] Ormond Rush, *Still Interpreting Vatican II: Some Hermeneutical Principles* (New York: Paulist Press, 2004), 55. See Paul Ricoeur, *Interpretation Theory: Discourse and the Surplus of Meaning* (Fort Worth, Tex.: Texas Christian University Press, 1976).

of the tensions inherent in human ecology. The cosmic hymn of praise ensures the inseparability of human and nonhuman creation as only both, together, make that chorus complete. Quieting a component of this praise or setting voices that comprise it against each other disrupts the harmony of the chorus. Moreover, this presentation need not flatten the unique role of human beings. As Benedict XVI began to suggest, humans play a uniquely priestly role in channeling this hymn of praise. The thoroughly theocentric character of this arrangement likewise guards against any anthropocentric, dominative excess, for creation finds its end in God, not in human beings. Indeed, setting care for creation in this doxological, eucharistic context demands an ethics of thanksgiving and solidarity rather than greed and individualism. The eucharistic liturgy is "*integrating* in that it articulates our relationship with all of humanity and with all that lives and moves on this earth, and with the earth itself."[153] Eucharistic praise can secure a more seamlessly integral vision of human and natural ecologies.

Yet, John Paul II and Benedict XVI did not integrate this radically Catholic and concrete vision of care for creation into their social approaches to the environmental crisis. In their pontificates, the ecological significance of the Eucharist furnished a topic for theological reflection rather than a framework for social and environmental ethics. Not only could framing the church's social approach to the ecological crisis through this doxological and eucharistic lens overcome divides between human and natural ecologies, so too might it make clearer the essential place of care for creation within Catholic identity. To make those Catholic responsibilities clearer, it became apparent that both John Paul II and Benedict XVI needed to specify how exactly eucharistic praise can help resolve the many structural and cultural dimensions of the ecological crisis.

These were the foundational pieces left by John Paul II and Benedict XVI, waiting to be put together in some future iteration of ecclesial reception. With some additional emphases and emerging from a different context, the next pontificate would take up the task. The observation that began this chapter becomes plainer now; the environmental insights of these two influential popes would indeed ground the decisive breakthrough expressed in *Laudato Si'*.

---

[153] Kevin W. Irwin, *Models of the Eucharist* (New York: Paulist, 2005), 41.

Chapter 2

The Integral Ecology of *Laudato Si'*

Laudato Si' is an encyclical sui generis. One commentator observes that it is "intended for as wide an audience as possible" and yet "also particularly and decisively Catholic in the worldview it expresses and presumes."[1] The encyclical's (and its author's) namesake embodies this paradox. Saint Francis of Assisi has enjoyed universal adulation while having lived as radical a Catholic life as possible.[2] In many ways, that same tension—between particularity and universality in ecclesial mission—marked the environmental thought of popes John Paul II and Benedict XVI. Both incipiently exhibited the robust contribution that Catholic social teaching can make toward healing the global scope of the ecological crisis and, in their reflections on the Eucharist, the decisively Catholic character of caring for creation. However, neither fully integrated these two poles despite the rich potential of doing so.

This chapter examines the unique character of *Laudato Si'* by exploring how Pope Francis integrates these two poles in his presentation of an integral ecology. On the one hand, it shows how Francis's introduction of integral ecology more adequately addresses the full scope of the ecological crisis, in both its human and natural dimensions. The integral ecology of *Laudato Si'* sets forth a vision and charge of care that responds to the cries of the earth and the poor and, through this broad lens, can contribute to a global conversation. On the other hand, it shows how a profoundly doxological, eucharistic ethos suffuses this integral ecology and in fact enflames its full enactment. That is, *Laudato Si'* furnishes a compelling synthesis of the universal and decisively Catholic in John Paul II and Benedict XVI's environmental thought, realizing the potential of their preliminary contributions. It is in this way that *Laudato Si'* maintains a decisively Catholic worldview while enjoying such universal appeal. And yet, as this chapter concludes,

---

[1] Kevin W. Irwin, *A Commentary on* Laudato Si': *Examining the Background, Contributions, Implementation, and Future of Pope Francis's Encyclical* (New York: Paulist Press, 2016), 99.

[2] A tension explored at length in Lawrence S. Cunningham, *Francis of Assisi: Performing the Gospel of Life* (Grand Rapids, Mich.: Eerdmans, 2004).

this feature of the encyclical requires an account of ecclesial mission if it is to endure. Such systematic reflection can secure the radicality of *Laudato Si'* and the tradition that grounds it, more clearly illustrating how the integral ecology of *Laudato Si'* weaves together the church's *ora et labora* in our common home.

INTEGRAL ECOLOGY

On June 18, 2015, Francis released his highly anticipated encyclical, *Laudato Si'*, subtitled "On Care for Our Common Home." Despite popular perception, the encyclical covers far more than climate change. Topics include global inequality, technology, biodiversity, bioethics, and urban design, along with many others. As Pope Francis would remark five years after its release, "*Laudato Si'* is not a green encyclical. It's a social encyclical. The green and social go hand in hand. The fate of creation is tied to the fate of all humanity."[3] Following his papal predecessors, Francis employs a wide lens in approaching the ecological crisis, viewing harm against creation as an especially clear symptom of a deeper moral crisis.

Prior to the release of the encyclical, early speculation indicated that Francis would emphasize human ecology in *Laudato Si'*. On January 24, 2014, in the initial announcement that the pope was penning an encyclical on ecology, Vatican spokesman Fr. Federico Lombardi declared that Francis planned to put a "particular emphasis" on human ecology in the forthcoming encyclical.[4] A few days later, Fr. Paul Haffner, a theologian at the Pontifical Gregorian University, confirmed this expectation, predicting that Francis would take a "humancentric approach" to the environmental crisis and condemn errors of "ecologism."[5] Following papal precedent, Francis seemed poised to frame the calls of *Laudato Si'* through human ecology.

It is surprising then that, in his official presentation of *Laudato Si'* a year and a half later, Cardinal Peter Turkson never mentioned "human ecology." Instead, he highlighted how "Pope Francis *puts the concept of integral ecology*

---

[3] Francis, with Austen Ivereigh, *Let Us Dream: The Path to a Better Future* (New York: Simon & Schuster, 2020), 32.

[4] Elise Harris, "Pope Francis' Writings on Ecology Could Become Encyclical," Catholic News Agency, January 27, 2014, https://www.catholicnewsagency.com/news/pope-francis-writings-on-ecology-could-become-encyclical.

[5] Edward Pentin, "Pope Francis to Emphasize 'Human Ecology' in Forthcoming Document, Says Theologian," *National Catholic Register*, January 30, 2014, www.ncregister.com/daily-news/pope-francis-to-emphasize-human-ecology-in-forthcoming-document-says-theolo.

at the center of the Encyclical as a paradigm able to articulate the fundamental relationships of the person with God, with him/herself, with other human beings, with creation."[6] In *Laudato Si'*, integral ecology provides the primary frame by which to assess and respond to the ecological crisis. Thus, Irwin calls the papal neologism "the most distinctive contribution of the encyclical" and "the most important theological insight about ecology in the document."[7] And yet, as Daniel Castillo admits, "for all the attention that *Laudato Si'* gives to the concept of integral ecology, the encyclical neither straightforwardly defines the concept nor clearly delineates its structure and dynamism."[8] In other words, the phrase "integral ecology" represents what Ladislaus Orsy calls a "seminal locution," a magisterial term that expresses truth without defining it precisely.[9] *Laudato Si'* invites readers to ruminate on the elusive meaning of its integral ecology.

Integral Ecology as a Vision: Synthesizing Human and Natural Ecologies

A vision of unity, communion, and reconciliation marks Francis's thought. Synthetic theologies of polarity—systems of thought that attempt to reconcile seemingly disparate realities—guide his vision, including the time before his election as pope. During his studies as a Jesuit, Jorge Mario Bergoglio cherished Gaston Fessard's dialectical interpretation of Jesuit spirituality and the tensions he highlighted between contemplation and action, grace and freedom, smallness and greatness.[10] This attraction likewise drew Bergoglio toward another Jesuit, Henri de Lubac, and his theological stress

---

[6] Peter Turkson, *Conferenza Stampa per la presentazione della Lettera Enciclica «Laudato si'» del Santo Padre Francesco sulla cura della casa commune: Intervento del Card. Peter Kodwo Appiah Turkson*, bulletin, June 18, 2015. Emphasis added.

[7] Irwin, *A Commentary on* Laudato Si', 102, 117. In magisterial texts, the term had been used once previously by the International Theological Commission, in *In Search of a Universal Ethic: A New Look at Natural Law* (May 20, 2009), 82.

[8] Daniel P. Castillo, *An Ecological Theology of Liberation: Salvation and Political Ecology* (Maryknoll, N.Y.: Orbis Books, 2019), 39.

[9] Ladislas Orsy, *The Church: Learning and Teaching* (Wilmington, Del.: Michael Glazier Books, 1987), 85–86.

[10] Massimo Borghesi, *The Mind of Pope Francis: Jorge Mario Bergoglio's Intellectual Journey*, trans. Barry Hudock (Collegeville, Minn.: Liturgical Press, 2018), 9–13. See Gaston Fessard, *La Dialectique des "Exercises Spirituels" de Saint Ignace de Loyola*, 3 vols. (Paris: Aubier, 1956–84); and Francis, with Antonio Spadaro, *My Door Is Always Open: A Conversation on Faith, Hope, and the Church in a Time of Change*, trans. Shaun Whiteside (New York: Bloomsbury Publishing, 2013), 21.

on paradox and communion.¹¹ De Lubac described the church, for instance, as a "*complexio oppositorum*," a catholic reality that mystically holds in tension divine perfection and human folly, locality and universality, the eternal and the temporal.¹² In 1986, after a leadership stint during which infighting almost capsized the Jesuit order in Argentina, Bergoglio began to write a dissertation in his "exile" to Cordoba. Entitled "Polar Opposition as Structure of Daily Thought and Christian Proclamation," the unfinished project fittingly examined Romano Guardini's 1925 *Der Gegensatz*, a philosophical plea for the synthesis and reconciliation of polarized divisions.¹³ Guardini's work enhanced Bergoglio's own burgeoning theology of polarity.

Francis has advanced this vision in his pontificate. In *Evangelii Gaudium*, a programmatic document for his papal ministry, he outlines four foundational principles. Two of them—"unity prevails over conflict" and "the whole is greater than the part"—showcase the centrality of this deeply catholic vision for his papal program.¹⁴ So too does this vision explain his pronounced endorsement of synodality in the life of the church, a confidence that "walking together" can secure harmony despite ecclesial difference.¹⁵ It likewise inspires his willingness to entertain more radical forms of inculturation as, for him, variety enriches catholicity.¹⁶ For Francis, this relational vision must guide the church both *ad intra* and *ad extra*.

This focus foregrounds his introduction of integral ecology in *Laudato Si'*. The term appears indebted to Pope Paul VI's notion of "integral development" from his 1967 social encyclical, *Populorum Progressio*, as well as its

---

[11] Francis, *My Door Is Always Open*, 9. See, e.g., Henri de Lubac, *Catholicism: Christ and the Common Destiny of Man*, trans. Lancelot C. Sheppard and Elizabeth Englund (San Francisco: Ignatius Press, 1988); and Henri de Lubac, *Paradoxes of Faith*, trans. Sadie Krielkamp (San Francisco: Ignatius Press, 1987).

[12] See Henri de Lubac, *The Church: Paradox and Mystery*, trans. James R. Dunne (Staten Island, N.Y.: Alba House, 1969).

[13] Borghesi, *The Mind of Pope Francis*, 101–7. For a detailed overview of this period of Bergoglio's life, see Paul Vallely, *Pope Francis: The Struggle for the Soul of Catholicism* (New York: Bloomsbury, 2015), 111–26.

[14] Francis, Apostolic Exhortation *Evangelii Gaudium* (November 24, 2013), 226–30, 234–37. The other two, "time is greater than space" and "realities are more important than ideas," are discussed later in this chapter.

[15] Concretely, Francis commissioned an ITC study on ecclesial synodality. See International Theological Commission, *Synodality in the Life and Mission of the Church* (March 2, 2018). So too did he announce synodality as the theme for the 2022 Synod of Bishops.

[16] *Evangelii Gaudium*, 115–18. See also Francis, Apostolic Letter *Magnum Principium* (September 9, 2017).

reiterations in Paul VI's successors.[17] In a speech commemorating the encyclical's fiftieth anniversary, Francis underscored "the very word integrate," a word he describes as "so dear to me."[18] While Catholic social encyclicals had focused previously on specific questions like labor, Paul VI employed the modern paradigm of development—and the economic, cultural, and social (though not explicitly environmental) facets it integrated—to broaden the concern of Catholic social teaching.[19] Likewise, against purely materialist presentations of development, Paul VI insisted that adequate theories of development must also integrate the spiritual dimension of human living.[20] In the integrative hopes of Paul VI, Francis's own reconciling vision finds a kindred spirit, especially as a way to delineate the church's social mission.

Besides relying on magisterial precedents, in *Laudato Si'* Francis also builds upon earlier uses of integral ecology. In 1995, along with Virgil Elizondo, the Brazilian liberation theologian Leonardo Boff called for an "integral ecology" that combined various approaches to the ecological crisis, including human ecology, "with a view to founding a new alliance between societies and nature."[21] Scientists and environmental advocates, especially those influenced by Ken Wilber's "integral theory," likewise deployed the term to encourage interdisciplinary approaches to ecological study. As Wilber wrote, "the word *integral* means comprehensive, inclusive, non-marginalizing, embracing. . . . In a certain sense, integral approaches are 'meta-paradigms,' or ways to draw together an already existing number of separate paradigms into an interrelated network of approaches that are mutually enriching."[22] Inspired by this framework and happening to parallel the integrating intent

---

[17] See Margaret R. Pfeil, "Fifty Years after *Populorum Progressio*: Understanding Integral Human Development in Light of Integral Ecology," *Journal of Catholic Social Thought* 15, no. 1 (2018): 5–17. Francis has noted the influence of Paul VI on several occasions, such as calling *Evangelii Gaudium* the *Evangelii Nuntiandi* of our time. See Francis, with Antonio Spadaro, *Open to God: Open to the World*, trans. Shaun Whiteside (London: Bloomsbury Publishing, 2018), 108.

[18] Francis, *Address to the Participants in the Conference Organized by the Dicastery for Promoting Integral Human Development, Marking the 50th Anniversary of the Encyclical* Populorum Progressio (April 4, 2017).

[19] Paul VI, Encyclical Letter *Populorum Progressio* (March 26, 1967), 13.

[20] *Populorum Progressio*, 14, 16. So too was this a key concern in Paul VI, Apostolic Exhortation *Evangelii Nuntiandi* (December 8, 1975), 31–36.

[21] See Leonardo Boff and Virgil Elizondo, "Ecology and Poverty: Cry of the Earth, Cry of the Poor—Editorial," *Concilium* 5 (1995): ix–xii, at ix. Around this time, Thomas Berry began to use this term as well; see his "An Ecologically Sensitive Spirituality," *Earth Ethics* 8, no. 1 (1996): 1–13.

[22] Ken Wilber, foreword to *Integral Medicine: A Noetic Reader*, ed. Marilyn Schlitz and Tina Hyman (Boston: Shambala Publications, 2004), xii–xiii.

of Paul VI, theorists Sean Esbjörn-Hargens and Michael Zimmerman proposed an "integral ecology" to ensure that standard presentations of ecology included both scientific and nonscientific (artistic, cultural, religious, etc.) approaches to the ecological crisis.[23] Not only do these articulations of integral ecology correspond well to the comprehensive approaches that John Paul II and Benedict XVI aspired to take to the environmental crisis, so too do they buttress Francis's embracing, inclusive, and catholic vision.

Several of Francis's references to integral ecology in *Laudato Si'* demonstrate his understanding of integral ecology as a vision of relationality. In the opening section of the encyclical, confirming that an integral ecology militates against reductionistic conceptions of ecology, the pope praises Saint Francis of Assisi for "help[ing] us to see that an integral ecology calls for *openness to categories* which transcends the language of mathematics and biology, and takes us to the heart of what it is to be human."[24] Francis likewise suggests that an integral ecology is needed "since everything is *closely interrelated*, and today's problems call for a *vision capable of taking into account every aspect of the global crisis*."[25] The multifaceted character of the ecological crisis requires that an integral ecology join disparate fields of knowledge: environmental, scientific, economic, political, cultural, philosophical, and religious. Appearing in some form nine other times, that "everything is interrelated" serves as a refrain of *Laudato Si'* and captures the spirit of its integral ecology.[26] So too does the pope note that an integral ecology entails an account of the common good spanning both time and space, since "an integral ecology is marked by this *broader vision*."[27] As the subtitle of the encyclical suggests, Francis asks people to envision the world as "our common home," dismantling any sense that creation is simply "mine."[28] The coinherent

---

[23] Sean Esbjörn-Hargens and Michael E. Zimmerman, *Integral Ecology: Uniting Multiple Perspectives on the Natural World* (Boston: Integral Books, 2009), 168–69. See also Sam Mickey, *On the Verge of a Planetary Civilization: A Philosophy of Integral Ecology* (New York: Rowman & Littlefield Publishers, 2014). On page 16, Mickey adds that the first use of "integral ecology" appeared in Hilary B. Moore, *Marine Ecology* (Hoboken, N.J.: Wiley, 1958), 7, wherein Moore called for an expansion of traditional scientific understandings of ecology.

[24] Francis, Encyclical Letter *Laudato Si'* (May 24, 2015), 11. Emphasis added.

[25] *Laudato Si'*, 137. Emphasis added.

[26] See *Laudato Si'*, 16, 70, 91, 92, 117, 120, 138, 142, 240.

[27] *Laudato Si'*, 159. Emphasis added.

[28] Irwin, *A Commentary on* Laudato Si', 95. As I discussed in the previous chapter, the phrase *our common home* finds precedent in Benedict XVI's writing. See Benedict XVI, *The Human Family, a Community of Peace* (January 1, 2008), 8.

worldview of an integral ecology, in which everything is interrelated, sustains this renewed vision.

This broader vision introduces a significant development regarding how Catholic social teaching approaches the ecological crisis. As became clear in the pontificates of John Paul II and Benedict XVI, the juxtaposition of two separate ecologies, human and natural, could jeopardize the comprehensive approach that they tried to take to the ecological crisis. In the release of *Laudato si'*, it had become apparent that human ecology would not enjoy the same focusing role that it did before. In the encyclical itself, human ecology plays a relatively minor role. Apart from a citation of John Paul II's preference for the term early in the encyclical, the other four references to human ecology all come in chapter 4, "Integral Ecology."[29] There, human ecology appears as one ecology alongside a variety of ecologies—including environmental ecology, economic ecology, social ecology, cultural ecology, and an ecology of daily life—under the broader umbrella of an integral ecology. As Francis explains in the chapter:

> When we speak of the "environment," what we really mean is a relationship existing between nature and the society which lives in it. Nature cannot be regarded as something separate from ourselves or as a mere setting in which we live. We are part of nature, included in it and thus in constant interaction with it. . . . Given the scale of change, it is no longer possible to find a specific, discrete answer for each part of the problem. It is essential to seek comprehensive solutions which consider the interactions within natural systems themselves and with social systems. *We are faced not with two separate crises, one environmental and the other social, but rather with one complex crisis which is both social and environmental.* Strategies for a solution demand an integrated approach to combating poverty, restoring dignity to the excluded, and at the same time protecting nature.[30]

The passage names well the scope of a genuinely integral ecology. The comprehensiveness of the crisis demands a solution equally comprehensive in scope, bridging all types of ecology. In securing the inseparability of the natural and the human, integral ecology best names the comprehensive approach taken by Catholic social teaching to address the ecological crisis.

29 See *Laudato Si'*, 5, 148, 152, 155.

30 *Laudato Si'*, 139. Emphasis added. Since then, Francis has called for the interdisciplinary perspective of an integral ecology to shape ecclesiastical universities and faculties; see Francis, Apostolic Constitution *Veritatis Gaudium* (January 29, 2018), 5.

Supported by Francis's depolarizing vision, the inclusivity of an integral ecology joins together what might be artificially sundered. As a more inclusive concept than either human ecology or natural ecology, integral ecology reconciles and fuses together those ecologies. And so, through this new category, Francis releases latent potential in the reflections of John Paul II and Benedict XVI. As Irwin concludes, with integral ecology, "any separation between 'natural' ecology and 'human' ecology . . . is transcended. This approach also reflects the best of the both/and rhetoric that marks much of the Catholic theological tradition."[31] Integral ecology extends this synthetic, catholic vision to the church's social mission as it relates to the environment.

Through the category of integral ecology, Francis places previous papal reflections on human ecology within a more expansive paradigm. Just as, in *Populorum Progressio*, Paul VI incorporated questions of labor into a broader context of integral development, so too, in *Laudato Si'*, Francis incorporates human ecology into a broader context of integral ecology. His use of integral ecology thus displays his intention, stated elsewhere, to place urgent matters of human ecology like abortion in a more seamless framework of Christian moral reflection.[32] In so doing, as numerous passages in *Laudato Si'* illustrate, Francis does not diminish the importance of these issues.[33] Instead, he shows how everything in the church's moral teaching is interconnected. In the U.S. Catholic Church, such efforts have "the potential to straddle, rather than worsen, some of the church's internal divides," especially those between "pro-life" and "social justice" Catholics.[34] Precisely through the ways that integral ecology connects everything, far from

---

[31] Irwin, *A Commentary on* Laudato Si', 119. See also Michael A. Perry, "From Assisi to Buenos Aires: The Cry of the Poor and the Cry of the Planet," in *Fragile World: Ecology and the Church*, ed. William T. Cavanaugh (Eugene, Ore.: Cascade Books, 2018), 84; and Donal Dorr, *Option for the Poor and for the Earth: From Leo XIII to Pope Francis*, rev. ed. (Maryknoll, N.Y.: Orbis Books, 2016), 422–23.

[32] See Francis, *My Door Is Always Open*, 62. See also *Evangelii Gaudium*, 34–39; and "In an Interview with *Corriere della Sera*, Bergoglio Talks about His Revolutionary First Year at the Head of the Church," Zenit (March 5, 2014), https://zenit.org/articles/english-translation-of-pope-francis-corriere-della-sera-interview/.

[33] See, e.g., *Evangelii Gaudium*, 213–14. The passages from *Laudato Si'* alluded to here are featured later in this chapter.

[34] Ross Douthat, *To Change the Church: Pope Francis and the Future of Catholicism* (New York: Simon & Schuster, 2018), 70. See also Charles C. Camosy, *Resisting Throwaway Culture: How a Consistent Life Ethic Can Unite a Fractured People* (Hyde Park, N.Y.: New City Press, 2019), who says that, while following in the footsteps of John Paul II and Benedict XVI, Francis "represents the leading edge" of the consistent ethic of life tradition (35).

detracting from the concerns of either human ecology or natural ecology, Francis indicates that neither can be preserved without the other.[35] Our common home includes both.

Insights from liberation theology help Francis link these two ecologies and hence uphold the relational vision of an integral ecology. Throughout his career, including before his election as pope, Francis has embraced themes from liberation theology, albeit critically. His endorsement of *la teología del pueblo*, an Argentinian strain of liberation theology, allowed him to take the best of liberation theology without acquiescing to its sometimes reductionistic, Marxist analysis of social inequality.[36] For him, disavowing this procrustean framework best attunes one's ears to hear the cry of the poor in their own voice. In various writings, Francis employs the inductive methodology characteristic of liberation theology, as captured by this "cry" language.[37] For instance, he structures *Laudato Si'* through "see-judge-act," asking readers first to "become aware of what is happening to our common home."[38] Only with this awareness might readers become aware of the full scope of the ecological crisis.

This inductive focus on the cries of history's victims can help explain how Francis connects human and natural ecologies together within an integral ecology. As already noted, the liberation theologian Leonardo Boff figures prominently in the background of *Laudato Si'*. Boff has admitted to sending the pope his writings during the drafting of the encyclical.[39] While not explicitly citing Boff's *Cry of the Earth, Cry of the Poor*, this influence shines through most lucidly in Francis's plea that "we have to realize that a true ecological approach *always* becomes a social approach; it must integrate

---

[35] In an interesting mirror to Benedict XVI's 2011 address to the German *Bundestag* (see n. 78 of chap. 1), in November 2014, Francis highlighted the need to preserve natural ecology alongside human ecology at a Vatican conference on male-female complementarity. See Francis, *Address to Participants in the International Colloquium on the Complementarity between Man and Woman* (November 17, 2014). See Austen Ivereigh, *Wounded Shepherd: Pope Francis and His Struggle to Convert the Catholic Church* (New York: Henry Holt and Company, 2019), 207–8.

[36] See Rafael Luciani, *Pope Francis and the Theology of the People*, trans. Phillip Berryman (Maryknoll, N.Y.: Orbis Books, 2017); and Juan Carlos Scannone, *La teología del pueblo: Raíces teológicas del papa Francisco* (Maliaño, Spain: Editorial Sal Terrae, 2017).

[37] See *Evangelii Gaudium*, 199–200. Likewise following this inductive approach is Francis, Post-Synodal Apostolic Exhortation *Amoris Laetitia* (March 19, 2016).

[38] *Laudato Si'*, 17.

[39] See Dawn M. Nothwehr, "Leonardo Boff's Franciscan Liberation Ecological Theology and 'Integral Ecology' in *Laudato Si'*," in *All Creation Is Connected: Voices in Response to Pope Francis's Encyclical on Ecology*, ed. Daniel R. DiLeo (Winona, Minn.: Anselm Academic, 2018), 107–8.

questions of justice in debates on the environment, so as to hear *both the cry of the earth and the cry of the poor.*"[40] To become aware of what is happening to our common home demands attentiveness to both the cry of the poor and the cry of the earth. He hails Francis of Assisi as "the example par excellence" of a figure who grasps the interrelatedness between care for the earth and care for the poor.[41] As Bruno Latour submits, social and environmental concern merge at these joined cries that *Laudato Si'* channels.[42] "Sister [earth] *cries* out to us" and "*groans* in travail" (Rom 8:22), indicating that "the earth herself, burdened and laid waste, is among the most abandoned and maltreated of our poor."[43] Rapid social and environmental decline "have caused sister earth, along with all the abandoned of our world, to *cry out, pleading* that we take another course."[44] In these sections, *Laudato Si'* introduces a "preferential option for the earth," alongside that of for the poor.[45]

Francis is not the first pope to make such a link. Particularly through the category of development, John Paul II and Benedict XVI correlated harm against the earth and harm against the poor. However, Francis's use of liberationist "cry" language signals a more profound link. In a way that development language cannot, the cries of the poor and of the earth connote the interruption of the cries of the poor and of the earth in history.[46] What distinguishes Francis here is his inductive approach and, through that method, the hermeneutical privilege he grants the poor and the earth in scrutinizing the harm done to our common home.[47] In *Laudato Si'*, viewed

---

[40] *Laudato Si'*, 49. Francis likewise speaks of the "intimate relationship between the poor and the fragility of the planet" (16). See also, e.g., 91, 93 and the final stanza of the "Christian Prayer in Union with Creation" that Francis includes at the end of the encyclical.

[41] *Laudato Si'*, 10.

[42] Bruno Latour, "La grande clameur relayée par le pape François," in Laudato si': *Encyclique, édition commentée: Texte intégral, réactions et commentaires*, ed. F. Louzeau and B. Toger (Paris: Parole et silence, 2015), 222–23.

[43] *Laudato Si'*, 2. Emphasis added.

[44] *Laudato Si'*, 53. Emphasis added.

[45] As, e.g., introduced by Peter Turkson, *Address to Santa Clara University:* Laudato Si' *from Silicon Valley to Paris* (November 3, 2015).

[46] See Johan Verstraeten, "Development as a Path to a Just World: Fifty Years of *Populorum Progressio*—A Critical Retrospective," *Louvain Studies* 40, no. 4 (2017): 396–409; and Gustavo Gutiérrez, *A Theology of Liberation: History, Politics, and Salvation*, rev. ed., trans. Caridad Inda and John Eagleson (Maryknoll, N.Y.: Orbis Books, 1988), 13–25.

[47] See Rohan M. Curnow, "Which Preferential Option for the Poor? A History of the Doctrine's Bifurcation," *Modern Theology* 31, no. 1 (January 2015): 27–59. Curnow shows how the pontificates of John Paul II and Benedict XVI differed in their interpretation of the "option for the poor"

through the relational lens of an integral ecology, the earth and the poor share a common, inseparable starting point "from below," namely the underside of human history.

Francis extends this cry to all who are vulnerable and, by so doing, discloses how an integral ecology weaves together both human and natural ecologies in a seamless garment. Including the unborn, a key concern for human ecology, as among those crying out, Francis writes: "Neglecting to monitor the harm done to nature and the environmental impact of our decisions is only the most striking sign of a disregard for the message contained in the structures of nature itself. When we fail to acknowledge as part of reality the worth of a poor person, a human embryo, a person with disabilities—to offer just a few examples—it becomes difficult to hear the *cry* of nature itself; everything is connected."[48]

As he questions readers, "How can we genuinely teach the importance of concern for other vulnerable beings, however troublesome or inconvenient they may be, if we fail to protect a human embryo, even when its presence is uncomfortable and creates difficulties?"[49] Because everything is connected, ignoring the cries bellowing from one of these vulnerable persons deafens one to the cries of others. In admonishing readers "to accept our body, to care for it, and to respect its fullest meaning," Francis extends this same logic to another key dimension of human ecology.[50] A disregard for one's body indicates a more general disregard for the giftedness of creation. He also applies this cohesive vision to the treatment of animals, explaining how indifference to and domination of animals coincides with indifference to and domination of fellow human persons.[51] An integral vision demands connecting efforts to preserve both human and natural ecologies, as Francis writes: "A sense of deep communion with the rest of

---

from the more hermeneutical interpretation liberation theologians afford it. While Curnow does not discuss him, Pope Francis quite clearly falls in the latter category. On this point, see, e.g., Gerard Whelan, "*Evangelii Gaudium* as 'Contextual Theology': Helping the Church 'Mount to the Level of Its Times,'" *Australian eJournal of Theology* 22, no. 1 (2015): 1–10.

48 *Laudato Si'*, 117. Emphasis added. See also Francis, *Homily for the World Day of the Poor* (November 18, 2018): "The *cry of the poor*: it is the stifled cry of the unborn, of starving children, of young people more used to the explosion of bombs than happy shouts of the playground."

49 *Laudato Si'*, 120.

50 *Laudato Si'*, 155. See Robert Ryan, "Pope Francis, Theology of the Body, Ecology, and Encounter," special issue, *Journal of Moral Theology* 6, no. 1 (2017): 56–73.

51 See also *Laudato Si'*, 92.

nature cannot be real if our hearts lack tenderness, compassion and concern for our fellow human beings. It is clearly inconsistent to combat trafficking in endangered species while remaining completely indifferent to human trafficking, unconcerned about the poor, or undertaking to destroy another human being deemed unwanted. This compromises the very meaning of our struggle for the sake of the environment."[52]

Since everything is related, an integral ecology yokes together all the cries emanating from the many vulnerable, fragile entities that populate both human and natural ecologies, from human bodies, the unborn, the economically downtrodden, nonhuman animals, and the earth. In an integrated manner, an integral ecology thus must also address the economic, political, cultural, human, and natural ecologies that sustain these populations. Through this privileging of the poor and vulnerable, broadly construed, Francis begins to surmount the obstacles that frustrated the comprehensive approach to the ecological crisis that John Paul II and Benedict XVI both sought.[53] Through the inclusive vision of an integral ecology, Francis unleashes the full contribution of this catholic, integrated approach to the ecological crisis.

Integral Ecology as Task: Care in the Ruins of the Technocratic Paradigm

Throughout his pontificate, Francis has bidden all to hear deeply and encounter these cries and, in resisting all forces that desensitize people to them, to establish an alternative culture of empathetic care. This task guides what the pope identifies as the church's missionary and pastoral "conversion" in a post-Christendom world.[54] The work of Alberto Methol Ferré—a prominent Uruguayan Catholic social critic in the second half of the

---

[52] *Laudato Si'*, 91. As Pope Francis would remark during the fifth anniversary of *Laudato Si'*:
> I called for an "integral ecology," an ecology that is about much more than caring for nature; it's about caring for each other as fellow creatures of a loving God, and all that this implies. In other words, if you think abortion, euthanasia, and the death penalty are acceptable, your heart will find it hard to care about the contamination of rivers and the destruction of the rainforest. And the reverse is also true. So even while people will argue strenuously that these issues are different in moral terms, as long as they insist that abortion is justified but not desertification, or that euthanasia is wrong but polluted rivers are the price to pay for economic progress, we will remain stuck in the same lack of integrity that put us where we are now. (*Let Us Dream*, 34–35)

[53] See Dorr, *Option for the Poor and for the Earth*, 458, 468–69.

[54] *Evangelii Gaudium*, 27.

twentieth century and close friend of Francis's prior to his papal election—shapes the pope's diagnosis and prognosis.[55] For Methol Ferré, the nihilistic and libertine positivism ultimately promoted by Western philosophers like Auguste Comte, Friedrich Nietzsche, and Marquis de Sade has produced a globalized culture oriented toward material opulence and spiritual emptiness that has come even to infect the church in its wintry season.[56] The will to power demolishes anything that might constrain this ceaseless consumerism, whether objective value or community. As typified in neoliberalism, this individualism dissolves social bonds, leaving the vulnerable especially susceptible to harm. At the same time, for Methol Ferré, Marxism fails to offer a worthy alternative, as it too alienates through its fragmenting soullessness and dissolution of community for the sake of class conflict. The stark social inequality and unrest of the twentieth century attests to the insufficiency of these economic systems and cultural worldviews. Both, as forms of imperialism, impose alien patterns of thought upon the lived experience of communities.

Methol Ferré believed that this toxic decadence demands an ecclesial *risorgimento* in Latin America. He urges the Latin American church to fulfill its unique destiny as "an agent of integration, a mechanism of synthesis" in the twentieth and twenty-first centuries.[57] For him, the signs of the times prime the Latin American church to become a "source church" able to reinvigorate the universal church. Against the chilly impersonalism of Western technocracy and its ideological impositions, the post-conciliar Latin American church can reveal to the world the prophetic path of becoming a church of the poor and embracing the lively warmth of popular religiosity, populist economics and politics, cultural diversity, and frank dialogue.[58] The Romantic origins of *la teología del pueblo* contributes much to this aim. Compared

[55] See Austen Ivereigh, *The Great Reformer: Francis and the Making of a Radical Pope* (New York: Henry Holt and Company, 2014), 233–37; Borghesi, *The Mind of Pope Francis*, 177–97.

[56] See Alberto Methol Ferré and Alver Metalli, *Il Papa e il filosofo* (Siena, Italy: Cantagalli, 2014), 38, 150–60, 205–6. First published in 2007, then-Cardinal Bergoglio presented the book, calling it a work of "metaphysical profundity." For Bergoglio's praise of Methol Ferré's cultural critique, see Jorge Mario Bergoglio, *Noi come cittadini, noi come popolo: Verso un bicentenario in giustizia e solidarietà 2010-2016* (Milan: Jaca Book, 2013), 35–36.

[57] Ivereigh, *Wounded Shepherd*, 235; see Alberto Methol Ferré, *Il risorgimento cattolico latinoamericano*, trans. P. Di Pauli and C. Perfetti (Bologna: CSEO-Incontri, 1983), 208; and Methol Ferré and Metalli, *Il Papa e il filosofo*, 28–29 (wherein they quote Bergoglio).

[58] See Alberto Methol Ferré, "El resurgimiento católico latinoamericano," in *Religión y cultura. Perspectivas de la evangelización de la cultura desde Puebla. Encuentro del equipo de reflexión del Celam y otros pensadores sobre el tema «Religión y cultura»*, ed. CELAM (Bogotá: Ed. CELAM, 1980).

with Marxist strains of liberation theology, this Argentine theology places a higher value on the devotional life of the Latin American poor and helped recover the sense of belonging to a people, rather than to a Marxist-defined class. Bergoglio concurred with Methol Ferré that retrieving a Latin American sense of *"patria grande"* and its familial connotations of home and belonging, could reverse the abstract, individualistic balkanization of a liquid modernity.[59] This mission of the Latin American church can provide a third way to approach modernity by sifting through and reconciling the root desires of the age, rather than outright condemnation or accommodation. Methol Ferré's work inspires the ecclesial vision outlined in the historic 2007 meeting of the Latin American church in Aparecida; in fact, Bergoglio redacted the meeting's final document.[60] Methol Ferré provided Bergoglio with a clear sense of the Latin American church's mission both to the world and as a source to the rest of the ecclesial communion.

With the election of Bergoglio as pope, this vision has indeed come to shape the church universal and catalyze what Francis hopes is its *risorgimento*. Showing the influence of Methol Ferré's cultural diagnosis, Francis often decries a "globalization of indifference." As he describes the phenomenon:

> To sustain a lifestyle which excludes others, or to sustain enthusiasm for that selfish ideal, a globalization of indifference has developed. Almost without being aware of it, we end up being incapable of feeling compassion at the outcry of the poor, weeping for other people's pain, and feeling a need to help them, as though all this were someone else's responsibility and not our own. The culture of prosperity deadens us; we are thrilled if the market offers us something new to purchase. In the meantime all those lives stunted for lack of opportunity seem a mere spectacle; they fail to move us.[61]

Rampant consumption hardens hearts and renders individuals deaf to the cries of the poor, making impossible the empathetic solidarity needed to feel their pain and respond to their pleas. The indifference to value and demands beyond oneself reveals a relativism that erodes any sense of collective respon-

---

59 Jorge Mario Bergoglio, prologue to Guzmán Carriquiry Lecour, *Il Bicentenario dell'indipendenza dei paesi latino-americani: Ieri e oggi* (Soveria Mannelli, Italy: Rubbettino, 2013), vii–ix. See Austen Ivereigh, "To Discern and Reform: The 'Francis Option' for Evangelizing a World in Flux," *The Way* 57, no. 4 (October 2018): 9–24.

60 See CELAM, "Aparecida Concluding Document: Fifth General Conference of Bishops of Latin America and the Caribbean" (May 2007).

61 *Evangelii Gaudium*, 54.

sibility, whereby "it becomes difficult for citizens to devise a common plan which transcends individual gain and personal ambitions."[62] This narrowed horizon dissipates any sense of belonging to a whole, to a people.

In this narcissistic worldview, usefulness and personal convenience determine the worth of something or someone else. Francis christens this worldview a "throwaway culture." Various forces, like the market, reduce the vulnerable and "inconvenient"—the poor, the young, the old, the unborn, the earth—to no more than objects worthy of consumption or discard.[63] As he denounces this utilitarian logic in *Amoris Laetitia*, "We treat affective relationships the way we treat material objects and the environment: everything is disposable; everyone uses and throws away, takes and breaks, exploits and squeezes to the last drop."[64] A throwaway culture endangers the very possibility of loving and caring for others in their own value. So too can these corrosive forces distort the mission of the church. Francis condemns contemporary forms of Gnosticism and Pelagianism, as both abstract Christian life from the concrete, social bonds of ecclesial vitality.[65] The globalization of indifference, the throwaway culture, and strains of ecclesial Gnosticism and Pelagianism all sap the pathos that colors life, roots a life of conversion, and brings people into contact with others. Without a change of heart, not only do the cries from the underside of history go unheard, but they also grow shriller as distant apathy enables people to trample continually upon them.

To these forces, again paralleling Methol Ferré's prognosis, Francis offers the warming balm of mercy and the conversion it can evoke. For Francis, the twenty-first century affords a unique *kairos* for a message of mercy.[66] "To

---

[62] *Evangelii Gaudium*, 61.

[63] *Evangelii Gaudium*, 53. See also Francis, Post-Synodal Apostolic Exhortation *Christus Vivit* (March 25, 2019), 78: "We also see how a certain kind of advertising teaches young people to be perpetually dissatisfied and contributes to the throwaway culture, in which young people themselves end up being discarded." This diagnosis likewise informs Francis's support of Paul VI's *Humane Vitae*, seeing it as prophetic in its rejection of an ideological "neo-Malthusianism" that deems only some worthy of birth, an instantiation of the throwaway culture. See, e.g., Francis, with Austen Ivereigh, "'A Time of Great Uncertainty': An Interview with Pope Francis," *Commonweal Magazine* (April 8, 2020), https://www.commonwealmagazine.org/time-great-uncertainty.

[64] *Amoris Laetitia*, 39.

[65] *Evangelii Gaudium*, 94, 233. See also Francis, Apostolic Exhortation *Gaudete et Exsultate* (March 19, 2018), 35–62; and Congregation for the Doctrine of the Faith, *Placuit Deo* (February 22, 2018), 3–4.

[66] Francis, with Andrea Tornielli, *The Name of God Is Mercy*, trans. Oonagh Stransky (New York: Random House, 2016), 6.

feel pity with the heart," the root meaning of *misericordia*, can overcome the heartless apathy that governs the world. Pope Francis relays often his own visceral encounter with the tender mercy of God that pierced through his hardened heart.[67] Hence, he chose *miserando atque eligendo*, "by showing mercy and by choosing him," as his episcopal motto. He declared 2016 as an Extraordinary Jubilee of Mercy. He has expressed preference for more mystical French over stricter ascetical Spanish forms of Jesuit spirituality, as the former can better cultivate a deeper gratefulness for divine mercy in one's life.[68] Frequently, he cites Benedict XVI's words that "[b]eing a Christian is not the result of an ethical choice or a lofty idea, but the encounter with an event, a person, which gives life a new horizon and a decisive direction."[69] Francis hopes to invite individual Christians toward this root, practically tactile, and Christocentric encounter with God's mercy.[70]

At the same time, Francis insists that this personal encounter is always simultaneously a missionary call and should blossom into what he calls a "culture of encounter." For him, an encounter with God's mercy should lead people to encounter others, to feel their pain with one's heart. As he shared in an interview, "Jesus does not look at reality from the outside, without letting himself be moved, as if he were taking a picture. He lets himself get involved. This kind of compassion is needed today to conquer the globalization of indifference. This kind of regard is needed when we find ourselves in front of a poor person, an outcast, or a sinner."[71] Francis's call to encounter affixes an affective component to the calls for solidarity made by both John Paul II and Benedict XVI.[72] Compassion, a "feeling with," can penetrate the unfeeling of indifference.

---

[67] See, e.g., Francis, with Antonio Spadaro, "A Big Heart Open to God," *America Magazine* (September 30, 2013), https://www.americamagazine.org/faith/2013/09/30/big-heart-open-god-interview-pope-francis.

[68] See Francis, *My Door Is Always Open*, 24; Francis, with Guillaume Goubert and Sébastien Maillard, "Interview with Pope Francis," trans. Stefan Gigacz, *La Croix*, May 17, 2016, https://www.la-croix.com/Religion/Pape/INTERVIEW-Pope-Francis-2016-05-17-1200760633; and Borghesi, *The Mind of Pope Francis*, 4–5, 45–46, 236–43.

[69] *Evangelii Gaudium*, 7. See Benedict XVI, Encyclical Letter *Deus Caritas Est* (December 25, 2005), 1.

[70] See *Evangelii Gaudium*, 3, 120, 264–67.

[71] Francis, *The Name of God Is Mercy*, 92.

[72] Uzochukwu Jude Njoku, for instance, worries that magisterial calls for solidarity often remain too abstract. See his "Rethinking Solidarity as a Principle of Catholic Social Teaching: Going Beyond *Gaudium et Spes* and the Social Encyclicals of John Paul II," *Political Theology* 9 (2008): 525–44, at 535.

In Francis's view, while a throwaway culture discards those deemed inconvenient, the church should embrace the vulnerable and the peripheries so as to enter into the "feeling pity with the heart" of its Savior. By fostering this culture of encounter, the church empowers the cries of the vulnerable to interrupt history: "the Gospel tells us constantly to run the risk of a face-to-face encounter with others, with their physical presence which challenges us, with their pain and their pleas, with their joy which infects us in our close and continuous interaction. . . . The Son of God, by becoming flesh, summoned us to the revolution of tenderness."[73] The church must model the Good Samaritan, who bothers to notice, love, and embrace.[74] "The hallmark of the Church is its proximity," Francis believes, and so conversely, a "Church that is not close to people is not a Church."[75] Against the disincarnate tendencies of neo-Gnosticism and neo-Pelagianism, Francis calls for a centrifugal church "bruised, hurting and dirty because it has been out in the streets," guided by shepherds stinking with the smell of their sheep.[76] The other two of his four foundational principles, "time is greater than space" and "realities are more important than ideas," both indicate the need not to rest secure simply in a vague sense of unity but to work toward the concrete solidarity that genuine unity requires.[77] While indifference hardens hearts and drives people apart, a culture of encounter leads to conversion. It "opens hearts" and brings people into close, concrete contact with each other.[78] In the words of one commentator, for Francis, "to be close and concrete in a technocratic world" defines the church's evangelizing mission in the twenty-first century.[79]

So too must this spirit guide the church's social mission. In *Laudato Si'*, the same drama marks our common home and specifies the requirements of an integral ecology. Several references within the encyclical illustrate that, along with being a vision, integral ecology is a task.[80] Francis of Assisi "is

---

[73] *Evangelii Gaudium*, 88. See Diego Fares, *Papa Francisco. La cultura del encuentro* (Buenos Aires: Edhasa, 2014).

[74] See Francis, Encyclical Letter *Fratelli Tutti* (October 3, 2020), 56–86.

[75] Francis, "Interview with Pablo Ordaz," January 20, 2017, https://english.elpais.com/elpais/2017/01/21/inenglish/1485026427_223988.html.

[76] *Evangelii Gaudium*, 49.

[77] *Evangelii Gaudium*, 231–33.

[78] *Evangelii Gaudium*, 171.

[79] Ivereigh, *Wounded Shepherd*, 223.

[80] See Vincent J. Miller, "Integral Ecology: Francis's Spiritual and Moral Vision of Interconnectedness," in *The Theological and Ecological Vision of Laudato Si': Everything Is Connected*, ed. Vincent J. Miller, 12–21 (New York: Bloomsbury T&T Clark, 2017).

the example par excellence . . . of an integral ecology *lived out* joyfully and authentically."[81] Religions can make a "rich contribution . . . toward an integral ecology."[82] An integral ecology, Francis adds elsewhere, "needs to take account of the value of labor," "includes taking time to recover a serene harmony with creation" and is "made up of simple daily gestures which break with the logic of violence, exploitation and selfishness."[83] As it does for the rest of Francis's pontificate, merciful proximity characterizes the task our common home requires.

What Francis refers to as the "technocratic paradigm," the root cause of the ecological crisis in *Laudato Si'*, impedes this task. The work of Guardini, cited the most of anyone other than a pope in *Laudato Si'*, undergirds this diagnosis. Given the pope's previous study of the theologian, this influence is unsurprising. Moreover, Guardini's disillusionment with industrialized, technological advance, as expressed in his *Letters from Lake Como* and *The End of the Modern World* (cited five times in *Laudato Si'*), complements well Methol Ferré's critiques of Western technocracy.[84] Just as Guardini laments the dislocation, fragmentation, and violence that accompanied the rise of modern technology, so too does Francis worry that, in a twenty-first century context, many of these same forces devastate our common home.

While acknowledging the achievements of technology and innovation, the pope submits that the attitudes presumed in the use of technology can and often do lose their moral bearings. Likewise, they can evolve into an entire "undifferentiated and one-dimensional paradigm" of seeing and doing, consequently distorting humans' relationships with each other, with creation, and with God.[85] Just as a globalization of indifference contracts one's horizon of concern, so too, by enlarging the objectifying tendencies of technology, the technocratic paradigm "leads to a loss of appreciation for the whole, for the relationships between things, and for the broader horizon."[86] Whether in ignoring the long-term consequences of actions or in

---

[81] *Laudato Si'*, 10. Emphasis added.

[82] *Laudato Si'*, 62.

[83] *Laudato Si'*, 124, 225, 230.

[84] See Romano Guardini, *Letters from Lake Como: Explorations on Technology and the Human Race*, trans. Geoffrey W. Bromiley (Grand Rapids, Mich.: Eerdmans, 1994); and *The End of the Modern World*, trans. Joseph Theman, Herbert Burke, and Elinor Castendyk Briefs (Wilmington, Del.: ISI Books, 1998).

[85] *Laudato Si'*, 106.

[86] *Laudato Si'*, 110.

reducing progress to profit maximization, the technocratic paradigm classifies "everything as irrelevant unless it serves one's own immediate interests."[87] This attitude reveals an "excessive anthropocentrism," a "practical relativism" that shrivels concern to oneself, enclosed from God, others, and creation.[88] These egocentric attitudes perpetuate the globalization of indifference as it buffers one against the cries of others and the responses that those cries should engender.[89]

So too do these technocratic attitudes sustain the heartlessness that underlie a throwaway culture. "The emptier a person's heart is," Francis submits, "the more he or she needs things to buy, own and consume."[90] The sharp bifurcation erected between oneself and the rest of the world reduces the latter into a mere object, a resource to be extracted. Anthropocentrism quickly becomes "tyrannical."[91] The control promised by modern technology produces what Francis denounces as "a Promethean vision of mastery over the world," a Baconian vision of confrontation that takes the form of "a throwaway culture which affects the excluded just as it quickly reduces things to rubbish."[92] These distortions are indiscriminate in their victims; Francis lists, among others, the old, the aborted, human trafficking victims, and endangered species.[93] The result is "a constant schizophrenia, wherein a technocracy which sees no intrinsic value in lesser beings coexists with the other extreme, which sees no special value in human beings."[94] The technocratic paradigm—and the globalization of indifference and throwaway culture it unites—causes the earth and the poor to cry out and numbs people to those cries. Illustrating yet again the close connection between preserving human and natural ecologies, Francis makes clear that the encompassing exploitative logic of the technocratic paradigm threatens all the vulnerable who inhabit those interconnected spheres.

An integral ecology, as a task, offers an integrated response to those cries smothered by the technocratic paradigm. Describing the attentive

---

87 *Laudato Si'*, 122.
88 *Laudato Si'*, 116, 122.
89 *Laudato Si'*, 25, 52.
90 *Laudato Si'*, 204.
91 *Laudato Si'*, 68, 83.
92 *Laudato Si'*, 116, 22.
93 *Laudato Si'*, 123.
94 *Laudato Si'*, 118.

seeing with which *Laudato Si'* begins, Francis states that "[o]ur goal is not to amass information or to satisfy curiosity, but rather to become painfully aware, to dare to turn what is happening to the world into our own personal suffering and thus to discover what each of us can do about it."[95] The cries of the earth and the poor demand this painful awareness, this close encounter and sympathetic solidarity in which the suffering of our common home becomes one's own.[96] Styled after the purgative first week of the *Spiritual Exercises* that guides his order, Francis implores his audience here to "feel pity with the heart" the devastation of our common home.[97] In this way might God's mercy start to heal the cries of the earth and the poor.

As the subtitle of the encyclical suggests, against the apathy fostered by the technocratic paradigm, the pope calls Christians to participate in this mercy by caring for our common home. The word *care* appears forty times in the encyclical to describe humans' relationship to creation, capping off an evolution from descriptors like *dominate* and *subdue*, as found in John Paul II, to relying primarily on the language of care, as introduced by Benedict XVI. Cardinal Peter Turkson, a chief architect of the encyclical, justified this shift away from traditional stewardship language at the time of the encyclical's release, remarking that "when one *cares* for something it is something one does with passion and love."[98] To care is to become painfully aware, to evoke a passion that shatters indifference. To speak of our

---

[95] *Laudato Si'*, 19.

[96] See *Evangelii Gaudium*, 215: "Thanks to our bodies, God has joined us so closely to the world around us that we can feel the desertification of the soil almost as a physical ailment, and the extinction of a species as a painful disfigurement."

[97] While an earlier draft of the encyclical initially began with a biblical theology of creation (later becoming chapter 2), Francis reportedly requested drafters to change the order of the material so as to reflect this opening penitential salvo, like the first chapter of the *Spiritual Exercises*. See Dorr, *Option for the Poor and for the Earth*, 417. For a reading of the encyclical in this way, see Marianne Farina, "Integral Ecology and the Care for Our Common Home," *Listening* 52, no. 1 (Winter 2017): 46–57.

[98] As recounted in Naomi Klein, "A Radical Vatican?" *The New Yorker* (July 10, 2015), https://www.newyorker.com/news/news-desk/a-visit-to-the-vatican. Emphasis added. Detailing the processes behind the encyclical's composition, Francis acknowledged Turkson's chief role:

> Cardinal Turkson and his team prepared the first draft. Then, with some help, I took it and worked on it, then with a few theologians I made a third draft and sent a copy to the Congregation for the Doctrine of the Faith, to the second section of the Secretariat of State, and to the Theologian of the Papal Household to take a look at it, so that I would not say anything "silly"! Three weeks ago I got their responses back, some of them this thick, but all of them constructive. Now I will take a week of March, an entire week, to complete it. I believe that by the end of March it will be finished and sent out for translation. (*Press Conference of His Holiness Pope Francis onboard the Flight from Colombo to Manila* [January 15, 2015])

common home, and the images of belonging and warmth it conjures, also bolsters this charge to care. Care becomes an obligation upon realizing that "all of us are linked by unseen bonds and together form a kind of universal family, a sublime communion which fills us with a sacred, affectionate and humble respect."[99] To counter liquid technocracy, Francis extends the Latin American sense of *patria grande* to include all creation.

The task of caring likewise counters the individualistic narcissism and dislocation that plagues our common home, instilling a renewed vision of the human person and securing the life of others. Francis writes:

> We are always capable of going out of ourselves toward the other. Unless we do this, other creatures will not be recognized for their true worth; we are unconcerned about caring for things for the sake of others; we fail to set limits on ourselves in order to avoid the suffering of others or the deterioration of our surroundings. Disinterested concern for others, and the rejection of every form of self-centeredness and self-absorption, are essential if we truly wish to care for our brothers and sisters and for the natural environment. These attitudes also attune us to the moral imperative of assessing the impact of our every action and personal decision on the world around us. If we can overcome individualism, we will truly be able to develop a different lifestyle and bring about significant changes in society.[100]

The compassionate anthropology of an integral ecology offers an alternative to the tyrannical anthropocentrism of the technocratic paradigm. What Marianne Heimbach-Steins and Andreas Lienkamp label the "anthropo-relational" vision of *Laudato Si'* tasks human beings with recognizing and ordering rightly the relationships that constitute our common home.[101] A culture of encounter requires no less. Francis remarks that, as revealed through the Trinity that human beings are made in the image of, "The human person grows more, matures more and is sanctified more to the extent that he or she enters into relationships, going out from themselves to live in communion with God, with others and with all creatures."[102] He

---

[99] *Laudato Si'*, 89.

[100] *Laudato Si'*, 208.

[101] Marianne Heimbach-Steins and Andreas Lienkamp, "Die Enzyklika *Laudato si'* von Papst Franziskus Auch ein Beitrag zur Problematik des Klimawandels und zur Ethik der Energiewende," *JCSW* 56 (2015): 155–179, at 160, 175–76.

[102] *Laudato Si'*, 240. As the passage concludes, "Everything is interconnected, and this invites us to develop a spirituality of that global solidarity which flows from the mystery of the Trinity."

notes elsewhere that this capacity for communion helps name the unique dignity of human beings:

> Christian thought sees human beings as possessing a particular dignity above other creatures; it thus inculcates esteem for each person and respect for others. Our openness to others, each of whom is a "thou" capable of knowing, loving and entering into dialogue, remains the source of our nobility as human persons. A correct relationship with the created world demands that we not weaken this social dimension of openness to others, much less the transcendent dimension of our openness to the "Thou" of God. Our relationship with the environment can never be isolated from our relationship with others and with God.[103]

Caring for our common home thus entails "respect[ing] the laws of nature and the delicate equilibria existing between the creatures of this world."[104] This attentive care and dialogical posture distinguish the human vocation.

Indeed, stemming from his philosophy of polarity, Francis has long insisted that communion must not erase difference. Otherwise, any attempts at reconciliation simply reproduce the homogenization characteristic of technocratic modernity.[105] As the passage quoted above demonstrates, Francis holds that human beings possess a unique dignity within creation. He accordingly rejects a biocentrism that would supplant the difference between human beings and the rest of creation.[106] At the same time, while his papal predecessors refrained from explicitly acknowledging the intrinsic value of creation (though Benedict XVI intimated it in his notion of a "grammar of creation"), Francis bids Christians "to recognize that other living beings have a value of their own in God's eyes."[107] Again representing a shift and emerging precisely from this affirmation of intrinsic value, Francis posits that harm committed against creation is sinful in itself. Echoing Patriarch Bartholomew I, the pope invites readers "to acknowledge our sins against creation."[108] In

---

[103] *Laudato Si'*, 119.

[104] *Laudato Si'*, 68.

[105] Borghesi, *The Mind of Pope Francis*, 60–62.

[106] *Laudato Si'*, 118.

[107] *Laudato Si'*, 69. See also 33, 84, 140. In fact, from March 7–8, 2018, the Pontifical Gregorian University hosted a conference entitled "Radical Ecological Conversion after *Laudato Si'*: Discovering the Intrinsic Value of All Creatures, Human & Non-human."

[108] *Laudato Si'*, 8. In particular, he cites Bartholomew I, *Message for the Day of Prayer for the Protection of Creation* (September 1, 2012) and Bartholomew I, *Address in Santa Barbara, California* (November 8, 1997).

the years following the release of the encyclical, Francis has endorsed the inclusion of "ecological sin" in the *Catechism of the Catholic Church*.[109] As he proposes in *Laudato Si'*, the opening chapters of Genesis present sin as a rupture of "three fundamental and closely intertwined relationships: with God, with our neighbor, and with the earth itself."[110] Harm committed in any one of these relationships reflects a break present in the other relationships.[111] Severing one of these relationships, such as with the earth, is thus sinful in itself. In making this claim, Francis still preserves the earlier insight of John Paul II, that a rupture in one of these relationships, in this case with creation, simultaneously remains a consequence of breaking one's relationship with God. That harm committed against creation can be both sinful in itself and a consequence of sin emerges from Francis's stress on the relational character of our common home and the care it deserves.

In a way that stewardship and dominion language cannot convey, the imperative to care extends to human and nonhuman creation alike. It makes more sense to say that one cares for a friend or a parent than that one has stewardship or dominion over them. Capturing the inclusivity of the call to care, Francis writes:

> Moreover, when our hearts are authentically open to universal communion, this sense of fraternity excludes nothing and no one. It follows that our indifference or cruelty toward fellow creatures of this world sooner or later affects the treatment we mete out to other human beings. We have only one heart, and the same wretchedness which leads us to mistreat an animal will not be long in showing itself in our relationships with other people. . . . Everything is related, and we human beings are united as brothers and sisters on a wonderful pilgrimage, woven together by the love God has for each of his creatures and which also unites us in fond affection with brother sun, sister moon, brother river and mother earth.[112]

---

[109] In 2018, Peter Turkson asserted "ecological sin" as a key theme in the encyclical. See Peter Turkson, *Integral Ecological Conversion*, Dicastery for Promoting Integral Human Development (March 7, 2018), http://www.laudatosiinstitute.org/en/integral-ecological-conversion-cardinal-peter-kodwo-appiah-turkson/. On the term's addition to the *Catechism of the Catholic Church*, see Francis, *Address to Participants at the World Congress of the International Association of Penal Law* (November 15, 2019).

[110] *Laudato Si'*, 66.

[111] *Laudato Si'*, 70, 92.

[112] *Laudato Si'*, 92.

Because everything is connected, the task of caring and becoming painfully aware answers the cries of the earth and the poor alike, safeguarding human and natural ecologies. The heart with which one must feel and become close is one, and so an integral ecology, as task, requires replacing the stony heart of technocracy with the fleshy heart of merciful care—indeed, a conversion.

And yet, the nature of the technocratic paradigm complicates this call toward conversion considerably. Michael Hanby notes that this concept "represents a real magisterial development of the teaching of John Paul II and Benedict XVI."[113] Prior papal engagements with questions of technology normally presumed an instrumentalist account: that various modern technologies were a neutral tool whose morality depended on the user and the situation. They largely failed to engage determinist theories that considered the ways that the very medium of certain technologies reshaped human knowing and action.[114] In part due to the influence of Guardini and Methol Ferré, Francis's discussion of the technocratic paradigm in *Laudato Si'* represents an evolution of this approach by offering a more critical reading of technology.[115]

That is, this discussion admits both the ways that contemporary technology, as a "paradigm," has come to reshape human life and the distinct set of challenges that this recognition brings.[116] Admonishing readers "to accept that technological products are not neutral," Francis submits "that many problems of today's world stem from the tendency, at times unconscious, to make the method and aims of science and technology an epistemological paradigm which shapes the lives of individuals and the workings of society."[117] Describing its "ironclad logic," Francis writes, "The idea of promoting

---

[113] Michael Hanby, "The Gospel of Creation and the Technocratic Paradigm: Reflections on a Central Teaching of *Laudato Si'*," *Communio: International Catholic Review* 42, no. 4 (Winter 2015): 724–47, at 726.

[114] See James F. Caccamo, "The Message on the Media: Seventy Years of Catholic Social Teaching on Social Communication," *Josephinum Journal of Theology* 15, no. 2 (2008): 390–426, at 424–25.

[115] A point made indirectly in R. R. Reno, "The Return of Catholic Anti-modernism," *First Things* (June 6, 2015), https://www.firstthings.com/web-exclusives/2015/06/the-return-of-catholic-anti-modernism.

[116] This is a point that also marks Francis's other writings; see *Christus Vivit*, 86: "It is no longer merely a question of 'using' instruments of communication, but of living in a highly digitalized culture that has had a profound impact on ideas of time and space, on our self-understanding, our understanding of others and the world, and our ability to communicate, learn, be informed and enter into relationship with others. An approach to reality that privileges images over listening and reading has influenced the way people learn and the development of their critical sense" (citing the Final Document of the Synod).

[117] *Laudato Si'*, 107.

a different cultural paradigm and employing technology as a mere instrument is nowadays inconceivable. The technological paradigm has become so dominant that it would be difficult to do without its resources and even more difficult to utilize them without being dominated by their internal logic."[118] The technocratic paradigm monopolizes all dimensions of human living, deeming any alternative as backward or impractical. The technocratic paradigm allows indifference and a throwaway mentality to infiltrate technological, cultural, political, and economic systems, exacerbating the cries of the earth and the poor. It leaves little room for exit.

And thus, given its dominance, the technocratic paradigm distorts various efforts to care for those cries. Believing that they rely too much on technocratic assumptions, Francis mourns the ineffectiveness and failure of various policy proposals, technological innovations, and economic reforms for fully resolving the crises that plague our common home. He remarks, for instance, how "the failure of global summits on the environment make it plain that our politics are subject to technology and finance."[119] So too does Francis rue how "[t]echnology, which, linked to business interests, is presented as the only way of solving these problems, in fact proves incapable of seeing the mysterious network of relations between things and so sometimes solves one problem only to create others."[120] More generally, the mediation of another, let alone their pain, through a technological medium domesticates the possibility of a genuine encounter. Contemporary media, Francis suggests, can "shield us from direct contact with the pain, the fears and the joys of others and the complexity of their personal experiences."[121] Viewing the world through a screen jeopardizes the visceral, empathetic feeling with the heart that caring for our common home requires. Modern technology attempts to disburden users from the friction, such as the pain of another, that a culture of encounter strives to embrace.[122] In the face of

---

[118] *Laudato Si'*, 108.

[119] *Laudato Si'*, 54.

[120] *Laudato Si'*, 20. See also *Laudato Si'*, 14, 56, 57, 142, 165, 166, 169.

[121] *Laudato Si'*, 47. See also *Amoris Laetitia*, 278; and Sherry Turkle, *Reclaiming Conversation: The Power of Talk in a Digital Age* (New York: Penguin Press, 2015), 3–9, 168–73.

[122] As Francis writes elsewhere, "when we allow ourselves to be caught up in superficial information, instant communication and virtual reality, we can waste precious time and become indifferent to the suffering flesh of our brothers and sisters." *Gaudete et Exsultate*, 108. See also Richard R. Gaillardetz, *Transforming Our Days: Finding God amid the Noise of Modern Life* (Liguori, Mo.: Liguori Publications, 2007), 50–51.

the cries of the earth and the poor, the technocratic paradigm can render people passive, making the groanings of creation a mere spectacle rather than a challenge encountered in the concrete. To acknowledge the pervasiveness of the technocratic paradigm is to acknowledge the deep obstacles that inhibit the task that an integral ecology commands.

A little over a year after the release of *Laudato Si'*, Francis instituted the World Day of Prayer for the Care of Creation in a message entitled *Show Mercy to Our Common Home*.[123] In it, Francis condemns indifference and resignation to the cries of the earth and the poor. He invites everyone in his audience instead to an examination of conscience, a painful awareness, of their own sins against creation, others, and God as well as a grateful awareness for the gift of creation. He continues that the encounter with mercy received through this confession should prompt repentance, a change of heart that takes the shape of "showing mercy to the earth as our common home and cherishing the world in which we live as a place for sharing and communion."[124] The need is so pressing that Francis adds caring for our common home as a complement to the traditional seven corporal and seven spiritual works of mercy. This message serves as an apt summary (and reception) of how Francis envisions integral ecology as a task in *Laudato Si'*. Our common home demands a mercy, a feeling with the heart, that might respond to the cries of the earth and the poor. Nevertheless, as has become clear, the nature of the technocratic paradigm makes this urgent task practically impossible. How will hearts be awakened, enlarged, and stirred in the face of the cold, cramped, and stifling ironclad logic of technocracy?

---

[123] Francis, *Message for the Celebration of the World Day of Prayer for the Care of Creation: Show Mercy to Our Common Home* (September 1, 2016).

[124] Francis, *Message for the Celebration of the World Day of Prayer for the Care of Creation*. See also the early Eastern Christian theologian, Isaac the Syrian:

> And what is a merciful heart? It is the heart's burning for the sake of the entire creation, for men, for birds, for animals, for demons, and for every created thing; and by the recollection of them the eyes of a merciful man pour forth abundant tears. From the strong and vehement mercy which grips his heart and from his great compassion, his heart is humbled and he cannot bear to hear or to see any injury or slight sorrow in creation. For this reason he offers up tearful prayer continually even for irrational beasts, for the enemies of the truth, and for those who harm him, that they be protected and receive mercy. And in like manner he even prays for the family of reptiles because of the great compassion that burns without measure in his heart in the likeness of God. ("Homily 71," in *The Ascetical Homilies of Saint Isaac the Syrian* [Boston: Holy Transfiguration Monastery, 1984], 344–45)

THE DOXOLOGICAL AND EUCHARISTIC FOUNDATIONS OF AN INTEGRAL ECOLOGY

Prior to his election as pope, Cardinal Bergoglio identified "spiritual worldliness" as "the worst thing that can happen to the church."[125] In the conclave that would elect him pope, he again decried an ecclesial "self-referentiality," wherein the church lives for and glorifies itself and does not live *ad majorem Dei gloriam*. This too betrays a "spiritual worldliness."[126] In both instances, Francis cited Henri de Lubac, who described spiritual worldliness as when "moral and even spiritual standards [are] based, not on the glory of the Lord, but on what is the profit of [ourselves]; an entirely anthropocentric outlook would be exactly what we mean by worldliness."[127] Spiritual worldliness denotes the reduction of the church to a purely human institution that only serves its own preservation. As pope, Francis has reiterated de Lubac's warning against spiritual worldliness in the church's life, calling it an "anthropocentric immanentism," in the form perhaps of clericalism or ecclesial careerism.[128] A church wrapped up in itself, shining a light on itself rather than reflecting the light of Christ and the always greater God, suffocates and dies.

A similar sentiment marks Francis's analysis of social problems. For such a seemingly modern pope, and in relative contrast to his immediate predecessors, Francis denounces idolatry with frequency.[129] Like spiritual worldliness, idolatry ensconces oneself in too little by divinizing the creaturely. Whereas spiritual worldliness refers to an ecclesial phenomenon, idolatry infects the entire social fabric. In *Evangelii Gaudium* and elsewhere, Francis condemns an "idolatry of money" in which financial gain and endless consumption garner the devotion of one's entire being.[130] The subjugation

---

[125] Jorge Mario Bergoglio, "What I Would Have Said at the Consistory: Interview with Sefania Falasca," 30 Days, Issue 11 (2007), http://www.30giorni.it/articoli_id_16457_l3.htm.

[126] See Jorge Mario Bergoglio, "Bergoglio's Intervention: A Diagnosis of the Problems in the Church," Vatican News, March 27, 2013, http://en.radiovaticana.va/news/2013/03/27/bergoglios_intervention:_a_diagnosis_of_the_problems_in_the_church/en1-677269.

[127] Henri de Lubac, *The Splendor of the Church*, trans. Michael Mason (San Francisco: Ignatius Press, 1986), 378.

[128] *Evangelii Gaudium*, 94.

[129] See William Cavanaugh, "Return of the Golden Calf: Economy, Idolatry, and Secularization since *Gaudium et Spes*," *Theological Studies* 76, no. 4 (December 2015): 698–717.

[130] *Evangelii Gaudium*, 55. See also Andrea Tornielli and Giacomo Galeazzi, *This Economy Kills: Pope Francis on Capitalism and Social Justice* (Collegeville, Minn.: Liturgical Press, 2015), 26–30.

of all meaning and worth to profit or consumption betrays a submission to something other than God. This tendency shows the inherently theological character of social malaises. In *Lumen Fidei*, idolatry stands as the opposite of faith. Francis warns against the recurrent temptation "to worship an idol, into whose face we can look directly and whose origin we know, because it is the work of our own hands. Before an idol, there is no risk that we will be called to abandon our security.... Idols exist, we begin to see, as a pretext for setting ourselves at the center of reality and worshiping the work of our own hands."[131] To fall into idolatry devastates the rest of creation. In *Laudato Si'*, Francis remarks that displacing the one true God is "how we end up worshipping earthly powers, or ourselves usurping the place of God, even to the point of claiming an unlimited right to trample his creation underfoot."[132] Like spiritual worldliness, idolatry betrays a self-grasping anthropocentrism, a posture that suffocates not only oneself but our entire common home.

At the heart of spiritual worldliness and idolatry lies the question of worship. Spiritual worldliness, glorifying only oneself, reveals a refusal to be drawn out of oneself in the glorification of God. Idolatry, to surrender one's entire being to something other than the one true God, reveals a refusal to yield to the only one worthy of the total self-abandon of praise. In both instances, the rejection of right worship results in a cramped, hardened anthropocentrism. The Principle and Foundation of the *Spiritual Exercises* reads: "God created human beings to praise, reverence, and serve God, and by doing this, to save their souls."[133] The Jesuit spirituality that shapes Bergoglio (and de Lubac) presumes that the human person is a *homo adorans*, that the human person finds ultimate fulfillment in opening one's heart and moving out of oneself in a "sacrifice of praise" (Heb 13:15) to God.[134] To settle for anything less leads to the death of oneself and the death of others, smothering all within the confines of a deadly, tyrannical anthropocentrism.

---

[131] Francis, Encyclical Letter *Lumen Fidei* (June 29, 2013), 13. It should be noted that Francis collaborated extensively with Benedict XVI on this document.

[132] *Laudato Si'*, 75.

[133] Ignatius of Loyola, *The Spiritual Exercises of Saint Ignatius*, trans. Anthony Mottola (New York: Doubleday, 1964), 47.

[134] Fessard, whose reading of the *Spiritual Exercises* shaped Bergoglio deeply, read the doxological orientation of the Principle and Foundation as a challenge to "idolatrous messianism," modern totalitarianisms like communism and Nazism. See Robert Barron, "Gaston Fessard and Pope Francis," in *Discovering Pope Francis*, 119–23.

For Francis, the church's mission consists in fostering "right praise," the doxological vocation of humanity and of all of creation. Worship also catalyzes ecclesial mission, as the centripetal movement of praise propels a church that goes out of itself in mission.[135]

Francis's radical vision informs his presentation of the church's social mission in *Laudato Si'* and explains its unique character. Unlike any other social encyclical, praise frames the entirety of *Laudato Si'*. Borrowing from a doxological hymn composed by Francis of Assisi, the very title of *Laudato Si'* (Praise be to you) signals the vital place of right praise within our common home. Much like the Principle and Foundation, the encyclical begins with words of praise. So too does it end with words of praise. In the official presentation of the encyclical, Cardinal Turkson proposed that this doxological bookending clarifies the meaning of *Laudato Si'*. Commenting on the eponymous prayer, Turkson stated that the "reference to St. Francis also indicates the attitude upon which the entire Encyclical is based, that of prayerful contemplation."[136] He also highlighted the two prayers at the encyclical's end, which illustrate that the document "concludes, as it opened, in a spirit of prayerful contemplation."[137] Reading *Laudato Si'* on one's knees allows one to participate in the right praise that it attempts to foster.

The summit of praise on earth is the Eucharist. Thus, so too does this spirit point toward the extended treatment of the Eucharist within *Laudato Si'*. "It is in the Eucharist," Francis posits, "that all that has been created finds its greatest exaltation."[138] Several sections of the encyclical expand this claim, and even more reference it implicitly. This emphasis also signals the unique nature of *Laudato Si'*. Besides John Paul II's *Sollicitudo Rei Socialis*, no other social encyclical mentions the Eucharist, let alone dedicates substantial attention to it in the way that Francis does here. As the previous chapter intimated, this doxological, eucharistic framework most firmly secures the integrated approach that Catholic social teaching takes to the ecological crisis. It is this distinct character of *Laudato Si'* that undergirds

---

[135] See Christopher Ruddy, "'In My End Is My Beginning': *Lumen Gentium* and the Priority of Doxology," *Irish Theological Quarterly* 79, no. 2 (2014): 144–64, at 162–63.

[136] Turkson, *Conferenza Stampa per la presentazione della Lettera Enciclica «Laudato si'» del Santo Padre Francesco sulla cura della casa commune*. Turkson reiterated this point twelve days later in his presentation of *Laudato Si'* in the ECOSOC Chamber at the United Nations.

[137] Turkson, *Conferenza Stampa per la presentazione della Lettera Enciclica «Laudato si'» del Santo Padre Francesco sulla cura della casa commune*.

[138] *Laudato Si'*, 236.

the richness of its integral ecology. As Christopher Thompson recognizes, "Integral ecology is doxology; there is no simpler way to put it."[139]

A Doxological and Eucharistic Vision

As detailed above, the synthetic vision of an integral ecology reconciles human and natural ecologies. The previous chapter made clear that, if those two ecologies remained bifurcated, partisan forces could co-opt the division and obscure their deep interconnectedness. Progressive and conservative factions, especially in the West, could quite easily appropriate the distinct concerns of natural ecology and human ecology as each roughly correspond to the concerns of their respective political interests. This polarization threatens to rend the seamless garment of the church's integrated approach to the ecological crisis. Domesticating Catholic social teaching by these political standards represents a form of spiritual worldliness, as it conforms this tradition too easily to the expectations of Western politics.[140] The doxological, eucharistic emphases of *Laudato Si'* place its integral ecology on a properly theological basis able to transcend and rectify these divides.

Just as, against purely materialistic understandings of development, Paul VI's presentation of integral human development in *Populorum Progressio* aimed to ensure that theories of development included and were grounded in a religious dimension, so too does Francis's presentation of an integral ecology in *Laudato Si'* aim to ensure a more capacious vision for theories of ecology. As Francis insists, "If we are truly concerned to develop an ecology capable of remedying the damage we have done, no branch of the sciences and no form of wisdom can be left out, and that includes religion and the language particular to it."[141] While "some dismiss as irrational the rich contribution which religions can make toward an integral ecology," a truly integral ecology necessarily includes this dimension of living.[142] Francis recommends dialogue between religion and other fields of knowledge, since any given discipline "can tend to become enclosed in its own

---

[139] Christopher J. Thompson, *The Joyful Mystery: Field Notes toward a Green Thomism* (Steubenville, Ohio: Emmaus Road Publishing, 2017), 171.

[140] As Paul VI worries, the reduction of the church's mission to purely worldly standards makes it susceptible to the "monopolization and manipulation by ideological systems and political parties." *Evangelii Nuntiandi*, 43.

[141] *Laudato Si'*, 63.

[142] *Laudato Si'*, 62.

language, while specialization leads to a certain isolation and the absolutization of its own field of knowledge"; likewise, dialogue with religion can help environmental advocates, "among which ideological conflicts are not infrequently encountered."[143] This polarization, whether ideological or disciplinary, truncates the comprehensive vision that an integral ecology requires. As proposed in *Laudato Si'*, the expansive horizon of religious meaning can broaden these narrowed visions.

This capacious vision can accordingly overcome the political polarization that threatens to fragment an integral ecology. The numerous policy proposals contained within *Laudato Si'* that cover matters of both human and natural ecology can allow one to cull sections that happen to fit one's ideological agenda. The reception of the encyclical within the United States attests to precisely that possibility.[144] As Mary Taylor argues though, the robust spirituality of *Laudato Si'* demonstrates that its integral ecology offers something more than a blend of a scientific manifesto, a collection of ethical principles, and a political tract.[145] Reading the encyclical and its integral ecology in this reductionistic manner makes it susceptible to polarizing forces. Instead, the doxological spirit of *Laudato Si'* reveals its thoroughly theocentric character. Issues of human ecology and issues of natural ecology "are not merely to be juxtaposed; they flow from one single source, a source that lies deeper than science, politics, or ethics."[146] This doxological framework furnishes the deeper meaning and unity behind the issues discussed in *Laudato Si'* that correspond to human and natural ecologies alike, even if, to the partisan eye, they seem at odds with each other. In the ways that it counters spiritual worldliness by focusing the church on its deepest purpose, doxology thus secures the roomy vision of an integral ecology. While Francis's linking of the cries of the poor and of the earth joined human and natural ecologies "from below," Francis's framing of *Laudato Si'* through doxology joins human and natural ecologies "from above."

Throughout the encyclical, Francis affirms the doxological orientation of all creation and so unites these ecologies. The pope highlights how the Psalms frequently join humans with sun and moon, stars and water, in a

---

[143] *Laudato Si'*, 201.

[144] See the discussion in the introduction to this book.

[145] Mary Taylor, "Ecology on One's Knees: Reading *Laudato Si'*," *Communio* 42, no. 4 (Winter 2015): 618–51, at 619.

[146] Taylor, "Ecology on One's Knees," 634.

single chorus of glorifying God.[147] He laments that, with the loss of biodiversity, "thousands of species will no longer give glory to God by their very existence."[148] In fact, Francis roots the intrinsic value of all creatures in their ability to "give [God] glory."[149] The pope echoes the Japanese bishops that "[t]o sense each creature singing the hymn of its existence is to live joyfully in God's love and hope."[150] In the canticle that gives *Laudato Si'* its name, Francis of Assisi praises God through "Brother Sun" and "Sister Moon," "Sister Water" and "Brother Fire."[151] The pope makes clear in *Laudato Si'* that praise directs all creation, across both human and natural ecologies, to its triune Creator. Dividing these ecologies renders this hymn cacophonous.

At the same time, as Francis of Assisi illustrates, humans play a priest-like role within the praise that *Laudato Si'* strains to channel. As an extension of his radically missionary spirit, it was Francis of Assisi who exhorted all creatures to glorify God.[152] The pope hails his namesake for "drawing all creatures into his praise" instead of viewing them through mere "intellectual appreciation or economic calculus."[153] As opposed to the twin errors of biocentrism and excessive anthropocentrism, people, like Francis of Assisi, "are called to lead all creatures back to their creator" by joining with yet also bringing forth creation's sacrifice of praise.[154] Mediating creation's praise conforms oneself to Christ's own cosmic priesthood, whereby "the creatures of this world no longer appear to us under merely natural guise because the risen One is mysteriously holding them to himself and directing them toward fullness as their end."[155] Developing Benedict XVI's earlier intima-

---

[147] *Laudato Si'*, 72.

[148] *Laudato Si'*, 33.

[149] *Laudato Si'*, 69.

[150] *Laudato Si'*, 85.

[151] *Laudato Si'*, 87.

[152] See Roger D. Sorrell, *St. Francis of Assisi and Nature: Tradition and Innovation in Western Christian Attitudes toward the Environment* (New York: Oxford University Press, 1988), 110–11, 140.

[153] *Laudato Si'*, 11.

[154] *Laudato Si'*, 83. As Willis Jenkins notes, the encyclical "requalifies dominion in contemplative terms, and thereby reconnects human dignity to the dignity of all creatures. Reinterpreted through the figure of Saint Francis, the dominion mandate refers to a uniquely human ability to learn the songs of other creatures and restore harmony in creation by joining in the ways creatures praise God." See Willis Jenkins, "The Mysterious Silence of Mother Earth in *Laudato Si'*," *Journal of Religious Ethics* 46, no. 3 (2018): 441–62, at 448.

[155] *Laudato Si'*, 100.

tions on this point, the encyclical's conception of the proper relationship between human beings and the rest of creation has a liturgical quality. The Eastern Orthodox theologian John Zizioulas presided at the official presentation of *Laudato Si'* and observed that the encyclical makes "human beings instead of proprietors of creation act as its priests" such that "the human being leads this cosmic chorus of glorification to the Creator as the priest of creation."[156] As Zizioulas argues elsewhere, a priestly anthropology can offer a less functional, more organic conception of humans' relationship with creation than the managerial connotations of stewardship can.[157] This priestly anthropology grounds the anthropo-relational vision of *Laudato Si'*, as humans join with all creation in the common praise of God.

The Eucharist concretizes this praise unsurpassably. Again, in the words of *Laudato Si'*, "It is in the Eucharist that all that has been created finds its greatest exaltation." Citing both John Paul II and Benedict XVI, Francis continues:

> Joined to the incarnate Son, present in the Eucharist, the whole cosmos gives thanks to God. Indeed the Eucharist is itself an act of cosmic love: "Yes, cosmic! Because even when it is celebrated on the humble altar of a country church, the Eucharist is always in some way celebrated on the altar of the world." The Eucharist joins heaven and earth; it embraces and penetrates all creation. The world which came forth from God's hands returns to him in blessed and undivided adoration: in the bread of the Eucharist, "creation is projected toward divinization, toward the holy wedding feast, toward unification with the Creator himself."[158]

The eucharistic celebration channels uniquely the praise of all creation, spanning human and natural ecology alike, toward its eschatological end. Moreover, it is in the Eucharist where Christians enact their vocation as priests, their participation in Christ's high priesthood, in a most explicit way.[159] In the eucharistic communion, all sing together the praise of God.

---

[156] John D. Zizioulas, "A Comment on Pope Francis' Encyclical *Laudato Si'* by Elder Metropolitan John (Zizioulas) of Pergamon" (June 18, 2015), https://www.patriarchate.org/-/a-comment-on-pope-francis-encyclical-laudato-si-.

[157] See John D. Zizioulas, *The Eucharistic Communion and the World* (New York: Bloomsbury T & T Clark, 2011), 133–41.

[158] *Laudato Si'*, 236. Francis here cites John Paul II, *Ecclesia de Eucharistia*, 8, and Benedict XVI, *Homily for the Mass of Corpus Christi* (June 15, 2006).

[159] See Paul McPartlan, "Praying with Creation: Cosmic Aspects of Eucharist," *Liturgy News* 40, no. 3 (September 2010): 6–10.

The cosmic scope of the Eucharist enlivens the expansive vision of *Laudato Si'*. As the summit of praise, the Eucharist supplies the deeper unity and meaning of its integral ecology as well as the many proposals concerning human and natural ecologies that comprise it. The above quotation fittingly includes a citation of both John Paul II and Benedict XVI, as it is here that Francis joins explicitly his predecessors' rich reflections on the ecological significance of the Eucharist with the integrated approach to the ecological crisis that they attempted to marshal. Precisely by incorporating this radically doxological, eucharistic framework into its proposed integral ecology, *Laudato Si'* secures the full breadth of the church's response to the ecological crisis. In eucharistic praise, the cries of the earth and the poor can be transformed into hymns of rejoicing.

The Eucharistic Shape of Caring for Our Common Home

At its root, the eucharistic liturgy is an encounter that re-forms the self. As Jeremy Driscoll writes:

> To say that the Mass is about love is to say that it is an encounter. It is an encounter with God, but not God as vaguely conceived. It is an encounter with God through Jesus. We encounter Jesus, and through him we encounter the one whom he calls God and Father. We do not encounter Jesus as vaguely conceived. Our encounter with him is nothing less than an encounter with one whom we must also call Lord and God. . . . The Jesus who was crucified under Pontius Pilate and whose Death is remembered during the course of the Mass is encountered there as risen from the dead and so known as Lord and God. This precisely defined encounter with God gives me freedom. It defines me. It offers me a new self in which I am defined through this new relationship.[160]

As an encounter with Christ, the eucharistic liturgy supplies a prime locus for conversion: the experience of God's mercy through Christ.[161] In engaging the entirety of one's being, the liturgy speaks a language of the heart, supplying the visceral character of this encounter. In the pope's words, the

---

[160] Jeremy Driscoll, *What Happens at Mass*, rev. ed. (Chicago: Liturgy Training Publications, 2011), vii.

[161] Innocent Smith, for example, shows how many of Francis's references to mercy emerge from liturgical contexts (especially through the work of Thomas Aquinas). See his "Liturgical Prayer and the Theology of Mercy in Thomas Aquinas and Pope Francis," *Theological Studies* 79, no. 4 (December 2018): 782–800, at 796–99.

liturgical homily should foster a "heart-to-heart communication," and the Eucharist is "a powerful medicine and nourishment for the weak."[162] Moreover, rooted in this encounter, the liturgy is always a communal reality. As Francis writes, "Thanks solely to this encounter—or renewed encounter—with God's love, which blossoms into an enriching friendship, we are liberated from our narrowness and self-absorption."[163] In the eucharistic liturgy, Christians encounter the mercy of God, which breaks open their hearts to encounter others in communion.

The Eucharist, as a sacrament of encounter, thus buttresses Francis's broader conception of the church's mission. A eucharistically formed heart roots a culture of encounter and, consequently, shatters all forms of anthropocentrism. In the words of one writer, "The logic of the Eucharist, the world of gifts, frees us from the calculations of technocracy."[164] This suggestion can begin to explain why Francis makes the Eucharist so central to *Laudato Si'* and why, for him, "[r]ather than a problem to be solved, the world is a joyful mystery to be contemplated with gladness and praise."[165] So too does can it begin to explain why Francis frames his proposed integral ecology through doxology and the Eucharist so thoroughly. To counter a culture of death, John Paul II stressed the unalienable dignity of the human person. To counter a dictatorship of relativism, Benedict XVI stressed the *Logos* prior to oneself. As the previous chapter showed, these respective contextual foils shaped the environmental writings of Francis's papal predecessors. For Francis, the merciful care that makes one painfully aware of what is happening to our common home demands "a spirituality [that] can motivate us to a more *passionate* concern for the protection of our world."[166] Guardini, who guides Francis throughout *Laudato si'*, saw Christian worship and its contemplative, embodied, and communal character as challenging the foundational tenets of modern technocracy.[167] In the face of a globalization of indifference, the eucharistic liturgy plays an indispensable role in breaking through the ironclad logic of the technocratic paradigm as

---

162 *Evangelii Gaudium*, 142, 47.

163 *Evangelii Gaudium*, 8.

164 Timothy Radcliffe, *Alive in God: A Christian Imagination* (New York: Bloomsbury Continuum, 2019), 321.

165 *Laudato Si'*, 12.

166 *Laudato Si'*, 216. Emphasis added.

167 See Romano Guardini, *The Spirit of the Liturgy*, trans. Ada Lane (New York: Crossroad Publishing, 1998), 85–95.

it awakens one's heart to imagine the world anew or, more accurately, to see the world as God intends it to be.[168] "Eucharist is the fulfillment of the practice of integral ecology," Thompson writes.[169] The task of an integral ecology, caring for our common home, has an indelibly eucharistic shape.

Compared with stewardship, the more organic character of a priestly anthropology captures the need to feel with one's heart the hymn of the universe throbbing through one's veins. Inasmuch as the eucharistic celebration enacts this vocation, one can recognize the ways that creation points to God, that the *telos* of creation is doxological. That is, the Eucharist offers a privileged encounter with this sacramentality of creation, God's incarnational logic:

> Grace, which tends to manifest itself tangibly, found unsurpassable expression when God himself became man and gave himself as food for his creatures. The Lord, in the culmination of the mystery of the Incarnation, chose to reach our intimate depths through a fragment of matter. He comes not from above, but from within, he comes that we might find him in this world of ours. In the Eucharist, fullness is already achieved; it is the living center of the universe, the overflowing core of love and of inexhaustible life.[170]

While the technocratic paradigm reduces creation to raw stuff to be manipulated, the Eucharist discloses the revelatory capacity of all creation, its capacity for praise. Thanksgiving (*eucharistia*), rather than ceaseless consumption, marks a properly eucharistic posture. Rather than seeing the end of creation in oneself—this is idolatrous anthropocentrism—the Eucharist involves one offering the gift of creation, formed through "the work of human hands," as a sacrifice back to God. This stretching forth, the position of praise, orients oneself alongside all creation toward God.

This eucharistic encounter with the sacramentality of creation opens human hearts to enter into communion with the praise of all creation. In the words of *Laudato Si'*, "[w]hen we can see God reflected in all that exists, our hearts are moved to praise the Lord for all his creatures and to worship

---

[168] See Walter Brueggemann, *The Prophetic Imagination*, 40th anniv. ed. (Minneapolis, Minn.: Fortress Press, 2018), xxxiv. As he writes from a U.S. context, "the cultural situation in the United States, satiated by consumer goods and propelled by electronic technology, is one of narcoticized insensibility to human reality. . . . [P]erhaps eucharistic imagination can . . . be a potential resistance and alternative to commodity satiation."

[169] Thompson, *The Joyful Mystery*, 173.

[170] *Laudato Si'*, 236.

him in union within them."[171] In a sacrament like the Eucharist, "we are invited to embrace the world on a different plane. Water, oil, fire and colors are taken up in all their symbolic power and incorporated in our act of praise."[172] The liturgical equivalent of Benedict XVI's "grammar of creation," it is this revelatory, doxological capacity of creation that grounds its intrinsic value. Sacramentality marks all creation, human and nonhuman alike: "The universe unfolds in God, who fills it completely. Hence, there is a mystical meaning to be found in a leaf, in a mountain trail, in a dewdrop, in a poor person's face."[173] Instead of seeing the world, in the words of Jacques Monod, as an "unfeeling immensity," a sacramental worldview sees the world as, in the words of Gerard Manley Hopkins, "charged with grandeur of God."[174] Instead of viewing the world through the lens of utility, a sacramental worldview demands encountering the unique worth of each created thing. Recognizing the doxological orientation of all creation and its revelatory capacity engenders the inclusive imperative to care contained within the integral ecology of *Laudato Si'*.

In a world of cold indifference and consumeristic narcissism, the celebration of the Eucharist opens one's heart to both the cries of the earth and the poor as well as the stream of praise, however disjointed, that swells from all creation. Francis notes how, besides the way it signals the doxological orientation of all creation, the sabbatical character of the Eucharist cultivates this attentiveness:

> On Sunday, our participation in the Eucharist has special importance. Sunday, like the Jewish Sabbath, is meant to be a day which heals our relationships with God, with ourselves, with others and with the world. Sunday is the day of the Resurrection, the "first day" of the new creation, whose first fruits are the Lord's risen humanity, the pledge of the final transfiguration of all created reality. It also proclaims "man's eternal rest in God." In this way, Christian spirituality incorporates the value of relaxation and festivity. We tend to demean contemplative rest as something unproductive and unnecessary, but this is to do away with the very thing

---

[171] *Laudato Si'*, 87.

[172] *Laudato Si'*, 235.

[173] *Laudato Si'*, 233.

[174] Jacques Monod, *Chance and Necessity: An Essay on the Natural Philosophy of Modern Biology*, trans. Austryn Wainhouse (New York: Vintage Books, 1972), 180; and Gerard Manley Hopkins, "God's Grandeur," in *Poems and Prose*, ed. W. H. Gardner (New York: Penguin Books, 1985), 27.

> which is most important about work: its meaning. We are called to include in our work a dimension of receptivity and gratuity, which is quite different from mere inactivity. Rather, it is another way of working, which forms part of our very essence. It protects human action from becoming empty activism; it also prevents that unfettered greed and sense of isolation which make us seek personal gain to the detriment of all else. The law of weekly rest forbade work on the seventh day, "so that your ox and your donkey may have rest, and the son of your maidservant, and the stranger, may be refreshed" (Ex 23:12). Rest opens our eyes to the larger picture and gives us renewed sensitivity to the rights of others. And so the day of rest, centered on the Eucharist, sheds it light on the whole week, and motivates us to greater concern for nature and the poor.[175]

As opposed to the idolatry of unceasing consumption, the stillness of Sabbath sensitizes one to others. The day of rest, according to the logic of *Laudato Si'*, stirs Christians to hear the cries of the earth and the poor or how creation fails to praise God, impelling Christians to bother to care in empathetic solidarity. In this, the Eucharist makes the church, animating the ecstatic movement of its mission of mercy within our common home.

Communion, sacramentality, a priestly anthropology, and sabbath all ground the care that an integral ecology necessitates. Care, then, amid the technocratic ruins, has a doxological and eucharistic shape. Tellingly, Francis extols the witness of Benedictine monasticism in this regard. In something of a paradigmatic statement of *Laudato Si'*, he writes: "Saint Benedict of Norcia proposed that his monks live in community, combining prayer and spiritual reading with manual labor (*ora et labora*). Seeing manual labor as spiritually meaningful proved revolutionary. Personal growth and sanctification came to be sought in the interplay of recollection and work. This way of experiencing work makes us more protective and respectful of the environment; it imbues our relationship to the world with a healthy sobriety."[176]

The church's work of praise must imbue its work for justice in caring for our common home and vice-versa. The integral ecology of *Laudato Si'*, precisely because everything is deeply interconnected, joins this *ora et labora* in a radical way. Care, if is to address truly the cries of the earth and the poor, must pattern itself through eucharistic praise.

---

[175] *Laudato Si'*, 237.
[176] *Laudato Si'*, 126.

THE CHURCH IN OUR COMMON HOME: SOME LINGERING QUESTIONS

It is clear that *Laudato Si'* offers a monumental contribution to the church's reflection on the ecological crisis. More subtly but equally significantly, *Laudato Si'* also implies a certain vision of the church; the encyclical is an "eminently ecclesiological document."[177] Several commentators have already noted the insights the document holds for the church's internal constitution.[178] Less noticed is how *Laudato Si'* envisions the church's mission. On the one hand, it incorporates definitively ecological concern into the church's conception of its mission. On the other hand—and, as this chapter suggests, relatedly—so too does it configure the church's mission, especially in its social form, in a radically doxological, eucharistic manner. In both ways does *Laudato Si'* represent an ecclesiological achievement.

Admittedly, however, this eucharistic vision of the church remains at the level of implication in *Laudato Si'*. Hence, as the introduction of this book noted, the eucharistic vision of *Laudato Si'* has gone largely unnoticed in theological commentary on the encyclical. More importantly, as the introduction also suggested, the polarization that has distorted the encyclical's reception in U.S. Catholicism indicates a failure to recognize this profoundly theological heart of *Laudato Si'*. As has become clear, grasping the doxological and eucharistic vision of *Laudato Si'* is grasping how the encyclical offers a comprehensive call to care for our common home across all ecologies; the failure to grasp that vision has fragmented the integral ecology of *Laudato Si'* and the call to conversion it poses. Insofar as social encyclicals tend to be ad hoc documents responding to contextual contingencies, it is no surprise that *Laudato Si'* itself does not provide a systematic exposition of how exactly eucharistic praise relates to the church's call to care for our common home, how exactly it safeguards an integrated response to human and natural ecologies, and how exactly it shapes the many conversions

---

[177] Judith Gruber, "Ec(o)clesiology: Ecology as Ecclesiology in *Laudato Si'*," *Theological Studies* 78, no. 4 (2017): 807–24, at 808.

[178] See Irwin, *A Commentary on* Laudato Si', 7–8, 37–49, 220–30; and Mathew Verghese, "American Catholicism, Sacramentality, and Care for Creation: Resources for a Local Ecological Ethic," in *American Catholicism in the 21st Century: Crossroads, Crisis, or Renewal?*, ed. Benjamin Peters and Nicholas Rademacher, 212–21, Annual Publication of the College Theology Society, vol. 42 (Maryknoll, N.Y.: Orbis Books, 2017). In particular, of note is the number of citations Pope Francis includes in *Laudato Si'* to local bishops' conferences as an exercise of collegiality; in fact, Francis sent a copy of *Laudato Si'* to all diocesan bishops, with a note that references Vatican II's teaching on episcopal collegiality.

needed to answer the cries of the earth and the poor amid the technocratic paradigm. That is, *Laudato Si'* demands an integral, systematic account of the church's mission grounded in its doxological and eucharistic essence—a liturgically cast social theory set within our common home.

The value of heeding such a call is twofold. First, systematically examining the encyclical's conception of ecclesial mission better secures the doxological, eucharistic vision of *Laudato Si'* and makes that vision a lasting achievement. Ecclesiology, as a systematic enterprise, seeks to assist the church appropriate its redemptive mission within the context it finds itself and the exigencies of the moment.[179] Naming the eucharistic vision of *Laudato Si'* can thus help realize the deep potential of that vision and counter those obstacles that might impede it. In this way ecclesiological reflection can enrich the aims of *Laudato Si'*. So too can *Laudato Si'* enrich ecclesiological reflection. Second then, the integral ecology of *Laudato Si'* can broaden systematic ecclesiology to consider the church's mission to all creation. The encyclical offers something constructive for ecclesiology. *Laudato Si'*, as has become clear, challenges theologians (and, by extension, ecclesiologists) to more fully incorporate certain claims—like the cry of the earth and the praise of all creation—in conceptions of the church's mission. Doing so, again, is to solidify those claims and, consequently, to help receive the integral ecology of *Laudato Si'* more fully both now and in the future. If it is to be received fully, both ecclesiastically and theologically, *Laudato Si'* requires an account of ecclesial mission able to account for its distinctive eucharistic vision.

CONCLUSION

Gestating in previous pontificates (especially Benedict XVI's), the intimate connection between the church's work of praise and its work of justice has emerged as a key theme within Francis's pontificate. Correctly understanding this relationship positions one to avoid the spiritual worldliness that Francis rejects so vociferously. While spiritual worldliness can take many forms, at no place is the temptation greater than at the intersection of worship and justice. According to Francis, spiritual worldliness can, on the one hand, manifest itself in "an ostentatious preoccupation for the liturgy . . . without any concern that the Gospel has a real impact on God's faithful

---

[179] See Nicholas M. Healy, *Church, World and the Christian Life: Practical-Prophetic Ecclesiology* (New York: Cambridge University Press, 2000), 38–43.

people and the concrete needs of the present time."[180] On the other hand, spiritual worldliness "lurks behind a fascination with social and political gain, or pride in their ability to manage practical affairs," that is, work for justice without a broader eucharistic raison d'etre.[181] Lacking this broader doxological purpose, Francis submits, "Christianity . . . becomes a sort of NGO stripped of the luminous mysticism so evident in the lives of Saint Francis of Assisi, Saint Vincent de Paul, Saint Teresa of Calcutta, and many others."[182] A proper, balanced understanding of the relationship the *ora et labora* of the church safeguards against both these poles of spiritual worldliness. Indeed, for Francis, Christian "worship becomes pleasing to God when we devote ourselves to living generously, and allow God's gift, granted in prayer, to be shown in our concern for our brothers and sisters."[183]

Francis exemplifies this integration—of the church's work of praise and the church's work of justice—most clearly in *Laudato Si'* and its eucharistic vision of caring for our common home. Furthermore, *Laudato Si'* represents the culmination of a development that spanned several pontificates. By presenting an integral ecology through a robustly doxological, eucharistic lens, Francis brings to fruition latent meaning in the teachings of his predecessors and moves Catholic social teaching to a broader plane of reflection as a response to the ecological crisis. Integral ecology supplies a new foundational category, even paradigm, for Catholic social teaching. And that paradigm is radically doxological and eucharistic. The wide-angle lens of praise in *Laudato Si'* secures the expansive character of integral ecology and reconciles human and natural ecologies. The turn to worship animates several key novelties within *Laudato Si'* as well. For example, Francis's acknowledgment of creation's intrinsic value derives from a recognition of creation's doxological, sacramental, and ultimately eucharistic potential. The prevalence of care language finds its basis in the priestly anthropology of *Laudato Si'* that situates human beings within a theocentric ecosystem of praise. Moreover, by making the Eucharist so central within *Laudato Si'*, Francis links its integral ecology to a pillar of Catholic identity. This move can accordingly demonstrate how "[l]iving our vocation to be protectors of God's handiwork is essential to a life of virtue; it is not an optional or a

---

[180] *Evangelii Gaudium*, 96.
[181] *Evangelii Gaudium*, 95.
[182] *Gaudete et Exsultate*, 100.
[183] *Gaudete et Exsultate*, 104. See also 105–8.

secondary aspect of our Christian experience."[184] The magisterial reception of *Laudato Si'* confirms that this doxological, eucharistic shift is an enduring one.[185] That this development does and will bear great fruit is clear.

And yet, at least in the United States today, the reception of *Laudato Si'* remains uneven, its integral ecology fragmented by polarization. As the previous chapter's conclusion noted, reception cannot but convey something about the text being received. In this case, the reduction of *Laudato Si'* to partisan sound bites reveals an inattention to the encyclical's theological heart outlined in this chapter, a disintegration of its integration of *ora et labora*.

Rectifying this problem requires a systematic account of the church's mission able to specify the eucharistic vision of *Laudato Si'* and its integral ecology. The next part of the book takes up that charge, turning to the thought of Bernard Lonergan to do so. Francis and Lonergan might at first appear as an odd couple. However, Lonergan himself hoped to formulate a systematic account of the church's mission—a theology of history. Moreover, Lonergan's Ignatian emphases, his suspicion of technocracy, and his radically theological vision of "social reconstruction" indicate further key theological similarities with the distinctive vision Francis enunciates in *Laudato Si'*. The vision of *Laudato Si'* in turn can enrich and enflesh the theological project of someone like Lonergan, unearthing the ecological and doxological potential of that project. Transposing *Laudato Si'* onto the plane of ecclesiological reflection in this way can best secure its eucharistic vision and the significance of its integral ecology in the life of the church.

---

184 *Laudato Si'*, 217.

185 A point discussed at greater length in the conclusion.

Part 2

Toward a Eucharistic Theology of History

Chapter 3

A Theory of Redemptive Agency for the Church's Mission

Considering that he never wrote on environmental questions, Bernard Lonergan may appear as a strange choice to provide grounding for the eucharistic vision of *Laudato Si'*. Nevertheless, his deeply pastoral agenda distinguishes him as a most suitable partner. In William Loewe's words, "Lonergan's faith drove him into a massive project of integration in the service of promoting the redemptive efficacy of Christ in the real historical world of science and technology, economics, politics, and culture."[1] This claim may also be surprising; well-known is Lonergan's proclivity for highly technical vocabulary and rarefied philosophical aims. And yet, this ostensibly esoteric style stems precisely from his pastoral agenda.

The particular way that Lonergan pursues his pastoral ends reflects his distinction between description and explanation. *Description* considers "things as related to us," a contextual, ad hoc knowledge that focuses on the observable and the practical significance of a certain object.[2] Descriptions, by their nature, opt for everyday language over a technical, formal vocabulary. And it is their practical and immediate focus that accounts for their limitations; they cannot address questions that transcend these descriptive confines. *Explanation*, in contrast, considers "the same things as related among themselves," allowing people to understand why they experience those things as they do. Often requiring a specialized language, explanations focus both on the essence of a certain object and on its relationships to other objects, neither of which are immediately perceptible to oneself. Explanation arises from and make intelligible the data gleaned through descriptions; "description supplies, as it were, the tweezers by which we hold things while explanations are being discovered or verified,

---

[1] William P. Loewe, review of Frederick Crowe, *Christ and History: The Christology of Bernard Lonergan from 1935 to 1982*, in *Horizons* 33, no. 1 (Spring 2006): 149–50, at 150.

[2] See Bernard J. F. Lonergan, *Insight: A Study of Human Understanding*, vol. 3 of CWL, ed. Frederick E. Crowe and Robert M. Doran (Toronto: University of Toronto Press, 2005), 196–207.

applied or revised."³ Descriptions assert that something is; explanations regard how and why that something is. Whereas description operates within the realm of practical common sense, explanation operates within the realm of reflective theory.⁴ Both description and explanation are legitimate ways of knowing, though each yields a different (while complementary) apprehension of reality.

Lonergan's pastoral concern takes an explanatory form, in what he calls a "theology of history." Specifically, Lonergan seeks to supply explanatory weight to the church's mission, a dynamism frequently described though rarely explained. While, because of its practical orientation, Catholic social teaching operates primarily from the descriptive realm of common sense, it is theory that can express the underlying dynamics of the church's social mission. Practical admonitions alone cannot name these dynamics. The inchoate vision of ecclesial mission of *Laudato Si'* and the questions it raises typify such limits. Lonergan's theology of history can thus furnish them with explanatory clarification.

This chapter presents this theology of history, the complexity of which matches the complexity of history. The explanatory character of Lonergan's "massive project of integration" can start to provide a vision of ecclesial mission that befits *Laudato Si'* and thus begin to capture the doxological, eucharistic character of its integral ecology. After all, the "redemptive efficacy of Christ" continues through the church and through the church's Eucharist, both of which constitute Christ's body in history (see 1 Cor 11:17–12:31). And yet, as also becomes clear later in the chapter, Lonergan's work is incomplete and needs further development. This chapter and the next hope to develop, with the help of Lonergan, a systematic account of ecclesial mission understood doxologically and eucharistically, sensitive to ecological concern. Only then can Lonergan's pastoral agenda and the radically doxological, eucharistic character of *Laudato Si'* be grasped fully.

AN INTEGRATING VISION AND AN INTEREST IN HISTORY

Both the boldness and breadth of Lonergan's vision are titanic, made most evident in his monumental work, *Insight: A Study of Human Understanding*. In fact, Lonergan quips that he wrote the book while listening to Beethoven

---

3 Lonergan, *Insight*, 316.

4 See Bernard J. F. Lonergan, *Method in Theology* (New York: Herder and Herder, 1972), 82–83.

because the music struck him as "titanic," matching the intensity of his own project.[5] In *Insight*, Lonergan engages mathematics, the natural sciences, neuropsychology, social theory, metaphysics, ethics, and philosophical theology, only to conclude with a heuristic solution to the problem of evil. Grounded in an attentiveness to the processes of human knowing, this comprehensive ambition exemplifies his broader intentions "to seek a common ground on which men of intelligence might meet," since, in Lonergan's estimation, "the plain fact is that the world lies in pieces before man and pleads to be put together again."[6] This catholic, integrating vision courses throughout Lonergan's work. In the face of world division, this hope signals the pastoral character of the Jesuit's project.[7] So too does it anticipate Pope Francis's own synthetic emphasis that "everything is connected," captured in the phrase "integral ecology," by over fifty years.

Lonergan's integrating intent animates his enduring interest in history. As he submits, "For it is in history that man's making of man occurs, that it progresses and regresses, that through such changes there may be discerned a certain unity in an otherwise disconcerting multiplicity."[8] Read in this light, Lonergan's hope for common ground is not oppressive; rather than a modern erasure of particularity for the sake of unity, Lonergan's turn to history discovers unity precisely in the particularity of contingency. Frederick Crowe goes so far as to claim that "the need to understand history, basic history, the history that happens, is the chief dynamic element in [Lonergan's] academic work: not insight, not method, not economics, not emergent probability, but history. I will call it the 'essential' Lonergan."[9] Lonergan's interest in the topic also arises from pastoral concerns. The Great Depression, two world wars, the emergence of communism and fascism,

---

[5] Bernard J. F. Lonergan, *Caring about Meaning: Patterns in the Life of Bernard Lonergan*, ed. Pierrot Lambert, Charlotte Tansey, and Cathleen Going (Montreal: Thomas More Institute Papers, 1982), 236.

[6] Lonergan, *Insight*, 7, 552.

[7] For instance, written during a period of rapid nuclear proliferation, the penultimate draft of *Insight* concluded, "and by infusing the charity, the dispassionate, unrelenting at-oneness with all the true, the real, the good, that outlasts the fire-ball of the atom bomb and immeasurably exceeds its power to change the living of man." See Lonergan, *Insight*, 806, note n.

[8] Bernard J. F. Lonergan, "Natural Right and Historical Mindedness," in *A Third Collection: Papers by Bernard J. F. Lonergan, S.J.* (hereafter *A Third Collection*), ed. Frederick E. Crowe (Mahwah, N.J.: Paulist Press, 1985), 171.

[9] Frederick E. Crowe, *Christ and History: The Christology of Bernard Lonergan from 1935 to 1982* (Ottawa: Novalis, 2005), 168.

and, faced with this "Crisis of the West," the church's effort to articulate its mission, all shaped Lonergan's theological vocation.[10] At the beginning of his career, in the 1930s, the Canadian Jesuit found himself in "a Church that needed to be renewed and reformed precisely in order effectively to bring its unique contribution to the common historical project."[11] This was a period of Catholic Action, the Feast of Christ the King, theological renewal, a stream of encyclicals, and ubiquitous references to "restoring all things in Christ" (Eph 1:10) that dovetailed with Lonergan's own synthesizing desire.

Lonergan responded to this ecclesiological ferment with explanatory reflection. In the earliest stages of his career, he "began to search for an understanding of the church's redemptive mission in the context of historical reality."[12] Likening his own project to the social project of Plato's *Republic*, Lonergan concluded that effective praxis needed grounding in adequate theory, which neither liberal nor Marxist understandings of history could afford.[13] In an early 1935 letter to his Jesuit superior, Lonergan, the precocious Jesuit scholastic, reported, "I am certain (and I am not one who becomes certain easily) that I can put together a Thomistic metaphysic of history that will throw Hegel and Marx, despite the enormity of their influence on this very account, into the shade."[14] At the time, he referred to this project as a *Summa Sociologica*. In an early, unpublished essay, he wrote:

---

[10] William A. Mathews, *Lonergan's Quest: A Study of Desire in the Authoring of Insight* (Toronto: University of Toronto Press, 2005), 49, 51–54, 65–67.

[11] Joseph A. Komonchak, "Lonergan's Early Essays on the Redemption of History," *Lonergan Workshop* 10 (1994): 159–77, at 169. See also Komonchak, "Returning from Exile: Catholic Theology in the 1930s," in *The Twentieth Century: A Theological Overview*, ed. Gregory Baum (Maryknoll, N.Y.: Orbis Books, 1999), 35–48.

[12] William P. Loewe, *Lex Crucis: Soteriology and the Stages of Meaning* (Minneapolis, Minn.: Fortress Press, 2016), 313.

[13] See, e.g., Bernard J. F. Lonergan, "Essay in Fundamental Sociology," in *Lonergan's Early Economic Research: Texts and Commentary*, ed. Michael Shute (Toronto: University of Toronto Press, 2010), 26, 33–34, 41. This unpublished early essay—likely the closest to a *Summa Sociologica* Lonergan ever offered—also begins with a citation of Plato's discussion of the philosopher king in *Republic*, 473d–e.

[14] Bernard J. F. Lonergan, "Letter of Bernard Lonergan to the Reverend Henry Keane," *Method: Journal of Lonergan Studies* 28, no. 2 (Fall 2014): 23–40, at 33–34. In another letter written to his superior the summer before his doctoral studies, Lonergan wrote, "As philosophy of history is as yet not recognized as the essential branch of philosophy that it is, I hardly expect to have it assigned me as my subject during the biennium. I wish to ask your approval for maintaining my interest in it, profiting by such opportunities as may crop up, and in general devoting to it such time as I prudently judge can be spared." Quoted in Frederick E. Crowe, *Lonergan* (Collegeville, Minn.: Liturgical Press, 1992), 24.

any reflection on modern history and its consequent "Crisis in the West" reveals unmistakably the necessity of a *Summa Sociologica*. A metaphysic of history is not only imperative for the church to meet the attack of the Marxian materialist conception of history and its realization in apostolic Bolshevism; it is imperative if man is to solve the modern politico-economic entanglement, if political and economic forces are to be subjected to the rule of reason, if cultural values and all the achievement of the past are to be saved both from the onslaughts of purblind statemen and from the perfidious diplomacy of the merely destructive power of communism.[15]

A *Summa Sociologica* could chart the vision of "social reconstruction" the church aspired to offer to the modern politico-economic entanglement. For this reason, Lonergan extolled Pope Pius XI's requirement in his social encyclical, *Quadragesimo Anno*, that "all candidates for the sacred priesthood must be adequately prepared . . . by the intense study of social matters."[16] At the same time, identifying the need for a project like his, Lonergan tendered that "this command has not yet been put into effect, nor can it be till there is a *Summa Sociologica*: without that we would only flounder in the blundering and false science that created the [social] problem."[17] He maintained that the burgeoning body of Catholic social thought required a theology of history if it were to take seriously the saving role of Christ, "King of the historical process," given the complexity of that historical process.[18]

Lonergan's interest in these questions lasted throughout his career, particularly during debates concerning the church's social mission after the Second Vatican Council. Post-conciliar Catholic social reflection, along with the controversies it generated, reflected the church's ongoing attempt to realize its redemptive mission as well as the theological work left to be done. As late as 1976, answering a questionnaire sent to Jesuit scholars across the world, Lonergan reported, "It has long been my conviction that if Catholics . . . are to live and operate on the level of the times, they must not only know about theories of history but also must work out their own. . . . To put it bluntly, until we move onto the level of historical dynamics, we shall

---

[15] Bernard J. F. Lonergan, "*Pantôn Anakephalaiôsis* [The restoration of all things]," *Method: Journal of Lonergan Studies* 9 (1991): 134–72, at 156. For a textual study of these early writings on history, see Michael Shute, *The Origins of Lonergan's Notion of the Dialectic of History: A Study of Lonergan's Early Writings on History* (Lanham, Md.: University Press of America, 1993).

[16] Pius XI, Encyclical Letter *Quadragesimo Anno* (May 15, 1931), 142.

[17] Lonergan, "*Pantôn Anakephalaiôsis*," 157.

[18] Lonergan, "Essay in Fundamental Sociology," 41. See also *Insight*, 764.

face our secularist and atheist opponents, as . . . Indians, armed with bows and arrows, faced European muskets."[19] The need was pressing, considering the exclusively secular accounts of history that seemed to dominate the Catholic theological landscape after the Council. Admitting that "perhaps the great weakness of Catholic social thought is its apparent lack of awareness of the need for technical knowledge," Lonergan concluded, "what priests need today is, not an understanding of Marx, but an understanding of the dynamics of history and of the vital role that Christians are called upon to play."[20] Even the final act of Lonergan's career reflected his interest in history; from 1978 to 1983, shortly before his death, he taught a seminar, Macroeconomics and the Dialectic of History, at Boston College.[21] As shown by the course, from his scholastic studies to his death, Lonergan remained interested in understanding the dynamics of history. Whether labeled a *Summa Sociologica*, a "metaphysic of history," an "analytic concept of history," a "theology of history," or a "dialectic of history," the formulation of this explanatory framework, Lonergan believed, could aid the church's understanding of its redemptive mission in history, especially as expressed in its social teaching.

While his contemporaries contented themselves with general assertions that the church saves, Lonergan concerned himself with specifically how, in theory, the church did save.[22] Lonergan aimed to elaborate "a dynamic theology of redemptive praxis" for the church as it grappled with both the advances and pitfalls of modernity.[23] In particular, Lonergan hoped to lend

---

[19] Bernard J. F. Lonergan, "Questionnaire on Philosophy: Response," in *Philosophical and Theological Papers 1965–1980*, vol. 17 of CWL, ed. Robert C. Croken and Robert M. Doran (Toronto: University of Toronto Press, 2004), 366.

[20] Lonergan, "Questionnaire on Philosophy: Response," 370.

[21] As Lonergan once wrote, "I feel that the basic step in aiding [the poor] in a notable manner is a matter of spending one's nights and days in a deep and prolonged study of economic analysis." Lonergan, "Sacralization and Secularization," in *Philosophical and Theological Papers 1965–1980*, 280. For Lonergan's economic works, see *For a New Political Economy*, vol. 21 of CWL, ed. Philip J. McShane (Toronto: University of Toronto Press, 1998); and *Macroeconomic Dynamics: An Essay in Circulation Analysis*, vol. 15 of CWL, ed. Patrick H. Byrne, Frederick G. Lawrence, and Charles Hefling Jr. (Toronto: University of Toronto Press, 1999).

[22] Komonchak, "Lonergan's Early Essays on the Redemption of History," 177; see also Arthur Kennedy, "Christopher Dawson's Influence on Bernard Lonergan's Project of 'Introducing History into Theology,'" *Logos: A Journal of Catholic Thought & Culture* 15, no. 2 (Spring 2012): 138–64, at 152–53.

[23] Michael Shute, "Economic Analysis within Redemptive Praxis: An Achievement of Lonergan's Third Decade," *Lonergan Workshop* 14 (1998): 243–64, at 256.

explanatory heft to the church's social mission and its often contextual, ad hoc admonitions. As Patrick Brown notes, "for Lonergan, [Catholic social teaching] fails to live on the level of the times to the extent that it lacks any theory of historical process or historical dynamics."[24] And yet, despite the value he so clearly placed on such a theory, Lonergan never penned a full-length *Summa* on the topic. He discerned the need to address more fundamental epistemological and metaphysical questions instead, withdrawing in expectation of an eventual return by himself or others to address social concerns more fully.[25]

For various reasons—laborious teaching responsibilities, health problems, and the complexity he discovered in that withdrawal—Lonergan never completed this full return. The rest of this book attempts to carry his thoughts further. The present focus considers the foundational insights that Lonergan gleans on historical process and the church's redemptive agency, strewn throughout his various philosophical and theological works. Just as Lonergan had hoped to contribute the needed theoretical framework to bolster the church's social teaching and its implementation, so too will the seeds sown by this theory ultimately serve the newest addition to this body of social reflection: the integral ecology of *Laudato Si'* and its eucharistic vision.

A DYNAMIC WORLDVIEW: EMERGENT PROBABILITY

In withdrawing from explicit social concern to address epistemological and metaphysical questions, Lonergan sought to offer a theologically viable, albeit critical, rapprochement with modernity.[26] At the forefront of this project stands the tectonic paradigm shift engendered by evolutionary biology, historical consciousness, and the dynamic worldview that both presuppose.[27] On the one hand, Lonergan wishes to exorcise the deterministic and reductionistic—indeed, technocratic—distortions often accompanying these transformations, as found in a thinker like Pierre-Simon

---

[24] Patrick Brown, "'Aiming Excessively High and Far': The Early Lonergan and the Challenge of Theory in Catholic Social Thought," *Theological Studies* 72 (September 2011): 620–44, at 628.

[25] Crowe, *Lonergan*, 27.

[26] See Bernard J. F. Lonergan, "The Response of the Jesuit Priest and Apostle in the Modern World," in *Collected Works of Bernard Lonergan: A Second Collection* (hereafter *A Second Collection*), ed. William F. J. Ryan and Bernard Tyrell (Philadelphia: The Westminster Press, 1974), 183, 186–87; "Belief: Today's Issue," in *A Second Collection*, 99; "The Future of Thomism," in *A Second Collection*, 43–44; and *Method in Theology*, 155.

[27] Lonergan, "Questionnaire on Philosophy: Response," 354.

Laplace.[28] On the other hand, Lonergan perceives how this worldview challenges the "anti-historical immobilism" of the regnant baroque, conceptualist scholasticism of his day.[29] In turn, he urges theologians to shift from a classicist to a historical worldview, from a classicist to an empirical conception of culture, and from abstract human nature to concrete human history.[30] Through these transitions, he intends to recover a dynamic worldview isomorphic with the vitality and open-endedness of the human spirit, a dynamism that Patrick Byrne highlights as the "fabric" of Lonergan's thought.[31] Lonergan once remarked, "All my work has been introducing history into Catholic theology."[32] This achievement, which includes his theology of history, rests upon a dynamic worldview that Lonergan christens "emergent probability."

Lonergan details this worldview most extensively in *Insight*.[33] There, he distinguishes between classical and statistical scientific inquiries. These procedures denote two ways to anticipate data and the relations between them. Classical methods discover systematic processes, pursuing universal explanations for regular occurrences, formulating a relationship like the law of thermodynamics. Statistical methods discover nonsystematic processes

---

28 See Matthew L. Lamb, *Solidarity with Victims: Toward a Theology of Social Transformation* (New York: Crossroad Publishing, 1982), 126–27, 131. As Laplace wrote:

> We may regard the present state of the universe as the effect of its past and the cause of its future. An intellect which at a certain moment would know all forces that set nature in motion, and all positions of all items of which nature is composed, if this intellect were also vast enough to submit these data to analysis, it would embrace in a single formula the movements of the greatest bodies of the universe and those of the tiniest atom; for such an intellect nothing would be uncertain and the future just like the past would be present before its eyes. (In *A Philosophical Essay on Probabilities*, trans. F. W. Truscott and F. L. Emory [New York: Dover Publications, 1951], 4)

29 Bernard J. F. Lonergan, "The Subject," in *A Second Collection*, 74.

30 See Bernard J. F. Lonergan, "The Transition from Classicism to Historical-Mindedness," in *A Second Collection*, 1–10; "Revolution in Catholic Theology," in *A Second Collection*, 231–38; and "The Future of Thomism," 49–52.

31 See Patrick H. Byrne, "The Fabric of Lonergan's Thought," *Lonergan Workshop* 5 (1986): 1–84, at 1–19, 68–69.

32 Bernard J. F. Lonergan, *Curiosity at the Center of One's Life: Statements and Questions of R. Eric O'Connor*, ed. J. Martin O'Hara (Montreal: Thomas More Institute, 1987), 427. See also Lonergan, "Belief: Today's Issue," 96.

33 Particularly helpful for this section were Cynthia Crysdale and Neil Ormerod, *Creator God, Evolving World* (Minneapolis, Minn.: Fortress Press, 2013), 19–40, 57–82; and Kenneth R. Melchin, *History, Ethics, and Emergent Probability*, 2nd ed. (The Lonergan Workshop, 1999), 97–122. For the sources behind emergent probability, see Patrick H. Byrne, "The Thomist Sources of Lonergan's Dynamic Worldview," *The Thomist* 46, no. 1 (January 1982): 108–45.

and seek the probabilities of various occurrences. They consider not how something happens but whether and how often it happens, such as the number of women currently living in Pittsburgh. Classical and statistical methods ask two different types of questions.

Lonergan distinguishes these two perspectives in order to unite them. Though Laplacian determinism bifurcates these two methods in hopes of ridding the world of genuine randomness, Lonergan insists that classical and statistical investigations complement each other.[34] Classical laws articulate a certain relationship with the implication, "all other things being equal." In other words, those relationships depend on certain conditions being met, even if those conditions remain implicit. For example, all chemical laws assume a certain temperature or pressure. Statistical laws express how frequently those conditions occur.[35] They consider how often the conditions for certain chemical laws actually are attained. As is the case in chemistry, both types of methods and laws need and imply each other.

The relationships expressed in these laws complement each other not only in scientific investigation but also, as the chemistry example shows, in the concrete world. The probability of a given event happening, let alone several in a sequence, is relatively low. The chances increase significantly, however, when a series of those events coils around in a circle (i.e., event A causes event B, which causes event C, which causes event A again), such that the fulfillment of any one of those events catalyzes the entire sequence of events.[36] Examples include the Krebs cycle as well as the evaporation and condensation of water. The science of ecology studies such relationships. Lonergan labels these sequences "schemes of recurrence." Classical laws govern the necessary and regular relationships within a given scheme (event A causing event B). Statistical laws determine, first, the probability of a scheme's actual emergence (the likelihood of events A or B occurring), which can be quite low but over enough time can eventually transpire. Second, they express the likelihood of a scheme's survival, accounting for the possibility of "breakdowns" and "blind alleys": schemes changing, being exhausted, or collapsing.[37] For instance, global warming changes weather patterns, causing certain ecosystems to break down by removing their con-

---

[34] Lonergan, *Insight*, 147.
[35] Lonergan, *Insight*, 117–18; 131–38; and *Caring about Meaning*, 212.
[36] Lonergan, *Insight*, 141–44.
[37] Lonergan, *Insight*, 150.

ditions of possibility. Schemes of recurrence illustrate how "classical and statistical laws can coalesce into a single unified intelligibility commensurate with the universe of our experience."[38]

The name for this singular unified intelligibility is *emergent probability*. Lonergan defines emergent probability as "the successive realization in accord with successive schedules of probability of a conditioned series of schemes of recurrence."[39] That is, a scheme can eventually serve as a condition for the emergence of novel, more complex schemes. Early planetary conditions set the condition for the circulation of water; the circulation of water conditions the possibility of plants' nitrogen cycle to emerge, which conditions the possibility of animals' digestive systems to emerge.[40] Processes like these reveal "a pyramid of schemes resting on schemes in a splendid ascent of novelty and creativeness."[41] The irreducible complexity of the universe attests to this splendid ascent.

As Lonergan's language implies, the universe has a "finality," meaning that "the objective universe is not at rest, not static, not fixed in the present, but in process, in tension, fluid."[42] Being, he would posit in the twilight of his career, has a "passionateness" in the way it constantly transcends itself.[43] An "upwardly but indeterminately directed dynamism toward ever fuller realization of being" marks the universe.[44] Specifically, the presence of nonsystematic, contingent processes makes the universe indeterminately directed. The creative drive toward the increasing organization of these events and schemes into novel, more complex schemes spurs the universe's upward dynamism. Emergent higher schemes integrate what was statistically incidental, the "coincidental manifold" that just happens to be together in space and time, on a lower level of schemes.[45]

---

[38] Lonergan, *Insight*, 140.

[39] Lonergan, *Insight*, 148–49; see also 145.

[40] Lonergan, *Insight*, 142.

[41] Lonergan, *Insight*, 75.

[42] Lonergan, *Insight*, 470. See also 472.

[43] Bernard J. F. Lonergan, "Mission and the Spirit," in *A Third Collection*, 29–30. See also Patrick H. Byrne, "The Passionateness of Being: The Legacy of Bernard Lonergan, S.J.," in *Finding God in All Things: Celebrating Bernard Lonergan, John Courtney Murray, and Karl Rahner*, ed. Mark Bosco and David Stagaman (New York: Fordham University Press, 2007), 35–51.

[44] Lonergan, *Insight*, 477. For an earlier, sustained exploration of this topic by Lonergan, see his "Finality, Love, Marriage," in *Collection*, vol. 4 of CWL, ed. Frederick E. Crowe and Robert M. Doran (Toronto: University of Toronto Press, 1988), 17–52.

[45] Lonergan, *Insight*, 477, 483–84.

Elsewhere, Lonergan describes this relationship as one of "sublation." Higher, more complex orders sublate lower, more basic ones. As he specifies, "what sublates goes beyond what is sublated, introduces something new and distinct, puts everything on a new basis, yet so far from interfering with the sublated or destroying it, on the contrary needs it, includes it, preserves all its proper features and properties, and carries them forward to a fuller realization within a richer context."[46] Each higher level depends upon lower levels and, while preserving the nature of lower levels, brings them to a fuller integration capable of more complex functions. Each higher level brings about something genuinely new and irreducible to lower levels. A new set of laws governs the higher scheme, frequently modifying the functioning of lower schemes, and, consequently, change in the higher scheme often involves change in lower schemes. Schemes of calculus, for example, sublate schemes of algebra; calculus cannot be performed apart from algebra, while still exhibiting a more advanced type of performance that brings algebraic functioning (and geometric functioning) to bear on a new set of questions.

Lonergan offers several concrete examples of this emergent, sublating finality in nature: "chemical elements and compounds are higher integrations of otherwise coincidental manifolds of subatomic events; organisms are higher integrations of otherwise coincidental manifolds of chemical processes; sensitive consciousness is a higher integration of otherwise coincidental manifolds of changes in neural tissues; and accumulating insights are higher integrations of otherwise coincidental manifolds of images or of data."[47] Photosynthesis sustains a tree, even while the functioning of a tree goes beyond chemistry. Consciousness depends on certain arrangements of neural synapses, without being reducible to them. In each case, lower orders preserve their integrity while supplying the schemes for higher orders. Likewise, higher orders make intelligible and synthesize what otherwise appear random on lower orders, allowing them to function in more complex, original ways.

As the above passage intimates, for Lonergan, emergent probability likewise captures the dynamism of the human person in history. In his words, "As in the fields of physics, chemistry and biology, so in the field of human

---

[46] Lonergan, *Method in Theology*, 241.

[47] Lonergan, *Insight*, 477. As Lonergan wrote toward the end of his career, "subatomic particles somehow enter into the elements of a periodic table; chemical elements enter into chemical compounds, compounds into cells, cells in myriad combinations and configurations into the constitution of plant and animal life." "Mission and the Spirit," 24.

events and relationships there are classical and statistical laws that combine concretely in cumulating sets of schemes of recurrence. For the advent of man does not abrogate the rule of emergent probability. Human actions are recurrent; their recurrence is regular; and the regularity is the functioning of the scheme."[48] The processes of knowing and choosing exhibit the emergent character of humanity. The finality of the universe parallels the insatiable, self-transcending eros of human wonder, the "unrestricted desire to know" that intends, ultimately, everything about everything.[49] Like being, so too does a passionateness thrust the human spirit to reach beyond itself ceaselessly.

The emergently probable structure of this desire includes no fewer than four transcending components, posits Lonergan. First, *experience* attends to the nonsystematic data—the coincidental manifold—of the senses and consciousness. Second, *understanding* emerges from experiencing, as people ask the question, "what is it?" about the data. The answer to that question builds upon experience but cannot be derived from experience alone. For Lonergan, as for Aquinas and Aristotle, insight is always insight into mental pictures (phantasms).[50] As a distinct, higher level, understanding integrates and organizes what otherwise appears as coincident in experience.[51] Still, simply discerning the intelligible unity of data cannot answer the question, "Is it true?" As Lonergan quips, "Insights are a dime a dozen."[52] By marshaling and weighing evidence, understanding yields to a third, distinct level: *judgment*. While aided by a series of insights, judgment transcends understanding in order to determine the truthfulness of a given understanding or the goodness of a particular action. Fourth and finally, then, some judgments beg the question, "should I do it?" and so lead to the level of *decision*.[53] This question builds upon judgments yet goes beyond them in seeking proper courses of action. Thus, faithfulness to the emergent eros of the human spirit—what Lonergan understands as "human authenticity"—demands that one be

---

48 Lonergan, *Insight*, 235.

49 See Lonergan, *Insight*, 470, 475. For a study of the development of this theme in Lonergan's work, see Elizabeth J. Snedden, *The Eros of the Human Spirit: The Writings of Bernard Lonergan, SJ* (New York: Paulist Press, 2017).

50 See Bernard J. F. Lonergan, *Verbum: Word and Idea in Aquinas*, vol. 2 of CWL, ed. Frederick E. Crowe and Robert M. Doran (Toronto: University of Toronto Press, 1997).

51 Lonergan, *Insight*, 292.

52 See, e.g., Lonergan, *Method in Theology*, 13.

53 See, e.g., Lonergan, "*Existenz* and *Aggiornamento*," in *Collection*, 223.

radically attentive (to experience), intelligent (in understanding), rational (in judgment), and responsible (in decision).[54] Furthermore, this fourfold structure of experiencing, understanding, judging, and deciding is constantly and cyclically self-correcting. The wisdom gleaned from one cycle of experiencing, understanding, judging, and deciding conditions future experiencing, which in turns continues to condition the recurring acts of understanding, judging, and deciding that emerge from it.[55] Human knowing and acting forms a scheme of recurrence, liable as well to the contingency that characterizes those schemes in general.

These intricate processes of knowing and choosing distinguish humans' unique place in an emergently probable world. Indeed, like Pope John Paul II, Lonergan advances a personalism that undergirds a robustly theological humanism while, at the same time, embedding human personhood within the natural world. That is, like Pope Francis, Lonergan shows how in fact everything is interconnected without flattening differences within the created order. As befits an integral ecology, emergent probability situates humanity within our broader common home. As emergent beings, humans are irreducible to, yet dependent on the lower, less complex levels that constitute them. The human person "is not just a higher system but a source of higher systems," as in that person "there occurs the transition from the intelligible to the intelligent."[56] One dwells in a "world of meaning"—horizons of collective experiences, understandings, judgments, and decisions—to which one incessantly contributes and develops.[57] As Lonergan explains, "if human affairs fall under the dominion of emergent probability, they do so in their own way. . . . Less and less importance attaches to the probabilities of appropriate constellations of circumstances. More and more importance attaches to the probabilities of the occurrence of insight, communication, persuasion, agreement, decision."[58] While

---

54 Lonergan refers to these charges as the "transcendental precepts." See *Method in Theology*, 20.

55 See Lonergan, *Insight*, 18, 30, 197, 303, 311–12.

56 Lonergan, *Insight*, 292.

57 Lonergan, *Method in Theology*, 28. See also *Insight*, 316; and "*Existenz* and *Aggiornamento*," 226. For a discussion of horizons, see *Method in Theology*, 235–37.

58 Lonergan, *Insight*, 235–36; see also 252. As he states this elsewhere: "So we come to history in its radical difference from nature. Nature unfolds in accord with classical and statistical laws. But history is an expression of meaning, and meaning is open both to enduring stationary states, to development, the fruit of authenticity, and to aberration that matches the unauthenticity of its source." "A Post-Hegelian Philosophy of History," in *A Third Collection*, 213–14.

lower schemes depend almost exclusively on conditions introduced through chance, people influence certain conditions deliberately. Even while circumstance influences how one knows and chooses, as well as the particular world of common meaning that one inhabits, people can and do condition their environment and themselves.[59] Human acts of meaning shift probabilities in history, generating the conditions for the possible emergence of even more complex orders: recurring schemes of meaning in the shape of communities and social structures.[60] As is explored in depth below, emergence, sublation, and finality also characterize these stratified schemes. "For a human society, like an ecology," Lonergan posits, "is an assembly of assemblies of schemes of recurrence. As interdependent they support one another. As subordinate they underpin higher orders of schemes. As higher they bring to fuller fruition their subordinates."[61] These recurring schemes of meaning condition future knowing and acting, along with other burgeoning schemes of meaning.[62]

The introduction of human intelligence and freedom into this ecology muddies the many-layered and already byzantine relationships that constitute it. World process "does not run along the iron laws laid down by determinists, nor on the other hand is it a nonintelligible morass of merely chance events."[63] Rather than controlling outcomes, in a world shot through with randomness, people set conditions for future possibilities that may or may not be realized, for good and for ill. In capturing both the contingency and the intelligibility of world process, emergent probability captures the

---

[59] Relevant here is Lonergan's distinction between essential and effective freedom, explained at *Insight*, 631–47. As he captures this distinction elsewhere: "Such is the autonomy of the individual, but it is not the whole story. From the community he has his existence, his concrete possibilities, the constraints that hem him in, the opportunities he can seize and make the most of, the psychological, social, historical achievements and aberrations that constitute his situation. One can perhaps think of destiny as the working out of individual autonomy within the community." From "The Mediation of Christ in Prayer," in *Philosophical and Theological Papers 1958–1964*, vol. 6 of CWL, ed. Robert C. Croken, Frederick E. Crowe, and Robert M. Doran (Toronto: University of Toronto Press, 1996), 173.

[60] See Kenneth R. Melchin, *Living with Other People: An Introduction to Christian Ethics Based on Bernard Lonergan* (Ottawa: Novalis, 1998), 47–53.

[61] Lonergan, *Macroeconomic Dynamics*, 93.

[62] In his early (unpublished) works on history, Lonergan employs the Aristotelian notion of premotion to make this point. See his "Essay Fundamental Sociology," 17, 18–19, 34; "*Pantôn Anakephalaiôsis*," 143, 146, 152; and "Analytic Concept of History," in *Method: Journal of Lonergan Studies* 11, no. 1 (Spring 1993): 1–36, at 10.

[63] Lonergan, *Insight*, 149.

risk that marks human living.[64] Just as schemes can dissipate in "dead-ends" and "blind-alleys," so too, in an emergently probable, nondeterministic universe, can people misuse their intelligence and freedom in ways that frustrate other schemes.[65] As conditioners of their environments, just as people can introduce formative schemes of recurring meaning that set the conditions for and increase the likelihood of continued acts of intelligence and freedom, so too can people introduce vicious schemes of recurring meaning that set the conditions for and increase the likelihood of continued acts of stupidity and enslavement. As Lonergan puts it, "If you change the normative meaning—not merely the effective meaning but what ought to be, what people think ought to be—you change the possible attainment of community."[66] Lonergan's dynamic worldview accounts for the density of historical process and the gravity of human responsibility. So too does it begin to capture the church's redemptive role within the drama of history and within our common home.

THREE VECTORS IN HISTORY

In his comprehensive, critical engagement with modernity, Lonergan found inspiration in Thomas Aquinas and the medieval synthesis he epitomized. The task that lay before theology was "not to repeat Aquinas today, but to do for the twentieth century what Aquinas did for the thirteenth."[67] The Jesuit found direction in Pope Leo XIII's promotion of Aquinas in *Aeterni Patris* and its injunction, "*vetera novis augere et perficere*"—"to enlarge and perfect the old by means of the new."[68] Lonergan strives to transpose Aquinas's insights into the historically conscious, dynamic worldview of modernity. Not only can this transposition strengthen Lonergan's project, so too can it demonstrate the perennial value of the Angelic Doctor's thought.

---

64 See Cynthia S. W. Crysdale, "Making a Way by Walking: Risk, Control, and Emergent Probability," *Theoforum* 39, no. 1 (2008): 39–58; and "Playing God? Moral Agency in an Emergent World," *Journal of the Society of Christian Ethics* 23, no. 2 (2003): 243–59.

65 Lonergan, *Insight*, 474; see also *Method in Theology*, 81.

66 Lonergan, "Mediation of Christ in Prayer," 172.

67 Bernard J. F. Lonergan, "Theology and Man's Future," in *A Second Collection*, 138. On the Thomistic roots of Lonergan, see, e.g., Jeremy D. Wilkins, *Before Truth: Lonergan, Aquinas, and the Problem of Wisdom* (Washington, D.C.: The Catholic University of America Press, 2018), 96–130.

68 Leo XIII, Encyclical Letter *Aeterni Patris* (August 4, 1879), 24. See, e.g., Lonergan, *Insight*, 768–69; "The Scope of Renewal," in *Philosophical and Theological Papers 1965–1980*, 298; and *Verbum*, 222, 226.

Lonergan's theology of history is one area of many in which he enlisted Aquinas. Recall how, in his very early letter to his Jesuit superior, Lonergan mentions a "*Thomistic* metaphysic of history." Alluding to Leo XIII, Lonergan explains further in the letter that "I take him at his word. I also accept his '*vetera novis augere et perficere*'; hence, my excursion into the metaphysic of history."[69] One Thomistic insight in particular guides this excursion. In his doctoral dissertation, Lonergan views Aquinas's systematization of Phillip the Chancellor's "theorem of the supernatural" as a "Copernican revolution."[70] In Lonergan's estimation, Phillip introduces a distinction between the natural and the supernatural, a distinction Aquinas eventually systematizes. Aquinas sets forth a threefold set of coordinates—grace, sin, and nature—that differs from the Augustinian binary dialectic of sin and grace.[71] This third category of nature grants integrity to a space neither sin nor grace.

Lonergan's theology of history, his Thomistic metaphysic of history, accordingly portrays human history as "a cord woven with three strands."[72] He transposes the categories of nature, sin, and grace onto a historical, emergently probable backdrop, animating these Thomistic coordinates.[73] Lonergan names these categories *progress*, *decline*, and *redemption*. He describes these coordinates and the relationships that arise between them as follows:

> through an analysis of human activity principles are established in the light of which we are able to grasp in a comprehensive view the entire movement of human history.... Hence, we ask the following questions: (1) What would human history be like if every human being always followed the dictates of reason? (2) How is the course of human history changed as a result of the fact that people choose to act contrary to the dictates of reason? (3) How can the reign of sin be destroyed and the human race brought back to living in conformity with reason?[74]

---

69 Lonergan, "Letter of Bernard Lonergan to the Reverend Henry Keane," 35.

70 Bernard J. F. Lonergan, *Grace and Freedom: Operative Grace in the Thought of St. Thomas Aquinas*, vol. 1 of CWL, ed. Frederick E. Crowe and Robert M. Doran (Toronto: University of Toronto Press, 2000), 17.

71 See Neil Ormerod, *Creation, Grace, and Redemption* (Maryknoll, N.Y.: Orbis Books, 2007), 113-15.

72 Lonergan, *Macroeconomic Dynamics*, 93–94.

73 Lonergan, "Analytic Concept of History," 14. See also Joseph A. Komonchak, *Foundations in Ecclesiology*, Lonergan Workshop (Boston: Boston College, 1995), 125.

74 Bernard J. F. Lonergan, "The Notion of Fittingness: The Application of Theological Method to the Question of the Purpose of the Incarnation," in *Early Latin Theology*, vol. 19 of CWL, ed.

This outline parallels Isaac Newton's threefold approximation of planetary movement.[75] Newton's first law regards the linear movement and constant velocity of planets apart from any other intervening force, his second law accounts for how gravity bends the planets toward the sun in an elliptical orbit, and his third law concerns how the pulls of other planets cause an irregular elliptical orbit. Just as these laws provide explanatory, theoretical constructs otherwise indistinct to the descriptive confines of common sense, so too, for Lonergan, "in the concrete all three [historical approximations] function together. They are intertwined. They do not exist in isolation, but they have to be described separately before they can be considered together."[76] As explanatory categories, the three approximations serve as differentials or vectors. Likely first borrowed from Lonergan's reading of John Stuart Mill's *Logic* early in his studies, these three vectors—progress, decline, and redemption—guide Lonergan's analysis of the dynamics of history throughout his career.[77] Eventually, it will be these categories that provide the explanatory scaffolding that captures the complexity of caring for our common home.

Progress

Progress expresses "the ideal line of history," the "history that would arise did all men under all conditions in all thoughts, words, and deeds obey the natural law, and this without the aid of grace."[78] This vector originates in human authenticity—being attentive to experience, intelligent in understanding, rational in judgment, and responsible in deciding—as one responds to the exigencies of human living. While Lonergan acknowledges other types of knowing, this practical focus characterizes "common-sense" knowing.[79] As Lonergan narrates its dynamic creativity:

Robert M. Doran and H. Daniel Monsour, trans. Michael G. Shields (Toronto: University of Toronto Press, 2011), 507.

75 Lonergan, "*Insight* Revisited," in *A Second Collection*, 271–72.

76 Bernard J. F. Lonergan, *Topics in Education*, vol. 10 of CWL, ed. Frederick E. Crowe and Robert M. Doran (Toronto: University of Toronto, 1993), 69.

77 Mathews, *Lonergan's Quest*, 39; and Shute, *The Origins of Lonergan's Notion of the Dialectic of History*, 42.

78 Lonergan, "Analytic Concept of History," 15.

79 Lonergan, *Insight*, 232–34.

Being attentive includes attention to human affairs. Being intelligent includes a grasp of hitherto unnoticed or unrealized possibilities. Being reasonable includes the rejection of what probably would not work but also the acknowledgement of what probably would. Being responsible includes basing one's decisions and choices on an unbiased evaluation of short-term and long-term costs and benefits to oneself, to one's group, to other groups. Progress, of course, is not some single improvement but a continuous flow of them. . . . Attention, intelligence, reasonableness, and responsibility are to be exercised not only with respect to the existing situation but also with respect to the subsequent, changed situation. It spots the inadequacies and repercussions of the previous venture to improve what is good and remedy what is defective. More generally, the simple fact of change of itself makes it likely that new possibilities will have arisen and old possibilities will have advanced in probability. So change begets further change and the sustained observance of the transcendental precepts makes these cumulative changes an instance of progress.[80]

Again, authentic human knowing and choosing forms a recurrent, self-correcting, and ever-expanding scheme. In an emergently probable world, authenticity increases the likelihood of future authenticity, and "things begin to roll."[81] Resolutions of questions at earlier instances condition the resolutions of more complex questions in the future.[82] Furthermore, these processes sublate themselves to address higher levels of human living in history. Because emergence characterizes these progressive and practical processes, creativity directs itself to at least three additional levels of the good within which people apply this single dynamic process differently.

First, the "particular good" concerns the objects that satisfy an individual's appetite.[83] One particular good is "spontaneous intersubjectivity," the human attraction toward relationship, captured in the practically visceral

---

[80] Lonergan, *Method in Theology*, 53; see also 44.

[81] Bernard J. F. Lonergan, *Understanding and Being: The Halifax Lectures on Insight*, vol. 5 of CWL, ed. Elizabeth A. Morelli and Mark D. Morelli, rev. Frederick E. Crowe (Toronto: University of Toronto Press, 2005), 235; see also *Topics in Education*, 50.

[82] Bernard J. F. Lonergan, *Phenomenology and Logic: The Boston College Lectures on Mathematical Logic and Existentialism*, vol. 18 of CWL, ed. Philip J. McShane (Toronto: University of Toronto Press, 2001), 302–3; "A Post-Hegelian Philosophy of History," 214; and *Insight*, 8.

[83] Lonergan, *Topics in Education*, 33–34.

bond of community between child and parent, husband and wife, kinsperson and kinsperson.[84] On a primordial level, humans both need and want to belong to others; spontaneous intersubjectivity names the relationality that constitutes human personhood. So too do people need and want other necessities. Other particular goods include the objects needed for survival: food, water, and shelter. Life lived only at this level, however, is arduous, primitive, and precarious. This exigency consequently yields to a higher order, a systemization of the precariousness.

Second, the "good of order"—also referred to as "the setup" or "civilization"—coordinates human efforts to secure the regular recurrence of particular goods.[85] Technologies develop to procure goods like food, water, and shelter more efficiently. In order to specialize the labor involved in this procurement and to distribute the goods reaped from this technology, an economy develops. In order to ensure the harmonious collaboration of specialized labor groups and the distribution of goods, a politics develops. Technology, the economy, and the political arrangement themselves all form a recurring, dynamic scheme. Each of them is the product of "practical intelligence," while politics in particular institutionalizes the pursuit of the good life in a community of relationships.[86] That is, human community evolves from simple bonds of kinship, as practicality and human relationality coalesce into civil communities that maintain and develop the good of order.

Still, the good of order does not encompass the entirety of human living. "For society to progress," Lonergan proffers, "it must fulfill one condition. It cannot be a titanothore, a beast with a three-ton body and a ten-ounce brain."[87] Questions beyond practicality, those concerning whether the order itself is good, condition the emergence of a third level, the "good of value" or "culture."[88] As Lonergan explains:

---

[84] Lonergan, *Insight*, 237–40. As Lonergan recounts, "My own illustration of that is from an experience I had. In my daily walk in Rome there is a ramp up which I go to enter the Borghese Gardens. One day there was a child running in front of its mother, and it stumbled on the concrete. I was at least thirty feet away but spontaneously I leaned forward to prevent the child from falling, although it was a quite useless gesture. There is a community that is prior to the distinction between 'I' and 'thou.'" See Lonergan, "The Analogy of Meaning," in *Philosophical and Theological Papers 1958–1964*, 187.

[85] Lonergan, *Insight*, 238; see also *Topics in Education*, 34–36.

[86] Lonergan, *Insight*, 238.

[87] Lonergan, *For a New Political Economy*, 20.

[88] Lonergan, *Topics in Education*, 36, 55; and *Insight*, 261.

> For men not only do things. They wish to understand their own doing. They wish to discover and to express the appropriateness, the meaning, the significance, the value, and the use of their way of life as a whole and in its parts. Such discovery and expression constitute the cultural and, quite evidently, culture stands to social order as soul to body, for any element of social order will be rejected the moment it is widely judged inappropriate, meaningless, irrelevant, useless, just not worthwhile.[89]

Culture concerns the sense humans make of their living, what they value within it, and how they do so. It encompasses the meaning people invest in their doing, giving structure to the good of order that underpins it and forming those who operate within it. It supplies the ideological substratum of the social order to which it gives meaning. Culture is the inescapable milieu that people inhabit and within which their structures stand.

Moreover, there are a myriad of ways that people make sense of their living. Crediting Christopher Dawson for this insight, Lonergan distinguishes between classical and empirical notions of culture.[90] Whereas classical understandings of culture make one culture—and, historically speaking, Western culture—normative for everyone, an empirical notion of culture defines culture more generally as "the set of meanings and values that informs a way of life."[91] This shift affords a more dynamic conception of culture. Besides admitting the possibility of development and decline, this recognition acknowledges the possibility of cultural contestation, competing meanings and values that inform a way of life, and a range of claims regarding the order itself. One can detect culture on an immediate, everyday level. Social assumptions, predominant career expectations and aspirations, and the functioning of symbols (such as those found in advertisements) are a few examples. This meaning can be "embodied or carried in human intersubjectivity, in art, in symbols, in language, and in the lives and deeds of persons."[92] Or, one can discern culture in more reflective expressions such as literature, science, and philosophy. All these carriers—from advertisements to literature—convey the meaning undergirding a particular community, the soul of its social order.

---

[89] Bernard J. F. Lonergan, "The Absence of God in Modern Culture," in *A Second Collection*, 102. See also "Belief: Today's Issue," in *A Second Collection*, 90–91.

[90] Lonergan, *Caring about Meaning*, 9.

[91] Lonergan, *Method in Theology*, xi. See also "Revolution in Catholic Theology," 195–99; and "Belief: Today's Issue," 92.

[92] Lonergan, *Method in Theology*, 57.

These meanings and values point to the persons who apprehend them. Specifically, for Lonergan, they point to the cognitive processes underlying authentic apprehensions of meaning and value.[93] The modern turn to the subject exemplifies this move to interiority, a turn that Lonergan hopes to retrieve through the best of the Christian tradition (e.g., Augustine, Aquinas, and Newman) in his overall project. For him, a mature grasp of meaning demands "[t]horoughly understand[ing] what it is to understand," a certain asceticism that discerns the common processes by which people come to know things.[94] Lonergan invites people to discern the fourfold scheme of experiencing, understanding, judging, and deciding in their own living. In coming to discern these operations in oneself, one can more consciously appropriate the wonder that characterizes the human spirit, the unrestricted desire to know, that desire to know everything about everything. Indeed, questions about one's own questioning raise questions about the goodness and intelligibility of the universe as well as the meaningfulness of moral deliberation.[95] Such grand questions intend the ultimate question of God—the origin and end of the created order to which the human heart stands restlessly oriented.

Through his portrayal of progress, Lonergan captures the intricate dynamism of human living in history. The need for particular goods, from food to human belonging, points to the emergence of the good of order, the political-technological-economic matrix that might secure them. The good of order points to the good of value, the cultural worldview that supplies meaning and value to that order. Finally, the ascertaining of that meaning and value by human persons points beyond to an ultimate source of meaning and value, truth and intelligibility. This heuristic supplies an invaluable backdrop with which to grasp the other vectors Lonergan identifies in decline and redemption.[96] Indeed, an expanded account is needed since the serenity that Lonergan assumes in his account of progress fails to approximate human experience in the concrete.

---

[93] Lonergan notes that the apprehension of this meaning and value progresses through various emergent "stages of meaning," with each level enriching the level that preceded it. It is here that Lonergan discusses the relationship between explanation and description referenced at the beginning of this chapter. See Lonergan, *Method in Theology*, 81–99.

[94] Lonergan, *Insight*, 22. Elsewhere, Lonergan describes this as "a heightening of consciousness that brings to light our conscious and intentional operations and thereby leads to the answers to three basic questions. What am I doing when I am knowing? Why is doing that knowing? What do I know when I do it?" *Method in Theology*, 25.

[95] Lonergan, *Method in Theology*, 101–3.

[96] See Komonchak, *Foundations in Ecclesiology*, 79–80, 124–25.

Decline

Over the course of his writings, Lonergan critiques the unbridled optimism of modernity. The horrific violence of the twentieth century belied the illusion of perpetual progress hailed by liberal depictions of history. "The cult of progress has suffered an eclipse," he laments in *Insight*, "because development does imply that perfection belongs not to the present but to the future. Had that implication of present shortcomings not been overlooked with such abandon, had the apostles of progress not mistaken their basic views for premature attainments of future perfection, then the disillusionment of the twentieth century could hardly have been at once so unexpected, so bitter, and so complete."[97] The progressive character of the human spirit does not guarantee historical progress. Earlier in the same work, Lonergan confesses:

> So we are brought to the profound disillusionment of modern man and to the focal point of his horror. He had hoped through knowledge to ensure a development that was always progress and never decline. He has discovered that the advance of human knowledge is ambivalent, that it places in man's hands stupendous power without necessarily adding proportionate wisdom and virtue, that the fact of advance and the evidence of powers are not guarantees of truth, that myth is the permanent alternative to mystery and mystery is what his hybris rejected.[98]

Prefiguring Pope Francis by over fifty years, Lonergan believes that such optimism betrays technocratic assumptions blind to the inherent ambiguity of technical advance. He even suggests that some theologians had overlooked the ambivalence of modern progress in their own theological accounts.[99] Accordingly, Lonergan insists on the need for differentials in any analysis of history. Since progress alone does not constitute human living, Lonergan includes an account of decline, that which deviates from progress, to his theology of history. Likewise, mirroring his exposition of progress, Lonergan attends to the social and cultural features of decline. By so doing, he anticipates the structural forms of sin featured in Catholic social thought after his death.

---

[97] Lonergan, *Insight*, 710. See also *Topics in Education*, 47, 66; and "Essay in Fundamental Sociology," 20.

[98] Lonergan, *Insight*, 572.

[99] In particular, Lonergan has in mind Marie-Dominique Chenu. Lonergan, "Sacralization and Secularization," 280.

Just as progress originates from human attentiveness, intelligence, rationality, and responsibility, decline originates from the refusal to heed those imperatives.[100] To account for this reality, Lonergan speaks of the "problem of development."[101] In a developing, emergent universe, lower levels tend to preserve their relative autonomy, despite the pull of higher levels toward increasingly complex syntheses.[102] In the human person, a tension exists between the unrestricted drive of the human spirit and the grounded, embodied character of being human. One simultaneously wants to know everything about everything, while also being grounded and situated in particular social and biological limits. The drama of an emergent universe—the tug-and-pull of lower and higher levels, of self-preservation and transcendence—characterizes the intersection between human experiencing and the drive toward understanding, between the psyche and the intelligence for which the psyche provides requisite images.

The tension helps explain the precariousness of progress and development in history in two ways. First is the possibility of "dramatic bias" in human subjects.[103] Neurological aberration or past trauma can elicit a psychic repression of the images and relevant questions that provide the grist for insight, a distortion what Lonergan labels *scotosis*. By blocking these elements, the psyche stunts insights that can otherwise direct the "dramatic artistry" of human living fruitfully.[104] Dramatic bias inhibits the deep attentiveness that human authenticity requires. The second, related way stems from the ability of human consciousness to image a virtually unlimited number and range of mental objects and images in a broad variety of ways, what Lonergan refers to as the "polymorphism of consciousness."[105] Humans, as animals, begin from a world biased toward immediacy, wherein the real is defined by what is immediately experienced and the good by what immediately satisfies. Another piece of cake appears much better than running four miles, the benefit of which is not immediately palpable! Rather than a world governed by the complexity of meaning, in a world of immediacy, human knowing and choosing concern simply the "already out there

---

[100] Lonergan, *Method in Theology*, 55.
[101] Lonergan, *Insight*, 497–99.
[102] Lonergan, *Insight*, 467–69.
[103] Lonergan, *Insight*, 214–31.
[104] Lonergan, *Insight*, 212–14.
[105] Lonergan, *Insight*, 410–12, 424.

now real." They are "constituted completely on the level of experience; neither questions for intelligence nor questions for reflection have any part in its genesis; and as questions do not give rise to it, neither can they undo it; essentially it is unquestionable."[106]

This tendency biases human knowing and choosing toward immediacy and away from the unrestricted demands of the human spirit. As the needs of survival and the achievements of common sense confirm, this type of knowing is not bad in itself; it simply needs to be distinguished from the full blossoming of human intelligence and freedom. Nevertheless, since experience conditions the understanding, judging, and deciding that emerge from it, its logic tends to entrench itself as the overriding criterion of all human existence, distorting and restricting the drive toward attentive, intelligent, rational, and responsible activity and trapping the human subject in its egocentric, myopic, and short-term logic of immediacy.[107] A form of dramatic bias can result, a lodged inattentiveness to the questions that might free one from this biased logic. Distorted individual development results in decline.

Like progress, decline recurs and cumulatively spirals beyond the individual. The individual is not only already shaped by historical decline but also contributes to a communal decline that shapes future persons. Just as Lonergan referred to the wheel of progress "rolling along," so too the "wheel of decline has a similar but opposite momentum, and far greater power of acceleration—until things just fall apart."[108] The repeated failure to heed the demands of human intelligence and freedom produces a sociohistorical surd: a cascading cycle of inattentiveness, unintelligence, irrationality, and irresponsibility biased toward egoistic immediacy. Decline sets the condition for future schemes of decline. As Lonergan puts it, "A civilization in decline digs its own grave with a relentless consistency."[109] Bias infects the communal fabric in no fewer than three ways.

---

[106] Lonergan, *Insight*, 277. See also 11–12, 17.

[107] Lonergan, *Insight*, 243, 269; see also "*Pantôn Anakephalaiôsis*," 146; *Grace and Freedom*, 45; and "Finality, Love, Marriage," 26.

[108] Lonergan, "A Post-Hegelian Philosophy of History," 215. See also "Notion of Fittingness," 509–11; *Phenomenology and Logic*, 303; and "Moral Theology and Human Sciences," in *Philosophical and Theological Papers, 1965–1980*, 305.

[109] Lonergan, *Method in Theology*, 55. See also Bernard J. F. Lonergan, "The Redemption: A Supplement," in *The Redemption*, vol. 9 of CWL, ed. Robert M. Doran, H. Daniel Monsour, and Jeremy D. Wilkins, trans. Michael G. Shields (Toronto: University of Toronto Press, 2018), 309. This unpublished work is also sometimes referred to as "*De Bono et Malo*"; subsequent references will preserve the editorial decision to call it "The Redemption: A Supplement."

First, *individual bias* names an egoism in which one values the satisfaction of one's desires—particular goods—to the exclusion of further questions and insights that ensure the functioning of the good of order.[110] Intelligence comes to serve one's personal whims at the expense of the good of one's community. During times of communal emergencies, for instance, individuals rush to hoard as many supplies as possible to the detriment of the entire suffering community. "Egoists find loop-holes in social arrangements, and they exploit them to enlarge their own share and diminish the share of others in current instances of the particular good."[111] And yet, because individual bias involves intelligence—for the sake of attaining one's own immediate, spontaneous desires—and so also its self-transcending character, this bias becomes ultimately incoherent. "The egoist's uneasy conscience is his awareness of his sin against the light," Lonergan adds.[112] At least in theory does this self-defeating mechanism exist, as larger forms of bias stymie its natural resolution.

One such form is a second type of myopia: *group bias*.[113] It corresponds to the good of order that requires the adaptive cooperation between spontaneous intersubjectivity and practical intelligence, relationality and practicality. Given the tensions of human development, these two elements can undermine each other. Spontaneous intersubjectivity can fail to adapt to the demands of practical intelligence. Technical development can appear as a threat to communal bonds. So too—as in the case of ethnocentrism, racism, and classism—can spontaneous intersubjectivity make the needs of one group appear more pressing than the needs of the whole and enlist practical intelligence for this narrow end. The social inequalities named in Catholic social teaching illustrate as much. "What is good for this group or that group, is mistakenly thought to be good for the country or mankind, while what is good for the country is postponed or mutilated. There emerge the richer classes and the poorer classes, and the richer become ever richer, while the poorer sink into misery and squalor."[114]

The needs of groups beyond one's own go unheeded. Groups' power, rather than intelligent creativity and the common good, comes to determine

---

[110] Lonergan, *Insight*, 244–47; and *Method in Theology*, 54.

[111] Lonergan, *Method in Theology*, 360. See also "The Role of the Catholic University in the Modern World," in *Collection*, 110.

[112] Lonergan, *Insight*, 247.

[113] Lonergan, *Insight*, 247–50.

[114] Lonergan, *Method in Theology*, 360. See also 244.

social development.[115] Competing factions alternate between oppressed and oppressors, slaves and masters, with each shift in power. Like individual bias, however, group bias contains principles for its own reversal. The social order can become so clearly unstable, its divisions so obvious that "there is no need to call upon the experts and specialists to discover whether anything has gone wrong, nor even to hit upon a roughly accurate account of what can be done."[116] Through intelligence, people can identify social problems and discover solutions to them. Again, however, due to a third form of bias, this opening remains an aspirational reality.

The third form, *general bias*, is the most insidious and will be examined the most closely. Arising from the nature of common sense, this bias erodes the good of value, the level of culture.[117] Since common sense focuses only on the practical and immediate, it cannot recognize itself as simply one form of knowing among others, since this insight arises from a metaphysical claim. As a result, common sense is "incapable of coming to grasp that its peculiar danger is to extend its legitimate concern for the concrete and the immediately practical into disregard of larger issues and indifference to long-term results."[118] This monopolization of knowing poses a distinct danger when an exclusive emphasis on short-term practicality absorbs the level of reflective criticism that culture provides. From a pragmatic perspective, art looks useless or at least must become a tool for a more practical end like advertising; the corporatization of higher education makes the humanities irrelevant (or forces them to justify themselves using market logic). As Lonergan laments, "by becoming practical, culture renounces its one essential function, and by that renunciation condemns practicality to ruin."[119] When bias entrenches itself on this level, it births the "longer cycle of decline" that is "characterized by the neglect of ideas to which all groups are rendered indifferent."[120] General bias "insists on palpable short-term benefits at the cost of long-term evils."[121] It regularizes individual and group

---

115 Lonergan, *Topics in Education*, 60; and *Method in Theology*, 54.
116 Lonergan, *Insight*, 250.
117 Lonergan, *Topics in Education*, 44–45, 62.
118 Lonergan, *Insight*, 251. See also *Insight*, 201; *Topics*, 72–73; and *Method in Theology*, 360–61.
119 Lonergan, *Insight*, 262.
120 Lonergan, *Insight*, 252.
121 Lonergan, "Moral Theology and Human Sciences," 305. See also *Method in Theology*, 53, 361.

biases by promoting pseudo-theories that direct praxis to conform to "the way things are," a Machiavellian realpolitik.[122] It marginalizes "detached and disinterested intelligence" to the private realm, blunting its critical edge and thwarting its ability to assuage social deterioration, even recruiting religiosity to serve practicality.[123] General bias distorts the very notion of progress, as an unquestioned myth of insatiable progress supplants a more critical account of progress.[124]

Lonergan's identification of general bias allies him with many twentieth-century cultural critiques suspicious of scientific positivism and instrumental rationality. The normalization of bias means for Lonergan that "we live in the midst of a sensate culture, in which very many men, insofar as they acknowledge any hegemony of truth, given their allegiance not to a divine revelation, nor to a theology, nor to a philosophy, nor even to an intellectualist science, but to science interpreted in a positivistic and pragmatic fashion."[125] William Loewe notes the similarities between Lonergan's diagnosis of decline with the secular, critical theory of Max Horkheimer and the Frankfurt School.[126] So too does Lonergan's diagnosis parallel the critiques leveled by both Alberto Methol Ferré and Romano Guardini against Western technocracy. Here is how Lonergan describes the consequences of general bias:

> This tendency of contemporary human science has combined with the spectacle of the gigantic enterprises of modern industry to give plausibility to the notion that the panacea for all human ills lies in a minutely designed organization both of human energy and of natural resources to secure a maximum productivity. Man as intelligent and reasonable, as free and responsible, is ruled out of consideration. In place of the free unfolding of human vitality there comes the blueprint and the quota. . . . One is assured that in due time the world will be a paradise of prosperity, security,

---

[122] Lonergan, "The Notion of Fittingness," 511–13; *Macroeconomic Dynamics*, 94; and "Essay in Fundamental Sociology," 31.

[123] Lonergan, *Insight*, 254–57; "The Notion of Fittingness," 513; *Topics in Education*, 46–47; and *Method in Theology*, 105.

[124] Lonergan, *Method in Theology*, 244.

[125] Lonergan, *Insight*, 766.

[126] William P. Loewe, "Dialectics of Sin: Lonergan's *Insight* and the Critical Theory of Max Horkheimer," *Anglican Theological Review* 61 (1979): 224–45. Loewe stresses that, despite these similarities, Lonergan's theological convictions ultimately differentiate his "solution" from the neo-Marxism, quasi-positivism of Horkheimer and others (244–45). See also Lamb, *Solidarity with Victims*, 28–55.

and peace. But, while men wait for the utopia promised by universal organization, there are wars, transplanted populations, refugees, displaced persons, unemployment, outrageous inequalities in living standards, the legalized robbery of devaluated currencies, and the vast but somewhat hidden numbers of the destitute.[127]

Lonergan recognizes the deadly decadence of deformations of practicality, both technological and scientific. An alienated world eventually alienates even the human person; general bias dissolves any parameters on who or what is worthy of discard. Indeed, as chapter 5 details, Lonergan's analysis of general bias and its effects anticipates Pope Francis's description of the technocratic paradigm and its throwaway logic in *Laudato Si'*.

Moreover, general bias entraps in its self-replicating logic. Whereas individual and social biases contain within them their own principles of reversal, general bias does not. By its nature, the immediacy of common sense dismisses the long-term, patient, often-laborious reflection on self and history that can supply an alternative recurring scheme of wisdom.[128] The general bias of common sense necessarily dismisses alternatives to its claim of omnicompetence since, precisely as alternatives, they are deemed impractical. From the eyes of common sense, something like philosophy appears useless or, at least, the province of the starry-eyed. Nor can practicality—economics, politics, or technology—reverse the longer cycle of decline, as practicality itself and its imperialistic tendencies comprise the problem. More bureaucracy cannot fix political corruption; more technology cannot fix technopoly. Seemingly nothing can question or challenge the distortions of general bias.[129]

General bias conditions the recurrence of all other forms of bias, significantly increasing the likelihood of continuing misuses of human intelligence and freedom, which is how Lonergan understands sin. After all, inauthenticity is a rejection of both the *imago Dei* in which one is made and God's continual offer of friendship that draws one out of oneself.[130] Inauthenticity is sustained by powers and principalities larger than the control

---

127 Bernard J. F. Lonergan, "Respect for Human Dignity," in *Shorter Papers*, vol. 20 of CWL, ed. Robert Croken, Robert M. Doran, and H. Daniel Monsour (Toronto: University of Toronto Press, 2007), 124–25.

128 Lonergan, *Insight*, 8–9, 201, 445; and *Method in Theology*, 55.

129 Lonergan, *Insight*, 258, 445.

130 Lonergan, "The Redemption: A Supplement," 315.

of any one human being (Eph 6:12). In *Insight*, Lonergan expresses the need for one not simply to acknowledge one's unrestricted desire of the human spirit but also to have the "universal willingness" to actually appropriate that desire, to live its eros. And yet the seductions of sin and the confines of bias neuter and shrink that capacious, unrestricted scope and desiccate the persuasive means that might activate this willingness.[131] Just the opposite, general bias normalizes the inertial drag with which the psyche limits the unrestricted desire of the human spirit. It normalizes an egoism in which people remain inattentive, unintelligent, irrational, and irresponsible, compromising the call toward constant self-transcendence that constitutes human authenticity. It perpetuates group biases, as the promotion of one's group appears the only practical tact. Together, all these effects render persons "morally impotent," confining them to biased, truncated horizons.[132] "How, indeed," Lonergan wonders, "is a mind to become conscious of its own bias when that bias springs from a communal flight from understanding and is supported by the whole texture of a civilization?"[133] Sustained human inauthenticity conditions growing distortions in the social and cultural fabric, animating a reverse cycle of antiprogress and a sociohistorical surd. History devolves into a "reign of sin."[134] Born into and shaped by this world, people remain seemingly powerless to mend it. Nevertheless, in an emergently probable world, nothing is determined totally and so, despite these conditions, hope for redemption endures. As Loewe tenders, Lonergan's analysis of decline "indicates the full dimensions of the redemptive task."[135] It indicates the integral character of conversion that caring for our common home implies.

Redemption

With redemption, Lonergan enters the specifically theological realm. "The facts of good and evil, of progress and decline, raise questions about the

---

[131] Lonergan, *Insight*, 646–47.

[132] Lonergan, *Insight*, 651. This description and what follows provide the systematic underpinnings for what the Christian tradition calls original sin; see Ormerod, *Creation, Grace, and Redemption*, 77–87.

[133] Lonergan, *Insight*, 8–9.

[134] Lonergan, *Insight*, 714–15. See also "*Pantôn Anakephalaiôsis*," 141, 161.

[135] William P. Loewe, "Towards a Responsible Contemporary Soteriology," in *Creativity and Method: Essays in Honor of Bernard Lonergan*, ed. Matthew Lamb (Milwaukee, Wis.: Marquette University Press, 1981), 224.

character of the universe."[136] Decline raises the "problem of evil," and with it, the question of God. For Lonergan, evil is only a problem, understood in the technical sense as something beckoning a solution, if there is a God. If God does exist and is all-powerful and all-good, then God can and does will a solution in history.[137] Lonergan discerns what God is doing about evil through the third vector he identifies: supernatural redemption.

For Lonergan, a genuine presentation of history requires this third vector.[138] In this, he mirrors Pope Pius XI's emphasis on the necessity of Christ and the church for social reconstruction, as captured in celebrations of "Christ the King," refrains of "restoring of all things in Christ," and the blossoming of Catholic social teaching. In this way, Lonergan sees his own theory of history as offering an alternative to dominant Marxist and liberal theories that dismissed this redemptive vector.[139] In addition, Lonergan's distinct understanding of the problem—general bias, the longer cycle of decline, and moral impotence—cannot but imply the necessity of a solution beyond human striving. "Cultural evils," posits Lonergan, "call for a heaven-sent redeemer."[140] The cumulative spiral of decline significantly lowers, if not eradicates, the possibility of alternatives that could emerge through natural means.

His consideration of one possible solution to decline confirms this supernatural need. In *Insight*, after examining decline, Lonergan considers how what he calls *cosmopolis* can reverse the distortions of general bias. He writes that "there is a convergence of evidence for the assertion that the longer cycle is to be met, not by any idea or set of ideas on the level of technology, economics, or politics, but only by the attainment of a higher viewpoint in man's understanding and making of man," which he sees as the function of culture.[141] Cosmopolis signifies a philosophical enterprise at this cultural level, a collective commitment to the pure, detached, and

---

[136] Lonergan, *Method in Theology*, 101.

[137] Lonergan, *Insight*, 709, 715–16.

[138] See Lonergan, "Essay in Fundamental Sociology," 33, 41; "*Pantôn Anakephalaiôsis*," 158–59; *Topics in Education*, 46–48; *Understanding and Being*, 236–37, 380; and *Method in Theology*, 117. See also R. Michael Clark, "Byway of the Cross: The Early Lonergan and Political Order," *Lonergan Workshop* 12 (1996): 27–44, at 35; and Loewe, "Dialectics of Sin," 243–45.

[139] Lonergan, "Questionnaire on Philosophy: Response," 368.

[140] Lonergan, "The Redemption: A Supplement," 317. See also "The Redemption: A Supplement," 367.

[141] Lonergan, *Insight*, 258, 261. See also "The Role of the Catholic University in the Modern World," 109.

unrestricted desire to know. At their best, universities strive to offer this cosmopolitan service. Cosmopolis witnesses to the possibility of authentic knowing precisely through its renunciation of force and partisanship. It is "supremely practical by ignoring what is thought to be really practical," a "withdrawal from practicality to save practicality."[142] This endeavor can counter the dominance and reductionism of general bias. Nonetheless, Lonergan admits the impossibility of the undertaking. Even cosmopolis cannot withstand the problem of moral impotence and the longer cycle of decline.[143] Redemption cannot come from universities alone. While the nature of cosmopolis hints at some elements of the solution, it does not suffice as a full solution. Instead, cosmopolis represents an asymptotic hypothesis that illustrates the futility of a purely natural renewal, and hence cosmopolis signals the radical need for grace in history.[144] "The solution," Lonergan concedes, "has to be a still higher integration of human living."[145] The exigencies of the human situation point to a higher order that sublates a human history overrun by bias and sin.

A supernatural solution, a "greater actuation of human potency," brings human history to a fuller realization and fulfillment.[146] In his analysis of decline, Lonergan discusses the developmental inertia found at the intersection of one's psyche, experience, and intelligence, as well as the consequent need for a universal willingness. Because he frames the problem in this fashion, Lonergan shows how the theological virtues of faith, hope, and love enable the requisite integration of the psyche and one's full subjectivity with the unrestricted demands of human development and authenticity.[147] Charity aligns a person's will with the unrestricted desire to know that ultimately inclines toward God and God's will for the universe. Charity inspires one to take a dialectical attitude toward the sociohistorical surd, an attitude that refuses to return evil for evil.[148] In view of the apparent impracticality

---

[142] Lonergan, *Insight*, 264, 266.

[143] Lonergan, "*Pantôn Anakephalaiôsis*," 156; *Insight*, 656, 712–13; *Understanding and Being*, 377; and *Method in Theology*, 346. See also Komonchak, *Foundations in Ecclesiology*, 21–22.

[144] Matthew L. Lamb, "The Social and Political Dimensions of Lonergan's Theology," in *The Desires of the Human Heart: An Introduction to the Theology of Bernard Lonergan*, ed. Vernon Gregson (New York: Paulist Press, 1988), 275–76.

[145] Lonergan, *Insight*, 655.

[146] Lonergan, *Grace and Freedom*, 45.

[147] Lonergan, *Insight*, 718.

[148] Lonergan, *Insight*, 720–22.

of that attitude, hope furnishes this willing with a confidence that unrestricted knowing and willing is not futile.[149] Faith grants the intellectual confirmation for this confidence, sanctioning one to rest secure in the existence of both God and a divine solution to evil.[150] While charity and hope correspond to the will, faith corresponds to the intellect.[151]

So too does this solution take the form of mystery so as to stabilize these virtues psychically and experientially—indeed, imaginatively. Since, as John Henry Newman recognized, "no man will be a martyr for a conclusion," religious conviction requires more than notional consent.[152] To this end, mystery provides a symbolic, affective analogue to a subject's orientation toward unrestricted knowing and willing, allowing one to appropriate this orientation fully.[153] Mystery stirs the heart and arouses the universal willingness needed for human authenticity. As an element of God's solution to evil, mystery serves as "at once symbol of the uncomprehended and sign of what is grasped and psychic force that sweeps living human bodies, linked in charity, to the joyful, courageous, wholehearted, yet intelligently controlled performance of the tasks set by a world order in which the problem of evil is not suppressed but transcended."[154] Mystery integrates one's full being—mind, will, and heart—with God's solution to evil, a participation that takes the shape of faith, hope, and love. So too, as the next chapter makes clear, does it start to illustrate the liturgical dimensions of healing.

Shifting away from faculty psychology to intentionality analysis post-*Insight*, Lonergan calls this greater actuation of human potency *religious conversion*. For Lonergan, religious conversion does not refer simply to switching one's religious allegiances but to something deeper. Religious conversion names one's appropriation of "being in love in an unrestricted fashion . . . without limits or qualifications or conditions or reservations," the

---

[149] Lonergan, *Insight*, 723–24.

[150] Lonergan, *Insight*, 724, 740–42.

[151] It should be noted that Lonergan uses the language of faculty psychology here, even while he engages in intentionality analysis in *Insight*. For other discussions of the theological virtues, see Lonergan, "The Notion of Fittingness," 515–18; *Topics in Education*, 67–68; and "Moral Theology and Human Sciences," 309.

[152] John Henry Newman, *An Essay in Aid of a Grammar of Assent* (Garden City, N.Y.: Doubleday, 1955), 89. On the importance of this work for Lonergan, see Lonergan, "*Insight* Revisited," 221. On the influence of Newman on Lonergan generally, see Richard M. Liddy, *Transforming Light: Intellectual Conversion in the Early Lonergan* (Collegeville, Minn.: Liturgical Press, 1993), 16–40.

[153] Lonergan, *Insight*, 569–70.

[154] Lonergan, *Insight*, 745.

response to "God's love poured onto our hearts" (Rom 5:5).[155] Whereas human effort alone cannot surmount the suffocating rubble of egoistic bias and sin, the love of and for another pulls people out of themselves. That is, love animates the self-transcendence that characterizes the restlessness of the human spirit at its best. Moreover, only an unrestricted and unconditioned—indeed, divine—love sates, albeit provocatively, the insatiable desire to know, to value, and to love everything about everything. Only a love that knows no bounds can enliven, elicit, and restore the unrestricted character of the human spirit oriented toward the infinite God. This love alone persuades, instilling a universal willingness in one's being. It pierces hearts and opens horizons, exploding the "radical . . . lovelessness" that marks the egocentrism of bias and sin.[156]

Owned by this otherworldly love, the subject in love perceives the world differently, as it opens one up to goodness and truth wherever they might be found; it empowers one to authentically be responsible, rational, intelligent, and attentive. This love provides a rock that sustains religious conversion, bearing fruit in "a deep-set joy that can remain despite humiliation, failure, privation, pain, betrayal, desertion," a "radical peace, the peace that the world cannot give," and a disciplined withdrawal from inauthenticity and bias.[157] As a response to this love, religious conversion establishes a new recurring scheme of choosing, judging, understanding, and experiencing; religious conversion renders more likely the occurrence of intellectual and moral conversion.[158] The response beckoned by this otherworldly love surfaces as an "inner word," a "quiet undertow," "a fateful call to a dreaded holiness," a "deep but obscure conviction that one cannot get out of trying to be holy."[159]

And yet, for beings who live in a world mediated by meaning, that love is not without form. That mysterious love, the quiet undertow that invites conversion, becomes realized through and is "constituted" by an "outer

---

[155] Lonergan, *Method in Theology*, 105–6.

[156] Lonergan, *Method in Theology*, 242.

[157] Lonergan, *Method in Theology*, 105, 110, 252.

[158] Lonergan, *Method in Theology*, 243, 267–68. In intellectual conversion, the true ceases to be simply a matter of "taking a good look" but becomes instead a compound of critical experiencing, understanding, and judging. In moral conversion, the good ceases to be simply a matter of what satisfies oneself but instead an opting for the authentic value of the entire universe as God intends it (see *Method in Theology*, 238–40).

[159] Lonergan, *Method in Theology*, 113; and "Horizons," in *Philosophical and Theological Papers 1965–1980*, 20.

word" that is God's loving, incarnate Word.[160] God's passionate love, and human participation in it, takes the shape of Jesus Christ; to use Pope Francis's (and Pope Benedict XVI's) parlance, religious conversion arises from an encounter with that Love become flesh, who "lays down his life for his friends" (Jn 15:13). It is Christ who enables people to affirm that undertow as a summons of the Holy Spirit, the love of a God who first loved us (1 Jn 4:19).[161] It is Christ, himself enflamed by the love of God, whose heart speaks to human hearts, making them "burn within us" (Lk 24:32) and who extends an offer of friendship that elevates humankind as adopted sons and daughters into God's triune life.[162] It is Christ who transforms one's subjectivity, such that it is "no longer I who live, but it is Christ who lives in me" (Gal 2:20), whereby one now experiences, understands, judges, and decides with the mind of Christ (Phil 2:5). One lives "in Christ Jesus as subject," "where the hand of the Lord ceases to be hidden," such that "being in love with God can be as full and dominant, as overwhelming and as lasting, an experience as human love."[163] Christ's offer of friendship enables one to appropriate, however proleptically and gropingly, the pulsing love of the ever-greater God ever cajoling persons to transcend themselves in love.

As the fate of Jesus illustrates, this love is cruciform insofar as it responds to the problem of sin and evil. Jesus lives, dies, and rises according to the "just and mysterious Law of the Cross." As Lonergan summarizes the law, "This is why the Son of God became man, suffered, died, and was raised again: because divine wisdom has ordained and divine goodness has willed,

---

160 Lonergan, *Method in Theology*, 113. See Avery Dulles, *The Assurance of Things Hoped For* (New York: Oxford University Press, 1994), 155, who stresses the importance of maintaining this inseparable, however distinct, relationship between inner and outer words in Lonergan's theology; see also Robert Imbelli, "Receiving Vatican II: Renewing the Christic Center," *Lonergan Workshop* 26 (2012): 187–209, at 200–8.

161 See Lonergan, "Mission and the Spirit," 31–33. See also Frederick E. Crowe, "Son and Spirit: Tension in the Divine Missions?" in *Appropriating the Lonergan Idea*, ed. Michael Vertin, 297–314 (Toronto: University of Toronto, 2006). Since it plays a more developed role in the following chapter, this chapter references only briefly the Trinitarian character of the grace that animates religious conversion for Lonergan.

162 On the role of the "heart" within Lonergan, see *Method in Theology*, 113, 115. The experience of grace, Lonergan adds, lets "—so gently and quietly—one's heart be touched." "Mission and the Spirit," 33.

163 Lonergan, "*Existenz* and *Aggiornamento*," 231. See also Frederick G. Lawrence, "Growing in Faith as the Eyes of Being-in-Love with God," in *The Fragility of Consciousness: Faith, Reason, and the Human Good*, ed. Randall S. Rosenberg and Kevin M. Vander Schel (Toronto: University of Toronto Press, 2017), 384–404; and Robert Barron, *The Priority of Christ: Toward a Postliberal Catholicism* (Grand Rapids, Mich.: Baker Academic, 2007), 167–71.

not to do away with the evils of the human race through power, but to convert those same evils into a supreme good."[164] Thus, to be in Christ as subject is not only to live in Christ but also to "have been crucified with Christ" (Gal 2:19). The Law of the Cross, as a precept, conveys the need to live this paschal wisdom, "a stumbling block to Jews and folly to Gentiles" (1 Cor 1:23). In Lonergan's words, one "has to learn and believe, that out of charity gladly feels together with Christ, lives in Christ, works through Christ, is one with Christ, so as to be assimilated and conformed to Christ in his dying and rising."[165] This precept encapsulates the shape of authenticity in a world disfigured by decline, conveying the need both to constantly die to one's own biases and to embrace the inevitably cruciform character that unrestricted, self-transcending loving takes in a violent world. Despite its seeming impracticality to the biased eye, to be in love unrestrictedly and to will the good and the true at all costs demands the laying down of one's whole life. The Resurrection reveals that such an endeavor will not be in vain and will indeed lead to new life; true liberation comes through the Cross. And hence, the Law of the Cross unveils sinful bias for what it is: destructive and absurd. As Lonergan captures the power of the paschal mystery in the face of the seemingly unconquerable biases of history, moral impotence, and the reign of sin:

> the possibilities of resisting the mechanisms and the determinisms that can emerge historically are heightened almost to an unlimited extent by Christianity. The death and resurrection of Christ express the victory of truth and goodness in spite of every kind of suffering: physical, in reputation, and in every other way. The example of Christ and the grace of God that comes to us through Christ constitute a historical force that, in Christ's own words, amounts really to this: Fear not, I have overcome the world. Christ himself overcame the world by resisting the powers of evil in suffering everything they would inflict upon him. And he rose again the third day. It is this Christian hope that is a supreme force in history. It is a fundamental and unchangeable ground that enables ordinary mortals to stand by the truth, and stand by what is right, no matter what the consequences.[166]

---

[164] Bernard J. F. Lonergan, "Theses 15–17 of *De Verbo Incarnato*," in *The Redemption*, 197. See also Lonergan, "The Transition from Classicism to Historical-Mindedness," 7; and "Moral Theology and Human Sciences," 309.

[165] Lonergan, "Theses 15–17 of *De Verbo Incarnato*," 205.

[166] Lonergan, *Topics in Education*, 257. See also Loewe, "Toward a Responsible Contemporary Soteriology," 217–19; and *Lex Crucis*, 367–68.

Through the Law of the Cross, Lonergan synthesizes the virtues of faith, hope, and love and conveys the intelligibility of the mystery that evokes and sustains religious conversion in a sin-torn history. Rooted in Jesus Christ, religious conversion bears a distinctive historical, social, and personal shape, a shape extended through the Gospel that Christ proclaimed and the community that he gathered.

God's redemptive offer is ongoing, for the church is Christ's mystical body in history. The meaning communicated through the Law of the Cross grounds the church's life and enlivens its redemptive dynamism, as the church mediates religious conversion personally, socially, and historically through its proclamation of Christ and his Gospel.[167] This evangelical witness of the church can overcome the determinisms of bias in all its forms. As Lonergan writes:

> The church is an out-going process. It exists not just for itself but for mankind. Its aim is the realization of the kingdom of God not only within its own organization but in the whole of human society and not only in the after life but also in this life. The church is a redemptive process. The Christian message, incarnate in Christ scourged and crucified, dead and risen, tells not only of God's love but also of man's sin. . . . As alienation and ideology are destructive of community, so the self-sacrificing love that is Christian charity reconciles alienated man to his true being, and undoes the mischief initiated by alienation and consolidated by ideology. This redemptive process has to be exercised in the church and in human society generally.[168]

And, in accord with the Law of the Cross, the mission of the church is not coercive. The cross entails an intentional surrender of control, a divine rejection of the *libido dominandi*. As revealed in Christ, God does away with evil not through force but rather through a transformative persuasion that works in tandem with human freedom. In an emergently probable world, the church thus sets conditions for transformation, a transformation that awaits final fulfillment only in the eschaton.[169] Against the reign of sin, the church establishes a "new order," a redemptive recurring scheme of meaning

---

[167] Lonergan, "Theses 15–17 of *De Verbo Incarnato*," 203–5; and "The Redemption: A Supplement," 615–17. See also Jeremy Blackwood, "Law of the Cross and the Mystical Body of Christ," in *Intellect, Affect, and God: The Trinity, History, and the Life of Grace*, ed. Joseph Ogbonnaya and Gerard Whelan (Milwaukee, Wis.: Marquette University Press, 2021), 274–91.

[168] Lonergan, *Method in Theology*, 363–64; see also 361.

[169] See Lonergan, "The Redemption: A Supplement," 459, 481. See also Cynthia S. W. Crysdale, "The Law of the Cross and Emergent Probability," in *Finding Salvation in Christ: Essays on*

initiated by Christ, the New Adam.[170] Particularly through the redemptive meanings and values to which its doctrines witness, the church "socializes" its members in this higher redemptive order.[171] For Lonergan, the church becomes intelligible only through its saving mission.

Unanswered Questions

And yet, Lonergan fails to articulate in detail how the church exercises this redemptive agency in history. Joseph Komonchak classifies ecclesiology as Lonergan's least developed theological topic.[172] For instance, in a discussion of the non-coercive character of ecclesial mission, Lonergan writes:

> Nor did the Lord at that time restore a kingdom of Israel (Acts 1:6) that would suddenly and with manifest power bring all things under its sway; he preferred rather to sow a grain of mustard seed (Matthew 13:31), which seems to grow slowly because interior fruit is ignored by the news media and also because the kingdom is proclaimed and propagated through secondary causes, namely, human beings. *This entire subject calls for a longer treatment.*[173]

Lonergan never provides a longer treatment to the subject in this work (which was unpublished) or elsewhere. In the epilogue of *Insight*, he states, "to the foregoing considerations that regard any individual that has embraced God's solution, there is to be added the consideration of the cumulative historical development, first of the chosen people and then of the Catholic church, both in themselves and in their role in the unfolding of all human history and in the order of the universe."[174] By his death, Lon-

---

Christology and Soteriology in Honor of William P. Loewe, ed. Christopher D. Denny and Christopher McMahon, 193–214 (Eugene, Ore.: Pickwick Publications, 2011).

170 Lonergan, "Essay in Fundamental Sociology," 36, 42; "Pantôn Anakephalaiôsis," 141; and "Finality, Love, Marriage," 27.

171 Lonergan, *Topics in Education*, 242; *Method in Theology*, 130, 311, 327. See also Komonchak, *Foundations in Ecclesiology*, 32–41, 141–66.

172 Joseph A. Komonchak, "The Church," in *The Desires of the Human Heart*, 223; and *Foundations in Ecclesiology*, 47. See also Mark T. Miller, *The Quest for God and the Good Life: Lonergan's Theological Anthropology* (Washington, D.C.: The Catholic University of America Press, 2013), 187, n. 36, who laments how little Lonergan wrote on ecclesiology.

173 Lonergan, "The Redemption: A Supplement," 365. Emphasis added. See also his "Theses 15–17 of *De Verbo Incarnato*," 251.

174 Lonergan, *Insight*, 763. See also his "Theses 15–17 of *De Verbo Incarnato*," 223.

ergan had failed to explain fully that "cumulative historical development," the outgoing process that is the church.

Whereas Lonergan accounts presciently for social and cultural forms of decline, he does not do the same for redemption. Instead, Lonergan's description of redemption concentrates primarily on how God's solution transforms individuals, how it actuates human potencies in response to the problem of development. In an early, unpublished work, Lonergan submits that "[t]he effect of [Christ's] total historical action is the total human good of order both external and cultural, past, present, and future."[175] How stands unexplained.[176] His occasional references to the social and cultural ramifications of this transformation lack the sophistication of his analysis of decline.[177] While Lonergan's analysis of individual conversion yields considerable insight, his account of the redemptive task is lopsided, especially if it is meant to counter the full dimensions of decline. Indeed, Crowe acknowledges Lonergan's enduring yet uncompleted interest in Christ's "historical causality."[178] Calling it "a tantalizing loose end," Loewe similarly highlights how Lonergan failed to resolve what the Canadian Jesuit terms "the general problem of integration" in the penultimate thesis of *De Verbo Incarnato*, his most sustained treatment of redemption.[179] As described above, Lonergan's integrating intent generates in him a hope to delineate the church's redemptive mission within the full scope of history. His inability to focus wholeheartedly on that project means that an account of the cultural and social shape of redemption remains a lacuna that begs further development. Resolving this question better positions Lonergan's theology of history to supply the needed theoretical context for understanding the church's mission, especially in the form of Catholic social teaching. It can better explain the complexity of the church's task to care for our common home. The eucharistic and doxological vision of ecclesial mission implied within *Laudato Si'* and its integral ecology demands as much.

---

[175] Lonergan, "The Redemption: A Supplement," 611.

[176] For an unearthing of latent potentialities in Lonergan's work in response to this need, see Ligita Ryliškytė, "*Cur Deus Cruciatus?*: Lonergan's Law of the Cross and The Transpositions of 'Justice over Power'" (PhD diss., Boston College, 2020), especially chap. 5.

[177] See, e.g., Lonergan, *Method in Theology*, 55, 117.

[178] Crowe, *Christ and History*, 18–19, 150–52. Komonchak recalls Lonergan telling him that ecclesiology had to be approached through these historical categories. See Komonchak, "The Church," 222; and *Foundations in Ecclesiology*, 77.

[179] Loewe, *Lex Crucis*, 307–8. Cf. Lonergan, "Theses 15–17 of *De Verbo Incarnato*," 143. See also William P. Loewe, "Lonergan and the Law of the Cross: A Universalist View of Salvation," *Anglican Theological Review* 59, no. 2 (1977): 162–74, at 164–68.

TWO POSSIBLE AIDS IN LATER DEVELOPMENTS

As discussed above, Lonergan leaves these questions unanswered because he withdrew from practicality to pursue more fundamental questions, as works like *Insight* and *Method in Theology* evidence. Still, even those projects are rushed ones. Lonergan needed to hastily "round-off" *Insight* before he left to teach in Rome, making it, as William Mathews acknowledges, more "a series of suggestions of possibilities in need of enlargement."[180] He authored *Method in Theology* under the specter of a cancer diagnosis, explaining what Frederick Lawrence describes as its "maddeningly dense, allusive, and elliptical style."[181] As a result, Lonergan leaves readers with only possible clues for an adequate understanding of the dynamics of historical redemption, the social mission of the church. Two themes deserve attention: "the scale of values" and "healing and creating." Both emerge most clearly in the final stages of his career; as the next chapter shows, both have since been employed by future commentary to complete Lonergan's theology of history.

The Scale of Values: An Organizing Principle?

Lonergan charts the vector of progress through what he calls "the invariant structure of the human good."[182] Specifically, as was shown, he references the particular good, the good of order, and the good of value in describing historical progress. By situating progress within the context of the good, Lonergan conveys how people, at least ideally, deliberate and prioritize as they form societies and contribute to history. These decisions objectify the otherwise implicit structure of the good.[183] For instance, people can pursue the good of order only after securing particular goods. Meanwhile, because the good of order maintains the regular recurrence of those particular goods, opting for a particular good over the good of order violates this

---

[180] Lonergan, "*Insight* Revisited," 268; and Mathews, *Lonergan's Quest*, 456.

[181] Frederick Lawrence, "Lonergan as Political Theologian," in *Religion in Context: Recent Studies in Lonergan*, ed. Timothy P. Fallon and Philip Boo Riley (Lanham, Md.: University Press of America, 1988), 16. See Lonergan, *Caring about Meaning*, 148–49. See also Michael Shute, *Lonergan's Discovery of the Science of Economics* (Toronto: University of Toronto Press, 2010), 238; and Crowe, *Lonergan*, 107. As the latter writes, "*Method* does suffer in comparison with *Insight*. It is schematic in style almost to the point of being laconic, and the content lacks the leisurely sweep of its great predecessor . . . one feels that the Lonergan of pre-surgery times would have greatly expanded them."

[182] Lonergan, *Topics in Education*, 27. For the most mature form of Lonergan's presentation of the structure of the good, see *Method in Theology*, 47–52.

[183] Lonergan, *Phenomenology and Logic*, 303.

invariant structure. The structure of the good hence anticipates an understanding of history. As Lonergan adds, "your idea of society is connected with your notion of the good . . . my notion of the human good is interconvertible with my notion of the structure of history."[184] Lonergan's understanding of history finds root in his structure of the good.

Lonergan honed his understanding of the good over time. In the latter half of his career, he pays closer attention to people's feelings, deliberations, decisions, and responsibilities as well as to the good and value that these intend.[185] In *Method in Theology*, Lonergan discusses how the feelings that guide decisions respond to certain values in an order of preference. That is, this preference anticipates the structure of the human good. It is here that Lonergan introduces the scale of values. The passage deserves quotation at length:

> Not only do feelings respond to values. They do so in accord with some scale of preference. We may distinguish vital, social, cultural, personal and religious values in an ascending order. Vital values, such as health and strength, grace and vigor, normally are preferred to avoiding the work, privations, pains involved in acquiring, maintaining, restoring them. Social values, such as the good of order which conditions the vital values of the whole community, have to be preferred to the vital values of individual members of the community. Cultural values do not exist without the underpinning of vital and social values, but none the less they rank higher. Not by bread alone doth man live. Over and above mere living and operating, men have to find meaning in their living and operating. It is the function of culture to discover, express, validate, criticize, correct, develop, improve such meaning and value. Personal value is the person in his self-transcendence, as loving and being loved, as originator of value in himself and in his milieu, as an inspiration and invitation to others to do likewise. Religious values, finally, are at the heart of the meaning and values of man's living and man's world.[186]

---

[184] Lonergan, *Topics in Education*, 24. See also "The Philosophy of History," in *Philosophical and Theological Papers 1958–1964*, 78: "The position of a developed philosophic notion of the good is extremely relevant to the questions historians get asked."

[185] Lonergan, "*Insight* Revisited," 277.

[186] Lonergan, *Method in Theology*, 31–32. See also, e.g., "Horizons," 14–15, 18; "Natural Right and Historical Mindedness," 173; and "An Interview with Fr. Bernard Lonergan, S.J.," ed. Philip McShane, in *Second Collection*, 221. For a more extended study of this topic in Lonergan, see Patrick H. Byrne, "What Is *Our* Scale of Value Preference?" *Lonergan Workshop* 21 (2008): 43–64; and Patrick H. Byrne, "Which Scale of Value Preference? Lonergan, Scheler, Von Hildebrand, and Doran," in *Meaning and History in Systematic Theology: Essays in Honor of Robert M. Doran, SJ*, ed. John Dadosky (Milwaukee, Wis.: Marquette University Press, 2009), 19–49; and *The Ethics*

The scale builds upon Lonergan's invariant structure of the good. On the one hand, vital values reflect the particular good, social values the good of order (a connection Lonergan makes explicitly), and cultural values the good of value.[187] They also form a sublating hierarchy. As Lonergan's allusion to "an ascending order" indicates, each higher level emerges from yet depends upon lower levels, while lower levels depend upon higher levels for their stability. These relationships mirror Lonergan's account of historical progress. On the other hand, in contrast to the structure of the good, Lonergan expands the scale of values to include personal and religious values. This inclusion is only implicit in his account of the good of value, as the expression of cultural meaning and value can generate a critical exigency, a turn to the person's self-transcending quality (personal value). That exigency in turn generates religious questions of ultimacy (religious values). Nevertheless, Lonergan made this path clearest only around the time of *Method in Theology*, toward the end of his career.

Lonergan's scale of values contains much potential. It furnishes a succinct, ordered framework for his heuristic of history, outlining the various levels oriented potentially to either progress or decline. Moreover, Lonergan's inclusion of religious values offers a hint for discerning the processes of redemption. From the perspective of Lonergan's threefold structure of the good, it is unclear how religious conversion affects those goods. In his scale of values, however, Lonergan carves out a possible place for religious conversion. Still, he only intimates its place in history and does not specify how it might affect lower values. Because Lonergan developed his scale so late in his career, he never states explicitly how, or even whether, the scale parallels the dynamics of history in the same way that his notion of the good does. The scale stands as another "maddeningly allusive" theme in *Method in Theology*.[188] Future commentary, the next chapter demonstrates, refines it further.

---

of Discernment: Lonergan's Foundations for Ethics (Toronto: University of Toronto Press, 2016), 241–84, 387–410.

[187] For an early (though unpublished) hierarchical ordering of the good that anticipates the scale of values, see Lonergan, "The Redemption: A Supplement," 297–99.

[188] See Byrne, "What Is *Our* Scale of Value Preference?" 44, 63; and "Which Scale of Value Preference?" 19.

Creating and Healing... in History?

An even later development in Lonergan's work leaves a second clue: development "from below" and "from above" and, eventually, the interplay of "creating" and "healing." While arguably the theme lay dormant in his earlier work, Lonergan thematized it only in the final few years of his career, after the publication of *Method in Theology*.[189] As he explains these two types of development:

> Human development occurs in two distinct modes. If I may use a spatial metaphor, it moves (1) from below upwards and (2) from above downwards. It moves from below inasmuch as it begins from one's personal experience, advances through ever fuller understanding and more balanced judgment, and so attains the responsible exercise of personal freedom. It moves from above downwards inasmuch as one belongs to a hierarchy of groups and so owes allegiance to one's home, to one's country, to one's religion. Through the traditions of the group one is socialized, acculturated, educated.[190]

Throughout his writings, Lonergan insists that human wonder, intelligence, and freedom operate from below. Experience gives rise to understanding, understanding gives rise to judgment, and judgment gives rise to decision, as higher levels sublate lower ones. At this later stage, Lonergan makes explicit the opposite dynamic, development from above, such that higher levels likewise influence lower ones in a recurrent scheme. As in the case of a child or a disciple, the group to which a person belongs can condition one's valuing, which in turn conditions one's beliefs, one's judgments. These beliefs condition one's understandings, which likewise shape one's experiencing.[191] Language, for instance, shapes the way that one experiences, understands, judges, and decides in the world. Thus, though he devotes most of his writing to the arduous work of development from below, Lonergan also makes explicit another way of human development: from above.

---

[189] For the genesis and development of this theme in Lonergan, see Frederick E. Crowe, "An Expansion of Lonergan's Notion of Value," in *Appropriating the Lonergan Idea*, 345–53, which has been especially helpful for this section.

[190] Lonergan, "Questionnaire on Philosophy: Response," 361. See also "Theology and Praxis," in *A Third Collection*, 196–97. Crowe correctly admonishes readers to interpret Lonergan's spatial imagery as a mnemonic device for grasping the differences between the two ways of development. See "An Expansion of Lonergan's Notion of Value," 346.

[191] Lonergan, "Natural Right and Historical Mindedness," 181.

Lonergan presented the dynamic of love and, by extension, religious conversion as prime examples of development from above.[192] In discussing religious conversion, he highlights how falling in love and, most especially, the pouring of God's love onto human hearts prove exceptions to the traditional Thomistic tag, "*nihil amatum nisi praecognitum*," that knowledge precedes love.[193] For recipients of religious conversion, "[o]ur love reveals to us values we had not appreciated, values of prayer and worship, or repentance and belief."[194] Lonergan recalls Blaise Pascal's remark that "the heart has reasons which reason does not know."[195] For Lonergan, the heart signifies the dynamic being in love that marks religious conversion and that precedes the experiencing, understanding, judging, and deciding that constitutes being human. The effect of this love moves downward in the human person. The transformation effected by religious conversion stirs a new apprehension of value, to value as God values. Faith, as Lonergan defines it, is "the knowledge born of religious love," the beliefs and judgments that flow from that shift.[196] These judgments determine one's understandings and experiences, aligning them with the unrestricted love of God. From above, the gift of God's love that grounds religious conversion unleashes the full eros of the human spirit.[197] Grace perfects human intentionality, even if that perfection proceeds in accord with the Law of the Cross.

In one of his last works, "Healing and Creating in History," Lonergan applies the downward development of love to historical process.[198] In the essay, Lonergan labels the cumulative process of practical insights, the "wheel of progress," as "creating" in history.[199] He then rehearses how biases disrupt this creative process.[200] Then, since "human development is of two quite different kinds," Lonergan turns to healing, "the transformation of

---

[192] Bernard J. F. Lonergan, "Mission and the Spirit," 32; and "Christology Today: Methodological Reflections," in *A Third Collection*, 76–77.

[193] Lonergan, *Method in Theology*, 122, 278, 283, 340.

[194] Lonergan, *Method in Theology*, 122.

[195] Lonergan, *Method in Theology*, 115.

[196] Lonergan, *Method in Theology*, 115.

[197] See Patrick H. Byrne, "Spirit of Wonder, Spirit of Love: Reflections on the Work of Bernard Lonergan," *Budhi: A Journal of Ideas and Culture* 2 (1997): 67–84.

[198] Bernard J. F. Lonergan, "Healing and Creating in History," in *A Third Collection*, 100–9.

[199] Lonergan, "Healing and Creating in History," 103–4.

[200] Lonergan, "Healing and Creating in History," 105.

falling in love," as a complement to creating and a balm for bias.[201] "Where hatred reinforces bias," he writes, "love dissolves it, whether it be the bias of unconscious motivation, the bias of individual or group egoism, or the bias of omnicompetent, short-sighted common sense."[202] For Lonergan, understanding healing in this manner distinguishes it from the violent, materialistic reformism of Karl Marx.[203] Finally, Lonergan adds that historical development requires both creativity and healing. As he writes, "intrinsic to the nature of healing, there is the extrinsic requirement of a concomitant creative process. For just as the creative process, when unaccompanied by healing, is distorted and corrupted by bias, so too the healing process, when unaccompanied by creating, is a soul without a body."[204] In both the subject and history, given the presence of bias, merely human efforts need aid in the form of healing. Just as religious conversion unleashes the *eros* of the human spirit, so too does healing unleash the full potential of creativity in history, albeit through the Cross.

Lonergan viewed this essay as critical for his theology of history. At Boston College, he assigned it in the last class of his career, Macroeconomics and the Dialectic of History, the culmination of his lingering interest in the topic.[205] In the essay, Lonergan incorporates the three vectors of history—progress, decline, and redemption—that he identified at an early point in his career.[206] He also hints at the precise dynamic of redemption in history, as Lonergan grants redemption a directionality and specifies its relation to the vectors of progress and decline. Whereas progress moves upward and bias skews this upward thrust, redemption moves downward, conceivably through all the levels that comprise progress and decline.[207] Nevertheless, despite implying that it does, Lonergan leaves unclarified how redemption affects those levels. As Gerard Whelan comments, especially since it postdated *Method in Theology*, Lonergan's thinking on the two ways of devel-

---

201 Lonergan, "Healing and Creating in History," 106.

202 Lonergan, "Healing and Creating in History," 106.

203 Lonergan, "Healing and Creating in History," 107.

204 Lonergan, "Healing and Creating in History," 107.

205 Lonergan, *Caring about Meaning*, 88; and Maurice Schepers, "Lonergan on the Person and the Economy: 'Reaching Up to the Mind of Aquinas,' In View of Responding to Pope Leo XIII, *Vetera Novis Augere et Perficere*," *New Blackfriars* 93, no. 1043 (January 2012): 99–115, at 105.

206 He refers to "vectors" in "Healing and Creating in History," 107.

207 See also Lonergan, *Caring about Meaning*, 93, where he identifies nature as "upward" and grace as "downward."

opment is "not systematically expounded."[208] As with the scale of values, Lonergan leaves this systematization to future commentators.

CONCLUSION

"If praxis is identified with practicality, then theology becomes an instance of praxis when it is converted into a tool for some distinct and praiseworthy end."[209] While praising the achievements of the liberation theologies that emerge from this premise, Lonergan adds that, for the ancients, genuine *praxis* (in contrast to *poiesis*) follows from *phronesis*—that is, deliberate action needs guidance from practical wisdom. Despite the seductions of general bias, producing certain goals is not the immediate goal of theology per se. Instead, theology, oriented toward praxis in this ancient sense, offers the practical wisdom that guides intentional deliberation and choice in missioned discipleship. Hence, as Lonergan posits in *Insight* and incarnated in his life, withdrawals from practicality can be for the sake of practicality. Never removed entirely from the needs of human living, such withdrawals allow one to cultivate this wisdom. Otherwise, praxis can be aimless or even exacerbate an existing situation.

Lonergan, like many theologians of his generation, wishes to "inspire and direct the ... Christian dynamic of history."[210] For him, that more radical meaning of praxis directs his endeavors. A withdrawal to explanatory theory in the form of a theology of history can afford the type of practical wisdom needed for a more intentional fidelity to the church's mission in a broken world. The practical character of Catholic social teaching makes it a clear potential beneficiary of this explanatory clarity. Otherwise, Catholic social teaching can lack a systematic wholeness, both making it susceptible to various distortions and obscuring its implementation. Lonergan's project can accordingly bear much fruit, especially in light of *Laudato Si'*, its sprawling admonitions, and its uneven reception. In this, a *Summa Sociologica* proves supremely practical.

Still, Lonergan never had the opportunity to return fully to the project and, as a result, left vague how that Christian dynamic functioned in history. His account of redemption does not match the complexity of decline in a

---

[208] Gerard Whelan, *Redeeming History: Social Concern in Bernard Lonergan and Robert Doran* (Rome: Gregorian & Biblical Press, 2013), 165.
[209] Lonergan, "Theology and Praxis," 184.
[210] Lonergan, "Questionnaire on Philosophy: Response," 381.

way that *Laudato Si'* invites. Thankfully, Lonergan left his project intentionally open-ended. The role of wonder, the upward yet undetermined dynamism of knowing, and the self-correcting process of learning all indicate the capacious character of his project. It invites collaboration, commentary, and further refinement. The preliminary nature of works like *Insight* and *Method in Theology* indicate as much.[211]

In the words of Brian Bajzek:

> New data emerge constantly, and Lonergan's method is designed to account for, openly accommodate, and expand in light of this. This openness and data-oriented dynamism is built into Lonergan's whole project, and it is the very thing that prevents that project from stagnation and calcification. It is a unique thing to be utilizing a framework which has the conditions for its own constant rejuvenation and expansion built into it from the very beginning.[212]

The existence of a "Lonerganism" betrays the spirit of the project and stagnates it. Lonergan's thought is not a closed system but rather an invitation to a renewed human and theological authenticity for the sake of the church and, by extension, for the sake of the world.

The unanswered questions left in Lonergan's work as well as the questions raised by *Laudato Si'* provide data that prevent the calcification of his work and invite the work of others to resolve these questions, as the next two chapters show. Lonergan's efforts lay critical foundations for scrutinizing the integral ecology that Pope Francis outlines in *Laudato Si'*. While Lonergan never wrote on environmental issues per se, the comprehensive approach taken by Catholic social teaching to the ecological crisis matches Lonergan's synthetic approach. In addition, his theology of history begins to capture the myriad relationships that comprise an integral ecology. Just

---

[211] See this from Lonergan as an example:
> What had to be undertaken was preliminary exploratory journey into an unfortunately neglected region. Only after specialists in different fields had been given the opportunity to discover the existence and significance of their insights could there arise the hope that some would be found to discern my intention where my expression was at fault, to correct my errors where ignorance led me astray, and with the wealth of their knowledge to fill the dynamic but formal structures I tried to erect. (*Insight*, 7)

See also Lonergan, "The Response of the Jesuit Priest and Apostle in the Modern World," 187.

[212] Quoted in Robert M. Doran, "The International Institute for Method in Theology: A Vision," 2017, https://www.loneganresource.com/pdf/lectures/Doran_-_International_Institute_for_Method_in_Theology.pdf.

as Lonergan understood himself as furnishing Catholic social teaching with a broader theoretical context, so too does an integral ecology require the same type of framework. What remains to be developed in that framework, however, is a liturgically cast, ecclesiological account of integral conversion. Given the lacunae in Lonergan's work, developing his theology of history further can uncover the dynamism of Christ's redemptive efficacy—perpetuated through the church's eucharistic mission—in our common home.

Chapter 4

The Integral Scale of Values and the Eucharist

The previous chapter highlighted Lonergan's ambition to "do for the twentieth century what Aquinas did for the thirteenth."[1] Just as Aquinas engages exigencies of his day—pastoral ones, like the theological underpinnings of penitential practice, and academic ones, like the theological value of Aristotelianism—Lonergan engages areas such as modern science, contemporary political theory, macroeconomics, and history. In this Thomistic spirit, to use his words, Lonergan strives "to operate on the level of our day."[2] Lonergan's understanding of theology follows suit: "theology mediates between a cultural matrix and the significance and role of a religion in that matrix."[3] This mediation—both dialogical and dialectical—permits theology to do for the current moment what Aquinas did for his.

The present chapter follows this spirit. While others have performed the indispensable work of excavating the Thomistic roots of Lonergan, arguably no other contemporary theologian has sustained this Thomistic spirit of Lonergan more than Robert Doran did. Thus, this chapter begins by focusing on Doran's work. In bringing Lonergan's work to bear on contemporary issues, Doran fills in the lacunae identified in the previous chapter. This effort can realize what he believes to be the "ultimate goal" of Lonergan's project: "the clarification of the constituents of collective responsibility for the social mediation of the human good."[4] That is, Doran proffers an account of cultural and social redemption that better allows Lonergan's theology of history to furnish a full explanatory framework for the church's saving mission, particularly as expressed in Catholic social teaching. With

---

[1] Bernard J. F. Lonergan, "Theology and Man's Future," in *A Second Collection*, ed. William F. J. Ryan and Bernard Tyrell (Philadelphia: The Westminster Press, 1974), 138.

[2] Bernard J. F. Lonergan, *Method in Theology* (New York: Herder and Herder, 1972), 367.

[3] Lonergan, *Method in Theology*, xi.

[4] Robert M. Doran, preface to *Redeeming History: Social Concern in Bernard Lonergan and Robert Doran*, by Gerard Whelan (Rome: Gregorian & Biblical Press, 2013), 1.

an eye toward the questions raised in *Laudato Si'*, this chapter presents Doran's development of Lonergan's theology of history through the scale of values. At the same time, bearing in mind the distinctly doxological and eucharistic character of *Laudato Si'*, this chapter also determines the role of eucharistic praise within this theology of history, a question left unaddressed by Lonergan and Doran alike. The framework outlined here—a doxological, eucharistic account of ecclesial mission—can shed explanatory light on the integral ecology of *Laudato Si'*. In this way Lonergan's theology of history can operate adequately at the level of our day and respond appropriately to the demands of today's cultural matrix, one marked by the call to care for our common home.

READING LONERGAN AMID SOCIAL CONCERN

Over the course of his life, Robert Doran devoted himself to carrying forward Lonergan's legacy in view of social concerns such as those raised by Catholic social teaching. The pastoral inclinations of Doran, a Jesuit like Lonergan, awakened this academic interest. Thus, as the next chapter makes clear, it is the pastoral concerns about what is happening to our common home that are the most deserving of a closer look through the thought of Doran and Lonergan alike. Like Lonergan, Doran came to believe that right responses to pastoral concerns depended on adequate theory. As Doran tells it, his fascination with Lonergan's theology blossomed during the social unrest of the late 1960s. At that time, chapter 7 of *Insight*—which provides Lonergan's most extensive examination of progress and decline in history by surveying the development of common sense and its biased corruptions—prompted a conversion for Doran. His recounting of the episode merits quotation at length:

> in terms of the framework provided by Lonergan, and of the horizon shift that his work effects, it was chapter 7 . . . of *Insight* that got me started, and it will be in terms of what he says there that my own proposals about culture and society will have to be judged. I had finally got this far in *Insight* in the summer of 1967. And I believed then, as I still do today, that chapter 7 was the most important piece of literature that I had ever read; that it was the product not only of philosophic genius, which I already knew from earlier chapters, indeed from the first page of the preface, but also of prophetic vision and so of grace, of a certain holiness, and no doubt a good deal of suffering. The call to conversion that is at the heart of all of

Lonergan's writings began to make its singular impact on me in the reading of this chapter. I can recall reading and rereading and being stirred as I never had been before to a profound sense of what it would be worth while to devote my life to. For the first time, I think, I had found concretely something of which I could say, "This is worth a lifetime."[5]

Amid the chaotic happenings of the late 1960s, he recalls, "Lonergan, for me, spoke to those coincidental manifolds in history calling for higher integration in a way and to a depth that nobody else did."[6] Doran's encounter with Lonergan's theology of history amid these social concerns stimulated his enduring devotion to Lonergan's thought.

Pastoral questions continually returned Doran to Lonergan's work. Shortly after 1967, Doran's Jesuit superiors assigned him to establish a campus ministry program at Marquette University. There, too, he found Lonergan's understanding of history helpful for that daunting task.[7] It was there that, before the Catholic magisterium began to focus at length on environmental concerns, Doran helped organized and concelebrated a liturgy to celebrate the first Earth Day in 1970.[8] Lonergan's theology also informed Doran's work with people with HIV and AIDS in Toronto later in his career.[9] This ministry likewise took on a liturgical dimension; the healing liturgies organized by Doran for this community helped named the workings of God's grace amid suffering and alienation. These were just a few "coincidental manifolds" that Lonergan's work helped make intelligible for Doran.

On a broader scale, Lonergan's thought helped Doran navigate the church's developing self-understanding in the tumultuous post-conciliar period. Doran believed, for instance, that Lonergan's work could clarify and substantiate the meaning behind the declaration of the 1971 Synod of

---

[5] Robert M. Doran, "From Psychic Conversion to the Dialectic of Community," in *Theological Foundations*, vol. 2, *Theology and Culture* (Milwaukee, Wis.: Marquette University Press, 1995), 37. See also Doran, "Bernard Lonergan: An Appreciation," in *Theological Foundations*, vol. 2, *Theology and Culture*, 307–8. This volume is a collection of Doran's early writings on history, most of which had been previously published elsewhere.

[6] Doran, "From Psychic Conversion to the Dialectic of Community," 38.

[7] Doran, "From Psychic Conversion to the Dialectic of Community," 39.

[8] See Brian Roewe, "Hymns, Teach-ins and a Horse Ride to School: Catholic Stories of the First Earth Day," *National Catholic Reporter*, April 20, 2020, https://www.ncronline.org/news/earthbeat/hymns-teach-ins-and-horse-ride-school-catholic-stories-first-earth-day.

[9] See Robert M. Doran, "AIDS Ministry as a Praxis of Hope," in *Jesus Crucified and Risen: Essays in Spirituality and Theology in Honor of Dom Sebastian Moore*, ed. William P. Loewe and Vernon J. Gregson, 177–93 (Collegeville, Minn.: Liturgical Press, 1998).

Bishops in *Justitia in Mundo* that working for justice is constitutive of evangelization.[10] Doran likewise maintained that Lonergan's work could steer a more responsible reception of the Thirty-Second Congregation of the Society of Jesus's defining its mission as "the service of the faith and the promotion of justice."[11] Overall, Doran found Lonergan helpful for rectifying Christian spiritualities "too thin, without substance, vacuous, and above all self-centered and narcissistic" and for instead founding a spirituality oriented toward self-transcendence in social, political, and cultural responsibility.[12] Lonergan's theology of history, in Doran's eyes, could answer such pastoral and ecclesial exigencies.

These concerns inspired Doran to dedicate his life to the study of Lonergan. In 1975, Doran completed a dissertation on Lonergan, a project that Lonergan himself praised as "remarkably creative."[13] The relationship between the two continued to grow, so much so that, shortly before Lonergan died, he told Doran, "It is in in your hands now."[14] Reflecting on that charge, for Doran, "[t]hat promise and the responsibility it demands to secure Lonergan's legacy as best I can have determined the course of my life ever since and will continue to do so until I can work no more."[15] Doran acted as a trustee of Lonergan's estate. He served as the general editor of *The Collected Works of Bernard Lonergan*, a twenty-five-volume critical edition of Lonergan's materials, both published and unpublished. In 1985, along with Frederick Crowe, he established the Toronto Lonergan Research Institute to promote Lonergan's work. In 2017, answering Lonergan's call

---

[10] Robert M. Doran, "Suffering Servanthood and the Scale of Values," in *Theological Foundations*, vol. 2, *Theology and Culture*, 218–19. See World Synod of Bishops, *Justitia in Mundo* (1971), 6.

[11] Doran, "From Psychic Conversion to the Dialectic of Community," 62–63. See *Jesuit Life & Mission Today: The Decrees and Accompanying Documents of the 31st–35th General Congregations of the Society of Jesus* (St. Louis, Mo.: Institute of Jesuit Sources, 2009), Congregation 32.

[12] Robert M. Doran, "Psychic Conversion and Spiritual Development," in *Theological Foundations*, vol. 2, *Theology and Culture*, 65–66; see also 74.

[13] Bernard J. F. Lonergan, *Caring about Meaning: Patterns in the Life of Bernard Lonergan*, ed. Pierrot Lambert, Charlotte Tansey, and Cathleen Going (Montreal: Thomas More Institute Papers, 1982), 115.

[14] As quoted in John D. Dadosky introduction to in *Meaning and History in Systematic Theology: Essays in Honor of Robert M. Doran, SJ*, ed. John D. Dadosky (Milwaukee, Wis.: Marquette University Press, 2009), 11–12.

[15] Robert M. Doran, "Bernard Lonergan and Daniel Berrigan," in *Faith, Resistance, and the Future: Daniel Berrigan's Challenge to Catholic Social Thought*, ed. James L. Marsh and Anna J. Brown (New York: Fordham University Press, 2012), 123.

in *Insight* for a more institutionalized collaboration, Doran founded the International Institute for Method in Theology—a joint venture of Marquette University, the University of Toronto, and the theology faculty of the Pontifical Gregorian University in Rome—to apply Lonergan's thought to a range of topics.[16] He published books and numerous articles that sharpen and develop Lonergan's ideas, foraying, for instance, into Lonergan's Trinitarian theology at the end of his career. Dying in January 2021 (shortly after the release of the final volume of the *Collected Works*), he without doubt fulfilled his desire to promote Lonergan's legacy "until he can work no more."

In his writings, Doran's respect for Lonergan is one not of slavish obedience but one of creative fidelity. As he writes, "It is to Lonergan's undying credit that he never claimed, at any step in the process . . . that he had gone the whole way. Always there was, and, I hope, always there will be, a next step."[17] He continues elsewhere, "it is more accurate to say that [Lonergan] has given us a first word, a foundational word on which even the improvements and nuances that are required can be built."[18] As discussed in the conclusion of the previous chapter, Lonergan's work contains a natural dynamism that summons further growth and application.

Doran cultivates this growth in numerous ways. However, given his overriding interest in the topic, this chapter focuses primarily on Doran's development of Lonergan's theology of history. As the previous chapter showed, Lonergan leaves incomplete the *Summa Sociologica* that he believes to be so integral for ecclesial mission. Doran realizes that unfinished theology of history mainly in his *Theology and the Dialectics of History*.[19] As he confesses there, "The . . . book, while not out of harmony with Lonergan's thought, reflects certain emphases and even clarifications that either add to what he has said or draw out implications of his work in ways that he did

---

[16] See Bernard J. F. Lonergan, *Insight, A Study of Human Understanding*, vol. 3 of CWL, ed. Frederick E. Crowe and Robert M. Doran (Toronto: University of Toronto Press, 2005), 7. For the launch of this endeavor, see Robert M. Doran, "The International Institute for Method in Theology: A Vision," 2017, https://www.lonerganresource.com/pdf/lectures/Doran_-_International_Institute_for_Method_in_Theology.pdf.

[17] Robert M. Doran, "Common Ground," in *Theological Foundations*, vol. 2, *Theology and Culture*, 329–30.

[18] Doran, "Bernard Lonergan: An Appreciation," 315.

[19] Robert M. Doran, *What Is Systematic Theology?* (Toronto: University of Toronto Press, 2005), 74. See also Whelan, *Redeeming History*; and Gerard Whelan, "Transformations, Personal and Social, in Bernard Lonergan and Robert Doran," *The Lonergan Review* 5, no. 1 (2014): 22–38.

not stress."[20] Specifically, Doran lifts up those "maddeningly allusive" themes explored at the end of the previous chapter—the "scale of values" and "healing and creating"—and marshals them to outline an account of cultural and social redemption in a way that Lonergan did not. In Doran's words, "*Theology and the Dialectics of History* more than implicitly affirms a social-political dimension of conversion."[21] Since the publication of the book, Doran has named this dimension *social grace*. "Just as theologians some thirty years ago placed stress on sin as social and spoke of sinful social structures, so today we must work out the constitution of grace-filled social structures."[22] Such an account fills precisely the lacunae that the previous chapter identified in Lonergan's writings on history. Furthermore, because of Doran's pastoral concerns outlined above, he situates Lonergan's theology of history within more recent ecclesial debates and developments. For instance, his work in ministry during the early stages of the environmental movement sensitizes Doran to ecological concern. In other words, Doran affords a crucial middle step to employ Lonergan's theology of history to the doxological, eucharistic vision of *Laudato Si'* and its integral call to care for our common home.

EXPANDING LONERGAN'S THEOLOGY OF HISTORY

In *Theology and the Dialectics of History*, Doran takes up what he believes to be "[t]he crucial challenge set for systematic theologians in our day," namely "to formulate a theological theory of history, a theory that will understand confessional and theological doctrines in categories expressive of the structure of history."[23] To do so, and to expand upon Lonergan's own theology of history, Doran develops Lonergan's understanding of the scale of values to discern the "immanent intelligibility of the process of world history" and the church's role in serving the "integral scale of values."[24] Doran also charts the role of creating and healing within the scale of values, transposing this framework into a historical, ecclesiological matrix.[25] In

---

20 Robert M. Doran, *Theology and the Dialectics of History* (Toronto: University of Toronto Press, 1990), 8.
21 Doran, *What Is Systematic Theology?*, 123–24.
22 Doran, *What Is Systematic Theology?*, 138.
23 Doran, *Theology and the Dialectics of History*, 5.
24 Doran, *Theology and the Dialectics of History*, 144; see also 10, 90.
25 Doran, *Theology and the Dialectics of History*, 31–33.

fact, Doran's presentation of the integral scale of values anticipates Pope Francis's call for an integral ecology; both attempt to position the church's healing mission within the intricate ecology of history.

The first vector within the integral scale is creating, the equivalent of Lonergan's notion of progress. According to Doran, creating moves up the scale of values from vital to social, social to cultural, cultural to personal, and personal to religious in an emergently probable, sublating fashion. Recurrent needs at lower, more basic schemes give rise to and set the questions to be met by more complex schemes. Stated conversely, higher levels enable the effective functioning of more basic schemes of recurrence.[26] *Vital values*—the "particular goods" Lonergan highlighted like food, water, and shelter—require regular distribution.[27] Thus, this level gives rise to *social values*—what Lonergan called the "good of order." As Lonergan noted, social values—technology, economics, and politics—are constituted by a tension between practical intelligence and spontaneous intersubjectivity, between practicality and relationality. The tension generates a "dialectic of contraries," that is, "any concrete unfolding of linked but opposed principles that are modified cumulatively by the unfolding."[28] Borrowing from Lonergan, Doran characterizes this dialectic generically as one between "limitation" and "transcendence," a tension, he claims, that permeates all human living.[29] Limitation connotes a principle of integration and conservation, while transcendence connotes a principle of change and becoming. These principles name a need for both preservation and evolution, respectively. On the level of social values, relationality represents the pole of limitation and practicality the pole of transcendence; the former holds together the social fabric while the latter facilitates advances in the social order. Healthy communities depend on both well-worn tradition and daring innovation. The tensive balance of the dialectic of community ensures the smooth functioning of the social order and, subsequently, the equitable distribution of vital values.

---

26 Doran, *Theology and the Dialectics of History*, 148.

27 Doran adds that vital values not only concern freedom from hunger and thirst but also "from servitude and personal degradation, hopelessness and meaninglessness." "Cosmopolis and the Situation: A Preface to Systematics and Communications," in *Theological Foundations*, vol. 2, *Theology and Culture*, 354.

28 Lonergan, *Insight*, 269. Cf. Doran, *Theology and the Dialectics of History*, 9–10, 68–71.

29 See Lonergan on the "law of limitation and transcendence" in human development in *Insight*, 497–502.

Cultural values—what Lonergan dubbed the "good of value"—arise from the need to maintain this balance.[30] Like Lonergan, Doran understands these to be the meanings and values that inform a particular way of life, the soul of the social order, and the breath that gives pathos to social structures.[31] Cultural values enmesh social values within a world of meaning and value. A dialectic of limitation and transcendence also constitutes the level of cultural values, a proposal that Doran confesses "is the most precarious and tentative of all my suggestions."[32] Borrowing from Eric Voegelin, he distinguishes between "cosmological" and "anthropological" poles in the cultural dialectic.[33] On the limitation pole, cosmological meanings and values are "rooted in the affective and thus biologically based sympathy of the human organism with the rhythms and processes of nonhuman nature."[34] As exemplified especially clearly in indigenous communities, this pole stresses the wisdom that can come from belonging to a land.[35] On the transcendence pole, anthropological meanings and values judge "history [to be] a process involving the contribution of human insight, reflection, deliberation, and decision."[36] The Western premium placed on scientific discovery serves as one example of this type of value. Cultural health comes from a tensive-yet-creative balance between these two poles. Politics mediates this balance to the social order in order to maintain the dialectical balance between practicality and intersubjectivity.[37]

Cultural health depends on human authenticity, thus leading to the emergence of *personal values*. Personal values capture the need for people

[30] Doran, *Theology and the Dialectics of History*, 473.

[31] Doran, *Theology and the Dialectics of History*, 95, 98–99.

[32] Doran, *Theology and the Dialectics of History*, 11.

[33] Cf. Eric Voegelin, *Collected Works of Eric Voegelin*, vol. 14, *Israel and Revelation* (Columbia, Mo.: University of Missouri Press, 2001), 56. See also Robert M. Doran, "Theology's Situation: Questions to Eric Voegelin," in *Theological Foundations*, vol. 2, *Theology and Culture*, 259–96.

[34] Doran, *Theology and the Dialectics of History*, 510; cf. 507, 511. As Lonergan writes, "Undoubtedly the organic and integral mentality fostered by a life in touch with nature has to spread through the whole fabric of society and completely oust the mechanist and fractional thinking that has landed us where we are." "Review of George Boyle, *Democracy's Second Chance*," in *Shorter Papers*, vol. 20 of CWL, ed. Robert Croken, Robert M. Doran, H. Daniel Monsour (Toronto: University of Toronto Press, 2007), 159.

[35] See, e.g., Robin Wall Kimmerer, *Braiding Sweetgrass: Indigenous Wisdom, Scientific Knowledge, and the Teachings of Plants* (Minneapolis, Minn.: Milkweed Editions, 2013). The work of the agrarian writer Wendell Berry likewise emphasizes this point.

[36] Doran, *Theology and the Dialectics of History*, 510.

[37] Doran, *Theology and the Dialectics of History*, 101, 105.

to either appropriate or critically judge the cultural values that shape their living. For Doran, following Lonergan, human authenticity comes through surrendering oneself to the unrestrictedly self-transcending character of "the search for direction in the movement of life," the "passionateness of being" itself.[38] Located at the intersection of experience and understanding, the release of this undertow comes through "psychic conversion," which Doran defines as "a transformation of the psychic component of what Freud calls 'the censor' from a repressive to a constructive agency in a person's development."[39] Psychic conversion furnishes the unrestricted character of the human spirit with an experiential, affective thrust while, at the same time, ensuring that the human spirit remains attentive to the importance of those visceral levels of being human, the natural schemes of recurrence that allow for the possibility of human life. That is, psychic conversion attunes oneself to the dialectical tension of limitation and transcendence that also marks this personal level. Befitting the integral ecology of *Laudato Si'*, Doran captures the inseparability of the human and the nonhuman, while preserving the distinction between the two. Human authenticity demands embracing the tension that is oneself, the transcendent insatiability of the human spirit and the biological-psychological limits of being embodied, the mix of *ruah* and clay that God has called together "very good" (Gn 2:7).

In the ways that personal authenticity integrates both affect and intellect, an aesthetic quality marks this creative unfolding. Doran proposes an "artistic paradigm of praxis" so as to underscore the "dramatic artistry" of human living.[40] As he describes it:

> As the artist who works with oils and clay, music and words, must be capable of this release of empirical consciousness from instrumentalization, so too the dramatic artist who would make a work of art out of his or her own life must be able to abide in an empirical freedom of consciousness that allows there to emerge from the materials of one's life an

---

[38] Doran, *Theology and the Dialectics of History*, 45–49, 80, 218, 358.

[39] Doran, *Theology and the Dialectics of History*, 59. Psychic conversion was the subject of Doran's dissertation. See Robert M. Doran, *Subject and Psyche: Ricoeur, Jung, and the Search for Foundations* (Washington, D.C.: University Press of America, 1977); and *Psychic Conversion and Theological Foundations* (Chico, Calif.: Scholars Press, 1981). Lonergan approved of the idea in two letters to Doran. See Dadosky, "Introduction," 10.

[40] Doran, *Theology and the Dialectics of History*, 72, 399–401. As Doran notes, Lonergan turns to drama and art when discussing authenticity in the everyday. See Lonergan, *Insight*, 210–31.

inevitability of form analogous to that of a painting, a work of sculpture, or a symphony.[41]

Located at the interplay of limitation and transcendence, psychic conversion alerts one to the work of art that one's life is becoming or failing to become. It allows one to imagine one's role on the stage of the world's drama. For this reason, "ethics is radically aesthetics."[42] Right action is deeper than is solving moral quandaries; instead, it involves holding together the true and the good through the beauty that one's life can communicate. As becomes clear later in this chapter, however, sustained personal authenticity and development occur only through the aid of divine grace, "God's love poured onto our hearts" (Rom 5:5), the level of *religious values*.

Doran's development of creating both follows from and expands Lonergan's understanding of progress. On the one hand, Doran employs the scale of values both to capture the dynamic of creating in history and to specify the stratification of society's many components.[43] This follows Lonergan's emergently probable account of historical development in his presentation of progress. On the other hand, Doran's use of the scale of values expands this account by incorporating—along with vital (particular goods), social (the good of order), and cultural (the good of value) values—personal and religious values. Doran also stresses that, besides authenticity, the creative unfolding of dialectical relationships and the appropriately differentiated ordering of the various values that constitute society propel progress in history.[44] That is, genuine progress depends on dialectical balances being struck between poles like between practicality and intersubjectivity. So too does progress depend on preserving right ordering and distinguishing between levels of value, such as between social and cultural values. The proper functioning of this ecology of relationships, both within and between levels of value, characterizes the integral scale of values.

Following his teacher, Doran also discerns the presence of decline in history. Inauthenticity, bias, disvalue, the misuse of human freedom and intelligence, the breakdown of dialectical relationships, and the collapse of

---

[41] Doran, *Theology and the Dialectics of History*, 54.
[42] Robert M. Doran, "Aesthetics and the Opposites," in *Theological Foundations*, vol. 1, *Intentionality and Psyche* (Milwaukee, Wis.: Marquette University Press, 1995), 123.
[43] Doran, *Theology and the Dialectics of History*, 10–11.
[44] Doran, *Theology and the Dialectics of History*, 551.

the scale's levels threaten this fragile ecology. As Doran describes it, globally imperialistic market forces dominate the contemporary situation, teetering on the brink of a posthistoric humanity.[45] The need to recognize these forces has only become more urgent since Lonergan's time; "the 'longer cycle' of decline is further 'advanced' today beyond its position in the early 1950s."[46] Indeed, Doran's analysis of decline complements Lonergan's.

Like Lonergan, Doran fears the suffocating domination of instrumental rationality and scientific positivism. Thus, Doran also approximates Pope Francis's attention to the technocratic paradigm. Understood through the scale of values, general bias undermines the dialectic of community by skewing it too far in the direction of transcendence: "the dominance of practicality has upset a delicate balance with intersubjectivity in the formation of human community. . . . Correlative to the distorted dialectic of community is an effective collapse into its most basic levels, which themselves are no longer grounded in the very conditions of their possibility at the higher levels of values."[47] Social and vital values come to dominate the scale, shrinking its scope and dissolving the differentiations between levels of value. The practical means to obtain practical ends like food, water, and shelter exclusively determine value; an appreciation for something like the arts simply distracts from these immediate and more practical purposes. Politics, which should mediate authentic cultural values to the social order, instead serves economic and technological interests.[48] The need to preserve the economic interests of specialized groups can trump the common good that politics should serve. In all cases, practicality alone comes to determine meaning and worth, subsuming religious, personal, and cultural values as a result.

So too can the dialectic of culture itself collapse. Whereas earlier cultures might have risked a fatalistic surrender to cosmological meaning and value (too much limitation), contemporary culture poses the opposite problem. At least in the West, the cultural dialectic skews toward transcendence.[49] Contemporary society suffers from what some have characterized

---

[45] Doran, *Theology and the Dialectics of History*, 37. See also 169.

[46] Doran, *Theology and the Dialectics of History*, 156.

[47] Doran, *Theology and the Dialectics of History*, 376–77.

[48] Doran, *Theology and the Dialectics of History*, 102–3. See also Doran, *What Is Systematic Theology?*, 194.

[49] Doran, *Theology and the Dialectics of History*, 514.

as a "nature-deficit disorder," an alienation from the earth.[50] Scientific innovation, for instance, can lose its rootedness in the natural world and see it instead, as Francis Bacon and René Descartes did, as something to be mastered or bound to our service.[51] Indeed, in words that prefigure Pope Francis's diagnosis of tyrannical anthropocentrism in *Laudato Si'*, for Doran cultural decline manifests itself as "the mechanomorphic imperialism of perverted anthropological truth."[52] Doran describes the results: the "rhythms of cosmic process, which once were hypostasized as intracosmic gods, lose our allegiance completely when our partnership with them is transmuted beyond recognition by our passion for mastery, control, and instrumental exploitation."[53] He continues:

> In the mechanomorphic societies the source of order becomes the human will for domination rather than participation. Transhuman sources—nature, the world-transcendent God, God in a gracious world-constitutive initiative—all disappear. The only attunement demanded is with the prevailing will of the social engineers, as this will is objectified in dominating structures equipped with the same overwhelming power that the cosmological mentality attributes to the rhythms of nature. The social engineers have usurped the prerogatives that the other modes of symbolization grant to what is other than human. The resulting alienation from nature, estrangement from the purposeful order, and meaninglessness culminate in nihilism, where the search for direction ... is rejected, and so the very ground of what it is to be human is removed from under the feet of persons and societies.[54]

---

50 See Richard Louv, *Last Child in the Woods: Saving Our Children from Nature-Deficit Disorder* (Chapel Hill, N.C.: Algonquin Books of Chapel Hill, 2005).

51 See René Descartes, "Discourse on Method," in vol. 1 of *Philosophical Works of Descartes*, trans. Elizabeth S. Haldane and G. R. T. Ross (Cambridge: Cambridge University Press, 1976), 119; and Francis Bacon, "The Masculine Birth of Time, or The Great Instauration of the Dominion of Man over the Universe," in *The Philosophy of Francis Bacon*, trans. Benjamin Farrington (Liverpool: Liverpool University Press, 1964), 62.

52 Doran, *Theology and the Dialectics of History*, 513. Doran credits Matthew Lamb for this term. See, e.g., Matthew L. Lamb, "Methodology, Metascience, and Political Theology," *Lonergan Workshop* 2 (1979): 280–380.

53 Doran, *Theology and the Dialectics of History*, 519.

54 Doran, *Theology and the Dialectics of History*, 543. See also 516, where Doran mentions how "agents of the distortions of the dialectic of community despoliate the natural environment," and 511, where he writes that "[t]he ecological crisis generated by the ... displacement [in the direction of transcendence] is due to our allowing the apparent linearity of humanly constituted history to play fast and loose with the apparent cycles of nature, interfering with them in such a cavalier fashion as to introduce into a disoriented culture another, mechanomorphic, process of experience and symbolization."

Since social values depend on cultural values, such a mechanomorphic distortion further exacerbates the recurrent breakdown of the social order (i.e., group biases) and the dominance of practicality at the expense of relationality. Since vital values depend on the health of social values, this mechanomorphic imperialism is a remote cause of the maldistribution of vital goods: global poverty. This insight anticipates the consequences of the technocratic paradigm described in *Laudato Si'*.

Though a genuine alternative to this form of decline must respect the integrity of personal values, salvation cannot come from human effort alone. Lonergan underscored the precarity of sustained human development. Doran illustrates even more clearly that, since lower levels on the scale dictate the premises and questions for higher levels, social and cultural decline distort personal values.[55] Besides this challenge, persons likewise struggle to maintain the balance between limitation and transcendence within themselves. The hubris of today's situation betrays the rejection of one's own limitations for the sake of transcendence, "which leads to the rootlessness of schizophrenia, to the fantastic vistas that offer too much possibility."[56] Just as Ratzinger rues the *Machbarkeit* that increasingly dominates Western society, Doran submits that, "at least for a typical secularized post-Enlightenment Westerner, the thematized instance of psychic conversion involves a fairly radical about-face, a basic correction of the Enlightenment illusion of autonomous instrumental rationality."[57] Instrumental rationality reduces life to a gray carbon copy, rather than an expressive work of art; it reduces the gift of the world to a product. The inability to effectively preserve the tension names yet another dimension of moral impotence.[58] The fragility of the entire scale of values and the relationships that comprise it point to the necessity of grace, the realm of religious values.

Along with the presence of creating in history, then, the presence of decline focuses the redemptive dynamics of healing in history. As the previous chapter showed, Lonergan speaks of the downward dynamic of healing only late in his career, gesturing toward its possible role in the historical process. Doran's work matures this intuition in examining the

---

55 Doran, *Theology and the Dialectics of History*, 521.

56 Doran, *Theology and the Dialectics of History*, 289. Generally, the tendency toward displacement in either direction is what the Christian tradition calls *concupiscence*, and the capitulation to either displacement is sin.

57 Doran, *Theology and the Dialectics of History*, 142.

58 Doran, *Theology and the Dialectics of History*, 331. See also 195, 198, 201.

relationship of higher to lower levels within the scale of values. While from below, lower levels enable and set the exigencies for developments at higher levels; conversely, "from above, these proportionate developments are the condition of possibility of the appropriate schemes of recurrent events at the more basic levels."[59] The effective realization and functioning of lower levels in the scale require transformations at higher levels. The integrity of the scale is recovered insofar as healing moves down the scale, from religious values downward, since a given level cannot resolve its breakdowns on its own.

The need for redemption contextualizes the role of religious values, understood as the entrance of grace, God's offer of salvific friendship, into history.[60] More recently, grounded in Lonergan's own Trinitarian theology, Doran has reflected upon the Trinitarian contours of God's gift of love poured onto human hearts (Rom 5:5). Sanctifying grace—the unfolding recollection of God's unconditioned love in one's self-presence (Augustinian *memoria*) and the affirmation of that love—is a created participation in the active spiration of the Father through the Son. The habit of charity—the ardent desire to return God's love that arises from this recognition—is a created participation in the passive spiration of the Holy Spirit. Moreover, in a perichoretic scheme of recurrence, that love returns human persons to abide more deeply in the love of God ceaselessly poured onto their hearts.[61] So too does this state of grace condition one's loving affirmation of all that is good, true, and intelligible; it conditions fidelity, however stumbling, to the search for direction in the movement of life. From above, the gift of God's love catalyzes religious, moral, intellectual, and psychic conversion. For instance, psychic conversion inspired by supernatural love sharpens human attentiveness, thawing the deeply

---

59 Doran, *Theology and the Dialectics of History*, 95. See also 148.

60 "Divine revelation," according to Lonergan, "is God's entry and his taking part in man's making of man. It is God's claim to have a say in the aims and purposes, the direction and development of human lives, human societies, human cultures, human history." "Theology in its New Context," in *A Second Collection*, 62.

61 See Robert M. Doran, *The Trinity in History: A Theology of the Divine Missions*, vol. 1, *Missions and Processions* (Toronto: University of Toronto Press, 2012), esp. x–xi. Before his death, Doran published two of three volumes of this complex work, leaving it to others to finish the project. Given this reality and since the focus of the present book is Lonergan's theology of history, the details of Doran's (and Lonergan's) Trinitarian theology go beyond this current work. For a more extensive discussion of the relationship between Doran's Trinitarian theology and his theology of history, see Jeremy W. Blackwood, "Trinitarian Love in the Dialectics of History," *Method: Journal of Lonergan Studies*, n.s. 4, no. 1 (Spring 2013): 1–16, at 1–8.

lodged scotoses that blind.⁶² All these conversions fuel the necessary integration of the subject—what Lonergan identified as the universal willingness to desire the good, intelligent, and true—that grounds authentic personal values. On how grace awakens this authenticity, Doran writes:

> Such willingness is awakened by persuasion, and so the question of the gift that God bestows is a question about the persuasiveness of grace in a human world infected by the surd of evil. Willingness is good insofar as it proceeds from detached willingness; the circle is broken by the communication of a willingness that conforms, not to inadequately developed human intelligence, but to God's understanding of the world order that God has chosen and created and that God sustains in being through the whole course of its emergent process.⁶³

Instead of one's own, one's life becomes God's work of art, inevitably cruciform in shape.⁶⁴ Through God's grace, one can "*learn and believe*, and come *freely to consent* to Christ, living in him, operating through him, being associated with him, so that [one] may be assimilated and conformed to him in his dying and rising."⁶⁵ Furthermore, because grace has a triune character, grace is necessarily interpersonal—indeed, ecclesial. The authentic personal values enabled by religious values, according to the logic of the scale, ensure the effective realization of genuine cultural values. Healing fosters a "soteriological culture" that can mediate between cosmological and anthropological distortions and restore the creative balance that cultural health requires.⁶⁶ Cultural authenticity in turn ensures the health of social values, the proper balance between practicality and intersubjectivity. Finally, social health ensures the equitable distribution of vital goods. Religious values thus ultimately condition the integrity of the entire scale of values. The sum total of this redeemed order is the integral scale of values.

---

62 Robert M. Doran, "Dramatic Artistry in the Third Stage of Meaning," in *Theological Foundations*, vol. 1, *Intentionality and Psyche*, 236.

63 Doran, *Theology and the Dialectics of History*, 201. See also 209. For Lonergan's discussion of willingness and persuasion, see *Insight*, 646–47.

64 Doran, *Theology and the Dialectics of History*, 206; see also 358. Thus, the Law of the Cross provides the measure to discern the presence of grace beyond the visible confines of the church; see Robert M. Doran, *The Trinity in History: A Theology of the Divine Missions*, vol. 2, *Missions, Relations, and Persons* (Toronto: University of Toronto Press, 2019), 39, 45–46.

65 Doran, *The Trinity in History*, vol. 2, *Missions, Relations, and Persons*, 43.

66 Doran, *Theology and the Dialectics of History*, 90, 502, 504, 551.

The healing impact of religious values on the entire scale is what Doran understands as social grace. "Grace becomes social as the meanings and values that inform given ways of living are transformed by the explicit revelation of the gift of God's love.... The integral functioning of the full scale of values is constitutive of what I mean by the 'social grace' that is set over against social sin."[67] Social grace enlivens authentic creating in history, liberating human creativity from the biases, collapses, and breakdowns that distort its effective functioning. By so doing, grace restores the integral scale of values, perfecting nature. For Doran, the integral scale of values, always anticipatory, expresses the shape of the reign of God on earth.[68]

As the mystical body of Christ, the church embodies Jesus's own service to this heavenly reign. Participating in the triune missions, its mission consists in a fidelity to the healing vector that secures the integral scale.[69] Through such praxis, it can evoke a situation alternative to the current one, as the church is a "living sacrament of God's catalytic agency in the world."[70] Specifying this sacramental presence further, Doran writes, that "[o]nly the deliberate resolve, faithfully executed, on the part of a creative minority of subjects truly committed to breaking the vicious circle of distortions both at the specific levels of value themselves and throughout the entire scale of values, can set things right."[71] The first task of the church is thus faithfulness to its divine calling.[72] This fidelity sets the conditions for the emergence of an alternative, redemptive scheme of recurrence in history. In a world infected by the surd of sin, that ministry will take the shape of the Law of the Cross and, Doran

---

67 Robert M. Doran, "Social Grace and the Mission of the Church," in *A Realist's Church: Essays in Honor of Joseph A. Komonchak*, ed. Christopher Denny, Patrick Hayes, and Nicholas Rademacher (Maryknoll, N.Y.: Orbis Books, 2015), 177–78. See also Doran, *What Is Systematic Theology?*, 182, 188; and *The Trinity in History*, vol. 1, *Missions and Processions*, 83–107.

68 Doran, *Theology and the Dialectics of History*, 12, 452.

69 Doran, *The Trinity in History*, vol. 1, *Missions and Processions*, 57, 63. See also Neil Ormerod, *Re-visioning the Church: An Experiment in Systematic-Historical Ecclesiology* (Minneapolis, Minn.: Fortress Press, 2014), 79, 85, 110–11, 113.

70 Doran, *Theology and the Dialectics of History*, 110.

71 Doran, *Theology and the Dialectics of History*, 522. See also 363. Joseph Ratzinger likewise spoke of the church as a leavening, creative minority in Joseph Ratzinger and Marcello Pero, *Without Roots: The West, Relativism, Christianity, Islam* (New York: Basic Books, 2006), 80, 120–26.

72 One is reminded of Stanley Hauerwas's admonition that the primary task of the church is not to change the world but to be the church. See, for example, Stanley Hauerwas, *The Peaceable Kingdom: A Primer in Christian Ethics* (Notre Dame, Ind.: University of Notre Dame Press, 1983), 105; and "The Servant Community: Christian Social Ethics" (1983), in *The Hauerwas Reader*, ed. John Berkman and Michael Cartwright (Durham, N.C.: Duke University Press, 2001), 374–78.

adds, that of the Deutero-Isaian Suffering Servant. "The cross," Doran contends, "is as inescapable a result of the church's seeking to do as Jesus did as it was of Jesus' own proclamation and praxis of the reign of God."[73] As Doran states even more boldly in the last article he ever published, "the reign of God, interpreted through the lens of the scale of values, is advanced in history through graced participation in the law of the cross."[74] Since the cross is the means and cost of promoting God's reign, the church's catalytic agency—including its charge to care for our common home—comes precisely inasmuch as it suffers vicariously in its mission for the world.

THREE ECCLESIOLOGICAL IMPLICATIONS OF THE SCALE

Doran's elaboration of healing in history, the shape of social grace, specifies the contours of social and cultural redemption within the integral ecology of history. It stands as arguably Doran's most significant development of Lonergan's work. While his presentation of the topic still invites further expansion, this framework identifies the church's mission as one that fosters healing processes in history. Doran buttresses Lonergan's original intention to provide a *Summa Sociologica* for the church's redemptive self-understanding. In so doing, he contributes additional insight on ecclesial mission otherwise left unsaid by Lonergan. In particular, Doran establishes systematically the centrality of the preferential option for the poor in the church's mission, the church's commitment to cultural transformation in particular, and the dependence of the entire scale of values on religious values.

The Preferential Option for the Poor

Doran's development of the scale of values offers three significant contributions to envisioning the mission of the church. The first concerns Doran's appreciation for the best of liberationist insights. Johann Baptist Metz's political critique of his teacher, Karl Rahner, epitomizes the conventional tension understood to exist between transcendental Thomism and liberation theologies.[75] In the integrating spirit of Lonergan, however, Doran joins

---

[73] Doran, *Theology and the Dialectics of History*, 120. See also Doran, *The Trinity in History*, vol. 1, *Missions and Processions*, 231–34.

[74] Robert M. Doran, "Redemption as End and Redemption as Mediation," *Gregorianum* 101, no. 4 (2020): 927–43, at 927–28.

[75] See Johann Baptist Metz, "Transcendental-Idealist or Narrative-Practical Christianity?" in *Faith in History and Society: Toward a Practical Fundamental Theology*, trans. J. Matthew Ashley (New York: Crossroad Publishing Company, 2007), 144–55.

the insights of both movements, along with *ressourcement* thinkers, through the scale of values.[76] Given its centrality in Pope Francis's ministry generally and *Laudato Si'* specifically, of special interest is Doran's focus on liberationist articulations of the preferential option for the poor. Through the scale of values, he captures the hermeneutical privilege of the poor and the inductive approach that the doctrine enjoins, as condensed in the biblical phrase "the cry of the poor."[77]

The emergent logic of the scale, the relationship between more basic levels and higher levels in particular, provides the meaning of this descriptive claim. Lower levels, it was noted earlier in this chapter, pose the questions that higher levels resolve. Hence, the global maldistribution of vital values signals the depth of communal decline: corrupt social institutions, technocratic cultural assumptions, short-sighted personal decisions, and even privatized religious practices.[78] This historical exigency, by extension, determines the character of the requisite healing, the church's saving mission, and, in the case of *Laudato Si'*, care for our common home. Social grace, the integrity of the scale of values, "is measured against its bottom line, namely, the equitable distribution of vital goods to the entire family of God's children. This measure tells us how far we have to go before what we pray for when we say 'Thy kingdom come,' actually occurs in our midst in any secure set of schemes of recurrence."[79] The scale makes the cry of the poor, and that cry's hermeneutical preferentiality, in the church's mission systematically intelligible. In this way might "[t]he voices of those who have been silenced must be released into speech."[80] Doran's exposition of the preferential option amplifies the cry of the marginalized and vulnerable, making it all the more piercing in the church's life.

Doran's achievement advances the church's ongoing appropriation of this claim in its social teaching. Rohan Curnow elaborates:

---

[76] Doran, *What Is Systematic Theology?*, 86–88. For his engagement with *ressourcement* theology, see Robert M. Doran, "Lonergan and Balthasar: Methodological Considerations," *Theological Studies* 58, no. 1 (1997): 61–84.

[77] See, for example, Jon Sobrino, "Central Position of the Reign of God in Liberation Theology," in *Mysterium Liberationis: Fundamental Concepts of Liberation Theology*, ed. Ignacio Ellacuría and Jon Sobrino (Maryknoll, N.Y.: Orbis Books, 1993), 374–76.

[78] Doran, *Theology and the Dialectics of History*, 422–24, 556.

[79] Doran, *The Trinity in History*, vol. 2, *Missions, Relations, and Persons*, 36.

[80] Doran, *Theology and the Dialectics of History*, 423.

The Church already directs its mission—as is evident in elements of Catholic Social Teaching—in such a manner as to attempt to address distortions in the dialectics of history and respond to some notion of a hierarchy of values. But it is not explicitly aware of the constitution of the dialectics of history or their interrelations. What Doran's theory of history offers, in terms of understanding the mission of the Church, is precisely this explicit formulation of the dialectics and the scale so that missional activity may be critically grounded to include the Option for the Poor as an integral element in that mission.[81]

The need for this critical grounding is pressing given the centrality of the option for the poor in the most recent incarnation of Catholic social teaching, *Laudato Si'*. As chapter 2 demonstrates, Francis's hermeneutical privileging of the cries of the poor and the earth helps connect human and natural ecologies in caring for our common home. Doran indicates how one can map the option for the poor within an integral ecology and its essential place within it. The status of an option for the earth within the scale, unmentioned by Doran, stands as a consideration for the chapter that follows.

The Importance of Cultural Transformation "From Above"

In explaining how the church should respond to the cry of the poor, Doran offers a second ecclesiological implication: namely, that the church should facilitate cultural transformation "from above." As this chapter's first section mentioned, through his theology of history Doran hopes to steer a responsible ecclesial reception of the developing sense that work for justice is essential to the work of evangelization. The questions raised by liberationist thought for ecclesial praxis—regarding the use of violence, the church's role in politics, and the recognition of structural evil—stood at the forefront of his religious order, the Society of Jesus, throughout the latter half of the twentieth century. Doran's transposition of the option for the poor into the scale represents part of his effort to respond to the legitimate concerns raised by liberation theologians. Another dimension of Doran's endeavor involves a more critical appropriation of liberationist insights. It is for this reason that *Theology and the Dialectics of History* contains a lengthy critique of the liberation theology of Juan Luis Segundo.[82] In a more general sense,

---

[81] Rohan Michael Curnow, *The Preferential Option for the Poor: A Short History and a Reading Based on the Thought of Bernard Lonergan* (Milwaukee, Wis.: Marquette University Press, 2012), 196.
[82] Doran, *Theology and the Dialectics of History*, 424–39.

Doran tries to remedy distortions found in certain strains of liberation theology predominantly influenced by the thought of Karl Marx.[83] Much like what attracts Pope Francis to *la teología del pueblo*, Doran hopes to articulate a theology that responds to the cry of the poor without imposing a reductionistic hermeneutic that ends up smothering it. In so doing, Doran lays the foundation for an appropriately thick account of caring for our common home that does not end up replicating the biases of the technocratic paradigm.

While valuing the concern for justice that drives Marxist social theory, Doran finds its conception of society's structure fundamentally flawed, if not destructive. For Doran, Marx identifies the basic social dialectic as one between the relations and forces of production. According to the structure of the scale, however, production is a component of practical intelligence, which itself is only one pole of the dialectic of community (social values). Marxist theory ignores the pole of limitation in the dialectic: the spontaneous intersubjectivity that names the human need for relationship.[84] This disregard typifies the technocratic assumptions at the heart of global injustice today. "Both Western technocracy and Marxism are in fact attempting ... to promote and implement an *exclusively* instrumentalized, technical orientation: an orientation that, as exclusive, would lead precisely to the world we know so well."[85] In this myopic worldview, human praxis ceases to be about making one's life a piece of art that balances limitation and transcendence. Instead, a "nearly exclusive emphasis [is] placed on production" and "instrumentalized technique," resulting in a vision of human dignity that loses its grounding in the limits of creatureliness.[86] The value of the human person—and, one might add, the earth—is reduced to productivity.

The technocratic truncation of the dialectic of community indicates a more fundamental problem embedded in Marxist social theory. Within the scale of values, the delicate dialectic of community is maintained only through a higher, synthesizing principle: the level of cultural values. Authentic, enduring societal change must accordingly attend to this cultural

---

[83] In this, he echoes some of the critiques offered in Congregation for the Doctrine of Faith, *Instruction on Certain Aspects of the "Theology of Liberation"* (August 6, 1984), 7.

[84] Doran, *Theology and the Dialectics of History*, 359–60.

[85] Doran, *Theology and the Dialectics of History*, 390.

[86] Doran, *Theology and the Dialectics of History*, 400–1, 410. See also 399, 415–16.

dimension of human living.⁸⁷ Marxist preoccupations with power, production, and practical intelligence overlook this constitutive role of culture for societal health.⁸⁸ In general, the belief that enduring change comes primarily through the transformation of economics, politics, or technology misses the need for change in the more fundamental meanings and values that underlie them.⁸⁹ Such a technocratic tendency betrays general bias and, by extension, hastens the longer cycle of decline. Doran remarks:

> If Marx's view ... of society is correct, we have no choice but to abandon the option of promoting autonomous cultural values as the radical key to the reversal of the longer cycle of social decline. But if Marx is not correct on this issue, then to accept his position, not as partial critique but as total world view, is to capitulate to the major surrender of intelligence at the root of the longer cycle.⁹⁰

By focusing exclusively on practicality (a social value), Marxist theory collapses the scale to social and vital values. Subsequently, along with cultural values, personal and religious values lose their significance for social processes. Only the violent overthrow of social structures, it is believed, can win success; anything higher is an opiate for the masses that saps the need for revolution. And yet, "[t]o abandon in principle as ideological illusion the promotion of autonomous cultural, personal, and religious values is to succumb to that major surrender of intelligence that is the radical reason for the longer cycle."⁹¹ Marxist social theory overlooks those questions about human living irreducible to economics, technology, or politics. It reduces what matters in human living to the tangibly practical, and, consequently,

---

87 Doran, *Theology and the Dialectics of History*, 409. See also "Psychic Conversion and Spiritual Development," 69: "social change of a major kind does not occur without cultural change, without a transformation of the meanings that people find in or give to their living and operating."

88 Doran, *Theology and the Dialectics of History*, 411. "The tendency or danger of liberation theologies in this regard is to overlook that it is *culture* that is responsible for social integrity. And the tendency or danger of theologies that are afraid of liberation emphases is to forget or repress the fact that one of the responsibilities of culture is precisely *social integrity*." In Doran, *What Is Systematic Theology?*, 176.

89 For instance, changing laws in a way that promote the life of the unborn are insufficient apart from developing the more general "culture of life" as promoted by John Paul II or racism is more than broken social interactions but is instead an entire range of broken meanings and values embedded in social institutions. See Bryan N. Massingale, *Racial Justice and the Catholic Church* (Maryknoll, N.Y.: Orbis Books, 2010), 1–42.

90 Doran, *Theology and the Dialectics of History*, 410. See also 208, 474.

91 Doran, *Theology and the Dialectics of History*, 395.

it perpetuates the biases of technocracy. Ironically then, Marxism replicates the very injustices that it tries to reverse.[92]

Stated otherwise, Marxist social theory conceives historical process solely from below, emphasizing the need for creating to the exclusion of the complementary need for healing.[93] As Doran describes Marx's account of historical process: "in other words, [culture] is an agent of social change only because of the class struggle that is prompted by relations of the dimensions of society from below upwards. . . . The constitution of a superstructure from below upwards results as well in *ideology*: that is, in various articulated forms of social self-consciousness whereby publicly effective conceptions are formulated to influence people's apprehension of themselves."[94]

According to this model, change—securing a more equitable distribution of vital goods, for example—comes only through practical shifts in technology, economics, and politics, not through seemingly imperceptible cultural shifts. When this kind of social transformation does enlist cultural meaning and value, it does so simply to replicate its own biases. Without doubt, practical changes from below carry significance. Exclusive reliance on them, however, can perpetuate the technocratic myopia of general bias and the longer cycle of decline that entraps a community. As Pope Francis makes clear in *Laudato Si'*, the current ecological crisis is one such instance of this tendency. Furthermore, Doran suggests, reform efforts exclusively from below are bound to fail, given the problem of development and the impotence of Promethean efforts to win redemption.[95] The scale of values indicates that redemption instead comes only through an alternative, soteriological culture born from personal authenticity and inspired by religious values, ultimately the result of healing from above. In other words, Marxist thought fails to grasp how distortions on the levels of vital and social values

---

92 Doran, *Theology and the Dialectics of History*, 94, 403, 553.

93 Doran, *Theology and the Dialectics of History*, 406, 410, 416–17, 477. As the previous chapter noted, Lonergan concurs. See his "Healing and Creating in History," in *A Third Collection: Papers by Bernard J. F. Lonergan, S.J.*, ed. Frederick E. Crowe (Mahwah, N.J.: Paulist Press, 1985), 107. For a liberation theology that appropriately incorporates this point, see Gustavo Gutiérrez, *A Theology of Liberation: History, Politics, and Salvation*, rev. ed., trans. Caridad Inda and John Eagleson (Maryknoll, N.Y.: Orbis Books, 1988), 104. See also Andrew Prevot, *Thinking Prayer: Theology and Spirituality Amid the Crises of Modernity* (Notre Dame, Ind.: University of Notre Dame Press, 2015), 218–79.

94 Doran, *Theology and the Dialectics of History*, 407.

95 Doran, *Theology and the Dialectics of History*, 416.

can only be fully rectified through transformations in higher levels of value, transformations that lower levels cannot supply on their own.

A genuine Christian alternative preserves the full scope of the integral scale of values and distinguishes the role of the second vector: healing. The possibility of truly redemptive ecclesial praxis consists in recognizing the importance of autonomous cultural and, by extension, personal values for redemptive recovery.[96] Discipleship consists in something far more radical than lobbying or voting for certain policies. It is significant then that, in outlining an integral ecology, Pope Francis identifies a cultural distortion—the technocratic paradigm—as the primary culprit behind the harm committed against our common home. Like Doran, he accordingly insists on the essential need for cultural transformation, a shift more challenging than is any change in economics, technology, or political policy. Precisely because of the ironclad logic that characterizes the technocratic paradigm, Francis stresses the need for a transformation from above, originating in religious values, to heal our common home.

The Dependence of the Integral Scale on Religious Values

In accounting for the source of cultural transformation from above, Doran distills a third ecclesiological implication: namely, the dependence of the integral scale of values on religious values. A receptivity to transformation from above and a recognition of the healing vector in history both point to the religious values that originate that dynamism. Mirroring Paul VI's assertion that a truly integral development must include a religious component, Doran posits that a truly integral scale of values necessarily includes religious values. Since the effective functioning of lower levels depends on the integrity of higher levels, the whole scale depends ultimately on those religious values.[97] As Doran concludes, "Grace is thus the ultimate condition of possibility of the integrity of the three dialectics constitutive of historical process,"

---

96 Doran, *Theology and the Dialectics of History*, 459. As Neil Ormerod points out, this claim ensures that the church is something other than yet another lobbying group (*Re-Visioning the Church*, 75, 85). See also Ormerod, "The Argument Has Vast Implications: Part II of *Deus Caritas Est*," in *Identity and Mission in Catholic Agencies*, ed. Neil Ormerod (Strathfield, Australia: St. Pauls Publications, 2008), 67–81. For an excellent case study of the pastoral value of recognizing the importance of cultural transformation, see Gerard Whelan, "Culture Building in Kenya: Employing Robert Doran's Thought in Parish Work," in *Meaning and History in Systematic Theology*, 487–508.

97 Doran, *Theology and the Dialectics of History*, 86, 90, 99–100; and *What Is Systematic Theology?*, 174.

since "integrity is a function, not of either of the two constitutive poles of the dialectic, but of a higher synthesis that, in the last analysis, is conditioned by religious values."[98] "Without this grace," he continues elsewhere, "a functioning relation of conditioning from above downwards among the levels of value is impossible."[99] Doran's elaboration of social grace underscores that insight, particularly as religious values generate personal authenticity and a soteriological culture, which in turn secure the health of social values and thus the equitable distribution of vital values. For this reason, he insists that religious values, and the personal values that arise from them, should not "be regarded as constituting a realm of privacy irrelevant to cultural and social process."[100] The logic of the scale of values suggests that the healing generated by religious values ultimately rectifies breakdowns at lower levels. "The Lord hears the cry of the poor" (cf. Ps 34:6); understood through the scale, religious values serve as the definitive response to that cry.

This insight too clarifies the integral ecology that Pope Francis sketches. Like the integral human development of Pope Paul VI, an integral ecology aspires to broaden ecological reflection to incorporate religious meaning and value. Chapter 2 highlights how, in *Laudato Si'*, Francis situates an integral ecology within a doxological, eucharistic context. Only by doing so explicitly can he preserve the comprehensive manner with which Popes John Paul II and Benedict XVI tried to redress the ecological crisis. The dependency of the scale on religious values begins to intimate how eucharistic praise does indeed buoy an integral ecology and spur the comprehensive care that our common home needs. Nevertheless, the exact place of doxology and the Eucharist in the scale of values remains unclear. Before transposing a doxological, eucharistic reading of an integral ecology into a theology of history, a more constructive proposal on the place of the Eucharist within the scale is needed.

THE PLACE OF EUCHARISTIC PRAISE WITHIN THE SCALE OF VALUES

Neither Lonergan nor Doran garners much attention for his liturgical theology. Joseph Komonchak admits that, in constructing a Lonerganian eccle-

---

[98] Doran, *Theology and the Dialectics of History*, 90.

[99] Doran, "The Analogy of Dialectic and the Systematics of History," in *Theological Foundations*, vol. 2, *Theology and Culture*, 524.

[100] Robert M. Doran, "The Analogy of Dialectic and the Systematics of History," 517.

siology, the liturgy and sacraments are areas that "need much further development."[101] Lonergan devotes most of his energy to cognitional theory and theological method. When he does write on theology proper, he invests most of his time pursuing questions in Christology and Trinitarian theology. He spends little time on ecclesiology and, by extension, on the role of the Eucharist in social transformation. Nevertheless, Lonergan did teach a course on sacraments from 1943–44 at the Collège de l'Immaculée-Conception in Montreal and delivered several lectures on the Eucharist in the years following at the Thomas More Institute. During that time, Lonergan penned a devotional piece entitled "The Mass and Man" in which he affirms and waxes poetic about Pope Pius XII's prayer intention for June 1947 that "from the Holy Sacrifice of the Mass be drawn the power of saving human society."[102] As the previous chapter notes, Lonergan belonged to a current of socially engaged Catholicism in the mid-twentieth century. As exemplified by someone like Virgil Michel, the Benedictine pioneer of the liturgical movement, strains of that movement proclaimed the indispensability of the Eucharist for social transformation.[103] Lonergan himself evidences this conviction in "The Mass and Man." Nevertheless, precisely because of his incomplete theology of history, Lonergan ultimately leaves this claim unsubstantiated.

Doran mentions only fleetingly the role of liturgy in *Theology and the Dialectics of History*. For instance, almost as an aside, he writes, "The ministry of the church . . . consists in the promotion, through prophetic witness, *sacramental worship*, and pastoral service of many kinds, of the integral scale of values that would constitute the new law on earth."[104] In the years following *Theology and the Dialectics of History*, Doran admits room for developing and integrating special theological categories like sacraments more fully within the scale.[105] Moreover, he suggests that the general categories provided by the integral scale of values can enrich one's understanding of topics like sacramental worship.[106] The question was a most pressing

---

[101] Joseph A. Komonchak, *Foundations in Ecclesiology*, Lonergan Workshop (Boston: Boston College, 1995), 199.

[102] Bernard J. F. Lonergan, "The Mass and Man," in *Shorter Papers*, 93, 97–98.

[103] See, e.g., Virgil Michel, "The Liturgy: The Basis of Social Regeneration," *Orate Fratres* 9 (1934–35): 536–45.

[104] Doran, *Theology and the Dialectics of History*, 107. Emphasis added.

[105] Doran, *What Is Systematic Theology?*, 70, 74.

[106] Doran, *What Is Systematic Theology?*, 71.

one for Doran's religious order as it emerged from the Second Vatican Council, pronouncing the inseparability of faith and justice for its charism. Pedro Arrupe, superior general of the Society of Jesus during Doran's most formative years, often discussed the relationship between the Eucharist and the church's social mission.[107] Nevertheless, despite the urgency of the question, Doran never specifies how eucharistic praise functions within the scale.[108] Thus, although both Lonergan and Doran acknowledge the importance of the Eucharist for social transformation, neither explains the meaning of such a confession at length. To begin to unpack this claim, one must probe Lonergan's thought in light of Doran's development of the scale of values to discover exactly how "from the Holy Sacrifice of the Mass be drawn the power of saving human society."[109]

A closer examination of the religious values that sustain the scale of values reveals their doxological character. Jeremy Wilkins rightly classifies "the normativity of love and worship" as "the point upon which [Lonergan's] thought was converging" in his career.[110] As Lonergan himself tenders, "Religious conversion is transferring oneself into the world of worship."[111] Thus, the love to which religious conversion responds "reveals to us values we had not appreciated, values of prayer and worship."[112] If religious conversion elicits the self-transcending nature of the human spirit, then it restores, however precariously, the human vocation to praise. Praise anticipates most closely the insatiability of the human spirit, as "[t]he reach, not of man's attainment, but of his intending is unrestricted. There lies within his horizon a region for the divine, a shrine for ultimate holiness."[113] That is, worship makes explicit the human capacity for self-transcendence and gratifies the hungry eros of the human heart. Like for the Jesuit Pope Fran-

---

[107] See, e.g., Pedro Arrupe, "The Eucharist and Hunger," in *Justice with Faith Today*, vol. 2 of *Selected Letters and Addresses*, ed. Jerome Aixala (St. Louis: Institute of Jesuit Sources, 1980), 171–81.

[108] The closest anyone comes is Ormerod, *Re-Visioning the Church*, 159. However, Ormerod's treatment is exceedingly brief and is done so only under the category of ordained ministry.

[109] See footnote 102 of this chapter.

[110] Jeremy D. Wilkins, *Before Truth: Lonergan, Aquinas, and the Problem of Wisdom* (Washington, D.C.: The Catholic University of America Press, 2018), 12.

[111] Bernard J. F. Lonergan, "An Interview with Fr. Bernard Lonergan, S.J.," ed. Philip McShane, in *A Second Collection*, 217. See also Timothy Brunk, "Worshipful Pattern," *Worship* 85, no. 6 (2011): 482–502

[112] Lonergan, *Method in Theology*, 122.

[113] Lonergan, *Method in Theology*, 103.

cis, for the Jesuit Lonergan, "God created human beings to praise, reverence, and serve God, and by doing this, to save their souls."[114] The constant self-transcendence demanded and enlivened by religious conversion is to always live *ad majorem Dei gloriam*. The radical openness of the religiously converted person mirrors the radical openness of the worshipper. Like praise, religious conversion entails a certain ecstatic self-forgetfulness, in which one continually surrenders the narrowness of one's immediate existence—and the egocentrism and biases that entrap one in that existence—and embraces God and God's ordering of the world. That is, conversion entails "the humble surrender of our own light to the self-revealing uncreated Light [that] makes the latter the loved law of all our assents."[115] It is to give oneself away lovingly to this deeper meaning and by so doing, to find one's life and to inhabit the world anew.[116] It is, as expressed in the Ignatian *Suscipe* prayer, a determination to return all that one has been gifted—one's liberty, memory, understanding, and entire will—to God in thanksgiving, a receptivity to the supernatural integration of one's being. The one in love is a *homo adorans*, restlessly oriented to and ablaze for the God in whom one alone finds rest. The quiet undertow, the inner word of God's love, beckons one to live a life of praise.

The "outer word" of God's Word in Christ reveals and evokes definitively this orientation toward praise.[117] To live in Christ Jesus as subject is to conform oneself to the doxological pattern that determined his life.[118] It is to undergo a transformation of one's subjectivity such that, in the spirit of Jesus, one opens oneself up in trusting love and dogged obedience to

---

[114] Ignatius of Loyola, *The Spiritual Exercises of Saint Ignatius*, trans. Anthony Mottola (New York: Doubleday, 1964), 47. See also James L. Connor, ed., *The Dynamism of Desire: Bernard J. F. Lonergan, SJ, on The Spiritual Exercises of Saint Ignatius of Loyola* (Saint Louis, Mo.: The Institute of Jesuit Sources, 2006), 56–69.

[115] Bernard J. F. Lonergan, *Verbum: Word and Idea in Aquinas*, vol. 2 of CWL, ed. Frederick E. Crowe and Robert M. Doran (Toronto: University of Toronto Press, 1997), 101.

[116] Lonergan, *Method in Theology*, 105–6; and *Understanding and Being: The Halifax Lectures on Insight*, vol. 5 of CWL, ed. Elizabeth A. Morelli and Mark D. Morelli, rev. Frederick E. Crowe (Toronto: University of Toronto Press, 2005), 377. See also Frederick G. Lawrence, "The Fragility of Consciousness: Lonergan and the Postmodern Concern for the Other," in *The Fragility of Consciousness: Faith, Reason, and the Human Good*, ed. Randall S. Rosenberg and Kevin M. Vander Schel (Toronto: University of Toronto Press, 2017), 274–75.

[117] See Charles Hefling, "Lonergan's *Cur Deus Homo*: Revisiting the 'Law of the Cross,'" in *Meaning and History in Systematic Theology*, 165.

[118] See, e.g., Edward Schillebeeckx, *Christ, the Sacrament of the Encounter with God* (New York: Sheed and Ward, 1963), 17–19, 30, 37–39.

the will of the Father, regardless of its costs. In this sacrificial spirit, one participates in the priesthood of Christ and, in a broken world, its inevitably cruciform shape.[119] In Lonergan's words, behind the Law of the Cross lies "the chief act of *religious worship*, the act of sacrifice. . . . It is the spirit of adoration . . . more simply and more solidly recognizing [God's] supreme dominion and surrendering to Him all that one is with all one's heart and all one's soul and all one's mind and all one's strength."[120] In the face of sin and bias, death accepted out of love becomes an act of self-pouring worship; rather than clinging to self-prerogatives, the loving offering of one's entire being exhibits an unwavering, trusting, self-transcending devotion to God and God's purposes.[121] Genuine dramatic artistry thus takes the form of outstretched arms on a cross, a "sacrifice of praise" pleasing to God (Heb 13:15). Doran desires to capture the "Trinitarian mysticism" of Lonergan.[122] Indeed, in the glorification of God the Father, through being conformed to Christ's priesthood in the Spirit, humans are drawn into the perichoretic doxology that is the triune God. "Father, . . . give glory to your son, so that your son may glorify you," Jesus prays in the face of death (Jn 17:1). The ecstasy of worship participates in the eternal ecstasy of the Trinity and, in this, worship saves.[123] To live in Christ and in fidelity to his Spirit, to surrender to the Father's love in praise, breaks one open to the trusting self-abandon that unrestricted knowing, valuing, and loving demands.

For Lonergan and the Catholic tradition alike, the ordinary means for this graced conversion and participation are the sacraments, chief among

---

[119] For a discussion of the priesthood of Christ, including in the context of the liturgy, see Bernard J. F. Lonergan, "Theses 15–17 of *De Verbo Incarnato*," in *The Redemption*, vol. 9 of CWL, ed. Robert M. Doran, H. Daniel Monsour, and Jeremy D. Wilkins, trans. Michael G. Shields (Toronto: University of Toronto Press, 2018), 53, 67, 73; and "The Redemption: A Supplement," in *The Redemption*, 621.

[120] Lonergan, "The Mass and Man," 95–96. Emphasis added. See also Bernard J. F. Lonergan, "The Notion of Sacrifice," in *Early Latin Theology*, vol. 19 of CWL, ed. Robert M. Doran and H. Daniel Monsour, trans. Michael G. Shields (Toronto: University of Toronto Press, 2011), 29–31, 37.

[121] See, e.g., Joseph Ratzinger, "Taking Bearings in Christology," in *Behold the Pierced One: An Approach to a Spiritual Christology*, trans. Graham Harrison (San Francisco: Ignatius Press, 1986), 22.

[122] Doran, *The Trinity in History* vol. 1, *Missions and Processions*, 157.

[123] For a developed account of the Trinity as a relationship of mutual glorification, see Khaled Anatolios, *Deification through the Cross: An Eastern Christian Theology of Salvation* (Grand Rapids, Mich.: Eerdmans, 2020), 229–63.

them the Eucharist.[124] In the Eucharist, one encounters most truly the mystery—as Lonergan understands mystery—of the "just and *mysterious* Law of the Cross."[125] Religious conversion entails something more than intellectual approval; instead, it requires universal willingness, the consent of one's whole being, such that one becomes a being in love through dying to self. After all, for both Lonergan and Doran, the human drama of vice and virtue arises at the intersection between the unrestricted demands of the human spirit and the experiential, psychic limitations of embodied living (cf. Rom 7:15–20). Mystery, the previous chapter made clear, elicits the human person's unrestricted orientation toward God, aligning not only one's intellect but also one's psyche, experience, and affective willingness—all that one has been gifted—toward this end. Lonergan suggests elsewhere that a mystery is a "symbol," "an image of a real or imaginary object that evokes a feeling or is evoked by a feeling."[126] Emphasized by Doran and illustrated by Pope Francis, this type of symbolic meaning can challenge a technocratic age that ignores the experiential, affective dimensions—the "heart"—of living.[127]

The central role of symbol for human authenticity grounds Lonergan's understanding of the soteriological centrality of the Eucharist. As he explains, "The eucharistic sacrifice is a proper symbol of the sacrificial attitude of Christ as Head, first, as that attitude is represented in the sacrifice of the cross, second, as flowing to the members of the church through multiplication of the eucharistic sacrifice, and third, as now multiplied in the members themselves through their active participation."[128] Participation in

---

[124] See Stephen Happel, "Sacrament: Symbol of Conversion," in *Creativity and Method: Essays in Honor of Bernard Lonergan*, ed. Matthew Lamb (Milwaukee, Wis.: Marquette University Press, 1981), 275–90.

[125] See Lonergan, "Theses 15–17 of *De Verbo Incarnato*," 205; and "The Redemption: A Supplement," 473. As Lonergan writes in *Insight*, without explicit reference to the Law of the Cross, "the emergent trend and the full realization of [God's] solution [to evil] must include the sensible data that are demanded by man's sensitive nature and that will command his attention, nourish his imagination, stimulate his intelligence and will, release his affectivity, control his aggressivity, and, as central features of the world of sense, intimate its finality, its yearning for God" (745).

[126] Lonergan, *Method in Theology*, 64. "You can't talk to your body without symbols," Lonergan says. "An Interview with Fr. Bernard Lonergan, S.J.," 225. See also Lonergan, "The Notion of Sacrifice," 7.

[127] Doran, *Theology and the Dialectics of History*, 512–13. Indeed, the affective, experiential side of living represents human "limitation," thus providing a check on anthropologies geared toward too much "transcendence."

[128] Lonergan, "The Notion of Sacrifice," 29; see also 21, 23. The cited passage confirms Frederick Crowe's assertion that Lonergan's enduring interest in Christ's historical causality

the mystery of the eucharistic celebration conforms all that one is—experientially, psychically, affectively, and intellectually—to the cruciform shape of the grace of Christ and, by extension, invites one to abide fully in his doxological spirit (Jn 15:5). Importantly, for Lonergan, symbol does not mean merely a symbol; it is only the real, enduring presence of Christ in the Eucharist that can offer congregants the full possibility for this transformative union with Christ and his Spirit, to become what they receive.[129] Participation in the Eucharist grants incorporation into Christ's "incarnate meaning," who Jesus was and what he wanted, the heart of his being.[130] Symbol, technically understood, serves that unitive end. The symbolic character of the Eucharist persuades, inspiring and moving Christians in their bodily existence to live in Christ as subject, to be a friend of God who experiences, understands, judges, and decides with the mind and heart of Christ.[131] The Eucharist offers worshippers entry into the mystery of the Law of the Cross *hic et nunc*; it arouses the religious conversion that sustains human authenticity, albeit dialectically. The Eucharist orients one to praise the always-greater God, to live for God's greater glory, and to withdraw from inauthenticity. Prayed through the Trinity, eucharistic worship thus proleptically elevates one into God's interpersonal life, simultaneously grounding unity in interpersonal relations on earth; everything is interconnected. Eucharistic worship reconfigures one's entire being, evoking the thirst for God intimated in the unrestricted yearning of the human spirit, the doxological telos of the human heart.

In this way the Eucharist makes the church, supplying both ground and goal of its redemptive mission as the body of Christ in history.[132]

---

manifested itself partly through his brief forays into sacramental theology. See his *Christ and History: The Christology of Bernard Lonergan from 1935 to 1982* (Ottawa: Novalis, 2005), 41–42.

[129] See Joseph C. Mudd, *Eucharist as Meaning: Critical Metaphysics and Contemporary Sacramental Theology* (Collegeville, Minn.: Liturgical Press, 2014), 201–24.

[130] On "incarnate meaning," see Lonergan, *Method in Theology*, 73. Lonergan introduces "incarnate meaning" with the Latin adage, "*cor ad cor loquitur.*"

[131] After a discussion of symbolic meaning, highlighting how the sacrifice of the Mass is a "memorial," Lonergan writes, "this external commemoration *arouses* a sacrificial attitude." "The Notion of Sacrifice," 21, emphasis added. He also states, "The efficacy of the sacrifice... operates at a deeper level, and is the source from which flow the power of the sacraments as well as both the *willingness* to receive them and the *dispositions* required for their fruitful reception." "The Notion of Sacrifice," 21, emphasis added.

[132] Raymond Moloney describes the ecclesiological character of Lonergan's theology of the Eucharist as "remarkable for its time." See "Lonergan on Eucharistic Sacrifice," *Theological Studies* 62, no. 1 (2001): 53–70, at 56.

Through the eucharistic celebration, the church brings Christ's real presence into history, living out that ecstatic, sacrificial presence in its very life as it participates in the ecstatic, sacrificial Trinitarian missions.[133] Against the quasi-idolatrous egocentrism of biases, the church's worship witnesses to the insufficiency of a purely natural conception of history, the dependency of the integral scale of values on religious values, the need for healing and mercy in history, and the passionate orientation of the cosmos to otherworldly, triune love. The church's work of praise witnesses to the claim that the world finds its end in worship, not biased practicality. Following the logic of the Law of the Cross, this noncoercive, nontechnocratic, and sacramental witness of praise introduces a redemptive scheme of recurrence into history that transforms all levels of value. Through this witness, the church mediates the healing vector in history, God's mercy to the world. The Eucharist joins the church to the heart of its crucified Lord, the sacrificial spirit that, as Doran suggested, marks service to the integral scale of values and the healing that restores it.[134] The work of God before it is the work of the people; eucharistic worship gradually socializes the church's members in a distinct set of redemptive meanings and values undergone "from above." The liturgy invites Christians to embody the meaning of the Eucharist throughout their entire lives, such that religious conversion permeates all of one's life, Christ governs one's (inter)subjectivity, the cross becomes the law of one's living, and one "glorifies the Lord by [one's] life." In an emergently probable world and despite its seeming impracticality, the celebration of the Eucharist, "sacrament of salvation," sets the conditions of possibility for the salvific transformation of the entire world.[135]

In other words, the Eucharist incarnates religious value—that on which the integrity of the scale rests—and, accordingly, mediates social grace, the downward vector of healing in history. As Lonergan concludes in "The Mass and Man," "It is on this prior and deeper level that the Sacrifice of the Mass

---

[133] See Eugene R. Schlesinger, *Missa Est! A Missional Liturgical Ecclesiology* (Minneapolis, Minn.: Fortress Press, 2017), 77–81.

[134] This is also a point fleshed out (from a non-Lonerganian angle) by Timothy P. O'Malley, *Liturgy and the New Evangelization: Practicing the Art of Self-Giving Love* (Collegeville, Minn.: Liturgical Press, 2014).

[135] See Christopher McMahon, "Cruciform Salvation and Emergent Probability: The Liturgical Significance of Lonergan's Precept," in *Approaching the Threshold of Mystery: Liturgical Worlds and Theological Spaces*, ed. Joris Geldhof, Daniel Minch, and Trevor Maine, 198–212 (Regensburg, Germany: Verlag Friedrich Pustet, 2015).

is the source of the power to save human society."[136] From this eucharistic encounter, all else follows; as Lonergan writes, those who undergo religious conversion are "ready to deliberate and judge and decide and act with the easy freedom of those that do all good because they are in love."[137] Doxology shapes one's sanctity; the Eucharist determines one's being. These authentic personal values condition the soteriological culture able to reverse the cultural and social distortions that inhibit the equitable distribution of vital goods. Stated otherwise, the Eucharist effects the healing mercy that ultimately responds to the cry of the poor, as understood through the scale. In this way, the church's sacramental worship promotes the full flourishing of the integral scale of values, both within and beyond its visible confines. Conversely, the scale of values helps explain how "from the Holy Sacrifice of the Mass be drawn the power of saving human society." In the words of the second eucharistic preface, "It is truly right and just, our duty and our salvation, always and everywhere to give you thanks, Father most holy, through your beloved Son, Jesus Christ." The theology of history described above begins to elucidate the mystery of how praise and thanksgiving (*Eucharistia*) is in fact our salvation. What remains to be explored is to understand how praise and thanksgiving is the salvation of our common home.

CONCLUSION

Reflecting upon Lonergan's definition of theology as the mediation between religion and a cultural matrix, Doran holds that "the situation which a theology addresses is as much a source of theology as are the data provided by the Christian tradition."[138] Without sacrificing the truth of the Christian tradition, Doran aspires to live out the Thomistic spirit that animated Lonergan's own capacious project and, by so doing, penetrate ever more deeply the permanently and perennially valid truth of the Christian tradition. That the situation plays a constitutive role for Doran's theology is clear. Pastoral exigencies spur his reflections: questions concerning the relationship between faith and justice, the contributions of liberation theologies, and the structural components of redemption that could match structural components of decline. Moreover, his engagement with the contemporary situation

---

[136] Lonergan, "The Mass and Man," 98.

[137] Lonergan, *Method in Theology*, 107.

[138] Doran, *Theology and the Dialectics of History*, 8; see also 12–16. See also Whelan, *Redeeming History*, 202–10.

is not facilely irenic. As his engagement with liberation theology typifies, Doran discerns charitably and dialectically both the insights and oversights that a given situation offers.

In this spirit, inspired by his times and his ministry, Doran begins to bring Lonergan's work into dialogue with care for our common home, a pillar of the situation today. He positions, for instance, the preferential option for the poor within a theology of history. He identifies the importance of cosmological meaning and value for cultural integrity, and he critiques mechanomorphic, anthropocentric distortions that would truncate this side of culture. On the level of personal authenticity, he attends more closely to the importance of recognizing one's limitations, one's being made *imago mundi*. He likewise explains how the church might mediate redemption in a way that avoids technocratic presuppositions. The synthetic breadth of Doran's integral scale of values largely mirrors the catholic vision behind the integral ecology set forth by Pope Francis.

The theology of history elaborated by Lonergan and Doran does more than parallel the integral ecology of *Laudato Si'*, however. Most importantly, it sanctions the placement of all these themes within the same explanatory matrix, such that the relationships between them might be related to each other. For instance, it can situate eucharistic praise in relationship to the cries of the earth and poor as well as to the technocratic paradigm. Coordinating these components in relationship to each other can solidify the comprehensive approach that Catholic social teaching takes to environmental concern and its doxological, eucharistic underpinnings. Indeed, it would better show how everything is in fact connected.

Still, in the spirit of the expansive dynamism of the Lonergan project, the engagement with today's situation remains incomplete. By no means repudiating the tradition that precedes him, Pope Francis has outlined the contours of the contemporary situation and the church's response to these exigencies in *Laudato Si'*. What remains is to bring Lonergan's theology of history, as interpreted by Doran, into dialogue with the integral ecology of *Laudato Si'*. This task has already begun; the doxological, eucharistic character of this integral ecology drives one to consider the central place of the eucharistic worship within this theology of history, a question left unanswered by both Lonergan and Doran. Indeed, prompted by *Laudato Si'*, this chapter has outlined a systematic, liturgically cast social theory and a eucharistic ecclesiology that can capture the radicality of its integral ecology. Other questions remain for developing such a theory, such as how to understand systematically an option for the earth, a priestly anthropology, or the praise of all creation. Thus, not only do the questions raised in *Laudato Si'* demand explanatory exploration, so too in no small way does *Laudato Si'* determine the shape of that explanatory exploration. In this way might the situation provide a fertile locus for continuing theological reflection, allowing one to do for our common home what Aquinas did for the thirteenth century.

Part 3

A Eucharistic Vision of Care for Our Common Home within a Eucharistic Theology of History

Chapter 5

A Eucharistic Integral Ecology

The previous two chapters adverted to Lonergan's distinction between explanation and description. They outlined what he viewed as an explanatory framework for the church's mission, more often described than explained. This final chapter goes a step further for, as Lonergan acknowledges, explanation is insufficient by itself. In his words, "But explanation does not give man a home. . . . [A]s explanation is reached through description, so it must be applied concretely by turning from explanation back to the descriptive world of things for us."[1] Turning Lonergan's theology of history back to the descriptive world of *Laudato Si'* captures the doxological and eucharistic character of the encyclical's integral ecology and the sources—especially the writings of popes John Paul II and Benedict XVI—that undergird it. As Gerard Whelan surmises, Lonergan's thought can add "explanatory depth" to the pastoral vision of Pope Francis.[2] Similarly expansive in scope, Lonergan's theology of history, especially as developed in the previous chapter, can make intelligible the eucharistic vision of *Laudato Si'*.

This chapter does more than apply Lonergan's thought to interpret an integral ecology, however. At one point, Lonergan likens the relationship between explanation and description to a pair of scissor blades.[3] An upper blade of explanation enriches the organization of descriptive data and shapes the way that one encounters, understands, and responds to that data. A lower blade of description, meanwhile, brings explanatory theories into contact with the real world, prompting their further refinement. That is, not only does explanation generate development in description, so too does description generate development in explanation.[4] By raising the questions

---

1 Bernard J. F. Lonergan, *Insight: A Study of Human Understanding*, vol. 3 of CWL, ed. Frederick E. Crowe and Robert M. Doran (Toronto: University of Toronto Press, 2005), 570.

2 Gerard Whelan, *A Discerning Church: Pope Francis, Lonergan, and a Theological Method for the Future* (New York: Paulist Press, 2019), xiv.

3 Lonergan, *Insight*, 114–15, 337–38, 546, 554, 600.

4 See Bernard J. F. Lonergan, *Method in Theology* (New York: Herder and Herder, 1972), 82. See also *Insight*, 316–24.

to be resolved through explanation, description sets the parameters for explanatory reflection, oftentimes stretching those parameters toward new insights. In this case, the calls of *Laudato Si'* can enlarge Lonergan's theology of history to better account for our common home, making the work of Lonergan more apt for the level of our day and more responsive to the contemporary situation. As chapter 4 concludes, the situation provides a genuine source for deepening theological insight.

Ecclesiological reflection arises in the space between these two scissor blades in the asymptotic attempt to complete the circle between description and explanation.[5] In bringing all the previous chapters together, this chapter operates in that space. It proffers a vision of the doxological, eucharistic character of the church's mission in our common home that both arises from and expands Lonergan's theology of history. Not only does the chapter demonstrate the enduring, flexible relevance of Lonergan's thought, so too does it crystallize the doxological, eucharistic character of the church's social and environmental mission as intimated by popes John Paul II and Benedict XVI in their environmental writings and described in a definitive way by Pope Francis in *Laudato Si'*. The radically theological character of Lonergan's theology of history makes clear the radically Catholic character of *Laudato Si'* and vice-versa.

DECLINE IN OUR COMMON HOME: THE CRY OF THE POOR AND THE CRY OF THE EARTH

A Breakdown in Vital and Elemental Values

In *Laudato Si'*, the cries of the earth and the poor connect the concerns of natural and human ecology "from below." Along with the more traditional preferential option for the poor, Francis includes a preferential option for the earth in describing the church's social mission. As confirmed by the inductive approach of *Laudato Si'* and its use of cry language, both options enjoy a hermeneutical privilege in the church's care for our common home. Both refer to breakdowns within the scale of values at its most fundamental levels. The cry of the poor describes breakdowns on the level of vital values: the maldistribution of necessities like food, water, and shelter; the breakdown of relationships, and, in sum, the breakdown of the possibility of

---

[5] Neil Ormerod, *Re-Visioning the Church: An Experiment in Systematic-Historical Ecclesiology* (Minneapolis, Minn.: Fortress Press, 2014), 8–10.

human life and its flourishing. The first chapter of *Laudato Si'* calls attention to social crises like global inequality, the squalor of cities, and the proliferation of environmental refugees.[6] Francis also stresses that this cry bellows from all vulnerable populations, including the unborn, a central preoccupation of the human ecology as first formulated by John Paul II.[7] The scale of values allows one to understand how attending to the cry of the poor attunes one to what is happening to our common home, at least in part.

Less clear is the place of the cry of the earth (or an option for the earth) within the scale of values. Francis implies that the cry of the earth functions similarly to the cry of the poor, though, given its novelty in Catholic social teaching, further explanation is needed. As Lonergan makes clear, an emergently probable worldview presumes the dependency of human persons on chemistry and biology, without making them reducible to either. While, as lower orders, these delicate ecologies possess their own integrity—an intrinsic value—certain biological and chemical schemes of recurrence set the conditions for the recurring schemes of vital values that sustain human life.[8] This claim deserves fuller development, given the exigencies named by *Laudato Si'*. Indeed, the integral ecology of *Laudato Si'* demands an expansion of the scale of values to incorporate what this book calls *elemental values*: the biological and chemical substrata that underpin vital values. Just as the cry of the poor names breakdowns within vital values, the cry of the earth names breakdowns within these elemental values and disruptions within their schemes of recurrence. The first chapter of *Laudato Si'* lists problems such as biodiversity loss, water pollution and depletion, excessive deforestation, and accelerating changes in climate.[9] As Francis teaches, and the logic of the scale of values corroborates, distortions within elemental values disrupt the equi-

---

[6] Francis, Encyclical Letter *Laudato Si'* (May 24, 2015), 43–52.

[7] *Laudato Si'*, 117.

[8] As Lonergan writes:

> [T]he intelligible orders that are invented, implemented, adjusted and improved by men are but further exploitations of prehuman intelligible orders; moreover, they fall within the universal order of generalized emergent probability, both as consequents of its fertility and as ruled by its more inclusive sweep. If the intelligible orders of human invention are a good because they systematically ensure the satisfaction of desires, then so also are the intelligible orders that underlie, condition, precede, and include man's invention. Finally, intelligible orders and their contents, as possible objects of rational choice, are values. *Insight*, 628.

See also Patrick H. Byrne, *The Ethics of Discernment: Lonergan's Foundations for Ethics* (Toronto: University of Toronto Press, 2016), 360–61, 393–400.

[9] *Laudato Si'*, 20–42.

table distribution of vital values. Extreme deforestation, for instance, not only destroys animal habitats. It also deprives human beings of an essential source of oxygen. And, as a region like the Amazon illustrates, the poor bear the brunt disproportionately when such elemental schemes of recurrence undergo disruption.[10] While the scale of values crystallizes the meaning of an option for the earth, so too does Francis's introduction of an option for the earth expand Lonergan's theology of history in a more ecological key.

The relationship between these two cries within the scale also helps explain some of the tensions discussed in chapter 1. Because the cry of the earth refers to breakdowns on levels lower than that of vital values (and certainly that of personal values), the concerns of human ecology lie higher on the scale than those of natural ecology. John Paul II's reference to the "more serious" need to preserve human ecology emphasizes this point.[11] However, the negotiation of complex value claims in the scale of values is not a rigid hierarchicalism in the sense that higher levels are more important at the expense of lower levels. Instead, insofar as they are located in an emergent and integral ecology, higher levels depend on lower levels even if higher levels perfect lower levels. The dependence of vital values on elemental values therefore signals the ultimate inseparability of the two levels. In order to secure the effective functioning of vital values and the flourishing of human life, elemental values must be secured and preserved. Elemental and vital values stand as inextricably tied. Together, the cry of the earth and the cry of the poor signal the depth of decline within our common home. Granting these cries hermeneutical priority requires examining how higher levels either exacerbate or answer them.

Social Decline

The many factors that amplify these cries manifest the social, cultural, personal, and religious dimensions of the ecological crisis. The comprehensive response to environmental concern taken by John Paul II, Benedict XVI, and Francis captures this key insight. On the level of social values—ideally, what secures the regular distribution of vital goods and thus respects the elemental values that underlie them—Francis decries the extreme imbalances to which the cries point. In his words,

---

[10] *Laudato Si'*, 38. See Francis, Post-Synodal Apostolic Exhortation *Querida Amazonia* (February 12, 2020), 47–52.

[11] John Paul II, Encyclical Letter *Centesimus Annus* (May 1, 1991), 38.

> A true "ecological debt" exists, particularly between the global north and south, connected to commercial imbalances with effects on the environment, and the disproportionate use of natural resources by certain countries over long periods of time. The export of raw materials to satisfy markets in the industrialized north has caused harm locally, as for example in mercury pollution in gold mining or sulphur dioxide pollution in copper mining.... The warming caused by huge consumption on the part of some rich countries has repercussions on the poorest areas of the world, especially Africa, where a rise in temperature, together with drought, has proved devastating for farming. There is also the damage caused by the export of solid waste and toxic liquids to developing countries, and by the pollution produced by companies which operate in less developed countries in ways they could never do at home, in the countries in which they raise their capital.[12]

Rampant consumption in the global north frequently comes at the expense of vital and elemental values in the global south. This situation betrays what Lonergan labels group bias, wherein the wants of wealthier populations appear more pressing than do the needs of poorer populations. Growing social inequalities only evidence the growing power of this bias.

A disordered relationship between politics, economics, technology (the operations of what Lonergan calls "practical intelligence"), and the bonds of human community (what Lonergan calls "spontaneous intersubjectivity") perpetuates this power. The cries of the earth and the poor reveal a broken dialectic between transcendence and limitation on the level of social values, the fragile relationship between the progressive dynamism of practical development and the inertial demands of social relationships, respectively. Francis worries how, in current times, instead of supporting human community, politics serves economic interests and economics serves a perverted understanding of technology. As opposed to a politics that serves the common good, a "politics concerned with immediate results, supported by consumerist sectors of the population, is driven to produce short-term growth," despite the costs to local and global communities.[13] Bereft of a genuine politics, the needs of human community are excluded for the ostensibly more practical sake of profit maximization and technological advance. Not only does this myopia displace the human

---

12 *Laudato Si'*, 51.
13 *Laudato Si'*, 178. See also 181, 189.

person, so too does it devastate the earth: "Where profits alone count, there can be no thinking about the rhythms of nature, its phases of decay and regeneration, or the complexity of ecosystems which may be gravely upset by human intervention."[14] Technology developed only for economic purposes supplants the limitations set by both the human community and the community of creation.[15] Furthermore, as the breakdown in politics suggests, seemingly no higher recourse—the possibility of asking whether this social arrangement is actually good—can enlarge this telos. The "alliance between the economy and technology ends up sidelining anything unrelated to its immediate interests."[16] The escalation of group biases, the breakdown of the relationship between community and practicality, and the failure to provide some alternative all indicate a corruption on an even more pervasive level than that of social values.

General Bias and the Technocratic Paradigm

At the heart of the ecological crisis, then, stands a cultural crisis. Both Francis and Lonergan save their level of deepest concern for this type of decline. Describing it as "a certain way of understanding human life and activity . . . gone awry," Francis identifies the "technocratic paradigm" as the root cultural corruption that causes the earth and the poor alike to cry out.[17] Francis's recognition of how technology reframes human living suggests that the technocratic paradigm shapes the meanings and values that inform a way of life, what Lonergan understands as the level of culture. Furthermore, as a higher order, culture synthesizes and sustains levels below it. Culture for Lonergan provides the soul of the social order, "the matrix within which persons develop."[18] As Francis ascertains, the technocratic paradigm "ends up conditioning lifestyles and social possibilities" and "tends to dominate economic and political life."[19] This paradigm, as a cultural phenomenon, conditions the meanings and values intended in the workings of practicality, as well as the possibility for life-giving community.

[14] *Laudato Si'*, 190.
[15] *Laudato Si'*, 113, 136.
[16] *Laudato Si'*, 54.
[17] *Laudato Si'*, 101.
[18] Bernard J. F. Lonergan, "Revolution in Catholic Theology," in *A Second Collection*, ed. William F. J. Ryan and Bernard Tyrell (Philadelphia: The Westminster Press, 1974), 233.
[19] *Laudato Si'*, 107, 109.

The technocratic paradigm represents something of an anticulture, however, setting the conditions for the impossibility of life-giving community and the unraveling of a practicality that genuinely serves this end. Under the technocratic paradigm, biased and short-sighted practicality governs the meanings and values that inform a way of life. With the rise of the technocratic paradigm, in Lonergan's words, "culture ceases to be an independent factor that passes a detached yet effective judgment upon capital formation and technology, upon economy and polity. To justify its existence, it ha[s] to be become more and more practical, more and more a factor within the technological, economic, political process, more and more a tool that serve[s] palpably useful ends."[20] As it subsumes culture, the immediate, nonreflective bent of practicality dissipates the long-term questions that cultural values should raise. Instead of serving the human person, practicality comes to rule human living, collapsing the entire scale of values. In words that could have come from *Laudato Si'*, Lonergan writes,

> What is settling everything is technological possibility. It is settling every aspect of the individual's private living, of the conditions of his living— what his cities are like, what his vacations are like, everything he does in his work. And who is running it? Concrete technological possibility. There is no room for personal decision, personal achievement, personal taste, personal significance. This is a case of economic determinism resulting from a lack of individuals who know their own minds and live their own lives.... The same result can appear on the level of science.... There can result an estrangement of man's world from man. Man sets up an inhuman order because he conceives man as a component in a machine; and man hates that machine.... The whole world, the whole social setup, is something alien to man.[21]

---

[20] Lonergan, *Insight*, 262.

[21] Bernard J. F. Lonergan, *Topics in Education*, vol. 10 of CWL, ed. Frederick E. Crowe and Robert M. Doran (Toronto: University of Toronto, 1993), 45–46. See also this from Lonergan:
> Applied science and consequent inventions have given us our vast industrial, commercial, financial, administrative, educational, military complex. Technicians are the people with the task of figuring out the most efficient use of currently available hardware. The more successful they are, the greater is the domain that they organize, and the less the domain under the control of old-style decision-makers, of managers, directors, mayors, governors, presidents. Again, the more brilliant they are, the less is it possible to explain to the uninitiated why things are done the way in which they done. Finally, the more thorough the application of the principle of efficiency, the more must men adapt themselves to its dictates in all their labor hours and in all the goods and services they purchase from the technological establishment. ("The Response of the Jesuit Priest and Apostle in the Modern World," in *A Second Collection*, 186)

This disillusionment with the world originates from the myopic despotism of a practicality that values only immediate benefit. A positivism reduces the world to simply what one can see, untethering it from its deeper meaning and call toward responsibility. As a result, the broader world vanishes from one's horizon of concern, and both creation and the social setup suffer accordingly.

The technocratic paradigm produces not simply an alien world but also the conditions of possibility for actions or, rather, inactions of alienation: the globalization of indifference. The sclerotic anthropocentrism of the technocratic paradigm betrays a "practical relativism" that anesthetizes people to the needs of others. Developing Benedict XVI's critique of a dictatorship of relativism, Francis explains that "[w]hen human beings place themselves at the center, they give absolute priority to immediate convenience and all else becomes relative."[22] The technocratic paradigm instantiates general bias, as it elevates the short-term, utilitarian logic of practicality to an exclusive norm, rendering one indifferent to all other considerations deemed impractical to oneself or one's group. As focused on the immediate, this cultural bias refuses a long view of history and shunts insights that question the sustainability of immediate gratification, ceaseless consumption, and delusions of luxury.

In normalizing the shortsightedness of bias, the technocratic paradigm conditions the recurrence of group and individual biases. It produces scotoses that blind one to the cries of the earth and the poor, as well as the privileged insights that those cries offer on what is happening in and what one

---

[22] *Laudato Si'*, 122. Francis decries this "practical relativism" on several occasions. See this from Francis:

> In many places, the problem is more that of widespread indifference and relativism, linked to disillusionment and the crisis of ideologies which has come about as a reaction to anything which might appear totalitarian. This not only harms the Church but the fabric of society as a whole. We should recognize how in a culture where each person wants to be bearer of his or her own subjective truth, it becomes difficult for citizens to devise a common plan which transcends individual gain and personal ambitions. (Apostolic Exhortation *Evangelii Gaudium* [November 24, 2013], 61)

See also this from Francis:

> Pastoral workers can thus fall into a relativism which, whatever their particular style of spirituality or way of thinking, proves even more dangerous than doctrinal relativism. It has to do with the deepest and inmost decisions that shape their way of life. This practical relativism consists in acting as if God did not exist, making decisions as if the poor did not exist, setting goals as if others did not exist, working as if people who have not received the Gospel did not exist. (*Evangelii Gaudium*, 80)

is doing to our common home.²³ The shrunken horizon of general bias decouples the human person from the natural and social limits that should characterize right living, as bias elevates self-concern to the detriment of all other concerns. The technocratic paradigm atrophies the solidarity that Benedict XVI understands as so central to resolving the current crisis. On the one hand, the technocratic paradigm divorces individuals from what Robert Doran calls cosmological meaning and value, the natural schemes of recurrence and elemental values that should limit human activity. Non-human creation becomes an intrusion to human living, rather than a grammar that beckons patient cooperation. On the other hand, the technocratic paradigm divorces individuals from the demands of human intersubjectivity. In the words of Francis, "When people become self-centered and self-enclosed, their greed increases. . . . It becomes almost impossible to accept the limits imposed by reality. In this horizon, a genuine sense of the common good also disappears. As these attitudes become more widespread, social norms are respected only to the extent that they do not clash with personal needs."²⁴ The egoism of bias shrivels the good to only oneself, and thus the general bias of the technocratic paradigm sets the conditions for a recurring cultural heartlessness.

In its disregard for limitations, general bias devastates our common home. Freed from one's dependence on the earth and on others, one can do as one pleases. In a way that Lonergan does not, Francis underscores the violent character of these forces:

> The culture of relativism is the same disorder which drives one person to take advantage of another, to treat others as mere objects, imposing forced labor on them or enslaving them to pay their debts. The same kind of thinking leads to the sexual exploitation of children and abandonment of the elderly who no longer serve our interests. It is also the mindset of those who say: Let us allow the invisible forces of the market to regulate the economy, and consider their impact on society and nature as collateral damage. In the absence of objective truths or sound principles other than the satisfaction of our own desires and immediate needs, what limits can be placed on human trafficking, organized crime, the drug trade, com-

---

23 Kate Ward, "Scotosis and Structural Inequality: The Dangers of Bias in a Globalized Age," in *Everything Is Interconnected: Towards a Globalization with a Human Face and an Integral Ecology*, ed. Joseph Ogbonnaya and Lucas Briola, 39–56 (Milwaukee, Wis.: Marquette University, 2019).

24 *Laudato Si'*, 204.

merce in blood diamonds and the fur of endangered species? Is it not the same relativistic logic which justifies buying the organs of the poor for resale or use in experimentation, or eliminating children because they are not what their parents wanted? This same "use and throw away" logic generates so much waste, because of the disordered desire to consume more than what is really necessary. We should not think that political efforts or the force of law will be sufficient to prevent actions which affect the environment because, when the culture itself is corrupt and objective truth and universally valid principles are no longer upheld, then laws can only be seen as arbitrary impositions or obstacles to be avoided.[25]

Such are the libertine consequences of bias when it provides the matrix within which the social order develops. Francis reiterates here that this phenomenon exists on the level of culture and, since cultural values provide the soul of social values, systematically distorts the entire social order: whether unfettered neoliberal capitalism, illegal trade, human trafficking, or abortion. The same throwaway logic likewise leads to the rapid depletion of natural resources and pollution.[26] The trade of blood diamonds, for instance, reveals the selfish valuing of profit over those victimized—both human and nonhuman—in diamond production. Across a range of problems, this throwaway culture victimizes both the earth and the poor, and so Francis's move to this more comprehensive level of cultural diagnosis allows him to link the concerns of natural and human ecologies. What Doran identifies as mechanomorphic imperialism threatens what Benedict XVI identifies as the common "grammar" that underlies human and natural ecologies alike. All cases evidence how the technocratic paradigm "exalts the concept of a subject who, using logical and rational procedures, progressively approaches and gains control over an external object."[27] Rather than a call to care, limitations—whether human community or the rest of creation—become obstacles to be ignored or manipulated for one's own immediate advantage. The heartlessness of general bias thus results from and produces a "tyrannical anthropocentrism" that not only refuses to hear the cries of the earth and the poor but also causes them to cry out more loudly.[28]

25 *Laudato Si'*, 123.
26 *Laudato Si'*, 20–22.
27 *Laudato Si'*, 106.
28 *Laudato Si'*, 68, 83.

From the biases of the technocratic paradigm emerge distorted personal values. A technocratic worldview envisions the human person as an isolated, apathetic, and domineering being set in a brutish, antiseptic, and mechanistic universe; the existential upshot of tyrannical anthropocentrism is the radical lovelessness of bias.[29] Human purpose is reduced to doing, making, and the practical rather than to caring and cultivating. The world is reduced to a mere setting or even a hindrance. The good becomes simply what satisfies immediately, and the true becomes simply what is visible at the present moment. A person wrapped up in self-interest suffocates in the narrow confines of biased immediacy, becoming something less than genuinely human and jeopardizing the very possibility of authentic personal values. "The truncated subject," Lonergan writes, "not only does not know himself but also is unaware of his ignorance and so, in one way or another, concludes that what he does not know does not exist."[30] Shriveling human persons into themselves, this truncation shields them from the religious need for self-transcendence, the ecstatic drive toward the other.

One becomes the center of the universe, revealing the idolatrous character of biased anthropocentrism and the truncation of genuine religious value. The rejection of self-transcendence in the name of technocratic practicality is "how we end up worshipping earthly powers, or ourselves usurping the place of God, even to the point of claiming an unlimited right to trample his creation underfoot."[31] Practicality instrumentalizes religious meaning to serve this anthropocentric, idolatrous end; recalling that "we are not God," Francis rejects misinterpretations of Genesis 1 that have "encouraged the unbridled exploitation of nature by painting him as domineering and destructive by nature" and have suggested that "our being created in God's image and given dominion over the earth justifies absolute

---

29 As Lonergan poses the existential questions of a technocratic age:

> Is moral enterprise consonant with this world? . . . [I]s the universe on our side, or are we just gamblers and, if gamblers, are we not, perhaps fools, individually struggling for authenticity and collectively endeavoring to snatch progress from the ever mounting welter of decline? The questions arise and, clearly, our attitudes and our resoluteness may be profoundly affected by the answers. Does there or does there not necessarily exist a transcendent, intelligent ground of the universe? Is that ground or are we the primary instances of moral consciousness? Are cosmogenesis, biological evolution, historical process basically cognate to us as moral beings or are they indifferent and so alien to us? (*Method in Theology*, 102–3)

30 Bernard J. F. Lonergan, "The Subject," in *A Second Collection*, 64.

31 *Laudato Si'*, 75.

domination over other creatures."[32] The crises in our common home are born out of the rejection of creatureliness that falsely promises to make us "gods" (Gen 3:5). The anthropocentrism of the technocratic paradigm, to put it in Lonergan's words, tempts humans to act and conceive of themselves "as if they were the First Cause."[33] And with this idolatry, the scale of values collapses to the *libido dominandi* of sin. The idolatrous reduction of religious value to lower levels—whether in idolizing oneself, the market, or technological possibility—truncates the scale and suffocates not only oneself but also the poor and the earth alike.

The Difficulties in Responding to the Cries of Our Common Home

Thus, the cries of the earth and the poor expose the breakdown of all levels of value, indeed the collapse of the entire scale of values. The twin cries accordingly exhibit the need for comprehensive healing, the need for radical social, cultural, personal, and religious transformations in our common home. Since lower levels set the questions to be resolved by higher levels within the scale of values, the breakdowns in those most basic levels also raise the question of how higher levels might heal them and condition the shape of that healing. This is the systematic meaning of granting the cries of the poor and the earth hermeneutical priority in the church's mission.

Nevertheless, the idolatrous reach of the technocratic paradigm hinders adequate responses of healing to those cries. As chapter 2 notes, Francis concedes the complexity of caring for our common home and expresses his doubt that technological, political, or economic shifts alone can fix the current crisis. Like Doran, Francis, in his preference for *la teología del pueblo*, disavows both Marxist and technocratic accounts of social process that reduce communal transformation simply to shifts in practicality.[34] In terms of the scale of values, attempts at transformation exclusively from below are bound to fail as long as they ignore and remain subject to the deeper corruptions that they hope to resist. After criticizing attempts to fix the ecological crisis purely through

---

32 *Laudato Si'*, 67.

33 Bernard J. F. Lonergan, "The Redemption: A Supplement," in *The Redemption*, vol. 9 of CWL, ed. Robert M. Doran, H. Daniel Monsour, and Jeremy D. Wilkins, trans. Michael G. Shields (Toronto: University of Toronto Press, 2018), 341. For a brief Lonerganian treatment of idolatry, see Randall S. Rosenberg, *The Givenness of Desire: Concrete Subjectivity and the Natural Desire to See God* (Toronto: University of Toronto, 2017), 192–94.

34 See Whelan, *A Discerning Church*, 113–16.

economic reform, for instance, Francis concludes, "We fail to see the deepest roots of our present failures, which have to do with the direction, goals, meaning and social implications of technological and economic growth."[35] Precisely as a cultural phenomenon, the technocratic paradigm pervades the level of social values, meaning that any shifts simply on the level of social values fail to challenge the more fundamental malaise. From below, nothing escapes the logic of the technocratic paradigm; idols are all-consuming.

This parasitic logic can also warp the church's social mission insofar as that mission is perceived as enacting change exclusively from below. Such an assumption reveals what Francis calls a "spiritual worldliness" by reducing the church's mediation of religious value to changes in social values, perhaps through an overly narrow focus on policy changes or, relatedly, realpolitik alliances with various factions.[36] This conception of ecclesial mission can reduce *Laudato Si'* to what it claims about, say, legislation regarding climate change or abortion, without attending to the theological heart of its integral ecology. So too can it lead to the co-optation of ecclesial mission by the standards assumed in the social setup today. This phenomenon explains the numerous examples throughout this book illustrating the divisions arising between pro-life (human ecology) and pro-environment (natural ecology) Catholics who mirror the polarizations of Western politics and replicate the very fragmentation that marks the technocratic paradigm.[37] As a result, Catholics themselves fall victim to the polarizing logic of group bias, sapping the church's redemptive mission.[38] This tendency

---

35 *Laudato Si'*, 109. See also 9, 26, 60, 111, 144, 200.

36 See Robert M. Doran:

> The religious and social values intended, respectively, by the terms faith and justice are related to one another through the intermediate values of personal integrity and autonomous cultural values. Without this mediation, attempts at the integration of religious and social values can result in a praxis that is too compact, and by its compactness susceptible of conscription by ideological forces that, far from contributing to the emergence of a genuine alternative to 'the murderous grotesque of our time,' will simply increase the probability of an eventual cataclysmic disaster. (*Theology and the Dialectics of History* [Toronto: University of Toronto Press, 1990], 459)

37 *Laudato Si'*, 110, 138.

38 Regarding the functional specialization of "communications" (in many ways, Lonergan's equivalent to ecclesial mission), Lonergan writes, "the divided community, their conflicting actions, and the messy situation are headed for disaster. For the messy situation is diagnosed differently by the divided community; action is ever more at cross-purposes; and the situation becomes still messier to provoke still sharper differences in diagnosis and policy, more radical criticism of one another's actions, and an ever deeper crisis in the situation." *Method in Theology*, 358.

domesticates ecclesial mission to something less than a radical transformation of social, cultural, personal, and religious values. Lonergan concurs that "one will be taking a superficial and rather sterile view of the constructive side of Christian action, if one thinks only of forming policies, planning operations, and carrying them out."[39] Neglecting the need for this more radical transformation and placing too much trust in changes in social values—economic, technological, or political shifts—ironically expands the imperialism of the technocratic paradigm, its fragmentating worldview, and the excessive premium that it places on practicality.

The technocratic tendency to rely exclusively on practicality for resolving problems in our common home constricts the emergence of alternative responses from below. General bias necessarily dismisses anything that fails to reflect its immediate and practical bent since, precisely as alternatives, they appear impractical. A determinism arises insofar as seemingly nothing can challenge this claim to omnicompetence. Through this myopic lens, for instance, worship appears quietist or irresponsible given the more urgent need to effect change and enact policy for the sake of our common home. This dynamic typifies the "ironclad logic" of the technocratic paradigm.[40] For Francis, a similar determinism characterizes the technocratic paradigm; as a form of general bias, the technocratic paradigm perpetuates itself.

The need for an alternative remains, however. Accordingly, in response to the nature of the technocratic paradigm and the failure to adequately respond to it, Francis admits that "[t]he problem is that we still lack the culture needed to confront this crisis," and hence urges "a bold cultural revolution."[41] After ruling out the possibility of satisfactory solutions to the decline emerging from the level of technology, economics, or politics, Lonergan similarly insists that "if men are to meet the challenge set by major decline and its longer cycle, it will be through their culture that they do so."[42] Precisely since it aims to ensure the effective functioning of social values, culture can and must perform a critical function toward a corruption like the dominance of practicality. So too can cultural transformation attend

---

[39] Lonergan, *Method in Theology*, 366. See also Michael Budde, *The (Magic) Kingdom of God: Christianity and Global Culture Industries* (Boulder, Colo.: Westview Press, 1997), 1.

[40] *Laudato Si'*, 108.

[41] *Laudato Si'*, 53, 114.

[42] Lonergan, *Insight*, 261.

to the same level of the technocratic paradigm by providing an alternative set of redemptive meanings and values.

Nevertheless, even cultural reform cannot solve the problem of general bias on its own, since its effective functioning depends on personal and religious values. Lonergan's recognition of the insufficiency of cosmopolis, a cultural commitment to wisdom, indicates as much. Chapter 2 proposes that the bold cultural revolution for which *Laudato Si'* calls depends on a "revolution of the heart."[43] Specifically, Francis identifies elsewhere the need for a "revolution of tenderness," arising from

> the love that comes close and becomes real. It is a movement that starts from our heart and reaches the eyes, the ears and the hands. Tenderness means to use our eyes to see the other, our ears to hear the other, to listen to the children, the poor, those who are afraid of the future. To listen also to the silent cry of our common home, of our sick and polluted earth. Tenderness means to use our hands and our heart to comfort the other, to take care of those in need.[44]

Lonergan too makes conversion central. Understood systematically, needed is what Lonergan identifies as a "universal willingness," a heart—the eros of one's entire being—open to self-transcendence toward creation, neighbor, and God. Only then can one "become painfully aware" of what is happening to our common home, feel with the heart the cries of the earth and the poor, and empathetically care to respond.[45] Only then can our common home receive the mercy for which it desperately longs.

And yet again, the imperialistic constrictions of the technocratic paradigm and its biases inhibit this possibility. This heart of care cannot be manufactured through sheer willpower. Bias instead enlists one's heart—the immediacy of experience and affectivity—to satisfy one's immediate needs. Within the technocratic paradigm, "[o]ur capacity to make decisions, a more genuine freedom and the space for each one's alternative creativity are diminished."[46] People stand morally impotent in the face of the ironclad logic of the technocratic paradigm. In view of general bias and the longer

---

43 This phrase is taken from Dorothy Day, *Loaves and Fishes* (Maryknoll, N.Y.: Orbis Books, 1997), 215. See also *Laudato Si'*, 218.

44 Francis, *Video Conference on the Occasion of the TED Conference in Vancouver*, April 26, 2017.

45 *Laudato Si'*, 19.

46 *Laudato Si'*, 116.

cycle of decline that it initiates, Lonergan calls for a "withdrawal from practicality for the sake of practicality."[47] "The solution," he confesses, "has to be a still higher integration of human living."[48] According to the logic of the scale of values, since this cultural distortion cannot resolve its own exigencies, then the solution must be generated and the cries of the earth and the poor must be answered from a higher level of value, "from above," not beholden to the dictates of the technocratic paradigm.

HEALING IN OUR COMMON HOME: EUCHARISTIC PRAISE AND A CULTURE OF CARE

A Doxological and Eucharistic Turn

"Rather than a problem to be solved," Francis submits, "the world is a joyful mystery to be contemplated with gladness and praise."[49] Given the entrapping biases of the technocratic paradigm, Francis conveys here the insufficiency of solving problems from below and the necessity of submitting oneself to healing from above. This healing can frame an adequate answer to the cries of the earth and of the poor. In the language of Lonergan, against the idolatries of tyrannical anthropocentrism and technocracy, praise supplies the proper withdrawal from practicality that ultimately saves practicality. It is for this reason that Francis offers *Laudato Si'* as a prayerful hymn of praise. Right praise sustains the integral scale of values, keeping it open toward the always greater God; in the case of *Laudato Si'*, doxology frames an integral ecology that heals our broken common home. In this way, the church promotes the doxological vocation of all creation, spanning human and natural ecologies alike. As Walter Brueggeman states:

> Praise is the duty and delight, the ultimate vocation of the human community; indeed, of all creation. Yes, all of life is aimed toward God and finally exists for the sake of God. Praise articulates and embodies our capacity to yield, submit, and abandon ourselves in trust and gratitude to the One whose we are. Praise is not only a human requirement and a human need, it is also a human delight. We have a resilient hunger to move beyond self, to return our energy and worth to the One from whom it has

---

[47] Lonergan, *Insight*, 266.
[48] Lonergan, *Insight*, 655.
[49] *Laudato Si'*, 12.

been granted. In our return to that One, we find our deepest joy. That is what is means to "glorify God and enjoy God forever."⁵⁰

The Eucharist makes the church and guides its mission to foster this right praise through Christ. Francis intimates in *Laudato Si'* that the climax of this doxological charge is the Eucharist. What follows takes the eucharistic liturgy as normative for understanding the right praise for which our common home cries.⁵¹

Eucharistic Praise: Religious and Personal Values

Authentic eucharistic praise evokes, however proleptically, the religious conversion that responds to God's Trinitarian offer of love.⁵² Celebrated through the Son, liturgical worship instantiates the graced recognition of the Father's adoptive love for the world and the Spirit-inspired desire to breathe forth that love; such praise elevates the entire cosmos into the eternal doxology of the Trinity.⁵³ Praise directed toward the triune God reveals that creation finds its end in something other than practicality. Worship is, as Herbert McCabe remarks, "not merely non-productive, non-money-making, but is even non-creative" as it invites all creation "into the waste of time which is the interior life of the Godhead," whose perichoretic "life is

---

50 Walter Brueggemann, *Israel's Praise: Doxology against Idolatry and Ideology* (Minneapolis, Minn.: Fortress Press, 1988), 1.

51 See pages 10 and 11 of the introduction. Throughout this section, I refer primarily to the "Ordinary Form" of the Roman Rite in order to make some of my claims more concrete. By no means is this emphasis meant to ignore the ecological significance of other rites in the Catholic Church (many of which make clearer connections between praise and care for creation); instead, I hope it supplements other studies of those rites done by people more familiar with them.

52 Of course, as theological reflections on the Eucharist must, all of what follows recognizes this proleptic character, the "not-yet" quality of worship that explains the gap between what happens in the Eucharist and what happens in the lives of those who partake in it. My hope, as the conclusion of this book suggests, is to narrow that gap.

53 As Robert Doran writes, "The state of grace is an interpersonal situation, where the founding persons are the divine Three, and where we are all invited to allow ourselves to be caught up, in prayer and in life, individually and communally, in the circumcession of divine life. Our participation in the divine relations through grace is an elevation also of our relatedness to our fellow men and women, *and in fact to all creation*." In *The Trinity in History: A Theology of the Divine Missions*, vol. 2, *Missions, Relations, and Persons* (Toronto: University of Toronto Press, 2019), 34. Emphasis added. For an extended treatment of the ecological significance of Doran's Trinitarian theology that complements what follows, see Eugene R. Schlesinger, "Ecological Conversion, Social Grace, and the Four-Point Hypothesis," in *Intellect, Affect, and God: The Trinity, History, and the Life of Grace*, ed. Joseph Ogbonnaya and Gerard Whelan, 19–33 (Milwaukee, Wis.: Marquette University Press, 2021).

not like the life of the worker or artist but of lovers wasting time with each other uselessly."[54] For those who partake in it, the Eucharist catalyzes a transformative encounter that gradually breaks through biased indifference and technocratic calculation, sets one's heart on fire with the love of God, and opens one's heart to intend God's order for the universe.

The Eucharist, as Lonergan makes clear, engages all of who one is: the experiencing, understanding, judging, and deciding that constitute being human. So too, for Lonergan, are these four levels of human knowing and doing perfected by God's love poured onto our hearts (Rom 5:5). In communicating this love then, a eucharistic revolution of the heart reorients all four of these levels and thus anticipates human salvation—indeed, the salvation of all creation. Lonergan specifies that, on the level of personal value, religious conversion can be understood as a development from above. That is, this encounter proceeds from decision, to judgment, to understanding, and to experience, grounding each level in love.

What follows correlates these four levels with four respective themes that have emerged in the teachings of John Paul II, Benedict XVI, and Francis: a priestly anthropology, sacramentality, communion, and sabbath.[55] On the level of decision, the Eucharist conforms one lovingly to the cosmic priesthood of Christ that mediates the praise of all creation. On the level of judgment, the Eucharist invites both the loving affirmation of one's creatureliness and, relatedly, the sacramentality of a world that glorifies God. On the level of understanding, the Eucharist entails a loving recognition that the world is united in its glorification of God as a communion of praise. On the level of experience, the Eucharist opens one's eyes to attend lovingly to the ways that all creation sings God's praises. At the same time, the recognition that creation fails to sing God's praises and fails to manifest God's glory draws one into the repentant, cruciform demands of caring for our common home. This eucharistic transformation of personal value roots the eucharistic transformation of cultural and social values, thus resolving disruptions to vital and elemental values.

---

[54] Herbert McCabe, "Prayer," in *The McCabe Reader*, ed. Brian Davies and Paul Kucharski (New York: Bloomsbury Publishing, 2016), 159.

[55] Thus, this material answers Doran's call to fill out in more detail the relationship between personal and religious values within the scale. See, e.g., Robert M. Doran, *The Trinity in History: A Theology of the Divine Missions*, vol. 1, *Missions and Processions* (Toronto: University of Toronto Press, 2012), 349.

On the existential level of decision, participation in the Eucharist conforms one to Christ—God's love become flesh—as subject. Participation in Christ, Lonergan stressed, is a participation in his doxological spirit of sacrifice, a conformity to his high priesthood. Developing Benedict XVI's writings, Francis underscores the cosmic dimensions of this priesthood and its bridge-like, mediatory character in *Laudato Si'*.[56] Christ joins with creation, grafting it to the God for whom it yearns in praise. Christ, as the New Adam, enacts the true mandate of Genesis 1, namely to "be an *angled mirror*, reflecting God's wise order into the world and reflecting the praises of all creation back to the Creator."[57] As a participation in Christ, care for our common home thus takes this sacerdotal shape. Understood through Doran's categories of limitation and transcendence, humans are embedded in creation by belonging to its chorus of praise (limitation). At the same time, this praise is mediated uniquely through the unrestricted drive of the human spirit (transcendence). On the one hand, a proper conception of a priestly anthropology must maintain the limitation pole of the dialectic, that humans join with and participate in creation's praise of God. Otherwise, this vision of the human person replicates the mechanomorphic distortions of the technocratic paradigm.[58] On the other hand, stressing limitation too much and neglecting the distinctive mediating role of humans within this praise produces the biocentrism rejected by Francis in *Laudato Si'*.[59] Lonergan tenders that "[m]an is nature's priest, and nature is God's silent communing with man."[60] The categories of limitation and transcendence provide systematic heft for understanding the bridge-like character of this calling to participate in Christ's cosmic priesthood.

---

[56] Lonergan too on occasion references the cosmic character of Christ. As he writes, "in his resurrection and exaltation [Christ] beckons us to the splendor of the children of God for which up to now the whole created universe groans in all its parts as if in the pangs of childbirth' (Rom 8:22). In that beckoning we discern not only the ground of our hope but also the cosmic dimension in the new creation of all things in Christ Jesus our Lord." "Christology Today: Methodological Reflections," in *A Third Collection: Papers by Bernard J. F. Lonergan, S.J.*, ed. Frederick E. Crowe (Mahwah, N.J.: Paulist Press, 1985), 94.

[57] N. T. Wright, "Excursus," in John H. Walton, *The Lost World of Adam and Eve* (Downers Grove, Ill.: InterVarsity Press, 2015), 175.

[58] See, e.g., Michael Northcott, *The Environment and Christian Ethics* (New York: Cambridge University Press, 1996), 131–32. See also Elizabeth Theokritoff, "Creation and Priesthood in Modern Orthodox Thinking," *Ecotheology* 10, no. 3 (2005): 344–63.

[59] *Laudato Si'*, 118.

[60] Lonergan, *Topics in Education*, 224–25. The material here and in the next paragraph has been developed at greater length in Lucas Briola, "Dramatic Artistry in Our Common Home: Robert

Dramatic artistry in our common home requires more than the maintenance of dialectical balances, however. In an emergently probable world that pulses with love, dramatic artistry is dynamic and ecstatic, the creative unfolding of linked but opposed principles of change. On the level of personal value, transcendence and limitation creatively unfold insofar as the unrestricted character of the human spirit operates not ex nihilo but by patiently attending to the elemental values that limit them, by respecting the grammar of creation. In so doing, humans participate in the upward, but indeterminately directed, dynamism of the universe and unleash the passionateness of being itself, now understood as creation's groundswell of praise that groans to be heard. As Doran writes, "What is good, is good for the whole person, and not simply for the upper reaches of consciousness. The lower manifolds are themselves energically, indeterminately, heading for the same good that higher conjugates understand, affirm, and choose. An intentionality open to things as they are is receptively instrumental in the flourishing of psyche and organism. The whole of creation groans in expectation of the liberation of the children of God."[61]

The priestly vocation of the human person includes restoring the lower manifolds of creation—elemental values—to their "higher good," their transcendent end in the God who is the "love that moves the sun and other stars."[62] In the words of the preface of the fourth eucharistic prayer, this

---

Doran and the Doxological Anthropology of *Laudato Si'*," in *Intellect, Affect, and God: The Trinity, History, and the Life of Grace*, ed. Joseph Ogbonnaya and Gerard Whelan, 3–18 (Milwaukee, Wis.: Marquette University Press, 2021).

[61] Robert M. Doran, *Psychic Conversion and Theological Foundations*, 2nd ed. (Milwaukee, Wis.: Marquette University Press, 2006), 230. See also Doran, "Dramatic Artistry in the Third Stage of Meaning," *Theological Foundations*, vol. 1, *Intentionality and Psyche* (Milwaukee, Wis.: Marquette University Press, 1995), 253, where after a similar passage, Doran states: "And so we have perhaps the starting point of a contemporary mediation through transcendental method of the biblical insight that the whole of creation groans in expectation, waiting for the liberation of the children of God."

[62] Dante Alighieri, *The Divine Comedy: Paradiso*, Canto XXXIII, 145, as quoted in *Laudato Si'*, 77. This by no means rejects creaturely integrity or the possibility of creation praising God apart from human beings. Respecting the doxological potential of nonhuman creation in part means to allow a creature to be as God intended it to be (which can certainly include serving as food, among other things), respecting what Lonergan the scholastic would refer to as a creature's "horizontal finality." Nevertheless, precisely through their conscious intentionality, human beings add something unique to creation's chorus of praise. On Lonergan's understanding of "horizontal finality," see his "Finality, Love, Marriage," in *Collection*, vol. 4 of CWL, eds. Frederick E. Crowe and Robert M. Doran (Toronto: University of Toronto Press, 1988), 22. For a Lonergan-inspired account of grace in this vein, see Benjamin J. Hohman, "The Glory to Be Revealed: Grace and Emergence in an Ecological Eschatology," in *Everything Is Interconnected*, 179–98.

charge means "giving voice to every creature under heaven." The subatomic movements, chemical processes, and biological phenomena that undergird human intentionality all transcend themselves insofar as one surrenders oneself in praise to the unrestricted character of being in love. As Lonergan himself remarks in his writings on the Eucharist, "the finality of a formal sacrifice is to be a compendious symbol of the universe towards God."[63] To seek the direction in the movement of life is thus to participate in and mediate this hymn of the universe, to offer this "sacrifice of praise" (Heb 13:15).

The Eucharist, as mediating the presence of Christ and his cosmic priesthood, conforms worshippers to this priestly vocation. In the words of *Laudato Si'*, "Joined to the incarnate Son, present in the Eucharist, the whole cosmos gives thanks to God."[64] The eucharistic celebration grafts worshippers onto the cosmic Christ in at least two ways. The first is the praying of a responsorial psalm. Francis mentions how the Psalms "frequently exhort us to praise God the Creator" and "also invite other creatures to join us in this praise."[65] When prayed in a liturgical setting, the Psalms, unlike other liturgical readings, prescribe the graced words of response for worshippers. In the Christian liturgy, the Psalms conform worshippers to Christ's own subjectivity, as tradition sees the Psalms as prayed most fittingly by Christ.[66] The integral ecology of *Laudato Si'* calls particular attention to the liturgical significance of those Psalms that bespeak creation's praise of God. Understood as such, they can begin to effect active human participation in the cosmic priesthood of Christ, forming a new horizon of meaning for those who pray the Psalms' words.

The preparation and offering of the gifts afford a second entry into Christ's cosmic priesthood, one that makes explicit the doxological orientation of the Psalms.[67] As chapter 1 notes, Benedict XVI suggests as much

---

[63] Bernard J. F. Lonergan, "The Notion of Sacrifice," in *Early Latin Theology*, vol. 19 of CWL, ed. Robert M. Doran and H. Daniel Monsour, trans. Michael G. Shields (Toronto: University of Toronto Press, 2011), 31.

[64] *Laudato Si'*, 236.

[65] *Laudato Si'*, 72.

[66] See Harry Nasuti, "The Sacramental Function of the Psalms in Contemporary Scholarship and Liturgical Practice," in *Psalms and Practice: Worship, Virtue, and Authority*, ed. Stephen Breck Reid (Collegeville, Minn.: Liturgical Press, 2001), 81–83. For an extended treatment of this formative character of the Psalms, see Catherine Petrany, *Pedagogy, Prayer and Praise: The Wisdom of the Psalter* (Tübingen: Mohr Siebeck, 2015).

[67] In the words of the Second Vatican Council, "the liturgy of the word and the eucharistic liturgy are so closely connected with each other that they form but one single act of worship." *Sacrosanctum Concilium* (December 7, 1963), 56.

in *Sacramentum Caritatis*.[68] Through the "work of human hands," congregants offer the gift that is the "fruit of the earth" and the "fruit of the vine" back to God, bringing the lower manifolds of creation toward the God whom their passionateness intends. Through this cosmic offering, worshippers realize the words of the third eucharistic prayer: "You are indeed Holy, O Lord, and all you have created rightly gives you praise." In this anaphoric action, humans participate in Christ's own sacrificial offering of creation, whereby Christ makes creation utterly transparent to the divine presence: "This is my body. . . . This is my blood." In the Eucharist, then, the "world which came forth from God's hands returns to him in blessed and undivided adoration: in the bread of the Eucharist, 'creation is projected towards divinization, towards the holy wedding feast, towards unification with the Creator himself.'"[69] To live the Eucharist and, by extension, Christ's cosmic priesthood demands returning creation to God lovingly through praise. Care for our common home, on the level of decision, has a priestly shape. So too does it imply certain judgments, understandings, and ways of experiencing that reflect this doxological vocation.

Indeed, from above, this existential calling conditions judgments of truth and value that reflect this eucharistic vocation: an affirmation both of one's creatureliness and of the sacramentality of creation. Living out a priestly vocation requires the yielding, decentering recognition that one's own praises are insufficient without those of creation. The eucharistic celebration in general situates one within an entire cosmic liturgy that includes all the angels, all the saints, and all creation; as the eucharistic preface for the Feast of Corpus Christi introduces the *Sanctus*, "all creatures of heaven and earth sing a new song in adoration, and we, with all the host of Angels, cry out, and without end we acclaim." For Lonergan, this affirmation of a world beyond oneself requires a series of judgments: namely, that oneself is, that something else is, and that oneself is not that something else.[70] Affirming the doxological potential of the rest of creation "reveals to man a universe of being in which he is but an item, and a universal order in which his desires and fears, his delight and anguish are but infinitesimal

---

[68] Benedict XVI, Post-Synodal Apostolic Exhortation *Sacramentum Caritatis* (February 22, 2007), 47, 92.

[69] *Laudato Si'*, 236. See also David L. Schindler, *Heart of the World, Center of the Church:* Communio *Ecclesiology, Liberalism, and Liberation* (Grand Rapids, Mich.: Eerdmans, 1996), 22.

[70] Lonergan, *Insight*, 399–400.

components," and as a result, one "is confronted with a universe of being in which [the self] finds itself, not the center of reference, but an object coordinated with other objects and, with them, subordinated to some destiny to be discovered or invented, approved or distained, accepted or repudiated."[71] Appreciating the doxological destiny of the universe and how one's own praise coordinates with that of the rest of creation can lead one to affirm one's creatureliness and, by extension, to reject all pretensions of idolatrous, tyrannical anthropocentrism. This judgment of humility entails a truthful and liberating acceptance of who one is (a creature) and who one is not (God), what one cannot control and on what one depends.[72] It is to acknowledge that one is "from the earth" (*hummus*), that one is a part, albeit a unique one, of the chorus of creation and not set against it. One judges that one is not the center of the universe but instead a creature set within a larger theocentric ecosystem.

A second judgment must complement this one if the universe is to be affirmed not as an unfeeling immensity but as a reality charged with the grandeur of God. Praise presumes a judgment about the goodness of the universe, namely that creation stands as a gift from God and, in its constant dependence on God, glorifies God.[73] Underlying the daring of praise, Josef Pieper contends, "is the conviction that . . . at bottom *everything that is, is good, and it is good to exist.*"[74] Coupled with the embrace that one is but an

---

[71] Lonergan, *Insight*, 498. While not essential to the liturgical celebration, in some cases church architecture can evoke this judgment on a visceral level. The disorienting immensity of a Gothic cathedral positions those who enter within a world much larger than themselves, a world of praise that includes both angels and nonhuman life. Chartres Cathedral, for instance, includes depictions of objects like plants, trees, animals, and planets. Laon Cathedral includes sculptures of the oxen that served as transports for material in its construction. See Robert Barron, *Heaven in Stone and Glass: Experiencing the Spirituality of the Great Cathedrals* (New York: Crossroad Publishing, 2002), 45–51. The green designs of some contemporary churches include windows that open toward the flooding of sunlight and, through these windows, stretch those who worship beyond themselves toward the horizons of creation that recede toward God. See Dean Dettloff, "A 'Green' Church in Toronto Teaches Theology through Design," *America* (October 14, 2019): 16–17.

[72] Norman Wirzba, *From Nature to Creation: A Christian Vision for Understanding and Loving Our World* (Grand Rapids, Mich.: Baker Academic, 2015), 101–7.

[73] As *Laudato Si'*, 76, reads, "In the Judeo-Christian tradition, the word 'creation' has a broader meaning than 'nature', for it has to do with God's loving plan in which every creature has its own value and significance. Nature is usually seen as a system which can be studied, understood and controlled, whereas creation can only be understood as a gift from the outstretched hand of the Father of all, and as a reality illuminated by the love which calls us together into universal communion."

[74] Josef Pieper, *In Tune with the World: A Theory of Festivity*, trans. Richard and Clara Winston (South Bend, Ind.: St. Augustine's Press, 1999), 20.

item in an entire universe oriented toward God, this conviction entails a stance of *eucharistia*. It is to accept, in the words of the offertory and like Israel's reception of manna in the desert, that "through [God's] goodness we have received the bread we offer [God]," that "through [God's] goodness we have received the wine we offer [God]." Affirming the passionateness of being, the stretching forth of creation toward God, is to affirm the goodness of creation as a home in which God dwells (Jn 1:14). "Faith," says Lonergan, "places human efforts in a friendly universe; it reveals an ultimate significance in human achievement; it strengthens new undertakings with confidence."[75] Through the lens of otherworldly love, one can judge that the dynamism of the entire universe sings of and thus reveals God's love, that "heaven and earth are full of God's glory."

The Eucharist, as a sacrament, forms worshippers to make such a judgment. Building on the insights of his predecessors concerning the sacramentality of creation, Francis remarks how, in liturgical worship, "we are invited to embrace the world on a different plane. Water, oil, fire and colors are taken up in all their symbolic power and incorporated in our act of praise."[76] Sacramentality marks the eucharistic liturgy since these elements—and, most uniquely, products of bread and wine—are transformed to mediate God's love.[77] Likewise, in the Eucharist, human beings also mediate this loving presence, whether in the figure of the priest who prays *in persona Christi capitis* or in the physical gathering of Christians. The eucharistic liturgy thus can invite the more general judgment that, in the words of *Laudato Si'*, there is an irreducible "mystical meaning to be found in a leaf, in a mountain trail, in a dewdrop, in a poor person's face."[78] Praise affirms the ultimate goodness, friendliness, and irreducible grammar of the created order—spanning human and natural ecologies—that should be approached not with grasping possessiveness but with receptive gratitude. The eucha-

---

[75] Lonergan, *Method in Theology*, 117. As Lonergan writes elsewhere in a similarly sacramental way, "It is as though a room were filled with music though one can have no sure knowledge of its source. There is in the world, as it were, a charged field of love and meaning; here and there it reaches a notable intensity; but it is ever unobtrusive, hidden, inviting each of us to join. And join we must if we are to perceive it, for our perceiving is through our own loving" (*Method in Theology*, 290). See also Patrick H. Byrne, "Intelligibility and Natural Science: Alienation or Friendship with the Universe?" *Lonergan Workshop* 24 (2010): 1–32.

[76] *Laudato Si'*, 235.

[77] On this "sacramental principle," see Kevin W. Irwin, *Context and Text: A Method for Liturgical Theology*, rev. ed. (Collegeville, Minn.: Liturgical Press, 2018), 123–86.

[78] *Laudato Si'*, 233.

ristic celebration thus invites Christians to make loving judgments about the goodness of creation: to embrace both one's creatureliness and to affirm the sacramental capacity of the universe to glorify God.

From above, these judgments condition a loving understanding that perceives the world through the lens of communion. For Lonergan, the act of understanding involves the grasp of "some intelligible unity or correlation."[79] Being conformed to Christ the cosmic priest and affirming the sacramentality of creation presumes a particular type of understanding. Being shaped by God's love allows one to grasp the intelligible unity of our common home as a communion of praise, a doxological ecology that mirrors God's triune life. That is, the relational character of creation is itself revelatory; for Francis, the "universe as a whole, in all its manifold relationships, shows forth the inexhaustible riches of God."[80] Affirming the sacramentality of creation thus leads one to understand the world as one in which "called into being by one Father, all of us are linked by unseen bonds and together form a kind of universal family, a sublime communion which fills us with a sacred, affectionate and humble respect."[81] One is but an item, though within a universal family of communion. To understand the world in this way is to grasp it as one bonded in love and praise.

The Eucharist trains its participants to understand the world as such. The eucharistic liturgy grants worshippers an "entry into an action, into a reality that is ongoing and bigger than we are," namely the praise sung together by all created things.[82] Again developing the contributions of his predecessors, Francis highlights how the Eucharist is "an act of cosmic love" wherein all creation comes together to glorify God.[83] In the Eucharist, creation forms "a uni-verse," a joined hymn of praise.[84] Whether through the sharing of food or the common orientation toward God, the Eucharist discloses that everything is interconnected through praise. Precisely by bringing creation into communion with God through praise, the Eucharist—the sacrament of communion—secures communion among

---

[79] Lonergan, *Insight*, 632.
[80] *Laudato Si'*, 86.
[81] *Laudato Si'*, 89.
[82] Edith P. Humphrey, *Grand Entrance: Worship on Earth as in Heaven* (Grand Rapids, Mich.: Brazos Press, 2011), 3.
[83] *Laudato Si'*, 236.
[84] See United Methodist–Roman Catholic Dialogue, *Heaven and Earth Are Full of Your Glory: A United Methodist and Roman Catholic Statement on the Eucharist and Ecology* (2008), 17.

all creation. In this way does the eucharistic celebration incorporate all creation into the mystical body of Christ, cosmic in scope (see Col 1:15). The Eucharist anticipates how, in the words of the fourth eucharistic prayer, "with the whole of creation, freed from the corruption of sin and death, may we glorify [God] through Christ our Lord, through whom [God] bestow[s] on the world all that is good." The Eucharist reveals that, through Christ, praise provides the intelligible unity of all creation, a unity that resides ultimately in the triune God.

From above, redeemed understanding elicits redeemed experiencing, in this case inviting one to be attentive to the hymn of creation to which one is inextricably tied. Lonergan's admonition to be attentive, as Robert Barron surmises, "means that the spiritually alert perceiver must see God everywhere, finding traces of his presence in all things and all places," prayerfully cultivating "a heightened attention to the depth dimension of the everyday and the commonplace, an act of real seeing."[85] This attentiveness joins one to the pulsing love of praise that animates creation and invites one to encounter the mystical meaning found in both a leaf and a poor person's face. From above, God's love heightens this attentiveness, evoking the "attentive love" with which Simone Weil equates prayer.[86] On the level of experience, for Lonergan, self-transcendence takes the form of "attend[ing] to the other."[87] That is, it takes the form of encountering an other in the full uniqueness of that other. As Francis stresses throughout his pontificate, receiving God's own attentive love demands encountering others with this attentive love that is the mercy of Jesus Christ.

The eucharistic celebration challenges those who gather to be attentive in this way. In *Laudato Si'*, Francis proposes that the sabbatical character of the Eucharist "heals our relationships with God, with ourselves, with others and with the world" insofar as it "opens our eyes to the larger picture and gives us renewed sensitivity to the rights of others."[88] In this way can eucharistic

---

[85] Robert Barron, "Why Bernard Lonergan Matters for Pastoral People," in *Exploring Catholic Theology: Essays on God, Liturgy, and Evangelization* (Grand Rapids, Mich.: Baker Academic, 2015), 177.

[86] As Simone Weil writes in *Gravity and Grace*, trans. Emma Crawford and Mario von der Ruhr (New York: Routledge Classics, 2002), 117: "Attention, taken to its highest degree, is the same thing as prayer. It presupposes faith and love. Absolutely unmixed attention is prayer." I owe this connection between Lonergan and Weil to Jennifer Crawford, *Spiritually-Engaged Knowledge: The Attentive Heart* (Burlington, Vt.: Ashgate Publishing, 2005), 97–98.

[87] Bernard J. F. Lonergan, "Mission and the Spirit," in *A Third Collection*, 29.

[88] *Laudato Si'*, 237.

participation train one to see with "the gaze of Jesus,"[89] and to participate in the "divine personal Listening" that is the Holy Spirit.[90] Indeed, in a recurring way, this attentiveness conforms one to Christ and his cosmic priesthood (decision), allowing one to affirm more deeply one's creatureliness and the world's sacramentality (judgment) and to perceive more clearly creation's communion of praise (understanding). The Eucharist evokes a revolution of tenderness by bringing those gathered into the feeling with the sacred heart of Christ, allowing one to live more fully and lovingly in Christ as subject and thus incorporating one into the true and merciful Mystical Body of Christ in history.

Cruciform Care for Our Common Home

Given the presence of decline in history, this participation takes a cruciform shape. The mystagogy of the Eucharist invites congregants both into Christ's priesthood and the foolish wisdom of the Law of the Cross that defines Christ's life of praise. Recalling Christ's victorious victimhood yields the "dangerous memories" of all those crying out for mercy in history and goads one to acknowledge one's own complicity in ignoring and exacerbating those cries.[91] That is, in a fallen world, giving glory to God also requires repenting for the ways that human sin—and the relationships it fractures—undermines the doxological vocation of creation.[92] For Lonergan, redemptive life in Christ entails not only a participation in his glorification of God, but it also entails a participation in his "utmost detestation for all sins and . . . extreme sorrow for all offense against God," sins that, by extension, include offense against neighbor and the rest of creation.[93] Religious conversion

---

[89] *Laudato Si'*, 96.

[90] For this Lonergan-inspired appellation for the Holy Spirit, see Jeremy D. Wilkins, *Before Truth: Lonergan, Aquinas, and the Problem of Wisdom* (Washington, D.C.: The Catholic University of America Press, 2018), 64.

[91] See Bruce T. Morrill, *Anamnesis as Dangerous Memory: Political and Liturgical Theology in Dialogue* (Collegeville, Minn.: Liturgical Press, 2000). While absent from *Laudato Si'*, this paschal emphasis emerges in the preparatory document for the Synod on the Amazon region: "At the same time, the blood of so many men and women that has been shed—bathing the Amazonian lands for the good of its inhabitants and of the territory—is joined to the Blood of Christ, which was poured out for all and for all creation." See Synod of Bishops, *Preparatory Document, Amazonia: New Paths for the Church and for an Integral Ecology* (June 8, 2018), 10.

[92] In this emphasis, I follow Khaled Anatolios's systematic soteriology that centers on "doxological contrition"; see Khaled Anatolios, *Deification through the Cross: An Eastern Christian Theology of Salvation* (Grand Rapids, Mich.: Eerdmans, 2020), 32.

[93] Bernard J. F. Lonergan, "Theses 15–17 of *De Verbo Incarnato*," in *The Redemption*, vol. 9 of CWL, eds. Robert M. Doran, H. Daniel Monsour, and Jeremy D. Wilkins, trans. Michael G. Shields

involves not only being in love unrestrictedly but is also "ever a withdrawal from unauthenticity."[94] Attentive love demands that one acknowledge in truth and with sorrow the scotoses that blind oneself to one's own brokenness and that render one indifferent to the victims of history.[95] The Eucharist, as a privileged encounter with the mercy of God, invites congregants to this repentant acknowledgment. In the eucharistic liturgy, as effected in the penitential act and the reception of God's mercy become flesh, the love of God poured onto one's heart can unleash insights or questions about the ecological crisis, and one's complicity in it, otherwise suppressed by bias. Indeed, in naming the truth of what is happening to our common home, the first chapter of *Laudato Si'* by design reads like a penitential litany. In a liturgical setting then, both the prayers of the faithful and the penitential act, insofar as they do name ecological sin, can facilitate this awareness. Confessing one's complicity in this sin sets the conditions for a painful awareness and conversion, a transformed dying to the many ways in which one disrupts the symphony of praise that should mark our common home. Moreover, the Eucharist can provoke this conversion by heightening a community's awareness of this disruption, the ways in which creation fails to give praise to God. Since, according to the logic of the scale of values, the cries of the earth and the poor condition the contours of social grace, the healing dynamism of the Eucharist takes shape as a response to those cries.[96] Just as it can reveal its presence, the Eucharist can signal the

---

(Toronto: University of Toronto Press, 2018), 191. See also Joseph C. Mudd, *Eucharist as Meaning: Critical Metaphysics and Contemporary Sacramental Theology* (Collegeville, Minn.: Liturgical Press, 2014), 19–36.

[94] Lonergan, *Method in Theology*, 110.

[95] As Doran explains the dynamics of psychic conversion from above, just as "the situation of the victimized elements of our own being is hermeneutically privileged in the interpretation of our own stories, so the situation of the poor is hermeneutically privileged in the interpretation of history. Contact with either one facilitates a truthful acknowledgement of the other." Doran, *Theology and the Dialectics of History*, 252. See also Robert M. Doran, *What Is Systematic Theology?* (Toronto: University of Toronto Press, 2005), 124.

[96] As Saint John Chrysostom preached:

> Do you wish to honor the body of Christ? Do not ignore him when he is naked. Do not pay him homage in the temple clad in silk only then to neglect him outside where he suffers cold and nakedness. He who said: 'This is my body' is the same One who said: 'You saw me hungry and you gave me no food', and 'Whatever you did to the least of my brothers you did also to me'. . . . What good is it if the eucharistic table is overloaded with golden chalices, when he is dying of hunger? Start by satisfying his hunger, and then with what is left you may adorn the altar as well. (*Homilies on the Gospel of Matthew*, 50, 3–4, as quoted in John Paul II, Apostolic Letter *Dies Domini* [May 31, 1998], 71)

absence of God's reign, the absence of a truly integral scale of values and the absence of a life-giving integral ecology.[97] For example, the "very liturgical use of what has been regarded as central bearers of divine revelation—water and food—may in fact bear the bad news that the goods of this good earth are no longer 'very good.' It is hard to sing the praises of 'brother sun and sister moon' when one's vision is clouded (literally) by urban pollution and smog."[98] Affirming one's own creatureliness and the sacramentality of creation defies the many ways that humans fail to actually live as such. Understanding the world as an intelligible unity of praise exposes the divisions people erect throughout the three "closely intertwined" relationships that Francis highlights in *Laudato Si'*: between themselves and God, among each other, and between themselves and the rest of creation.[99] The place where heaven and earth intersect, the eucharistic celebration supplies an alternative narrative from above that dispels the technocratic myth of "the way things are." While the technocratic paradigm anesthetizes one to the cries of the earth and the poor through selfish indifference, fruitful eucharistic participation should open the ears of one's heart to hear those cries.

The paschal heart of the eucharistic liturgy makes clear that the response to the absence of grace in our common home requires cruciform dying and sacrificial service; authentic deciding, judging, understanding, and experiencing must bear the imprint of Christ's Cross. To participate in Christ is to be conformed to the cruciform, repentant shape of his doxological spirit. Fittingly, the stigmata marked the hands and feet of Saint Francis of Assisi, the example par excellence of an integral ecology lived out. The embrace of one's creatureliness requires a cruciform surrender of mechanomorphic control and the submission of oneself to a higher, divine order. The affirmation that the world reveals God by singing the praises of God requires a self-dying to the biased illusion that one sings God's praises

---

[97] Mary Catherine Hilkert notes how preaching can name, along with grace, "dis-grace" in the world. See *Naming Grace: Preaching and the Sacramental Imagination* (New York: Continuum, 1997), 111–12. On the liturgical interplay between absence and presence, see Louis-Marie Chauvet, *Symbol and Sacrament: A Sacramental Reinterpretation of Christian Existence* (Collegeville, Minn.: Liturgical Press, 1995), 159–89.

[98] Kevin W. Irwin, "Sacramentality and the Theology of Creation: A Recovered Paradigm for Sacramental Theology," *Louvain Studies* 23, no. 2 (1998): 159–79, at 167–68.

[99] *Laudato Si'*, 66. On how the eucharistic celebration subverts the sin of racism in this way, for instance, see M. Shawn Copeland, *Enfleshing Freedom: Body, Race, and Being* (Minneapolis, Minn.: Fortress Press, 2010), 107–28.

as a virtuoso performer rather than as a part, albeit a privileged part, of creation. The perception that praise joins the world together in communion requires one to sacrifice pretensions of autonomous independence from God, one's neighbor, and the earth. Attentiveness demands a bothering to love, a willingness to feel pity with the heart even when it is painful, and an acceptance of a concern that transcends oneself. Christian discipleship under the sign of the Cross embraces the friction of caring for our common home.

So too does the Law of the Cross assure that this bothering to love will lead to new life. For Lonergan, the personal authenticity that originates in God's love surmounts the structural determinisms of decline, a point echoed in John Paul II's prophetic personalism. In *Laudato Si'*, Francis suggests that "ecological conversion" means practicing something akin to Saint Thérèse of Lisieux's "little way of love," caring for our common home through "simple daily gestures" like wearing warmer clothes in cold weather to save energy costs or saying grace before meals.[100] Attentive love demands no less. Even more so, as Dorothy Day suggests, Thérèse's little way carries political implications. The gentle smallness of these gestures escapes the violent and domineering dictates of the technocratic paradigm.[101] This kenotic love of the everyday not only escapes, but also unmasks, the distorted understanding of power presumed by the technocratic paradigm. Romano Guardini, so influential for Francis and *Laudato Si'*, makes the paschal character of this alternative politics clear in his critique of Western technocracy. As one commentator unearths this Guardinian conviction in *Laudato Si'*:

> Francis discerns with Guardini that the real drama of postmodernity turns not on technology per se but on the mind-set of power that flourishes in a technocratic age. In the incarnation, Guardini observed, God had revealed true power, which is the power of service, in which freedom is subject to and constrained by the essence of things and the limits of human nature. Jesus's unmasking of the false power of domination and

---

[100] *Laudato Si'*, 230, 211, and 227. On a Lonergan-inspired reading of ecological conversion, see Neil Ormerod and Cristina Vanin, "Ecological Conversion: What Does It Mean?" *Theological Studies* 77, no. 2 (2016): 328–52.

[101] See, e.g., Dorothy Day, *Thérèse* (Springfield, Ill.: Templegate Publishing, 1979), 174–75. See also Frederick Christian Bauerschmidt, "The Politics of the Little Way: Dorothy Day Reads Thérèse of Lisieux," in *American Catholic Traditions: Resources for Renewal*, ed. Sandra Yocum Mize and William L. Portier, 77–95 (Maryknoll, N.Y.: Orbis Books, 1997).

violence was the triumph of the Cross, his kenosis, which Guardini calls "supreme power converted into humility."[102]

The Cross reveals that true power shines forth in seemingly insignificant acts of worship and care, not the totalizing machinations of the technocratic paradigm. From this stance, Francis trusts that personal transformations and actions can gradually reverse cycles of ecological decline: "We must not think that these efforts are not going to change the world. They benefit society, often unbeknown to us, for they call forth a goodness which, albeit unseen, inevitably tends to spread."[103] In an emergently probable world, and despite the suggestions of technocratic determinism, true power does not coerce, but rather it sets the conditions for the possibility of new, redeemed life through vulnerable love. The pursuit of everyday holiness, to use Lonergan's words, "is in the night; our control is only rough and approximate; we have to believe and trust, to risk and dare."[104] Francis's confidence in personal actions for caring in our common home only becomes intelligible if this risk participates in the alternative, redemptive scheme of recurrence generated by the Eucharist from above. The Eucharist, as John Paul II and Benedict XVI both suggest, is a way of life.[105] Personal authenticity requires caring enough to do as one worships, daring to believe and trust that the glorification of God by one's life sets the conditions for a truly integral ecology.

A Seamless Culture of Care for Human and Natural Ecologies

Right praise likewise conditions and presumes a set of distinct, redemptive meanings and values that care for the cries of the earth and the poor. Francis has urged the promotion of a "eucharistic culture" that "impels us to express in our way of life and our thinking the grace of Christ who gave of himself

---

[102] Austen Ivereigh, *Wounded Shepherd: Pope Francis and His Struggle to Convert the Catholic Church* (New York: Henry Holt, 2019), 212. Ivereigh is citing here Romano Guardini, *The End of the Modern World*, trans. Joseph Theman, Herbert Burke, and Elinor Castendyk Briefs (Wilmington, Del.: ISI Books, 1998), 143.

[103] *Laudato Si'*, 211.

[104] Bernard J. F. Lonergan, "Self-transcendence: Intellectual, Moral, and Religious," in *Philosophical and Theological Papers 1965–1980*, vol. 17 of CWL, ed. Robert C. Croken and Robert M. Doran (Toronto: University of Toronto Press, 2004), 315.

[105] See, e.g., John Paul II, Encyclical Letter *Ecclesia de Eucharistia* (April 17, 2003), 20; and Benedict XVI, *Sacramentum Caritatis*, 92.

to the full."[106] Within the scale of values, a eucharistic culture is a "soteriological culture," as named by Doran. Within an integral ecology, a eucharistic culture is what Francis christens a "culture of care."[107] The cultivation of this culture enables a critique of technocratic biases. Francis goes on to say that a culture of care "cannot be reduced to a series of urgent and partial responses to the immediate problems of pollution, environmental decay and the depletion of natural resources. There needs to be a distinctive way of looking at things, a way of thinking, policies, an educational program, a lifestyle and a spirituality which together generate resistance to the assault of the technocratic paradigm."[108] Given the ironclad logic of the technocratic paradigm, Francis deems insufficient "a series of urgent and partial responses" only on the level of social values. Change must instead come from above and, as such, provide a coordinated response to the incursions of the technocratic paradigm. While changes coming exclusively from below remain mired in the myopia of the technocratic paradigm, eucharistic praise can secure the needed cultural transformation from above to be able to reverse the deepest roots of the ecological crisis.[109]

In *Laudato Si'*, Francis makes clear the eucharistic contours of these redemptive meanings and values, this culture of care. Against the mechanistic worldview of technocracy, a culture of care promotes a sacramental worldview, values of "gratitude and gratuitousness, a recognition that the world is God's loving gift, and that we are called quietly to imitate his generosity in self-sacrifice and good works."[110] Against a throwaway logic, a culture of care values an embrace of one's own creatureliness, a "capacity to be happy with little" that is resistant to the need to always use, consume, and discard more.[111] Against the myopic biases of excessive

---

[106] See Francis, *Udienza ai Partecipanti alla Plenaria del Pontificio Comitato per i Congressi Eucaristici Internazionali* (October 11, 2018).

[107] *Laudato Si'*, 231: "along with the importance of little everyday gestures, social love moves us to devise larger strategies to halt environmental degradation and to encourage a 'culture of care' which permeates all of society." See also 229.

[108] *Laudato Si'*, 111.

[109] See *Laudato Si'*, 215. It is for this reason that Donal Dorr proposes "first to focus on the cultural aspect [of the encyclical] because it underpins the other aspects of transformation involved in an integral and comprehensive ecological conversion." See Donal Dorr, *Option for the Poor and for the Earth: From Leo XIII to Pope Francis*, rev. ed. (Maryknoll, N.Y.: Orbis Books, 2016), 426.

[110] *Laudato Si'*, 220.

[111] *Laudato Si'*, 222. See also 78.

anthropocentrism, a culture of care recognizes the common doxological unity of all creation, "entail[ing] a loving awareness that we are not disconnected from the rest of creatures, but joined in a splendid universal communion."[112] Finally, against a frenetic hyperreality that globalizes indifference, a culture of care fosters a "serene attentiveness" that "includes taking time to recover a serene harmony with creation, reflecting on our lifestyle and our ideals, and contemplating the Creator who lives among us and surrounds us."[113] This loving attentiveness, a merciful feeling pity with the heart, means that a culture of care instantiates the culture of encounter so central for Francis's pontificate. This culture of care, as generated through the eucharistic celebration, can reverse the indifference and throwaway logic of the technocratic paradigm.

Viewed through the lens of healing from above, the Eucharist weaves cultural meanings and values into a seamless garment of ecclesial social concern. Doran tenders that "the integration of faith and justice *through personal conversion and cultural transformation* will be recognized as defining the ministry of... Pope Francis."[114] Indeed, the scale of values manifests the intimate connection between eucharistic praise and the culture of care within the integral ecology of *Laudato Si'*. The clarification of this connection settles a significant question identified in this book's first and second chapters, explaining how the turn to doxology and the Eucharist in *Laudato Si'* enables the comprehensive vision of an integral ecology. From below, and without reference to the Eucharist and doxology per se, respective matters of human and natural ecologies can appear as competing values, especially given that, from below, vital values rank higher on the scale than do the elemental values that underpin them. So too, from below, does concern for these two ecologies remain privy to the social values that mediate them—political, technological, and economic policy—and thus susceptible to the polarization that so frequently marks those social values. As is clear from the reception of John Paul II's initial presentation of the terms, the concerns of human and natural ecologies can appear as competitors as a result.

The recognition that, from above, the Eucharist evokes this culture of care underscores how eucharistic praise sublates the redemptive meanings

---

[112] *Laudato Si'*, 220. See also 89–92.

[113] *Laudato Si'*, 225–26.

[114] Robert M. Doran, foreword to *A Discerning Church*, by Gerard Whelan, xi. Cf. n. 37 of this chapter.

and values that can heal human and natural ecologies alike. In fact, while left unstated in his social teaching, Benedict XVI intimates that the Eucharist concretizes the grammar of creation and solidarity that, together, secure human and natural ecologies, a point made more explicit by Francis in *Laudato Si'*. From above, then, the Eucharist generates a culture of care that heals the broken worldview that joins seemingly disparate crises, from human trafficking to abortion to climate change. A culture of care translates into a respect for the giftedness of all life, a disavowal of the will to dominate, and a willingness to be bothered by the vulnerability of earth, embryo, and all the marginalized.[115]

The same redemptive meanings and values answer the cries of the earth and the poor. All originate in the celebration of the Eucharist. In other words, the turn to the Eucharist and praise in *Laudato Si'* allows its integral ecology to sublate human and natural ecologies, bringing them to a fuller, more integrated realization. Conversely, neglecting the higher synthesizing context provided by eucharistic praise risks forsaking the larger whole for the sake of the parts that one happens to prefer, disrupting the interdependence of the common meanings and values that anchor both human and natural ecologies.[116] Lonergan's theology of history shows how the eucharistic

---

[115] For an expanded exploration of this point, see Lucas Briola, "The Integral Ecology of *Laudato Si'* and a Seamless Garment: The Sartorial Usefulness of Lonergan and Doran's Turn to Culture," *The Lonergan Review* 9 (2018): 31–48.

[116] The scale of values thus explains a critical emphasis found in Francis's description of ecclesial mission:

> Just as the organic unity existing among the virtues means that no one of them can be excluded from the Christian ideal, so no truth may be denied. The integrity of the Gospel message must not be deformed. What is more, each truth is better understood when related to the harmonious totality of the Christian message; in this context all of the truths are important and illumine one another. When preaching is faithful to the Gospel, the centrality of certain truths is evident and it becomes clear that Christian morality is not a form of stoicism, or self-denial, or merely a practical philosophy or a catalogue of sins and faults. Before all else, the Gospel invites us to respond to the God of love who saves us, to see God in others and to go forth from ourselves to seek the good of others. . . . All of the virtues are at the service of this response of love. If this invitation does not radiate forcefully and attractively, the edifice of the Church's moral teaching risks becoming a house of cards, and this is our greatest risk. It would mean that it is not the Gospel which is being preached, but certain doctrinal or moral points based on specific ideological options. (*Evangelii Gaudium*, 39)

That is, situating the personal, cultural, and social dimensions of Christian morality properly within religious values—the encounter with God in the Eucharist, for instance—secures their essential unity against divisive forces that ideologically colonize them. On this general theme in Francis, see Massimo Borghesi, *The Mind of Pope Francis: Jorge Mario Bergoglio's Intellectual Journey*, trans. Barry Hudock (Collegeville, Minn.: Liturgical Press, 2018), 275–91.

vision of *Laudato Si'* can preserve the church's comprehensive approach to the many crises that endanger our common home.

A Eucharistic Reorientation of Social Values

This culture of care, this unified vision of life, these soteriological meanings and values must shape social values, rather than vice-versa. "We should not think," Francis declares, "that political efforts or the force of law will be sufficient to prevent actions which affect the environment because, when the culture itself is corrupt and objective truth and universally valid principles are no longer upheld, then laws can only be seen as arbitrary impositions or obstacles to be avoided."[117] Enduring changes in social values depend ultimately on the redemptive transformation of culture. An alternative culture of care, as embodied in the Eucharist, can make intelligible and secure Francis's call for a new politics, economics, and technology in *Laudato Si'*.[118] To assume otherwise domesticates the radicality of this call and reduces an integral ecology to a set of policy positions located on the level of social values. In hopes of inviting further reflection from others and cognizant of the room for prudential judgments at this level,[119] what follows is a selective presentation of how the Eucharist can reorient social values—politics, economics, and technology, respectively—in light of the cries of the earth and the poor.[120]

While, in the technocratic paradigm, economic interests bias politics, a eucharistic politics mediates genuine cultural values of care to the social order. The communal character of the eucharistic celebration grounds a

---

[117] *Laudato Si'*, 123. See also 211: "If . . . laws are to bring about significant, long-lasting effects, the majority of the members of society must be adequately motivated to accept them, and personally transformed to respond."

[118] See, e.g., *Laudato Si'*, 112, 129, 189, 190, 194, 195, 197.

[119] *Laudato Si'*, 188: "There are certain environmental issues where it is not easy to achieve a broad consensus. Here I would state once more that the Church does not presume to settle scientific questions or to replace politics. But I am concerned to encourage an honest and open debate so that particular interests or ideologies will not prejudice the common good."

[120] This section remains mindful of Lonergan's caution against moral exhortations leveled against the economic order that do not sufficiently grasp the intricacies of actual economic theory. See Bernard J. F. Lonergan, *Caring about Meaning: Patterns in the Life of Bernard Lonergan*, ed. Pierrot Lambert, Charlotte Tansey, and Cathleen Going (Montreal: Thomas More Institute Papers, 1982), 163–64. As Stephen Martin suggests, Catholic social teaching concerns itself primarily with healing from above by holding up redemptive meanings and values that might reverse decline and assist creative efforts from below. What follows occurs in that space. See Stephen L. Martin, *Healing and Creativity in Economic Ethics: The Contribution of Bernard Lonergan's Economic Thought to Catholic Social Teaching* (Lanham, Md.: University Press of America, 2007), xiii–xiv, 163, 167–68, 174–77.

politics that serves the common good, which, given the crises of our common home, "becomes . . . a summons to solidarity and a preferential option for the poorest of our brothers and sisters."[121] The Eucharist reimagines space such that worshippers are united with the mystical body of Christ, rather than divided by socioeconomic class or ethnicity, mindful of the victims of history and the dangerous memories they represent. The intergenerational character of the common good likewise means that such a politics attends to the long-term good for future generations.[122] The Eucharist, by recalling the past and anticipating the future amid the present, reimagines time; the person in love finds oneself within a community that transcends the premium placed on the present by technocratic biases. The gift character and doxological orientation of creation relativize claims of absolute ownership, revealing the ultimately universal destination of the fruit of the earth and work of human hands.[123] From above, the Eucharist embodies a politics that ensures that practicality does not eclipse relationship (which Lonergan And Doran dubbed "spontaneous intersubjectivity") but rather cooperates with it.

In the ways that it heals this social dialectic, the Eucharist represents an alternative economics to the predominant technocratic one. The Eucharist, the one food that satisfies, calls into question the restless consumption and discard of things, instead bringing people into communion with all creation.[124] In the face of neoliberal and socialist economic systems that overshadow actual communities, the eucharistic communion epitomizes an economics oriented toward relationship. In *Laudato Si'*, Francis calls for an "economic ecology" that, against exclusive focuses on profit and consumption, incorporates the many social and natural relationships that constitute our common home.[125] The humble acknowledgment of one's own creature-

---

[121] *Laudato Si'*, 158.

[122] *Laudato Si'*, 159.

[123] *Laudato Si'*, 93.

[124] William T. Cavanaugh, *Being Consumed: Economics and Christian Desire* (Grand Rapids, Mich.: Eerdmans, 2008), 94–95.

[125] *Laudato Si'*, 141. See also this from Francis:

> The principle of the maximization of profits, frequently isolated from other considerations, reflects a misunderstanding of the very concept of the economy. As long as production is increased, little concern is given to whether it is at the cost of future resources or the health of the environment; as long as the clearing of a forest increases production, no one calculates the losses entailed in the desertification of the land, the harm done to biodiversity or the

liness means that an economic ecology respects the limits supplied by the human community and the rest of creation, promoting an "economy of care" as if people and the earth mattered in forms such as cooperative economies.[126] Lonergan himself expresses admiration for cooperative economies, like those of the Antigonish Movement.[127] In his macroeconomic theory, against theories that make self-interest central to economic activity, Lonergan tenders that sustainable economies are themselves fragile ecologies that participate in social and natural schemes of recurrence, human and natural ecologies.[128] Like the Eucharist, economic activity understood in this way is always enmeshed within community. Just as the liturgical calendar aligns with rhythms of nature (e.g., in the Northern Hemisphere, the interplay of natural darkness and Advent), so too must economic activity be embedded in elemental value and cosmological meaning.[129] As exemplified in practices like regenerative agriculture, an economics that befits an integral ecology must respect the grammar of creation, a grammar that

---

increased pollution. In a word, businesses profit by calculating and paying only a fraction of the costs involved. (*Laudato Si'*, 195)

This economic ecology finds precedent in Benedict XVI's trenchant call for "forms of economic activity marked by quotas of gratuitousness and communion." Encyclical Letter *Caritas in Veritate* (June 29, 2009), 39. For a contemporary example of what a "Eucharistic economy" might look like, see the efforts of the Simone Weil Catholic Worker House in Portland, Oregon.

126 See E. F. Schumacher, *Small Is Beautiful: Economics As If People Mattered* (New York: Harper & Row, 1973). For Pope Francis's discussion of an "economy of care," see Francis, *Video Message to the Participants in the 7th World Day of Prayer, Reflection, and Action against Human Trafficking*, February 8, 2021. For Pope Francis's promotion of cooperative economies, see *Laudato Si'*, 180.

127 On this appreciation, see Darlene O'Leary, "Economic Democracy: Lonergan and the Antigonish Movement," *The Lonergan Review* 3, no. 1 (2011): 208–18. For an extended application of Lonergan's economic work to several contemporary case studies of social economies, see Morag McAleese, "The Canadian Social Economy and Values: Insights from Bernard Lonergan's Theological Ethics" (ThD diss., Saint Paul University, 2017).

128 See Patrick Byrne, "Ecology, Economy, and Redemption as Dynamic: The Contributions of Jane Jacobs and Bernard Lonergan," *Worldviews: Global Religions, Culture, and Ecology* 7, no. 1–2 (January 2003): 5–25. Lonergan's economic theory then can help answer Francis's lament that "[w]e have not yet managed to adopt a circular model of production capable of preserving resources for present and future generations, while limiting as much as possible the use of nonrenewable resources, moderating their consumption, maximizing their efficient use, reusing and recycling them" (*Laudato Si'*, 22).

129 Joseph Ratzinger, "The Spirit of the Liturgy," in *Joseph Ratzinger Collected Works*, vol. 11, *Theology of the Liturgy*, ed. Michael J. Miller (San Francisco: Ignatius Press, 2014), 56–69. Ratzinger here acknowledges the complex questions this point raises for inculturation; at the very least, the more general point that the liturgical calendar—and thus the liturgy itself—historically finds some intelligibility in the natural rhythms of the cosmos stands.

reflects the rhythms of praise that ring out from creation. Just as the Eucharist embeds one within a broader community of creation, so too must economic activity respect the human and nonhuman schemes of recurrence that mark our common home.

Spontaneous, intersubjective bonds of relationship arise through personal encounters and physical presence, and so an economic ecology also values locality.[130] Economic activity can reflect Thérèse's "little way" by rooting economic transaction in a culture of attentive care. The Eucharist, sacrament of catholicity, makes clear that genuine universal communion arises only by plunging more deeply into the local.[131] Worship spaces built from local materials, whether it be local wood in lecterns or local stone in altars, can make this claim and its social consequences tangible.[132] In *Laudato Si'*, Francis cautions against forms of intensive, globalized forms of production because, in their disregard of locality, they ignore the natural and social schemes of recurrence in a given community.[133] As an alternative, and as shown in the attention given to the Amazon region in the reception of *Laudato Si'*, Francis calls for the support of small-scale production that respects the particularity of local cultures.[134] He writes, "Liberation from the dominant technocratic paradigm does in fact happen sometimes, for example, when cooperatives of small producers adopt less polluting means of production, and opt for a non-consumerist model of life, recreation and community."[135] As demonstrated by events like local farmer's markets (sometimes sponsored by local churches), not only does this economic paradigm respect the gift of creation, so too does it balance the demands of both practicality and relationship by situating economic transactions within relational contexts.

---

130 On Lonergan's discussion of subsidiarity, see *Method in Theology*, 366.

131 See William T. Cavanaugh, *Theopolitical Imagination: Discovering the Liturgy as a Political Act in an Age of Global Consumerism* (New York: Bloomsbury T & T Clark, 2002), 112–22. On the potential links between Lonergan's thought and communitarianism, see Gerard Whelan, "Communitarian Solutions to the Ecological Crisis: Michael Northcott, Bernard Lonergan, and Robert Doran in Dialogue," in *Everything Is Interconnected*, 109–16.

132 For a concrete example of liturgical practice in this vein, see Lucas Briola, "Sustainable Communities and Eucharistic Communities: *Laudato Si'*, Northern Appalachia, and Redemptive Recovery," Special issue, *Journal of Moral Theology* 6 (March 2017): 22–33, at 29–31.

133 *Laudato Si'*, 143–46.

134 *Laudato Si'*, 129.

135 *Laudato Si'*, 112.

This alignment of practicality with relationship better attunes one to encounter concretely and attend lovingly to the particularities of the human and natural conditions of one's place. While the technocratic paradigm fosters scotoses that blind one to brutalizing supply chains in distant lands,[136] an economic ecology grounded in the Eucharist draws attention to the processes of production, "reconnecting the fruit of the earth" with the "work of human hands."[137] The Eucharist demands repenting for the ways that the fruit of the earth and work of human hands, in its form today, obscures God's glory. Praying over the Eucharist accordingly demands the release of insights that call into question the senseless violence, against human and nonhuman creation, that characterizes the production of goods like food and undermine genuine communion.[138] In these ways can a eucharistically shaped economics remain attentive to the cries of the earth and the poor.

This type of economics likewise resists the technocratic imperialization of technology, presuming an alternative understanding of labor.[139] While the technocratic paradigm makes practicality an idol, entrapping people and the earth in frenetic activity, eucharistic praise places this *labora* within a more expansive context of *ora*, the "work of human hands" within the surrender of sacrificial offering.[140] Like economics, labor too should be oriented

---

[136] As Francis suggests, the neglect of the problems of the excluded "is due partly to the fact that many professionals, opinion makers, communications media and centers of power, being located in affluent urban areas, are far removed from the poor, with little direct contact with their problems" (*Laudato Si'*, 49).

[137] Mary E. McGann, *The Meal That Reconnects: Eucharistic Eating and the Global Food Crisis* (Collegeville, Minn.: Liturgical Press, 2020), 189.

[138] See the United Methodist–Roman Catholic Dialogue:

> Bread and wine are necessary for the Eucharist, but wheat and grapes may come from oppressive agricultural practices. Nevertheless, a vigorous eucharistic theology and practice would require us to care about agricultural practices, and not only for wheat and grapes. Because bread and wine are manufactured, the issues of safe and suitable work environments and just wages are at the heart of the church's social justice concerns as derived from our eucharistic practice. . . . We call both Methodists and Catholics to attend more carefully to the production of the sacramental bread and wine both in itself and as a sign of the interconnection of worship, economy and nature. To participate in the Eucharist without discerning these interconnections is the result of indolence and may lead to diminished communion with the Lord. (*Heaven and Earth Are Full of Your Glory*, 26, 34)

[139] As Francis defines the scope of this topic in *Laudato Si'*, "the meaning and purpose of all human activity . . . has to do not only with manual or agricultural labor but with any activity involving a modification of existing reality, from producing a social report to the design of a technological development" (125).

[140] *Laudato Si'*, 126. See also Jonathan Malesic, *The End of Burnout: Why Work Drains Us and How to Live Better Lives* (Oakland, Calif.: University of California Press, 2022), 165–90.

toward communion: human, nonhuman, and divine. The good of human labor must be preserved, since, rather than an all-consuming idol, work should provide "the setting for . . . rich personal growth, where many aspects of life enter into play: creativity, planning for the future, developing our talents, living out our values, relating to others, *giving glory to God*."[141] In this way might genuine human creativity be unleashed from technocratic truncations, instead intending the entire scale of values: from social flourishing to cultural good to personal authenticity and to the glorification of God. Human creativity healed through the Eucharist, in a redemptive scheme of recurrence, can thus condition the emergence of further healing from above.[142] Against myopically biased understandings of progress, this creativity can secure "another type of progress, one which is healthier, more human, more social, more integral" tethered to community and oriented ultimately to God.[143] In the Eucharist, praise both secures and orients the progressive dynamism of the human spirit in a way that respects the full scope of an integral ecology, hears the cries of the earth and the poor, and bothers to care for our common home. Eucharistic praise provides the requisite withdrawal from practicality that saves practicality, directing all creation to the praise of God.

CREATING IN OUR COMMON HOME: DIALOGUE THROUGH EUCHARISTIC FIDELITY

Laudato Si' is a document of dialogue. The word *dialogue* appears twenty-four times throughout the encyclical. While other social encyclicals address themselves to the church or to people of good will, Francis expresses his wish at the beginning of *Laudato Si'* "to enter into dialogue with all people about our common home," *sine glossa*.[144] In this way can the encyclical facilitate "a new dialogue about how we are shaping the future of our planet," a "conversation which includes everyone, since the environmental challenge we are undergoing, and its human roots, concern and affect us all."[145] In chapter 5 of *Laudato Si'*, Francis accordingly urges dialogue within the

---

[141] *Laudato Si'*, 127. Emphasis added.

[142] See Maurice Schepers, "Human Development: From Below Upward and From Above Downward," *Method: Journal of Lonergan Studies* 7, no. 2 (1989): 141–44, at 143–44.

[143] *Laudato Si'*, 112. See also 191, 194, 197.

[144] *Laudato Si'*, 3.

[145] *Laudato Si'*, 14.

entire international community, within national and local communities, within economic and technological decision-making, between politics and human fulfillment, and between religion and science. For the pope, such dialogue and conversation, precisely by connecting everyone and everything, can promote a truly integral ecology and encourage genuine care for our common home.

As chapter 2 stresses, the decisively Catholic worldview of *Laudato Si'*—the distinctly doxological, eucharistic healing emphasized so strongly throughout this book—seemingly stands in tension with this expansive call to dialogue. Enveloping integral ecology within eucharistic praise may appear too churchy, overly introverted, and irresponsibly parochial given the type of public voice such global crises demand. Nevertheless, as Francis explains the unique character of *Laudato Si'*:

> although this Encyclical welcomes dialogue with everyone so that together we can seek paths of liberation, I would like from the outset to show how faith convictions can offer Christians, and some other believers as well, ample motivation to care for nature and for the most vulnerable of their brothers and sisters.... *It is good for humanity and the world at large when we believers better recognize the ecological commitments which stem from our convictions.*[146]

Paradoxically, the more deeply Christian believers engage their own faith convictions, the more truly they serve the other. The dilution of this identity for the sake of dialogue jeopardizes authentic dialogue. For the church to withhold its very essence hinders the truthful self-disclosure needed for dialogue. Not only does such dishonesty belie the trust that enables dialogue, so too does it leave faith convictions susceptible to nontheological parameters, such as the eclectic polarizations of Western politics. The decisively Catholic is indispensable for this wide-ranged conversation, and so it cannot be hidden under a bushel basket if it is in fact to be good for the world at large.

In this way might the healing embodied in and generated through eucharistic praise enable the genuine creating of all those who dwell in our common home. The relationship between healing and creating explains Lonergan's insistence that the redemptive efforts of the church coordinate with efforts beyond its visible confines.[147] In the "Mass and Man"—wherein

---

[146] *Laudato Si'*, 64. Emphasis added.
[147] Lonergan, *Method in Theology*, 366–67.

Lonergan asserts the indispensability of the Eucharist for social transformation—Lonergan adds:

> Can then "from the Holy Sacrifice of the Mass be drawn the power to save human society?" One must make no mistake. One is not to think that human society is going to have its endless cultural, social, political, economic problems solved by some astonishing series of miracles. If problems are to be solved, they will be solved by men who have taken the time and the trouble to discover their nature, who possess the talent to think out solutions, who are gifted with the judgment necessary to proceed from abstract theory to concrete policy.[148]

Likewise, in the twilight of his career, Lonergan speaks of the complementarity of healing and creating.[149] Amid the biased confines of the technocratic paradigm, this healing vector can liberate authentic creating, both within and beyond the institutional church.[150] As Francis maintains, dialogue with religious traditions can curb the tendencies of natural and human sciences "to become enclosed in [their] own language" that "leads to a certain isolation and the absolutization of [their] own field[s] of knowledge."[151] Healing can sublate these realms of knowledge and action, bringing them toward a fuller realization and wisdom as well as reorienting these deformed understandings of creating. The church mediates this healing and, by extension, redeemed creating in a unique way.

Through this lens, the primary way that the church can promote care for our common home is to remain faithful to this healing vector, to remain faithful to the demands of the eucharistic praise that makes the church in its religious, personal, cultural, and social dimensions. Genuine eucharistic fidelity

---

[148] Bernard J. F. Lonergan, "The Mass and Man," in *Shorter Papers*, vol. 20 of CWL, ed. Robert C. Croken, Robert M. Doran, and H. Daniel Monsour (Toronto: University of Toronto, 2007), 97.

[149] Bernard J. F. Lonergan, "Healing and Creating in History," in *A Third Collection*, 107.

[150] Lonergan writes:

> It is not propaganda and it is not argument but religious faith that will liberate human reasonableness from its ideological prisons. It is not the promises of men but religious hope that can enable men to resist the vast pressures of social decay. If passions are to quiet down, if wrongs are to be not exacerbated, not ignored, not merely palliated, but acknowledged and removed, then human possessiveness and human pride have to be replaced by religious charity, by the charity of the suffering servant, by self-sacrificing love. (*Method in Theology*, 117)

[151] *Laudato Si'*, 201.

consists in attending to this integral conversion.¹⁵² In his own work, Lonergan trusts that human authenticity produces genuine objectivity and that surrender to the demands of authenticity leads ultimately to the God who heals.¹⁵³ For him, the common ground on which people might meet and converse stands not on some ahistorical, supposedly neutral lowest common denominator but on authenticity, truthfulness to oneself as called by the God of Jesus Christ. Ecclesial authenticity in turn means faithfulness to God's ever-greater merciful presence and, accordingly, faithfulness to the full scope of the church's healing mission, from religious values downward, in their full specificity. So too, conversely, does such witness mean humbly acknowledging the ways that the church can fail to witness to this healing vector, the gaps between its worship and one's actual life. Staying true to this mission fosters the possibility of genuine dialogue.¹⁵⁴ Thus, the church can most authentically be for the world by being most authentically the church.

That is, the church's dialogical witness to this healing vector in history, through its fidelity to eucharistic praise, sets the indispensable conditions of possibility for genuine, holy care throughout our common home. Reducing dialogue to contestations of power betrays both the church's mission and the nature of genuine dialogue. "Healing," Lonergan states, "is not to be confused with the dominating and manipulating to which the reforming materialist is confined by his own principles."¹⁵⁵ In accord with the Law of

---

152 And thus the Eucharist is not a thing to be instrumentalized for the sake of some extrinsic end. See Chauvet, *Symbol and Sacrament*, 99–109; and Eugene R. Schlesinger, *Missa Est! A Missional Liturgical Ecclesiology* (Minneapolis, Minn.: Fortress Press, 2017), 154.

153 For instance, as Lonergan describes theological method:

> the theologian's strategy will be, not to prove his own position, not to refute counter-positions, but to exhibit diversity and to the point to the evidence for its roots. In this manner he will be attractive to those that appreciate full human authenticity and he will convince those that attain it. Indeed, the basic idea of the method we are trying to develop takes its stand on discovering what human authenticity is and how to appeal to it. It is not an infallible method, for men easily are unauthentic, but it is a powerful method, for man's deepest need and most prized achievement is authenticity. (*Method in Theology*, 254)

This conviction—Lonergan's "wisdom of the concrete"—receives particular emphasis in Wilkins, *Before Truth*, 61–95.

154 As Benedict XVI writes in *Caritas in Veritate*, 4: "Truth, in fact, is *lógos* which creates *diá-logos*, and hence communication and communion. Truth, by enabling men and women to let go of their subjective opinions and impressions, allows them to move beyond cultural and historical limitations and to come together in the assessment of the value and substance of things. Truth opens and unites our minds in the *lógos* of love: this is the Christian proclamation and testimony of charity."

155 Lonergan, "Healing and Creating in History," 107.

the Cross, the church witnesses to God's mercy in the world not through control but through sowing seeds of conversion and healing that may or may not fall on fertile ground. While from a technocratic lens, eucharistic worship appears impractical and irrelevant, *Laudato Si'* makes clear that it is praise that will set the conditions for and secure a truly integral ecology. Lonergan calls the church "an out-going process," an entity that "exists not just for itself but for mankind. Its aim is the realization of the kingdom of God not only within its own organization but in the whole of human society and not only in the after life but also in this life."[156] Developing the missionary emphases of John Paul II and Benedict XVI, Francis illustrates in *Laudato Si'* that the sacrificial ecstasy of dialogical service arises from the sacrificial ecstasy of worship, the outgoing process that defines the church and God's own triune life.[157]

CONCLUSION

Pope Francis has been labeled a "radical," neither conservative nor liberal.[158] "To me," he once recounted in an interview, "the greatest revolution is what goes to the roots."[159] Lonergan, in the words of Frederick Crowe, also hopes to "get to the bottom of things" throughout his theological work.[160] Lonergan's theology of history makes clear that, with *Laudato Si'*, Francis suggests that right praise addresses truly the "roots" (*radices*) of what is happening to our common home. Itself a radical project, Lonergan's theology of history highlights how *Laudato Si'* realizes the radical vision—the eucharistic roots—of Catholic social teaching anticipated by John Paul II, Benedict

---

[156] Lonergan, *Method in Theology*, 363–64.

[157] See Eugene R. Schlesinger, *Sacrificing the Church: Mass, Mission, and Ecumenism* (Lanham, Md.: Lexington Books, 2019), 104–5. Reflecting on the Parable of the Good Samaritan, Francis writes, "belief in God and the worship of God are not enough to ensure that we are actually living in a way pleasing to God. . . . The guarantee of an authentic openness to God, on the other hand, is a way of practicing the faith that helps open our hearts to our brothers and sisters." Encyclical Letter *Fratelli Tutti* (October 3, 2020), 74.

[158] Austin Ivereigh, *The Great Reformer: Francis and the Making of a Radical Pope* (New York: Henry Holt, 2014), 380–91; and Walter Kasper, *Pope Francis' Revolution of Tenderness and Love: Theological and Pastoral Perspectives*, trans. William Madges (New York: Paulist Press, 2015), 23, 27, 90.

[159] Francis, "Interview in *La Vanguardia*," June 12, 2014, https://www.catholicnewsagency.com/news/pope-francis-interview-with-la-vanguardia—-full-text-45430.

[160] Frederick E. Crowe, "Lonergan as Pastoral Theologian," *Gregorianum* 67, no. 3 (1986): 451–70, at 456.

XVI, and Francis. The radical vision of *Laudato Si'* in turn unearths the ecological potential of Lonergan's theology of history, illustrating the radical responsiveness of the Lonergan project to the situation described in the encyclical. This radicalism promises much to a world and church fragmented by the superficiality of polarization.

It is precisely this radical vision of the church's mission that marked what was arguably Francis's most important political address after the release of *Laudato Si'*. In September of 2015, during his visit to the United States, Francis referenced *Laudato Si'* twice in his highly anticipated and widely watched address to Congress. Both references occur as he discusses the Catholic radical, Dorothy Day, whose "social activism, . . . passion for justice and for the cause of the oppressed, were inspired by the Gospel, her faith, and the example of the saints."[161] To a gridlocked legislature, the allusion spoke volumes. Day's radicalism, referenced several times in this chapter, confounds camps that have formed both in the United States and the church in the past several decades. Her unyielding concern for the poor matched her fierce defense of the unborn; her hunger for social justice expressed her unyielding fidelity to the Eucharist.[162] In locating the calls of *Laudato Si'* within Day's witness, Francis seemingly implies that the encyclical can only be understood through a similar type of radical, integrative vision. In a polarized world and church, the radicalism of *Laudato Si'* confounds in its passionate protection of the earth and the unborn, its decisively Catholic worldview and its broad-minded attentiveness to far-reaching social concerns. Lonergan makes clear that, as was the case for Day, the radical call to conversion in *Laudato Si'* finds root in a eucharistic vision.

---

[161] Francis, *Visit to the Joint Session of the United States Congress* (September 24, 2015).

[162] See Mark and Louise Zwick, *The Catholic Worker Movement: Intellectual and Spiritual Origins* (Mahwah, N.J.: Paulist Press, 2005), 295–320.

Conclusion

Receiving the Eucharistic Vision of *Laudato Si'*

This book has offered a sustained, systematic exploration of the eucharistic vision of *Laudato Si'*. Popes John Paul II and Benedict XVI lay the foundation. Pope Francis articulates the vision itself. The work of Bernard Lonergan, especially when read in tandem with Robert Doran, solidifies this vision systematically and ecclesiologically. The theme of ecclesial reception has played an essential role in the development of this argument. The reception of human ecology points to the insufficiency of the category on its own; the reception of *Laudato Si'* and its integral ecology points to the need for a more robust account of ecclesial mission and integral conversion grounded in eucharistic praise. The proof of magisterial teaching can, in part, be found in the pudding of reception. Since the release of *Laudato Si'*, three key moments of reception attest that the radically doxological and eucharistic contours of its integral ecology are not pious anomalies but rather an enduring achievement that deserves expansion through ongoing systematic reflection.

The first moment came on February 26, 2019. On that day, Pope Francis released his annual Lenten message, taking the opportunity to meditate on Romans 8:19: "For creation waits with eager longing for the revealing of the children of God."[1] The message stuns in its cosmic and, indeed, integral scope. It speaks of how human cooperation with God's redemptive purposes can help redeem all creation and bring it into communion with the God who is Communion. Moreover, Francis underscores the doxological, priestly shape of this grace-enabled cooperation: "When the love of Christ transfigures the lives of the saints in spirit, body and soul, they give praise to God. Through prayer, contemplation and art, they also include other creatures in that praise, as we see admirably expressed in the 'Canticle of the Creatures' by Saint Francis of Assisi."[2] Praising God through Christ is creation's salvation,

---

1 Francis, *Message of His Holiness Pope Francis for Lent* (February 26, 2019).
2 Francis, *Message of His Holiness Pope Francis for Lent*, 1.

as "[a]ll creation is called, with us, to go forth 'from its bondage to decay and obtain the glorious liberty of the children of God' (Rom 8:21)."[3] What Francis identifies as "idolatry"—the temptation to "'devour' everything to satisfy our voracity" and "hoarding everything for ourselves in the illusory belief that we can secure a future that does not belong to us"—imprisons creation.[4] The message concludes that Lent requires, in the face of this sinful idolatry, embracing instead the cruciform shape of doxology. Lenten practices train Christians to begin to feel pity with an outstretched heart, to care for our common home in a way that leads to new life.

The second moment came on July 6, 2019, a moment that deepened this doxological charge and bared its eucharistic character. On that day, Francis addressed members of *Laudato Si'* Communities, an Italian Catholic movement that promotes the aims of the encyclical.[5] Francis offers three words to guide the praxis of these communities and, by extension, the character of an integral ecology. The first is doxology: "Faced with the good of creation . . . it is necessary to assume the attitude of praise." Praise leads one to respect creation. Specifically, the awe and wonder of praise shakes one out of indifference, making one attentive to the signs of God in creation. The second word, Eucharist, denotes the distinctively Christian shape of this care. "The eucharistic attitude, faced with the world and its inhabitants, knows how to grasp the status of gift that every living being carries within itself." As opposed to an excessive anthropocentrism that reduces creation to a thing to be greedily possessed, the Eucharist reveals that creation is a gift to be shared in common. The Eucharist discloses how creation, precisely as gift, reveals the glory of God. The third word, asceticism, ensures that doxology and the Eucharist become an entire way of life. Needed are practices that nurture the doxological and eucharistic shape of an integral ecology such that it becomes this entire way of life. In this way might communities committed to the calls of *Laudato Si'* serve as a "germ of a renewed way of living in the world, to give it a future, to preserve its beauty and integrity for the good of every living being, *ad majorem Dei gloriam*." In following this charge, ecclesial communities can facilitate the doxological vocation of our entire common home.

---

3 Francis, *Message of His Holiness Pope Francis for Lent*, 3.

4 Francis, *Message of His Holiness Pope Francis for Lent*, 3.

5 Francis, *Message to the Participants in the Second Forum of the* Laudato Si' Communities in Amatrice, Italy (July 6, 2019).

The third moment came on February 12, 2020. On that day, Francis promulgated *Querida Amazona*, a post-synodal apostolic exhortation on the church's mission in the Amazon region, wherein the cries of the earth and the poor intersect most clearly.[6] The document complements the final document of the Synod of Bishops released several months prior, *The Amazon: New Paths for the Church and for an Integral Ecology*.[7] Not only do these documents demonstrate that integral ecology continues to supply a new foundational category for Catholic social teaching, so too do they remain doxological and eucharistic. In the words of one commentator, *Querida Amazonia* "has a specific contemplative slant" in the ways it outlines an integral ecology.[8] As Francis reasons, this emphasis can challenge the ironclad logic of the technocratic paradigm, its positivism, and the indifference it perpetuates against the cries of the earth and of the poor. Explaining his frequent references to Amazonian poets throughout the text, he states, "Those poets, contemplatives and prophets, help free us from the technocratic and consumerist paradigm that destroys nature and robs us of a truly dignified existence."[9] Given that "[f]requently we let our consciences be deadened," Francis beseeches his audience to "awaken our God-given aesthetic and contemplative sense that so often we let languish."[10] Francis accordingly structures the entire document around four "dreams" for the region, an imaginative exercise meant to shatter the reductionistic positivism of technocracy.[11]

These contemplative emphases of *Querida Amazonia* have an unmistakably doxological, eucharistic bent. Quoting the poet Sui-Yun, Francis writes, "if we enter into communion with the forest, our voices will easily blend with its own and become a prayer: 'as we rest in the shade of an ancient eucalyptus, our prayer for light joins in the song of the eternal

---

6 Francis, Post-Synodal Apostolic Exhortation *Querida Amazonia* (February 12, 2020).

7 Synod of Bishops, *The Amazon: New Paths for the Church and for an Integral Ecology* (October 28, 2019). On the authoritative relationship between the two documents, see *Querida Amazonia*, 2–4.

8 Antonio Spadaro, "*Querida Amazonia*: Commentary on Pope Francis' Apostolic Exhortation," *La Civiltà Cattolica* (February 12, 2020), https://www.laciviltacattolica.com/querida-amazonia-commentary-on-pope-francis-apostolic-exhortation/.

9 *Querida Amazonia*, 46.

10 *Querida Amazonia*, 53, 56.

11 *Querida Amazonia*, 7. In Spadaro's words, "A dream combines a warm, affective and inner connotation with issues that are sometimes thorny and complex." In "Commentary on Pope Francis' Apostolic Exhortation."

foliage.'"[12] Humans are called to enter into and mediate the praise of creation. This contemplative sensibility not only assumes but awakens a sacramental, eucharistic perspective in those willing to hear. Again, in the words of Francis, "[Jesus Christ] is present in a glorious and mysterious way in the river, the trees, the fish and the wind, as the Lord who reigns in creation without ever losing his transfigured wounds, while in the Eucharist he takes up the elements of this world and confers on all things the meaning of the paschal gift."[13] The church's eucharistic identity witnesses to this reality. Remarking that the sacraments are "the fulfillment of creation, in which nature is elevated to become a locus and instrument of grace," Francis reechoes the words of *Laudato Si'* on the Eucharist and its Sunday celebration.[14] Thus, it this sacramental praxis that can break through the technocratic paradigm so as to awaken a new dream for the Amazon as well as for our entire common home. That is, an integral ecology bears the imprint of eucharistic praise.

In all three instances, Francis continues to stress the doxological and eucharistic contours of an integral ecology and indeed of the church's social mission. All three instances evince Francis's ongoing willingness to plunge more deeply into the decisively Catholic for the sake of a problem that spans the globe. He shows that turning to the decisively Catholic need not jeopardize the broadly catholic mission of the church. Francis completes a turn begun by popes John Paul II and Benedict XVI in this regard. For Francis, care for our common home is irreducible to common-sense solutions and has an unmistakably ecclesial bent. The theological depth of this integral ecology challenges all those forces that would diminish it to a collection of policy positions. The church's mediation of an integral ecology offers something other than more technocratic solutions mired in polarization. Indeed, that which makes the church—its work of praise, the *opus Dei*—provides the source and summit, the *Urbild* and telos, of this mission. To a church burdened by division—between left and right, between justice and worship—the integral ecology of *Laudato Si'* suggests a path forward. An integral ecology, if it is to in fact promote the interconnectedness of everything, demands a radical wedding of the church's *ora et labora*. This insight must be a lasting legacy of *Laudato Si'*. Insofar as it can account for the integral

---

12 *Querida Amazonia*, 56.

13 *Querida Amazonia*, 74.

14 *Querida Amazonia*, 81–83. Francis cites liberally from *Laudato Si'*, 235–36, here.

breadth and eucharistic depth of *Laudato Si'*, Lonergan's theology of history perpetuates this legacy.

Given the uneven reception of *Laudato Si'*, much more work remains. The church's response to the impact of the COVID-19 pandemic has made this work all the more urgent. The pandemic hit amid celebrations of the encyclical's fifth anniversary, a coincidence that seems to illustrate their relevance to each other. As he has outlined the church's mission in the wake of the pandemic, Pope Francis proposes that "the future we are called to build has to begin with an integral ecology."[15] The comprehensive approach named by the integral ecology of *Laudato Si'* can help address the environmental, social, cultural, moral, and religious crises that the pandemic has unearthed. At the same time, in their own response to the impact of COVID-19, the U.S. Catholic bishops have called for a three-year "eucharistic revival" beginning on the Feast of Corpus Christi, 2022.[16] This initiative hopes to deepen both a devotion to the Eucharist and an understanding of its significance for Christian life. The eucharistic vision of *Laudato Si'* confirms that both responses support each other. Cardinal Michael Czerny, who played a central role in recent synodal deliberations regarding the implementation of an integral ecology in the Amazon region, asks, "How is that over 40 years a priest I never before noticed how we are called to be fully engaged, as fellow creatures with the universe and all it contains, in offering praise and thanksgiving to our Creator, through Jesus Christ, His Son, our Lord? To me it seems that our worship, as expressed in both Offertory and Canon, is far ahead of our praxis in ecology and stewardship."[17] Eucharistic coherence demands recognizing and living such connections, and so, liturgical catechesis and mystagogy can continue to help care for creation catch up to the church's worship. Some parishes have begun to close this gap. Some liturgical theologians have started to make such connections more explicit. In either case, the call of this book's vision and the exigencies of the present moment demands a deeper fidelity to eucharistic worship

---

15 Francis, with Austen Ivereigh, *Let Us Dream: The Path to a Better Future* (New York: Simon & Schuster, 2020), 35.

16 Maria Wiering, "National Eucharistic Revival Aims to 'to Light Fire' among the Faithful," *Our Sunday Visitor*, June 21, 2021, https://osvnews.com/2021/06/21/national-eucharistic-revival-aims-to-to-light-fire-among-the-faithful/. See also J. D. Flynn, "'We Want to Light a Fire': A Pillar Interview with Bishop Andrew Cozzens," The Pillar, June 16, 2021, https://www.pillarcatholic.com/p/we-want-to-light-a-fire-usccb-plans.

17 As quoted in Christopher J. Thompson, *The Joyful Mystery: Field Notes toward a Green Thomism* (Steubenville, Ohio: Emmaus Road Publishing, 2017), 165.

itself, a worship that finds verification in the concrete acts of care for our common home that it evokes. A task that without doubt will be aided with a recovery of Lonergan's theology of history, this book stands as an invitation for continuing efforts that show connections between the church's worship and care for our common home and, as a result, deepen the conversion called for by the eucharistic vision of *Laudato Si'*.

Bibliography

Agliardo, Michael. "The Reception of *Laudato Si'* in the United States in Secular and Sacred Arenas." In *All Creation Is Connected: Voices in Response to Pope Francis's Encyclical on Ecology*, edited by Daniel R. DiLeo, 44–62. Winona, Minn.: Anselm Academic, 2018.

Allen, John L., Jr. *The Rise of Benedict XVI: The Inside Story of How the Pope Was Elected and Where He Will Take the Catholic Church*. New York: Doubleday, 2005.

Anatolios, Khaled. *Deification through the Cross: An Eastern Christian Theology of Salvation*. Grand Rapids, Mich.: Eerdmans, 2020.

Aquinas, Thomas. *Summa theologiae*. New York: Editiones Paulinae, 1962.

Arrupe, Pedro. "The Eucharist and Hunger." In *Selected Letters and Addresses*. Vol. 2 of *Justice with Faith Today*, edited by Jerome Aixala. St. Louis, Mo.: The Institute of Jesuit Sources, 1980.

Ashley, Mary. "If You Want Responsibility, Build Relationship: A Personalist Approach to Benedict XVI's Environmental Vision." In *Environmental Justice and Climate Change: Assessing Pope Benedict XVI's Ecological Vision for the Catholic Church in the United States*, edited by Jame Schaefer and Tobias Winright, 19–42. Lanham, Md.: Lexington Books, 2013.

Associated Press–NORC Center for Public Affairs Research. "Speaking Out on Global Warming: Public Attitudes toward the Papal Encyclical on Climate Change." August 2015. http://www.apnorc.org/PDFs/PopeGlobalWarming/Speaking%20Out%20on%20Global%20Warming%20Issue%20Brief.pdf.

Augustine. "On Free Will." In *Augustine: Earlier Writings*, 102–217. Translated by John H. S. Burleigh. Philadelphia: Westminster Press, 1953.

———. *The Confessions of St. Augustine*. Translated by John K. Ryan. Garden City, N.Y.: Image Books, 1960.

———. *On the Psalms*. Vol. 29 of *Ancient Christian Writers*. Translated by Scholastica Hebgin and Felicitas Corrigan. New York: Newman Press, 1960.

Bacon, Francis. "The Masculine Birth of Time, or The Great Instauration of the Dominion of Man over the Universe." In *The Philosophy of Francis Bacon*, 61–72. Translated by Benjamin Farrington. Liverpool: Liverpool University Press, 1964.

Barron, Robert. *Heaven in Stone and Glass: Experiencing the Spirituality of the Great Cathedrals*. New York: Crossroad Publishing, 2002.

———. "Evangelizing the American Culture." *Bridging the Great Divide: Musings of a Post-Liberal, Post-Conservative Evangelical Catholic*, 256–72. Lanham, Md.: Rowman & Littlefield Publishers, 2004.

———. *The Priority of Christ: Toward a Postliberal Catholicism*. Grand Rapids, Mich.: Baker Academic, 2007.

_____. "Why Bernard Lonergan Matters for Pastoral People." *Exploring Catholic Theology: Essays on God, Liturgy, and Evangelization*, 175–84. Grand Rapids, Mich.: Baker Academic, 2015.

_____. "Gaston Fessard and Pope Francis." In *Discovering Pope Francis: The Roots of Jorge Mario Bergoglio's Thinking*, edited by Brian Y. Lee and Thomas L. Knoebel, 114–29. Collegeville, Minn.: Liturgical Press, 2019.

Basil. *On the Hexameron, in Exegetic Homilies*. Translated by Agnes Clare Way. Washington, D.C.: The Catholic University of America Press, 1963.

Bauerschmidt, Frederick Christian. "The Politics of the Little Way: Dorothy Day Reads Thérèse of Lisieux." In *American Catholic Traditions: Resources for Renewal*, edited by Sandra Yocum Mize and William L. Portier, 77–95. Maryknoll, N.Y.: Orbis Books, 1997.

Baur, Michael. "Natural Law and the Natural Environment: Pope Benedict XVI's Vision beyond Utilitarianism and Deontology." In *Environmental Justice and Climate Change: Assessing Pope Benedict XVI's Ecological Vision for the Catholic Church in the United States*, edited by Jame Schaefer and Tobias Winright, 43–58. Lanham, Md.: Lexington Books, 2013.

Baxter, Michael J. "Reintroducing Virgil Michel: Towards a Counter-Tradition of Catholic Social Ethics in the United States." *Communio* 24 (Fall 1997): 499–528.

_____. "'Blowing the Dynamite of the Church': Catholic Radicalism from a Catholic Radicalist Perspective." In *The Church as Counterculture*, edited by Michael L. Budde and Robert W. Brimlow, 195–212. Albany: State University of New York Press, 2000.

_____. "Murray's Mistake." *America* (September 23, 2013): 13–18.

Baxter, Michael J., and William T. Cavanaugh. "Reply to 'A View from Abroad' by Massimo Faggioli." *America* (April 21, 2014): 8.

Benedict. *RB 1980: The Rule of St. Benedict*. Translated by Timothy Fry. Collegeville, Minn.: Liturgical Press, 1981.

Benedict XVI. *Homily for the Solemn Inauguration of the Petrine Ministry*. April 24, 2005.

_____. *Deus Caritas Est*. Encyclical Letter. December 25, 2005.

_____. *The Human Person, the Heart of Peace*. January 1, 2007.

_____. *Sacramentum Caritatis*. Post-Synodal Apostolic Exhortation. February 22, 2007.

_____. *Spe Salvi*. Encyclical Letter. November 30, 2007.

_____. *The Human Family, a Community of Peace*. January 1, 2008.

_____. *Caritas in Veritate*. Encyclical Letter. June 29, 2009.

_____. *If You Want to Cultivate Peace, Protect Creation*. January 1, 2010.

_____. *Address to the German Bundestag*. September 22, 2011.

Benedict XVI, with Peter Seewald. *Light of the World: The Pope, the Church, and the Signs of the Times*, translated by Michael J. Miller and Adrian J. Walker. San Francisco: Ignatius Press, 2010.

Bergoglio, Jorge Mario. "What I Would Have Said at the Consistory: Interview with Sefania Falasca." *30 Days*, 11 (2007). http://www.30giorni.it/articoli_id_16457_l3.htm.

———. "Bergoglio's Intervention: A Diagnosis of the Problems in the Church." Vatican News. March 27, 2013. http://en.radiovaticana.va/news/2013/03/27/bergoglios_intervention:_a_diagnosis_of_the_problems_in_the_church/en1-677269.

———. *Noi come cittadini, noi come popolo: Verso un bicenternario in giustizia e solidarietà 2010-2016*. Milan: Jaca Book, 2013.

———. Prologue to *Il Bicentenario dell'indipendenza dei paesi latino-americani: Ieri e oggi*, by Guzmán Carriquiry Lecour, vii–ix. Soveria Mannelli: Rubbettino, 2013.

Berry, Thomas. "An Ecologically Sensitive Spirituality." *Earth Ethics* 8, no. 1 (1996): 1–13.

Blackwood, Jeremy W. "Trinitarian Love in the Dialectics of History." *Method: Journal of Lonergan Studies*, n.s. 4, no. 1 (Spring 2013): 1–16.

———. "Law of the Cross and the Mystical Body of Christ." In *Intellect, Affect, and God: The Trinity, History, and the Life of Grace*, edited by Joseph Ogbonnaya and Gerard Whelan, 274–91. Milwaukee, Wis.: Marquette University Press, 2021.

Boff, Leonardo, and Virgil Elizondo. "Ecology and Poverty: Cry of the Earth, Cry of the Poor—Editorial." *Concilium* 5 (1995): ix–xii.

Borghesi, Massimo. *The Mind of Pope Francis: Jorge Mario Bergoglio's Intellectual Journey*. Translated by Barry Hudock. Collegeville, Minn.: Liturgical Press, 2018.

Briola, Lucas. "Sustainable Communities and Eucharistic Communities: *Laudato Si'*, Northern Appalachia, and Redemptive Recovery." Special issue, *Journal of Moral Theology* 6, 1 (March 2017): 22–33.

———. "The Integral Ecology of *Laudato Si'* and a Seamless Garment: The Sartorial Usefulness of Lonergan and Doran's Turn to Culture." *The Lonergan Review* 9 (2018): 31–48.

———. "Responding to the One Cry of Earth and Poor: An Integral Ecology, the Scale of Values, and Eucharistic Healing," in *Everything Is Interconnected: Toward a Globalization with a Human Face and an Integral Ecology*, ed. Joseph Ogbonnaya and Lucas Briola, 119–35 (Milwaukee, Wis.: Marquette University Press, 2019).

———. "Praise Rather Than Solving Problems: Understanding the Doxological Turn of *Laudato Si'* through Lonergan," *Theological Studies* 81, no. 3 (September 2020): 119–35.

———. "Dramatic Artistry in Our Common Home: Robert Doran and the Doxological Anthropology of *Laudato Si'*." In *Intellect, Affect, and God: The Trinity, History, and the Life of Grace*, edited by Joseph Ogbonnaya and Gerard Whelan, 3–18. Milwaukee, Wis.: Marquette University Press, 2021.

Brown, Patrick. "'Aiming Excessively High and Far': The Early Lonergan and the Challenge of Theory in Catholic Social Thought." *Theological Studies* 72, no. 3 (September 2011): 620–44.

Brown, William P. *Seeing the Psalms: A Theology of Metaphor*. Louisville, Ky.: Westminster John Knox Press, 2002.

Brueggemann, Walter. *Israel's Praise: Doxology against Idolatry and Ideology*. Minneapolis, Minn.: Fortress Press, 1988.

———. *The Prophetic Imagination*. 40th anniv. ed. Minneapolis, Minn.: Fortress Press, 2018.

Brunk, Timothy. "Worshipful Pattern." *Worship* 85, no. 6 (2011): 482–502.

Budde, Michael. *The (Magic) Kingdom of God: Christianity and Global Culture Industries*. Boulder, Colo.: Westview Press, 1997.

———. "The Alice's Restaurant of Catholic Social Teaching: Global Order in *Caritas in Veritate*." In *Jesus Christ: The New Face of Social Progress*, edited by Peter Casarella, 137–51. Grand Rapids, Mich.: Eerdmans, 2015.

Byrne, Patrick H. "The Thomist Sources of Lonergan's Dynamic Worldview." *The Thomist* 46, no. 1 (January 1982): 108–45.

———. "The Fabric of Lonergan's Thought." *Lonergan Workshop* 5 (1986): 1–84.

———. "Spirit of Wonder, Spirit of Love: Reflections on the Work of Bernard Lonergan." *Budhi: A Journal of Ideas and Culture* 2 (1997): 67–84.

———. "Ecology, Economy, and Redemption as Dynamic: The Contributions of Jane Jacobs and Bernard Lonergan." *Worldviews: Global Religions, Culture, and Ecology* 7, n. 1–2 (January 2003): 5–25.

———. "The Passionateness of Being: The Legacy of Bernard Lonergan, S.J." In *Finding God in All Things: Celebrating Bernard Lonergan, John Courtney Murray, and Karl Rahner*, edited by Mark Bosco and David Stagaman, 35–51. New York: Fordham University Press, 2007.

———. "What Is *Our* Scale of Value Preference?" *Lonergan Workshop* 21 (2008): 43–64.

———. "Which Scale of Value Preference? Lonergan, Scheler, Von Hildebrand, and Doran." In *Meaning and History in Systematic Theology: Essays in Honor of Robert M. Doran, SJ*, edited by John Dadosky, 19–49. Milwaukee, Wis.: Marquette University Press, 2009.

———. "Intelligibility and Natural Science: Alienation or Friendship with the Universe?" *Lonergan Workshop* 24 (2010): 1–32.

———. *The Ethics of Discernment: Lonergan's Foundations for Ethics*. Toronto: University of Toronto Press, 2016.

Caccamo, James F. "The Message on the Media: Seventy Years of Catholic Social Teaching on Social Communication." *Josephinum Journal of Theology* 15, no. 2 (2008): 390–426.

Caldecott, Stratford. "At Home in the Cosmos: The Revealing of the Sons of God." *Nova et Vetera*, English ed., 10, no. 1 (2012): 105–20.

Camosy, Charles C. *Resisting Throwaway Culture: How a Consistent Life Ethic Can Unite a Fractured People*. Hyde Park, N.Y.: New City Press, 2019.

Carmody, John. *Ecology and Religion: Toward a New Christian Theology of Nature*. New York: Paulist Press, 1983.

Castillo, Daniel P.. *An Ecological Theology of Liberation: Salvation and Political Ecology*. Maryknoll, N.Y.: Orbis Books, 2019.

Catton, William R. "Foundations of Human Ecology." *Sociological Perspectives* 37, no. 1 (1994): 75–95.

Cavanaugh, William T. *Theopolitical Imagination: Discovering the Liturgy as a Political Act in an Age of Global Consumerism*. New York: Bloomsbury T & T Clark, 2002.

———. *Being Consumed: Economics and Christian Desire*. Grand Rapids, Mich.: Eerdmans, 2008.

———. *Migrations of the Holy: God, State, and the Political Meaning of the Church*. Grand Rapids, Mich.: Eerdmans, 2011.

———. "Return of the Golden Calf: Economy, Idolatry, and Secularization since *Gaudium et Spes*." *Theological Studies* 76, no. 4 (December 2015): 698–717.

CELAM. "Aparecida Concluding Document: Fifth General Conference of Bishops of Latin America and the Caribbean." May 2007.

Center for Applied Research in the Apostolate. "CARA Catholic Poll (CCP) 2016: Attitudes about Climate Change." 2016. https://cara.georgetown.edu/climate%20summary.pdf.

Chapp, Larry. "Liberalism, the Church, and the Unreality of God." *Communio: International Catholic Review* 48, no. 3 (Fall 2021): 518–35.

Chauvet, Louis-Marie. *Symbol and Sacrament: A Sacramental Reinterpretation of Christian Existence*. Collegeville, Minn.: Liturgical Press, 1995.

Chryssavgis, John. *Creation as Sacrament: Reflections on Ecology and Spirituality*. New York: Bloomsbury T & T Clark, 2019.

Clark, R. Michael. "Byway of the Cross: The Early Lonergan and Political Order." *Lonergan Workshop* 12 (1996): 27–44.

Cloutier, David. "Working with the Grammar of Creation: Benedict XVI, Wendell Berry, and the Unity of the Catholic Moral Vision." *Communio* 37 (Winter 2010): 606–33.

———. "Cavanaugh and Grimes on Structural Evils of Violence and Race: Overcoming Conflicts in Contemporary Social Ethics," *Journal of the Society of Christian Ethics* 37, no. 2 (2017): 59–78.

Collins, Christopher S. *The Word Made Love: The Dialogical Theology of Joseph Ratzinger*. Collegeville, Minn.: Liturgical Press, 2013.

Congregation for the Doctrine of Faith. *Instruction on Certain Aspects of the "Theology of Liberation."* August 6, 1984.

———. *Placuit Deo*. February 22, 2018.

Connor, James L., ed. *The Dynamism of Desire: Bernard J. F. Lonergan, SJ, on The Spiritual Exercises of Saint Ignatius of Loyola*. Saint Louis: The Institute of Jesuit Sources, 2006.

Copeland, M. Shawn. *Enfleshing Freedom: Body, Race, and Being.* Minneapolis, Minn.: Fortress Press, 2010.

Corkery, James. *Joseph Ratzinger's Theological Ideas: Wise Cautions and Legitimate Hopes.* New York: Paulist Press, 2009.

———. "John Paul II: Universal Pastor in a Global Age." In *The Papacy since 1500: From Italian Prince to Universal Pastor,* edited by James Corkery and Thomas Worcester, 223–42. New York: Cambridge University Press, 2010.

Cowdin, Daniel M. "John Paul II and Environmental Concern: Problems and Possibilities." *Living Light* 28 (1991): 44–52.

Crawford, Jennifer. *Spiritually-Engaged Knowledge: The Attentive Heart.* Burlington, Vt.: Ashgate Publishing, 2005.

Crowe, Frederick. "Lonergan as Pastoral Theologian." *Gregorianum* 67, no. 3 (1986): 451–70.

———. "An Expansion of Lonergan's Notion of Value." In *Appropriating the Lonergan Idea,* edited by Michael Vertin, 344–59. Washington, D.C.: The Catholic University of Press, 1989.

———. *Lonergan.* Collegeville, Minn.: Liturgical Press, 1992.

———. *Christ and History: The Christology of Bernard Lonergan from 1935 to 1982.* Ottawa: Novalis, 2005.

———. "Son and Spirit: Tension in the Divine Missions?" In *Appropriating the Lonergan Idea,* edited by Michael Vertin, 297–314. Toronto: University of Toronto, 2006.

Crysdale, Cynthia S. W. "Playing God? Moral Agency in an Emergent World." *Journal of the Society of Christian Ethics* 23 (2003): 398–426.

———. "Making a Way by Walking: Risk, Control, and Emergent Probability." *Theoforum* 39 (2008): 39–58.

———. "The Law of the Cross and Emergent Probability." In *Finding Salvation in Christ: Essays on Christology and Soteriology in Honor of William P. Loewe,* edited by Christopher D. Denny and Christopher McMahon, 193–214. Eugene, Ore: Pickwick Publications, 2011.

Crysdale, Cynthia S. W., and Neil Ormerod. *Creator God, Evolving World.* Minneapolis, Minn.: Fortress Press, 2013.

Cunningham, Lawrence S. *Francis of Assisi: Performing the Gospel of Life.* Grand Rapids, Mich.: Eerdmans, 2004.

Curnow, Rohan Michael. *The Preferential Option for the Poor: A Short History and a Reading Based on the Thought of Bernard Lonergan.* Milwaukee, Wis.: Marquette University Press, 2012.

———. "Which Preferential Option for the Poor? A History of the Doctrine's Bifurcation." *Modern Theology* 31, no. 1 (January 2015): 27–59.

Curran, Charles. *American Catholic Social Ethics*. South Bend, Ind.: University of Notre Dame Press, 1982.

D'Antonio, William V., Michelle Dillon, and Mary L. Gautier. *American Catholics in Transition*. Lanham, Md.: Rowman & Littlefield Publishers, 2013.

Dadosky, John D. Introduction to in *Meaning and History in Systematic Theology: Essays in Honor of Robert M. Doran, SJ*, edited by John D. Dadosky, 9–18. Milwaukee, Wis.: Marquette University Press, 2009.

———. "Is There a Fourth Stage of Meaning?" *Heythrop Journal* 51 (2010): 768–80.

Day, Dorothy. *Thérèse*. Springfield, Ill.: Templegate Publishing, 1979.

———. *Loaves and Fishes*. Maryknoll, N.Y.: Orbis Books, 1997.

De Lubac, Henri. *The Church: Paradox and Mystery*. Translated by James R. Dunne. Staten Island, N.Y.: Alba House, 1969.

———. *The Splendor of the Church*. Translated by Michael Mason. San Francisco: Ignatius Press, 1986.

———. *Paradoxes of Faith*. Translated by Sadie Krielkamp. San Francisco: Ignatius Press, 1987.

———. *Catholicism: Christ and the Common Destiny of Man*. Translated by Lancelot C. Sheppard and Elizabeth Englund. San Francisco: Ignatius Press, 1988.

———. *At the Service of the Church: Henri de Lubac Reflects on the Circumstances That Occasioned His Writings*. Translated by Anne Elizabeth Englund. San Francisco: Ignatius Press, 1989.

Deane-Drummond, Celia. "Joining in the Dance: Catholic Social Teaching and Ecology." *New Blackfriars* 93, no. 1044 (2012): 193–212.

Descartes, René. "Discourse on Method." In Vol. 1 of *Philosophical Works of Descartes*, 80–130. Translated by Elizabeth S. Haldane and G. R. T. Ross. Cambridge: Cambridge University Press, 1976.

Dettloff, Dean. "A 'Green' Church in Toronto Teaches Theology through Design." *America* (October 14, 2019): 16–17.

Doran, Robert M. *Subject and Psyche: Ricoeur, Jung, and the Search for Foundations*. Washington, D.C.: University Press of America, 1977.

———. *Psychic Conversion and Theological Foundations*. Chico, Calif.: Scholars Press, 1981.

———. *Theology and the Dialectics of History*. Toronto: University of Toronto Press, 1990.

———. "Aesthetics and the Opposites." In *Intentionality and Psyche*. Vol. 1 of *Theological Foundations*, 105–32. Milwaukee, Wis.: Marquette University Press, 1995.

———. "The Analogy of Dialectic and the Systematics of History." In *Theology and Culture*. Vol. 2 of *Theological Foundations*, 503–33. Milwaukee, Wis.: Marquette University Press, 1995.

———. "Bernard Lonergan: An Appreciation." In *Theology and Culture*. Vol. 2 of *Theological Foundations*, 297–318. Milwaukee, Wis: Marquette University Press, 1995.

———. "Common Ground." In *Theology and Culture*. Vol. 2 of *Theological Foundations*, 319–30. Milwaukee, Wis.: Marquette University Press, 1995.

———. "Cosmopolis and the Situation: A Preface to Systematics and Communications." In *Theology and Culture*. Vol. 2 of *Theological Foundations*, 331–62. Milwaukee, Wis.: Marquette University Press, 1995.

———. "Dramatic Artistry in the Third Stage of Meaning." In *Intentionality and Psyche*. Vol. 1 of *Theological Foundations*, 231–78. Milwaukee, Wis.: Marquette University Press, 1995.

———. "From Psychic Conversion to the Dialectic of Community." In *Theology and Culture*. Vol. 2 of *Theological Foundations*, 35–64. Milwaukee, Wis.: Marquette University Press, 1995.

———. "Psychic Conversion and Spiritual Development." In *Theology and Culture*. Vol. 2 of *Theological Foundations*, 65–94. Milwaukee, Wis.: Marquette University Press, 1995.

———. "Suffering Servanthood and the Scale of Values." In *Theology and Culture*. Vol. 2 of *Theological Foundations*, 217–58. Milwaukee, Wis.: Marquette University Press, 1995.

———. "Theology's Situation: Questions to Eric Voegelin." In *Theology and Culture*. Vol. 2 of *Theological Foundations*, 259–96. Milwaukee, Wis.: Marquette University Press, 1995.

———. "Lonergan and Balthasar: Methodological Considerations." *Theological Studies* 58 (1997): 61–84.

———. "AIDS Ministry as a Praxis of Hope." In *Jesus Crucified and Risen: Essays in Spirituality and Theology in Honor of Dom Sebastian Moore*, edited by William P. Loewe and Vernon J. Gregson, 177–93. Collegeville, Minn.: Liturgical Press, 1998.

———. *What Is Systematic Theology?* Toronto: University of Toronto Press, 2005.

———. "Bernard Lonergan and Daniel Berrigan." In *Faith, Resistance, and the Future: Daniel Berrigan's Challenge to Catholic Social Thought*, edited by James L. Marsh and Anna J. Brown, 119–31. New York: Fordham University Press, 2012.

———. *Missions and Processions*. Vol. 1 of *The Trinity in History: A Theology of the Divine Missions*. Toronto: University of Toronto Press, 2012.

———. Preface to *Redeeming History: Social Concern in Bernard Lonergan and Robert Doran*, by Gerard Whelan. Rome: Gregorian & Biblical Press, 2013.

———. "Social Grace and the Mission of the Church." In *A Realist's Church: Essays in Honor of Joseph A. Komonchak*, edited by Christopher Denny, Patrick Hayes, and Nicholas Rademacher, 169–84. Maryknoll, N.Y.: Orbis Books, 2015.

———. "The International Institute for Method in Theology: A Vision." 2017. https://www.lonerganresource.com/pdf/lectures/Doran_-_International_Institute_for_Method_in_Theology.pdf.

———. Foreword to *A Discerning Church: Pope Francis, Lonergan, and a Theological Method for the Future*, by Gerard Whelan, vii–xi. New York: Paulist Press, 2019.

———. *Missions, Relations, and Persons*. Vol. 2 of *The Trinity in History: A Theology of the Divine Missions*. Toronto: University of Toronto Press, 2019.

———. "Redemption as End and Redemption as Mediation." *Gregorianum* 101, no. 4 (2020): 927–43.

Dorr, Donal. *Option for the Poor and for the Earth: From Leo XIII to Pope Francis*. Rev. ed. Maryknoll, N.Y.: Orbis Books, 2016.

Douthat, Ross. *To Change the Church: Pope Francis and the Future of Catholicism*. New York: Simon & Schuster, 2018.

Driscoll, Jeremy. *What Happens at Mass*. Rev. ed. Chicago: Liturgy Training Publications, 2011.

Dulles, Avery. *The Assurance of Things Hoped For*. New York: Oxford University Press, 1994.

———. "The Prophetic Humanism of John Paul II." In *Church and Society: The Laurence J. McGinley Lectures, 1988–2007*, 142–56. New York: Fordham University Press, 2008.

Edwards, Denis. *Ecology at the Heart of Faith: The Change of Heart That Leads to a New Way of Living on Earth*. Maryknoll, N.Y.: Orbis Books, 2006.

Esbjörn-Hargens, Sean, and Michael E. Zimmerman. *Integral Ecology: Uniting Multiple Perspectives on the Natural World*. Boston: Integral Books, 2009.

Faggioli, Massimo. "A View from Abroad." *America* (February 24, 2014): 20–23.

Fares, Diego. *Papa Francisco. La cultura del encuentro*. Buenos Aires: Edhasa, 2014.

Farina, Marianne. "Integral Ecology and the Care for Our Common Home." *Listening* 52, no. 1 (Winter 2017): 46–57.

Fessard, Gaston. *La Dialectique des "Exercises Spirituels" de Saint Ignace de Loyola*. Three vols. Paris: Aubier, 1956–84.

Flynn, J. D. "'We Want to Light a Fire': A Pillar Interview with Bishop Andrew Cozzens." *The Pillar*. June 16, 2021. https://www.pillarcatholic.com/p/we-want-to-light-a-fire-usccb-plans.

Fraga, Brian. "Political Role Reversal: Democrats Praise Encyclical, While GOP Remains Cautious." *National Catholic Register*. June 26, 2015. https://www.ncregister.com/daily-news/political-role-reversal-democrats-praise-encyclical-while-gop-remains-cauti.

Francis. *Lumen Fidei*. Encyclical Letter. June 29, 2013.

———. *Evangelii Gaudium*. Apostolic Exhortation. November 24, 2013.

———. "In an Interview with *Corriere della Sera*, Bergoglio Talks about His Revolutionary First Year at the Head of the Church." Zenit, March 5, 2014. https://zenit.org/articles/english-translation-of-pope-francis-corriere-della-sera-interview/.

———. "Interview in *La Vanguardia*." June 12, 2014. https://www.catholicnewsagency.com/news/pope-francis-interview-with-la-vanguardia—-full-text-45430.

———. *Address to Participants in the International Colloquium on the Complementarity between Man and Woman*. November 17, 2014.

———. *Press Conference of His Holiness Pope Francis onboard the Flight from Colombo to Manila*. January 15, 2015.

———. *Laudato Si'*. Encyclical Letter. May 24, 2015.

———. *Visit to the Joint Session of the United States Congress*. September 24, 2015.

———. *Amoris Laetitia*. Post-Synodal Apostolic Exhortation. March 19, 2016.

———. *Message for the Celebration of the World Day of Prayer for the Care of Creation: Show Mercy to Our Common Home*. September 1, 2016.

———. "Interview with Pablo Ordaz." January 20, 2017. https://english.elpais.com/elpais/2017/01/21/inenglish/1485026427_223988.html.

———. *Address to the Participants in the Conference Organized by the Dicastery for Promoting Integral Human Development, Marking the 50th Anniversary of the Encyclical* Populorum Progressio. April 4, 2017.

———. *Video Conference on the Occasion of the TED Conference in Vancouver*. April 26, 2017.

———. *Magnum Principium*. Apostolic Letter. September 9, 2017.

———. *Veritatis Gaudium*. Apostolic Constitution. January 29, 2018.

———. *Gaudete et Exsultate*. Apostolic Exhortation. March 19, 2018.

———. *Udienza ai Partecipanti alla Plenaria del Pontificio Comitato per i Congressi Eucaristici Internazionali*. October 11, 2018.

———. *Homily for the World Day of the Poor*. November 18, 2018.

———. *Message of His Holiness Pope Francis for Lent*. February 26, 2019.

———. *Christus Vivit*. Post-Synodal Apostolic Exhortation. March 25, 2019.

———. *Message to the Participants in the Second Forum of the* Laudato Si' *Communities in Amatrice, Italy*. July 6, 2019.

———. *Address to Participants at the World Congress of the International Association of Penal Law*. November 15, 2019.

———. *Querida Amazonia*. February 12, 2020. Post-Synodal Apostolic Exhortation.

———. *Fratelli Tutti*. Encyclical Letter. October 3, 2020.

———. *Video Message to the Participants in the Seventh World Day of Prayer, Reflection, and Action against Human Trafficking*. February 8, 2021.

Francis, with Guillaume Goubert and Sébastien Maillard. "Interview with Pope Francis." Translated by Stefan Gigacz. *La Croix*. May 17, 2016. https://www.la-croix.com/Religion/Pape/INTERVIEW-Pope-Francis-2016-05-17-1200760633.

Francis, with Austen Ivereigh. *Let Us Dream: The Path to a Better Future*. New York: Simon & Schuster, 2020.

———. "'A Time of Great Uncertainty': An Interview with Pope Francis." *Commonweal Magazine*. April 8, 2020. https://www.commonwealmagazine.org/time-great-uncertainty.

Francis, with Antonio Spadaro. "A Big Heart Open to God." *America Magazine*. September 30, 2013. https://www.americamagazine.org/faith/2013/09/30/big-heart-open-god-interview-pope-francis.

———. *My Door Is Always Open: A Conversation on Faith, Hope, and the Church in a Time of Change*. Translated by Shaun Whiteside. New York: Bloomsbury Publishing, 2013.

———. *Open to God: Open to the World*. Translated by Shaun Whiteside. London: Bloomsbury Publishing, 2018.

Francis, with Andrea Tornielli. *The Name of God Is Mercy*. Translated by Oonagh Stransky. New York: Random House, 2016.

Francis of Assisi. "The Canticle of Brother Sun." In *Francis and Clare: The Complete Works*, 37–39. Translated by Regis. J. Armstrong and Ignatius C. Brady. New York: Paulist Press, 1982.

———. "The Second Version of the Letter to the Faithful." In *Francis and Clare: The Complete Works*, 66–73. Translated by Regis. J. Armstrong and Ignatius C. Brady. New York: Paulist Press, 1982.

Fretheim, Terence E. *God and World in the Old Testament: A Relational Theology of Creation*. Nashville, Tenn.: Abingdon Press, 2005.

Gaillardetz, Richard R. *Transforming Our Days: Finding God amid the Noise of Modern Life*. Liguori, Mo.: Liguori Publications, 2007.

Gruber, Judith. "Ec(o)clesiology: Ecology as Ecclesiology in *Laudato Si'*." *Theological Studies* 78, no. 4 (2017): 807–24.

Guardini, Romano. *Letters from Lake Como: Explorations on Technology and the Human Race*. Translated by Geoffrey W. Bromiley. Grand Rapids, Mich.: Eerdmans, 1994.

———. *The End of the Modern World*. Translated by Joseph Theman, Herbert Burke, and Elinor Castendyk Briefs. Wilmington, Del.: ISI Books, 1998.

———. *The Spirit of the Liturgy*. Translated by Ada Lane. New York: Crossroad Publishing, 1998.

Guerriero, Elio. *Benedict XVI: His Life and Thought*. Translated by William J. Melcher. San Francisco: Ignatius Press, 2018.

Gutiérrez, Gustavo. *A Theology of Liberation: History, Politics, and Salvation*. Rev. ed. Translated by Caridad Inda and John Eagleson. Maryknoll, N.Y.: Orbis Books, 1988.

Hanby, Michael. "The Gospel of Creation and the Technocratic Paradigm: Reflections on a Central Teaching of *Laudato Si'*." *Communio* 42, no. 4 (Winter 2015): 724–47.

Happel, Stephen. "Sacrament: Symbol of Conversion." In *Creativity and Method: Essays in Honor of Bernard Lonergan*, edited by Matthew Lamb, 275–90. Milwaukee, Wis.: Marquette University Press, 1981.

Harris, Elise. "Pope Francis' Writings on Ecology Could Become Encyclical." Catholic News Agency. January 27, 2014. https://www.catholicnewsagency.com/news/pope-francis-writings-on-ecology-could-become-encyclical.

Hauerwas, Stanley. *The Peaceable Kingdom: A Primer in Christian Ethics.* Notre Dame, Ind.: University of Notre Dame Press, 1983.

———. "The Servant Community: Christian Social Ethics." In *The Hauerwas Reader*, edited by John Berkman and Michael Cartwright, 371–91. Durham, N.C.: Duke University Press, 2001.

Hawley, Amos. *Human Ecology: A Theory of Community Structure.* New York: Ronald Press, 1950.

Healy, Nicholas M. *Church, World and the Christian Life: Practical-Prophetic Ecclesiology.* New York: Cambridge University Press, 2000.

Hefelfinger, Scott G. "Human, Social, and Natural Ecology: Three Ecologies, One Cosmology, and the Common Good." In *Environmental Justice and Climate Change: Assessing Pope Benedict XVI's Ecological Vision for the Catholic Church in the United States*, edited by Jame Schaefer and Tobias Winright, 61–82. Lanham, Md.: Lexington Books, 2013.

Hefling, Charles. "Lonergan's *Cur Deus Homo*: Revisiting the 'Law of the Cross.'" In *Meaning and History in Systematic Theology: Essays in Honor of Robert M. Doran, SJ*, edited by John Dadosky, 145–66. Milwaukee, Wis.: Marquette University Press, 2009.

Heimbach-Steins, Marianne, and Andreas Lienkamp. "Die Enzyklika „Laudato si'" von Papst Franziskus Auch ein Beitrag zur Problematik des Klimawandels und zur Ethik der Energiewende." *JCSW* 56 (2015): 155–79.

Heyer, Kristen. *Prophetic and Public: The Social Witness of U.S. Catholicism.* Washington, D.C.: Georgetown University Press, 2006.

Hilkert, Mary Catherine. *Naming Grace: Preaching and the Sacramental Imagination.* New York: Bloomsbury Continuum, 1997.

Hohman, Benjamin J. "The Glory to Be Revealed: Grace and Emergence in an Ecological Eschatology." In *Everything Is Interconnected: Towards a Globalization with a Human Face and an Integral Ecology*, edited by Joseph Ogbonnaya and Lucas Briola, 179–98. Milwaukee, Wis.: Marquette University, 2019.

Hopkins, Gerard Manley. *Poems and Prose.* Edited by W. H. Gardner. New York: Penguin Books, 1985.

Humphrey, Edith P. *Grand Entrance: Worship on Earth as in Heaven.* Grand Rapids, Mich.: Brazos Press, 2011.

Hütter, Reinhard. "The Ecological Crisis: A Common Responsibility." The Institute for Human Ecology. October 22, 2019. https://ihe.catholic.edu/the-ecological-crisis-a-common-responsibility/.

Ignatius of Loyola. *The Spiritual Exercises of Saint Ignatius.* Translated by Anthony Mottola. New York: Doubleday, 1964.

Imbelli, Robert. "Receiving Vatican II: Renewing the Christic Center." *Lonergan Workshop* 26 (2012): 187–209.

———. "Benedict and Francis." In *Go into the Streets! The Welcoming Church of Pope Francis*, edited by Thomas P. Rausch and Richard Gaillardetz, 11–27. New York: Paulist Press, 2016.

International Theological Commission. *In Search of a Universal Ethic: A New Look at Natural Law*. May 20, 2009.

———. *Synodality in the Life and Mission of the Church*. March 2, 2018.

Irwin, Kevin W. "Sacramentality and the Theology of Creation: A Recovered Paradigm for Sacramental Theology." *Louvain Studies* 23 (1998): 159–79.

———. *Models of the Eucharist*. New York: Paulist Press, 2005.

———. "The World as God's Icon: Creation, Sacramentality, Liturgy." In *Environmental Justice and Climate Change: Assessing Pope Benedict XVI's Ecological Vision for the Catholic Church in the United States*, edited by Jame Schaefer and Tobias Winright, 149–72. Lanham, Md.: Lexington Books, 2013.

———. *A Commentary on* Laudato Si': *Examining the Background, Contributions, Implementation, and Future of Pope Francis's Encyclical*. New York: Paulist Press, 2016.

———. "Background to and Contributions of *Laudato Si'*: On Care for Our Common Home." In *All Creation Is Connected: Voices in Response to Pope Francis's Encyclical on Ecology*, edited by Daniel R. DiLeo, 15–30. Winona, Minn.: Anselm Academic, 2018.

———. *Context and Text: A Method for Liturgical Theology*. Rev. Ed. Collegeville, Minn.: Liturgical Press, 2018.

———. *Pope Francis and the Liturgy: The Call to Holiness and Mission*. New York: Paulist Press, 2020.

Isaac the Syrian. *The Ascetical Homilies of Saint Isaac the Syrian*. Boston: Holy Transfiguration Monastery, 1984.

Ivereigh, Austen. *The Great Reformer: Francis and the Making of a Radical Pope*. New York: Henry Holt, 2014.

———. "To Discern and Reform: The 'Francis Option' for Evangelizing a World in Flux." *The Way* 57, no. 4 (October 2018): 9–24.

———. *Wounded Shepherd: Pope Francis and His Struggle to Convert the Catholic Church*. New York: Henry Holt, 2019.

Jenkins, Willis. *Ecologies of Grace: Environmental Ethics and Christian Theology*. New York: Oxford University Press, 2008.

———. "After Lynn White: Religious Ethics and Environmental Problems." *Journal of Religious Ethics* 37 no. 2 (2009): 283–309.

———. "The Mysterious Silence of Mother Earth in *Laudato Si'*." *Journal of Religious Ethics* 46, no. 3 (2018): 441–62.

John of the Cross. "The Spiritual Canticle." In *The Collected Works of St. John of the Cross*, 461–632. Translated by Kieran Kavanaugh and Otilio Rodriguez. Washington, D.C.: ICS Publications, 1973.

John Paul II. *Redemptor Hominis*. Encyclical Letter. March 4, 1979.

_____. *Laborem Exercens*. Encyclical Letter. September 14, 1981.

_____. *Dominum et Vivificantem*. Encyclical Letter. May 18, 1986.

_____. *Sollictudo Rei Socialis*. Encyclical Letter. December 30, 1987.

_____. *Christifideles Laici*. Post-Synodal Apostolic Exhortation. December 30, 1988.

_____. *Peace with God the Creator, Peace with All of Creation*. January 1, 1990.

_____. *Evangelium Vitae*. Encyclical Letter. March 25, 1991.

_____. *Centesimus Annus*. Encyclical Letter. May 1, 1991.

_____. *Veritatis Splendor*. Encyclical Letter. August 6, 1993.

_____. *Orientale Lumen*. Apostolic Letter. May 2, 1995.

_____. *Dies Domini*. Apostolic Letter. May 31, 1998.

_____. *Ecclesia in Oceania*. Post-Synodal Apostolic Exhortation. November 22, 2001.

_____. *Ecclesia de Eucharistia*. Encyclical Letter. April 17, 2003.

_____. *Pastores Gregis*. Post-Synodal Apostolic Exhortation. October 16, 2003.

Kasper, Walter. *Pope Francis' Revolution of Tenderness and Love: Theological and Pastoral Perspectives*. Translated by William Madges. New York: Paulist Press, 2015.

Keenan, Marjorie. *From Stockholm to Johannesburg: An Historical Overview of the Concern of the Holy See for the Environment: 1972–2002*. Vatican City: Vatican Press, 2002.

Kelly, Anthony J. *Laudato Si': An Integral Ecology and the Catholic Vision*. Adelaide: ATF Theology, 2016.

Kennedy, Arthur. "Christopher Dawson's Influence on Bernard Lonergan's Project of 'Introducing History into Theology.'" *Logos: A Journal of Catholic Thought & Culture* 15, no. 2 (Spring 2012): 138–64.

Kimmerer, Robin Wall. *Braiding Sweetgrass: Indigenous Wisdom, Scientific Knowledge, and the Teachings of Plants*. Minneapolis, Minn.: Milkweed Editions, 2013.

Klein, Naomi. "A Radical Vatican?" *The New Yorker*. July 10, 2015. https://www.newyorker.com/news/news-desk/a-visit-to-the-vatican.

Koenig-Bricker, Woodeene. *Ten Commandments for the Environment: Pope Benedict XVI Speaks Out for Creation and Justice*. Notre Dame, Ind.: Ave Maria Press, 2009.

Koester, Craig R. *Revelation and the End of All Things*. Grand Rapids, Mich.: Eerdmans, 2001.

Komonchak, Joseph A. "The Church." In *The Desires of the Human Heart: An Introduction to the Theology of Bernard Lonergan*, edited by Vernon Gregson, 222–36. New York: Paulist Press, 1988.

_____. "Lonergan's Early Essays on the Redemption of History." *Lonergan Workshop* 10 (1994): 159–77.

_____. *Foundations in Ecclesiology*. Lonergan Workshop. Boston: Boston College, 1995.

———. "Returning from Exile: Catholic Theology in the 1930s." In *The Twentieth Century: A Theological Overview*, edited by Gregory Baum, 35–48. Maryknoll, N.Y.: Orbis Books, 1999.

Lamb, Matthew L. "Methodology, Metascience, and Political Theology." *Lonergan Workshop* 2 (1979): 280–380.

———. *Solidarity with Victims: Toward a Theology of Social Transformation*. New York: Crossroad Publishing, 1982.

———. "The Social and Political Dimensions of Lonergan's Theology." In *The Desires of the Human Heart: An Introduction to the Theology of Bernard Lonergan*, edited by Vernon Gregson, 255–84. New York: Paulist Press, 1988.

Lamoureux, Patricia A. "Commentary on *Laborem Exercens* (*On Human Work*)." In *Modern Catholic Social Teaching: Commentaries and Interpretations*, edited by Kenneth R. Himes, 389–414. Washington, D.C.: Georgetown University Press, 2005.

Laplace, Pierre-Simon. *A Philosophical Essay on Probabilities*. Translated by F. W. Truscott and F. L. Emory. New York: Dover Publications, 1951.

Latour, Bruno. "La grande clameur relayée par le pape François." In *Laudato si': Encyclique, édition commentée: Texte intégral, réactions et commentaires*, edited by F. Louzeau and B. Toger, 221–30. Paris: Parole et silence, 2015.

Lawler, Ronald. "Personalism in the Thought of John Paul II." In *Catholic Social Thought and the Teaching of John Paul II*. Proceedings of the Fifth Convention (1982) of the Fellowship of Catholic Scholars, edited by Paul L. Williams. Scranton, Pa.: Northeast Books, 1983.

Lawrence, Frederick G. "Lonergan as Political Theologian." In *Religion in Context: Recent Studies in Lonergan*, edited by Timothy P. Fallon and Philip Boo Riley, 1–21. Lanham, Md.: University Press of America, 1988.

———. "The Fragility of Consciousness: Lonergan and the Postmodern Concern for the Other." In *The Fragility of Consciousness: Faith, Reason, and the Human Good*, edited by Randall S. Rosenberg and Kevin M. Vander Schel, 229–77. Toronto: University of Toronto Press, 2017.

———. "Growing in Faith as the Eyes of Being-in-Love with God." In *The Fragility of Consciousness: Faith, Reason, and the Human Good*, edited by Randall S. Rosenberg and Kevin M. Vander Schel, 384–404. Toronto: University of Toronto Press, 2017.

Leo XIII. *Aeterni Patris*. Encyclical Letter. August 4, 1879.

Li, Nan, et al. "Cross-pressuring Conservative Catholics? Effects of Pope Francis' Encyclical on the U.S. Public Opinion on Climate Change." *Climatic Change* 139, no. 3 (December 2016): 367–80.

Liddy, Richard M. *Transforming Light: Intellectual Conversion in the Early Lonergan*. Collegeville, Minn.: Liturgical Press, 1993.

Linden, Ian. *Global Catholicism: Diversity and Change Since Vatican II*. New York: Columbia University Press, 2009.

Lipka, Michael, and Gregory A. Smith. "Like Americans Overall, U.S. Catholics Are Sharply Divided by Party." Pew Research Center. January 24, 2019. https://www.pewresearch.org/fact-tank/2019/01/24/like-americans-overall-u-s-catholics-are-sharply-divided-by-party/.

Loewe, William P. "Lonergan and the Law of the Cross: A Universalist View of Salvation." *Anglican Theological Review* 59 (1977): 162–74.

_____. "Dialectics of Sin: Lonergan's *Insight* and the Critical Theory of Max Horkheimer." *Anglican Theological Review* 61 (1979): 224–45.

_____. "Towards a Responsible Contemporary Soteriology." In *Creativity and Method: Essays in Honor of Bernard Lonergan*, edited by Matthew Lamb, 213–28. Milwaukee, Wis: Marquette University Press, 1981.

_____. "Review of Frederick Crowe, *Christ and History: The Christology of Bernard Lonergan from 1935 to 1982*." In *Horizons* 33, no. 1 (Spring 2006): 149–50.

_____. Lex Crucis: *Soteriology and the Stages of Meaning*. Minneapolis, Minn.: Fortress Press, 2016.

Lonergan, Bernard J. F. *Method in Theology*. New York: Herder and Herder, 1972.

_____. "The Absence of God in Modern Culture." In *Collected Works of Bernard Lonergan: A Second Collection*, edited by William F. J. Ryan and Bernard Tyrell, 101–16. Philadelphia: The Westminster Press, 1974.

_____. "Belief: Today's Issue." In *Collected Works of Bernard Lonergan: A Second Collection*, edited by William F. J. Ryan and Bernard Tyrell, 87–100. Philadelphia: The Westminster Press, 1974.

_____. "The Future of Thomism." In *Collected Works of Bernard Lonergan: A Second Collection*, edited by William F. J. Ryan and Bernard Tyrell, 43–54. Philadelphia: The Westminster Press, 1974.

_____. "*Insight* Revisited." In *Collected Works of Bernard Lonergan: A Second Collection*, edited by William F. J. Ryan and Bernard Tyrell, 263–78. Philadelphia: The Westminster Press, 1974.

_____. "An Interview with Fr. Bernard Lonergan, S.J.," edited by Philip McShane. In *Collected Works of Bernard Lonergan: A Second Collection*, edited by William F. J. Ryan and Bernard Tyrell, 209–30. Philadelphia: The Westminster Press, 1974.

_____. "The Response of the Jesuit Priest and Apostle in the Modern World." In *Collected Works of Bernard Lonergan: A Second Collection*, edited by William F. J. Ryan and Bernard Tyrell, 165–88. Philadelphia: The Westminster Press, 1974.

_____. "Revolution in Catholic Theology." In *Collected Works of Bernard Lonergan: A Second Collection*, edited by William F. J. Ryan and Bernard Tyrell, 231–38. Philadelphia: The Westminster Press, 1974.

_____. "The Subject." In *Collected Works of Bernard Lonergan: A Second Collection*, edited by William F. J. Ryan and Bernard Tyrell, 69–86. Philadelphia: The Westminster Press, 1974.

———. "Theology and Man's Future." In *Collected Works of Bernard Lonergan: A Second Collection*, edited by William F. J. Ryan and Bernard Tyrell, 135–48. Philadelphia: The Westminster Press, 1974.

———. "The Transition from Classicism to Historical-Mindedness." In *Collected Works of Bernard Lonergan: A Second Collection*, edited by William F. J. Ryan and Bernard Tyrell, 1–10. Philadelphia: The Westminster Press, 1974.

———. *Caring about Meaning: Patterns in the Life of Bernard Lonergan*. Edited by Pierrot Lambert, Charlotte Tansey, and Cathleen Going. Montreal: Thomas More Institute Papers, 1982.

———. "Christology Today: Methodological Reflections." In *A Third Collection: Papers by Bernard J. F. Lonergan, S.J.*, edited by Frederick E. Crowe, 74–99. Mahwah, N.J.: Paulist Press, 1985.

———. "Healing and Creating in History." In *A Third Collection: Papers by Bernard J. F. Lonergan, S.J.*, edited by Frederick E. Crowe, 100–9. Mahwah, N.J.: Paulist Press, 1985.

———. "Mission and the Spirit." In *A Third Collection: Papers by Bernard J. F. Lonergan, S.J.*, edited by Frederick E. Crowe, 23–34. Mahwah, N.J.: Paulist Press, 1985.

———. "Natural Right and Historical Mindedness." In *A Third Collection: Papers by Bernard J. F. Lonergan, S.J.*, edited by Frederick E. Crowe, 169–83. Mahwah, N.J.: Paulist Press, 1985.

———. "A Post-Hegelian Philosophy of History." In *A Third Collection: Papers by Bernard J. F. Lonergan, S.J.*, edited by Frederick E. Crowe, 202–23. Mahwah, N.J.: Paulist Press, 1985.

———. "Theology and Praxis." In *A Third Collection: Papers by Bernard J. F. Lonergan, S.J.*, edited by Frederick E. Crowe, 184–201. Mahwah, N.J.: Paulist Press, 1985.

———. *Curiosity at the Center of One's Life: Statements and Questions of R. Eric O'Connor*. Edited by J. Martin O'Hara. Montreal: Thomas More Institute, 1987.

———. "Dimensions of Meaning." In *Collection*, edited by Frederick E. Crowe and Robert M. Doran, 232–45. Vol. 4 of *Collected Works of Bernard Lonergan*. Toronto: University of Toronto Press, 1988.

———. "*Existenz* and *Aggiornamento*." In *Collection*, edited by Frederick E. Crowe and Robert M. Doran, 222–31. Vol. 4 of *Collected Works of Bernard Lonergan*. Toronto: University of Toronto Press, 1988.

———. "Finality, Love, Marriage." In *Collection*, edited by Frederick E. Crowe and Robert M. Doran, 17–52. Vol. 4 of *Collected Works of Bernard Lonergan*. Toronto: University of Toronto Press, 1988.

———. "The Role of the Catholic University in the Modern World." In *Collection*, edited by Frederick E. Crowe and Robert M. Doran, 108–13. Vol. 4 of *Collected Works of Bernard Lonergan*. Toronto: University of Toronto Press, 1988.

———. "*Pantôn Anakephalaiôsis* [The restoration of all things]." *Method: Journal of Lonergan Studies* 9 (1991): 134–72.

———. "Analytic Concept of History." *Method: Journal of Lonergan Studies* 11, no. 1 (Spring 1993): 1–36.

———. *Topics in Education.* Vol. 10 of *Collected Works of Bernard Lonergan,* edited by Frederick E. Crowe and Robert M. Doran. Toronto: University of Toronto, 1993.

———. "The Analogy of Meaning." In *Philosophical and Theological Papers 1958–1964,* edited by Robert C. Croken, Frederick E. Crowe, and Robert M. Doran, 183–213. Vol. 6 of *Collected Works of Bernard Lonergan.* Toronto: University of Toronto Press, 1996.

———. "The Mediation of Christ in Prayer." In *Philosophical and Theological Papers 1958–1964,* edited by Robert C. Croken, Frederick E. Crowe, and Robert M. Doran, 160–82. Vol. 6 of *Collected Works of Bernard Lonergan.* Toronto: University of Toronto Press, 1996.

———. "The Philosophy of History." In *Philosophical and Theological Papers 1958–1964,* edited by Robert C. Croken, Frederick E. Crowe, and Robert M. Doran, 54–79. Vol. 6 of *Collected Works of Bernard Lonergan.* Toronto: University of Toronto Press, 1996.

———. *Verbum: Word and Idea in Aquinas.* Vol. 2 of *Collected Works of Bernard Lonergan,* edited by Frederick E. Crowe and Robert M. Doran. Toronto: University of Toronto Press, 1997.

———. *For a New Political Economy.* Vol. 21 of *Collected Works of Bernard Lonergan,* edited by Philip J. McShane. Toronto: University of Toronto Press, 1998.

———. *Macroeconomic Dynamics: An Essay in Circulation Analysis.* Vol. 15 of *Collected Works of Bernard Lonergan,* edited by Patrick H. Byrne, Frederick G. Lawrence, and Charles Hefling Jr. Toronto: University of Toronto Press, 1999.

———. *Grace and Freedom: Operative Grace in the Thought of St. Thomas Aquinas.* Vol. 1 of *Collected Works of Bernard Lonergan,* edited by Frederick E. Crowe and Robert M. Doran. Toronto: University of Toronto Press, 2000.

———. *Phenomenology and Logic: The Boston College Lectures on Mathematical Logic and Existentialism.* Vol. 18 of *Collected Works of Bernard Lonergan,* edited by Philip J. McShane. Toronto: University of Toronto Press, 2001.

———. "Horizons." In *Philosophical and Theological Papers 1965–1980,* edited by Robert C. Croken and Robert M. Doran, 10–29. Vol. 17 of *Collected Works of Bernard Lonergan.* Toronto: University of Toronto Press, 2004.

———. "Moral Theology and Human Sciences." In *Philosophical and Theological Papers 1965–1980,* edited by Robert C. Croken and Robert M. Doran, 301–12. Vol. 17 of *Collected Works of Bernard Lonergan* Toronto: University of Toronto Press, 2004.

———. "Questionnaire on Philosophy: Response." In *Philosophical and Theological Papers 1965–1980,* edited by Robert C. Croken and Robert M. Doran, 352–83. Vol. 17 of *Collected Works of Bernard Lonergan.* Toronto: University of Toronto Press, 2004.

———. "Sacralization and Secularization." In *Philosophical and Theological Papers 1965–1980*, edited by Robert C. Croken and Robert M. Doran, 259–81. Vol. 17 of *Collected Works of Bernard Lonergan*. Toronto: University of Toronto Press, 2004.

———. "The Scope of Renewal." In *Philosophical and Theological Papers 1965–1980*, edited by Robert C. Croken and Robert M. Doran, 282–98. Vol. 17 of *Collected Works of Bernard Lonergan*. Toronto: University of Toronto Press, 2004.

———. "Self-transcendence: Intellectual, Moral, and Religious." In *Philosophical and Theological Papers 1965–1980*, edited by Robert C. Croken and Robert M. Doran, 313–31. Vol. 17 of *Collected Works of Bernard Lonergan*. Toronto: University of Toronto Press, 2004.

———. *Insight: A Study of Human Understanding*. Vol. 3 of *Collected Works of Bernard Lonergan*, edited by Frederick E. Crowe and Robert M. Doran. Toronto: University of Toronto Press, 2005.

———. *Understanding and Being: The Halifax Lectures on Insight*. Vol. 5 of *Collected Works of Bernard Lonergan*, edited by Elizabeth A. Morelli and Mark D. Morelli, revised by Frederick E. Crowe. Toronto: University of Toronto Press, 2005.

———. "The Mass and Man." In *Shorter Papers*, edited by Robert Croken, Robert M. Doran, and H. Daniel Monsour, 92–98. Vol. 20 of *Collected Works of Bernard Lonergan*. Toronto: University of Toronto Press, 2007.

———. "Respect for Human Dignity." In *Shorter Papers*, edited by Robert Croken, Robert M. Doran, and H. Daniel Monsour, 121–28. Vol. 20 of *Collected Works of Bernard Lonergan*. Toronto: University of Toronto Press, 2007.

———. "Review of George Boyle, *Democracy's Second Chance*," In *Shorter Papers*, edited by Robert Croken, Robert M. Doran, and H. Daniel Monsour, 157–59. Vol. 20 of *Collected Works of Bernard Lonergan*. Toronto: University of Toronto Press, 2007.

———. "Essay in Fundamental Sociology." In *Lonergan's Early Economic Research: Texts and Commentary*, edited by Michael Shute, 15–43. Toronto: University of Toronto Press, 2010.

———. "The Notion of Fittingness: The Application of Theological Method to the Question of the Purpose of the Incarnation." In *Early Latin Theology*, edited by Robert M. Doran and H. Daniel Monsour and translated by Michael G. Shields, 482–533. Vol. 19 of *Collected Works of Bernard Lonergan*. Toronto: University of Toronto Press, 2011.

———. "The Notion of Sacrifice." *Early Latin Theology*, edited by Robert M. Doran and H. Daniel Monsour and translated by Michael G. Shields, 3–52. Vol. 19 of *Collected Works of Bernard Lonergan*. Toronto: University of Toronto Press, 2011.

———. "Letter of Bernard Lonergan to the Reverend Henry Letter to Keane." *Method: Journal of Lonergan Studies* 28, no. 2 (Fall 2014): 23–40.

———. "The Redemption: A Supplement." In *The Redemption*, edited by Robert M. Doran, H. Daniel Monsour, and Jeremy D. Wilkins and translated by Michael G. Shields, 265–659. Vol. 9 of *Collected Works of Bernard Lonergan*. Toronto: University of Toronto Press, 2018.

———. "Theses 15–17 of *De Verbo Incarnato*." *The Redemption*, edited by Robert M. Doran, H. Daniel Monsour, and Jeremy D. Wilkins and translated by Michael G. Shields, 3–263. Vol 9 of *Collected Works of Bernard Lonergan*. Toronto: University of Toronto Press, 2018.

Lorbiecki, Marybeth. *Following St. Francis: John Paul II's Call for Ecological Action*. New York: Rizzoli Ex Libris, 2014.

Louv, Richard. *Last Child in the Woods: Saving Our Children from Nature-Deficit Disorder*. Chapel Hill, N.C.: Algonquin Books of Chapel Hill, 2005.

Luciani, Rafael. *Pope Francis and the Theology of the People*. Translated by Phillip Berryman. Maryknoll, N.Y.: Orbis Books, 2017.

Maibach, E., Leiserowitz, A., Roser-Renouf, C., Myers, T., Rosenthal, S. & Feinberg, G. *The Francis Effect: How Pope Francis Changed the Conversation about Global Warming*. Fairfax, Va.: George Mason University Center for Climate Change Communication, 2015.

Malesic, Jonathan. *The End of Burnout: Why Work Drains Us and How to Build Better Lives*. Oakland, Calif.: University of California Press, 2022.

Martin, Stephen L. *Healing and Creativity in Economic Ethics: The Contribution of Bernard Lonergan's Economic Thought to Catholic Social Teaching*. Lanham, Md.: University Press of America, 2007.

Massingale, Bryan N. *Racial Justice and the Catholic Church*. Maryknoll, N.Y.: Orbis Books, 2010.

Mathews, William A. *Lonergan's Quest: A Study of Desire in the Authoring of* Insight. Toronto: University of Toronto Press, 2005.

McAleese, Morag. "The Canadian Social Economy and Values: Insights from Bernard Lonergan's Theological Ethics." ThD dissertation, Saint Paul University, 2017.

McCabe, Herbert. "Prayer." In *The McCabe Reader*, edited by Brian Davies and Paul Kucharski, 145–59. New York: Bloomsbury Publishing, 2016.

McDonagh, Sean. *Passion for the Earth: The Christian Vocation to Promote Justice, Peace, and the Integrity of Creation*. Maryknoll, N.Y.: Orbis Books, 1994.

McGann, Mary E. *The Meal That Reconnects: Eucharistic Eating and the Global Food Crisis*. Collegeville, Minn.: Liturgical Press, 2020.

McMahon, Christopher. "Cruciform Salvation and Emergent Probability: The Liturgical Significance of Lonergan's Precept." In *Approaching the Threshold of Mystery: Liturgical Worlds and Theological Spaces*, edited by Joris Geldhof, Daniel Minch, and Trevor Maine, 198–212. Regensburg: Verlag Friedrich Pustet, 2015.

McPartlan, Paul. "Praying with Creation: Cosmic Aspects of Eucharist." *Liturgy News* 40, no. 3 (September 2010): 6–10.

Melchin, Kenneth R. *Living with Other People: An Introduction to Christian Ethics Based on Bernard Lonergan*. Ottawa: Novalis, 1998.

———. *History, Ethics, and Emergent Probability*. 2nd ed. The Lonergan Workshop, 1999.

Methol Ferré, Alberto. "El resurgimiento católico latinoamericano." In *Religión y cultura. Perspectivas de la evangelización de la cultura desde Puebla. Encuentro del equipo de reflexión del Celam y otros pensadores sobre el tema «Religión y cultura»*, edited by CELAM, 63–214. Bogotá: Ed. CELAM, 1980.

———. *Il risorgimento cattolico latinoamericano*. Translated by P. Di Pauli and C. Perfetti. Bologna: CSEO-Incontri, 1983.

Methol Ferré, Alberto, and Alver Metalli. *Il Papa e il filosofo*. Siena, Italy: Cantagalli, 2014.

Metz, Johann Baptist. "Transcendental-Idealist or Narrative-Practical Christianity?" In *Faith in History and Society: Toward a Practical Fundamental Theology*, 144–55. Translated by J. Matthew Ashley. New York: Crossroad Publishing Company, 2007.

Michel, Virgil. "The Liturgy: The Basis of Social Regeneration." *Orate Fratres* 9 (1934–35): 536–45.

Mickey, Sam. *On the Verge of a Planetary Civilization: A Philosophy of Integral Ecology*. New York: Rowman & Littlefield Publishers, 2014.

Miller, Mark T. *The Quest for God and the Good Life: Lonergan's Theological Anthropology*. Washington, D.C.: The Catholic University of America Press, 2013.

Miller, Vincent J. "Integral Ecology: Francis's Spiritual and Moral Vision of Interconnectedness." In *The Theological and Ecological Vision of Laudato Si': Everything Is Connected*, edited by Vincent J. Miller, 11–28. New York: Bloomsbury T & T Clark, 2017.

Modras, Ronald. "The Thomistic Personalism of Pope John Paul II." *The Modern Schoolman* 59, no. 1 (January 1982): 117–26.

Moloney, Raymond. "Lonergan on Eucharistic Sacrifice." *Theological Studies* 62 (2001): 53–70.

Monod, Jacques. *Chance and Necessity: An Essay on the Natural Philosophy of Modern Biology*. Translated by Austryn Wainhouse. New York: Vintage Books, 1972.

Moore, Hilary B. *Marine Ecology*. Hoboken, N.J.: Wiley, 1958.

Morill, Bruce T. *Anamnesis as Dangerous Memory: Political and Liturgical Theology in Dialogue*. Collegeville, Minn.: Liturgical Press, 2000.

Morris, Jeffrey. "Pope Benedict XVI on Faith and Reason in Western Europe." *Pro Ecclesia* 17, no. 3 (2008): 326–42.

Mudd, Joseph C. *Eucharist as Meaning: Critical Metaphysics and Contemporary Sacramental Theology*. Collegeville, Minn.: Liturgical Press, 2014.

Mullarkey, Maureen. "Where Did Pope Francis's Extravagant Rant Come From?" The Federalist. June 24, 2015. http://thefederalist.com/2015/06/24/where-did-pope-francissextravagant-rant-come-from/.

Nairn, Thomas A. "The Roman Catholic Social Tradition and the Question of Ecology." In *The Ecological Challenge: Ethical, Liturgical, and Spiritual Responses*, edited by Richard N. Fragomeni and John T. Pawlikowski, 27–38. Collegeville, Minn.: Liturgical Press, 1994.

Nasuti, Harry. "The Sacramental Function of the Psalms in Contemporary Scholarship and Liturgical Practice." In *Psalms and Practice: Worship, Virtue, and Authority*, edited by Stephen Breck Reid, 78–89. Collegeville, Minn.: Liturgical Press, 2001.

Newman, John Henry. *An Essay in Aid of a Grammar of Assent*. Garden City, N.Y.: Doubleday, 1955.

Njoku, Uzochukwu Jude. "Rethinking Solidarity as a Principle of Catholic Social Teaching: Going beyond *Gaudium et Spes* and the Social Encyclicals of John Paul II." *Political Theology* 9 (2008): 525–44.

Northcott, Michael. *The Environment and Christian Ethics*. New York: Cambridge University Press, 1996.

Nothwehr, Dawn M. "Leonardo Boff's Franciscan Liberation Ecological Theology and 'Integral Ecology' in *Laudato Si'*." In *All Creation Is Connected: Voices in Response to Pope Francis's Encyclical on Ecology*, edited by Daniel R. DiLeo, 94–112. Winona, Minn.: Anselm Academic, 2018.

Ogbonnaya, Joseph. *Lonergan, Social Transformation, and Sustainable Human Development*. Eugene, Ore.: Pickwick, 2013.

O'Leary, Darlene. "Economic Democracy: Lonergan and the Antigonish Movement." *The Lonergan Review* 3, no. 1 (2011): 208–18.

O'Malley, Timothy P. *Liturgy and the New Evangelization: Practicing the Art of Self-Giving Love*. Collegeville, Minn.: Liturgical Press, 2014.

Ormerod, Neil. *Creation, Grace, and Redemption*. Maryknoll, N.Y.: Orbis Books, 2007.

———. "The Argument Has Vast Implications: Part II of *Deus Caritas Est*." In *Identity and Mission in Catholic Agencies*, edited by Neil Ormerod, 67–81. Strathfield, Australia: St. Pauls Publications, 2008.

———. *Re-Visioning the Church: An Experiment in Systematic-Historical Ecclesiology*. Minneapolis, Minn.: Fortress Press, 2014.

Ormerod, Neil, and Shane Clifton. *Globalization and the Mission of the Church*. New York: Bloomsbury T & T Clark, 2009.

Ormerod, Neil, and Cristina Vanin. "Ecological Conversion: What Does It Mean?" *Theological Studies* 77, no. 2 (2016): 328–52.

Orsy, Ladislas. *The Church: Learning and Teaching*. Wilmington, Del.: Michael Glazier, 1987.

Panjabi, Ranee K. L. *The Earth Summit at Rio: Politics, Economics, and the Environment*. Boston: Northeastern University Press, 1997.

Paul VI. *Populorum Progressio*. Encyclical Letter. March 26, 1967.

———. *Evangelii Nuntiandi*. Apostolic Exhortation. December 8, 1975.

Pentin, Edward. "Pope Francis to Emphasize 'Human Ecology' in Forthcoming Document, Says Theologian." *National Catholic Register*. January 30, 2014. www.ncregister.com/daily-news/pope-francis-to-emphasize-human-ecology-in-forthcoming-document-says-theolo.

Perry, Michael A. "From Assisi to Buenos Aires: The Cry of the Poor and the Cry of the Planet." In *Fragile World: Ecology and the Church*, edited by William T. Cavanaugh, 63–88. Eugene, Ore.: Cascade Books, 2018.

Petrany, Catherine. *Pedagogy, Prayer and Praise: The Wisdom of the Psalter*. Tübingen: Mohr Siebeck, 2015.

Pfeil, Margaret R. "Fifty Years after *Populorum Progressio*: Understanding Integral Human Development in Light of Integral Ecology." *Journal of Catholic Social Thought* 15, no. 1 (2018): 5–17.

Phan, Peter C. "Pope John Paul II and the Ecological Crisis." *Irish Theological Quarterly* 60, no. 1 (1994): 59–69.

Pieper, Josef. *In Tune with the World: A Theory of Festivity*. Translated by Richard and Clara Winston. South Bend, Ind.: St. Augustine's Press, 1999.

Pius XI. *Quadragesimo Anno*. Encyclical Letter. May 15, 1931.

Porathur, Liju. "Ecology vis-à-vis Human Ecology after Pope Benedict XVI." *Journal of Dharma* 39, no. 2 (April–June 2014): 405–22.

Portier, William L. "Here Come the Evangelical Catholics." *Communio* 31, no. 1 (Spring 2004): 35–66.

Prevot, Andew. *Thinking Prayer: Theology and Spirituality Amid the Crises of Modernity*. Notre Dame, Ind.: University of Notre Dame Press, 2015.

Radcliffe, Timothy. *Alive in God: A Christian Imagination*. New York: Bloomsbury Continuum, 2019.

Rademacher, Nicholas K. *Paul Hanly Furfey: Priest, Scientist, Social Reformer*. New York: Fordham University Press, 2017.

Ratzinger, Joseph. "Neuheidentum." In *Lexikon für Theologie und Kirche* VII, edited by Josef Höfer and Karl Rahner, 907–9. Freiburg: Verlag Herder, 1962.

———. "Sühne: V. Systematisch." In *Lexikon für Theologie und Kirche* IX, edited by Josef Höfer and Karl Rahner, 1156–58. Freiburg: Verlag Herder, 1964.

———. "Taking Bearings in Christology." In *Behold the Pierced One: An Approach to a Spiritual Christology*, 13–46. Translated by Graham Harrison. San Francisco: Ignatius Press, 1986.

———. *Principles of Catholic Theology*. San Francisco: Ignatius Press, 1987.

———. *Eschatology: Death and Eternal Life*. 2nd ed. Translated by Michael Waldstein and Aidan Nichols. Washington, D.C.: The Catholic University of America Press, 1988.

———. *A Turning Point for Europe? The Church in the Modern World—Assessment and Forecast*. Translated by Brian McNeil. San Francisco: Ignatius Press, 1994.

———. *"In the Beginning...": A Catholic Understanding of the Story of Creation and the Fall*. Translated by Boniface Ramsey. Grand Rapids, Mich.: Eerdmans, 1995.

———. *Called to Communion: Understanding the Church Today*. Translated by Adrian Walker. San Francisco: Ignatius Press, 1996.

———. Foreword to *Catholicism: Christ and the Common Destiny of Man*, by Henri de Lubac, 11–12. Translated by Lancelot C. Sheppard and Elizabeth Englund. San Francisco: Ignatius Press, 1998.

———. *Milestones, Memoirs: 1927–1977*. Translated by Erasmo Leiva-Merikakis. San Francisco: Ignatius Press, 1998.

———. *God and the World: A Conversation with Peter Seewald*. Translated by Henry Taylor. San Francisco: Ignatius Press, 2002.

———. *Introduction to Christianity*. Translated by J. R. Foster and Michael J. Miller. San Francisco: Ignatius Press, 2004.

———. *Pilgrim Fellowship of Faith: The Church as Communion*. Translated by Henry Taylor. San Francisco: Ignatius Press, 2005.

———. *The Feast of Faith: Approaches to a Theology of the Liturgy*. Translated by Graham Harrison. San Francisco: Ignatius Press, 2006.

———. *Europe: Today and Tomorrow*. Translated by Michael J. Miller. San Francisco: Ignatius Press, 2007.

———. *From the Baptism in the Jordan to the Transfiguration*. Pt. 1 of *Jesus of Nazareth*. Translated by Adrian Walker. New York: Doubleday, 2007.

———. *Homily at the Mass Pro Eligendo Romano Pontifice*. February 24, 2007.

———. "Think of Acting According to the Spirit." In *Seek That Which Is Above: Meditations through the Year*, 109–14. Translated by Graham Harrison. 2nd ed. San Francisco: Ignatius Press, 2007.

———. "The Christian and the Modern World: Reflections on the Pastoral Constitution of the Second Vatican Council." In *Dogma and Preaching: Applying Christian Doctrine to Daily Life*, edited by Michael J. Miller, 162–80. Translated by Michael J. Miller and Matthew J. O'Connell. San Francisco: Ignatius Press, 2011.

———. *Holy Week: From the Entrance into Jerusalem to the Resurrection*. Pt. 2 of *Jesus of Nazareth*. Translated by Philip J. Whitmore. San Francisco: Ignatius Press, 2011.

———. "On the Understanding of 'Person' in Theology." In *Dogma and Preaching: Applying Christian Doctrine to Daily Life*, edited by Michael J. Miller, 181–96. Translated by Michael J. Miller and Matthew J. O'Connell. San Francisco: Ignatius Press, 2011.

———. "Eastward- or Westward-Facing Position? A Correction." In *Theology of the Liturgy*, edited by Michael J. Miller, 388–95. Vol. 11 of *Collected Works: Theology of the Liturgy*. San Francisco: Ignatius Press, 2014.

———. "The Spirit of the Liturgy." In *Theology of the Liturgy*, edited by Michael J. Miller, 3–152. Vol. 11 of *Collected Works: Theology of the Liturgy*. San Francisco: Ignatius Press, 2014.

Ratzinger, Joseph, with Vittorio Messori. *The Ratzinger Report: An Exclusive Interview on the State of the Church*. Translated by Salvator Attanasio and Graham Harrison. San Francisco: Ignatius Press, 1985.

Ratzinger, Joseph, and Marcello Pera. *Without Roots: The West, Relativism, Christianity, Islam.* New York: Basic Books, 2006.

Reno, R. R. "The Return of Catholic Anti-modernism." *First Things.* June 6, 2015. https://www.firstthings.com/web-exclusives/2015/06/the-return-of-catholic-anti-modernism.

Richards, Jay W. "What Exactly Is Human Ecology?" *The Spotlight—A Monthly Digest from The Institute for Human Ecology at The Catholic University of America* (September 2017). https://ihe.catholic.edu/exactly-human-ecology/.

Ricoeur, Paul. *Interpretation Theory: Discourse and the Surplus of Meaning.* Fort Worth, Tex.: Texas Christian University Press, 1976.

Roewe, Brian. "Hymns, Teach-ins and a Horse Ride to School: Catholic Stories of the First Earth Day." *National Catholic Reporter.* April 20, 2020. https://www.ncronline.org/news/earthbeat/hymns-teach-ins-and-horse-ride-school-catholic-stories-first-earth-day.

Rosenberg, Randall S. *The Givenness of Desire: Concrete Subjectivity and the Natural Desire to See God.* Toronto: University of Toronto, 2017.

Ruddy, Christopher. "'For the Many': The Vicarious-Representative Heart of Joseph Ratzinger's Theology." *Theological Studies* 75 (September 2014): 564–84.

———. "'In My End Is My Beginning': *Lumen Gentium* and the Priority of Doxology." *Irish Theological Quarterly* 79, no. 2 (2014): 144–64.

———. "*Deus Adorans, Homo Adorans*: Joseph Ratzinger's Liturgical Christology and Anthropology." In *The Center Is Jesus Christ Himself: Essays on Revelation, Salvation, and Evangelization in Honor of Robert P. Imbelli*, edited by Andrew Meszaros, 173–88. Washington, D.C.: The Catholic University of America Press, 2021.

Rush, Ormond. *Still Interpreting Vatican II: Some Hermeneutical Principles.* New York: Paulist Press, 2004.

Ryan, Maura A. "A New Shade of Green? Nature, Freedom, and Sexual Difference in *Caritas in Veritate*." *Theological Studies* 71, no. 2 (June 2010): 335–49.

Ryan, Robert. "Pope Francis, Theology of the Body, Ecology, and Encounter." Special issue, *Journal of Moral Theology* 6, no. 1 (2017): 56–73.

Ryliškytė, Ligita. "Non-*Communio* Trinitarian Ecclesiology: Furthering Neil Ormerod's Account." *Irish Theological Quarterly* 83, no. 2 (2018): 107–27.

———. "*Cur Deus Cruciatus?*: Lonergan's Law of the Cross and The Transpositions of 'Justice over Power.'" PhD diss., Boston College, 2020.

Savino, Damien Marie. "Nature, Soil, and God: Soils and the 'Grammar of Nature.'" In *Jesus Christ: The New Face of Social Progress*, edited by Peter Casarella, 311–26. Grand Rapids, Mich.: Eerdmans, 2015.

Scannone, Juan Carlos. *La teología del pueblo: Raíces teológicas del papa Francisco.* Maliaño, Spain: Editorial Sal Terrae, 2017.

Schaefer, Jame. *Theological Foundations for Environmental Ethics: Reconstructing Patristic and Medieval Concepts.* Washington, D.C.: Georgetown University Press, 2009.

———. "Solidarity, Subsidiarity, and Preference for the Poor: Extending Catholic Social Teaching in Response to the Climate Crisis." In *Confronting the Climate Crisis: Catholic Theological Perspectives*, edited by Jame Schaefer, 389–426. Milwaukee, Wis.: Marquette University Press, 2012.

Scheid, Daniel P. "Common Good: Human, or Cosmic?" *Journal of Religion & Society Supplement* 9 (2013): 5–15.

Schepers, Maurice. "Human Development: From Below Upward and From Above Downward." *Method: Journal of Lonergan Studies* 7, no. 2 (1989): 141–44.

———. "Lonergan on the Person and the Economy: 'Reaching up to the Mind of Aquinas,' in View of Responding to Pope Leo XIII, *Vetera Novis Augere et Perficere*." *New Blackfriars* 93, no. 1043 (January 2012): 99–115.

Schillebeeckx, Edward. *Christ, the Sacrament of the Encounter with God*. New York: Sheed and Ward, 1963.

Schindler, David L. *Heart of the World, Center of the Church:* Communio *Ecclesiology, Liberalism, and Liberation*. Grand Rapids, Mich.: Eerdmans, 1996.

———. "The Anthropological Vision of *Caritas in Veritate* in Light of Economic and Cultural Life in the United States." *Communio* 37, no. 4 (Winter 2010): 558–79.

Schlesinger, Eugene R. *Missa Est! A Missional Liturgical Ecclesiology*. Minneapolis, Minn.: Fortress Press, 2017.

———. *Sacrificing the Church. Mass, Mission, and Ecumenism*. Lanham, Md.: Lexington Books, 2019.

———. "Ecological Conversion, Social Grace, and the Four-Point Hypothesis." In *Intellect, Affect, and God: The Trinity, History, and the Life of Grace*, edited by Joseph Ogbonnaya and Gerard Whelan, 19–33. Milwaukee, Wis.: Marquette University Press, 2021.

Schumacher, E. F. *Small Is Beautiful: Economics As If People Mattered*. New York: Harper & Row, 1973.

Selak, Annie. "Inheriting Climate Controversies: Reception in a Polarized Church." Presentation to the Catholic Theological Society of America. June 9, 2017.

Shute, Michael. *The Origins of Lonergan's Notion of the Dialectic of History: A Study of Lonergan's Early Writings on History*. Lanham, Md.: University Press of America, 1993.

———. "Economic Analysis within Redemptive Praxis: An Achievement of Lonergan's Third Decade." *Lonergan Workshop* 14 (1998): 243–64.

———. *Lonergan's Discovery of the Science of Economics*. Toronto: University of Toronto Press, 2010.

Silecchia, Lucia A. "Environmental Ethics from the Perspectives of NEPA and Catholic Social Teaching: Ecological Guidance for the 21st Century." *William & Mary Environmental Law and Policy Review* 28, no. 3 (2004): 659–798.

Smith, Innocent. "Liturgical Prayer and the Theology of Mercy in Thomas Aquinas and Pope Francis." *Theological Studies* 79, no. 4 (December 2018): 782–800.

Snedden, Elizabeth J. *The Eros of the Human Spirit: The Writings of Bernard Lonergan, SJ.* New York: Paulist Press, 2017.

Sobrino, Jon. "Central Position of the Reign of God in Liberation Theology." In *Mysterium Liberationis: Fundamental Concepts of Liberation Theology*, edited by Ignacio Ellacuría and Jon Sobrino, 350–88. Maryknoll, N.Y.: Orbis Books, 1993.

Society of Jesus. *Jesuit Life & Mission Today: The Decrees and Accompanying Documents of the 31st–35th General Congregations of the Society of Jesus.* Saint Louis: Institute of Jesuit Sources, 2009.

Somplatsky-Jarman, William, Walter Grazer, and Stan L. LeQuire. "Partnership for the Environment among U.S. Christians: Report from National Partnership for the Environment." In *Christianity and Ecology: Seeking the Well-Being of Earth and Humans*, edited by Dieter T. Hessel and Rosemary Radford Reuther, 573–90. Cambridge, Mass.: Harvard University Press, 2000.

Sorrell, Roger D. *St. Francis of Assisi and Nature: Tradition and Innovation in Western Christian Attitudes toward the Environment.* New York: Oxford University Press, 1988.

Spadaro, Antonio. "*Querida Amazonia*: Commentary on Pope Francis' Apostolic Exhortation." *La Civiltà Cattolica*. February 12, 2020. https://www.laciviltacattolica.com/querida-amazonia-commentary-on-pope-francis-apostolic-exhortation/.

Synod of Bishops. *Preparatory Document, Amazonia: New Paths for the Church and for an Integral Ecology.* June 8, 2018.

_____. *The Amazon: New Paths for the Church and for an Integral Ecology.* October 28, 2019.

Taylor, Mary. "Ecology on One's Knees: Reading *Laudato Si'*." *Communio* 42, no. 4 (Winter 2015): 618–51.

Theokritoff, Elizabeth. "Creation and Priesthood in Modern Orthodox Thinking." *Ecotheology* 10, no. 3 (2005): 344–63.

Thompson, Christopher J. *The Joyful Mystery: Field Notes toward a Green Thomism.* Steubenville, Ohio: Emmaus Road Publishing, 2017.

Tornielli, Andrea, and Giacomo Galeazzi. *This Economy Kills: Pope Francis on Capitalism and Social Justice.* Collegeville, Minn.: Liturgical Press, 2015.

Turkle, Sherry. *Reclaiming Conversation: The Power of Talk in a Digital Age.* New York: Penguin Press, 2015.

Turkson, Peter. *Conferenza Stampa per la presentazione della Lettera Enciclica «Laudato si'» del Santo Padre Francesco sulla cura della casa commune: Intervento del Card. Peter Kodwo Appiah Turkson.* June 18, 2015.

_____. *Address to Santa Clara University: Laudato Si' from Silicon Valley to Paris.* November 3, 2015.

_____. *Integral Ecological Conversion.* Dicastery for Promoting Integral Human Development. March 7, 2018. http://www.laudatosiinstitute.org/en/integral-ecological-conversion-cardinal-peter-kodwo-appiah-turkson/.

United Methodist-Roman Catholic Dialogue. *Heaven and Earth Are Full of Your Glory: A United Methodist and Roman Catholic Statement on the Eucharist and Ecology.* 2008.

United States Catholic Conference of Bishops. *Communities of Salt and Light: Reflections on the Social Mission of the Parish.* Washington, D.C.: United States Catholic Conference of Bishops, 1994.

_____. "*Laudato Si'* Roundtable," May 26, 2020. Video. https://www.youtube.com/watch?v=2wF4AnOn7OI.

Vallely, Paul. *Pope Francis: The Struggle for the Soul of Catholicism.* New York: Bloomsbury, 2015.

Vatican Council II. *Sacrosanctum Concilium.* December 7, 1963.

_____. *Lumen Gentium.* November 21, 1964.

_____. *Ad Gentes.* December 7, 1965.

_____. *Presbyterorum Ordinis.* December 7, 1965.

Verghese, Mathew. "American Catholicism, Sacramentality, and Care for Creation: Resources for a Local Ecological Ethic." In *American Catholicism in the 21st Century: Crossroads, Crisis, or Renewal?*, edited by Benjamin Peters and Nicholas Rademacher, 212-21. Vol. 42 of the *Annual Publication of the College Theology Society.* Maryknoll: N.Y.: Orbis Books, 2017.

Verstraeten, Johan. "Development as a Path to a Just World: Fifty Years of *Populorum Progressio* - A Critical Retrospective." *Louvain Studies* 40, no. 4 (2017): 396-409.

Voegelin, Eric. *Collected Works of Eric Voegelin,* Vol. 14 of *Israel and Revelation.* Columbia, Mo.: University of Missouri Press, 2001.

Ward, Kate. "Scotosis and Structural Inequality: The Dangers of Bias in a Globalized Age." In *Everything Is Interconnected: Towards a Globalization with a Human Face and an Integral Ecology,* edited by Joseph Ogbonnaya and Lucas Briola, 39-56. Milwaukee, Wis.: Marquette University, 2019.

Weigel, George. *Witness to Hope: The Biography of Pope John Paul II.* New York: Cliff Street Books, 2001.

_____. *The End and the Beginning: Pope John Paul II—The Victory of Freedom, the Last Years, the Legacy.* New York: Image Books, 2010.

Weil, Simone. *Gravity and Grace.* Translated by Emma Crawford and Mario von der Ruhr. New York: Routledge Classics, 2002.

Whelan, Gerard. "Culture Building in Kenya: Employing Robert Doran's Thought in Parish Work." In *Meaning and History in Systematic Theology: Essays in Honor of Robert M. Doran, SJ,* edited by John Dadosky, 487-508. Milwaukee, Wis.: Marquette University Press, 2009.

_____. *Redeeming History: Social Concern in Bernard Lonergan and Robert Doran.* Rome: Gregorian & Biblical Press, 2013.

———. "Transformations, Personal and Social, in Bernard Lonergan and Robert Doran." *The Lonergan Review* 5, no. 1 (2014): 22–38.

———. "*Evangelii Gaudium* as 'Contextual Theology': Helping the Church 'Mount to the Level of Its Times.'" *Australian eJournal of Theology* 22, no. 1 (2015): 1–10.

———. "Communitarian Solutions to the Ecological Crisis: Michael Northcott, Bernard Lonergan, and Robert Doran in Dialogue." In *Everything Is Interconnected: Towards a Globalization with a Human Face and an Integral Ecology*, edited by Joseph Ogbonnaya and Lucas Briola, 109–16. Milwaukee, Wis.: Marquette University, 2019.

———. *A Discerning Church: Pope Francis, Lonergan, and a Theological Method for the Future*. New York: Paulist Press, 2019.

Whelan, Matthew Philipp. "The Grammar of Creation: Agriculture in the Thought of Pope Benedict XVI." In *Environmental Justice and Climate Change: Assessing Pope Benedict XVI's Ecological Vision for the Catholic Church in the United States*, edited by Jame Schaefer and Tobias Winright, 103–24. Lanham, Md.: Lexington Books, 2013.

White, Lynn. "The Historical Roots of Our Ecologic Crisis." *Science* 155 (1967): 1203–7.

Wiering, Maria. "National Eucharistic Revival Aims 'to Light Fire' among the Faithful," *Our Sunday Visitor*. June 21, 2021. https://osvnews.com/2021/06/21/national-eucharistic-revival-aims-to-to-light-fire-among-the-faithful/.

Wiker, Benjamin. *In Defense of Nature: The Catholic Unity of Environmental, Economic, and Moral Ecology*. Steubenville, Ohio: Emmaus Road Publishing, 2017.

Wilber, Ken. Foreword to *Integral Medicine: A Noetic Reader*, edited by Marilyn Schlitz and Tina Hyman. Boston: Shambala Publications, 2004.

Wilkins, Jeremy D. *Before Truth: Lonergan, Aquinas, and the Problem of Wisdom*. Washington, D.C.: The Catholic University of America Press, 2018.

Winters, Michael Sean. "*Laudato Si'—Magistra No*." *National Catholic Reporter*. June 19, 2015. https://www.ncronline.org/blogs/distinctly-catholic/laudato-si-magistra-no.

Wirzba, Norman. *From Nature to Creation: A Christian Vision for Understanding and Loving Our World*. Grand Rapids, Mich.: Baker Academic, 2015.

Wojtyla, Karol. *The Acting Person*. Translated by Andrzej Potocki. Boston: D. Reidel Publishing Company, 1979.

———. *Fruitful and Responsible Love*. New York: Seabury Press, 1979.

World Synod of Bishops. *Justitia in Mundo*. 1971.

Wright, N. T. "Excursus." In *The Lost World of Adam and Eve*, by John H. Walton, 169–80. Downers Grove, Ill.: InterVarsity, 2015.

Yocum, Sandra. "Liturgy: The Exaltation of Creation." In *The Theological and Ecological Vision of* Laudato Si', edited by Vincent J. Miller, 127–44. New York: Bloomsbury T & T Clark, 2017.

Zizioulas, John D. *The Eucharistic Communion and the World*. Edited by Luke Ben Tallon. New York: Bloomsbury T & T Clark, 2011.

———. "A Comment on Pope Francis' Encyclical *Laudato Si'* by Elder Metropolitan John (Zizioulas) of Pergamon. June 18, 2015. https://www.patriarchate.org/-/a-comment-on-pope-francis-encyclical-laudato-si-.

Zwick, Mark, and Louise. *The Catholic Worker Movement: Intellectual and Spiritual Origins*. Mahwah, N.J: Paulist Press, 2005.

Index

abortion: as a concern of human ecology, 23, 39, 41, 44, 46, 52; and cultural transformation, 175n89; in *Laudato Si'*, 1–3, 70, 73–74, 77, 81, 193, 200, 203, 224, 235

Aeterni Patris, 121

Africa, 22n4, 195

agriculture, 227, 229

Amazon (region), 12, 194, 217n91, 228, 239–41. See also *Querida Amazonia*; Synod of Bishops on the Amazon Region

Amoris Laetitia, 71n37, 77, 87n121

anthropocentrism: and Benedict XVI, 53, 57–58; as critique of Christianity, 34; and John Paul II, 29; and *Laudato Si'*, 81, 83, 94, 198, 200–2, 206, 223; as mechanomorphism/general bias, 166, 187, 200–2; priestly anthropology as alternative to, 57–58, 94, 98, 213; spiritual worldliness as, 89–90; worship as freeing from, 53, 97–98. See also mechanomorphism; technocratic paradigm

Antigonish Movement, 227

Aquinas, Thomas: on the distinction between exterior and interior worship, 10–11; influence on John Paul II, 27; influence on Lonergan, 118, 121–22, 127, 155

Arrupe, Pedro, 180

attentiveness: as demanded by cries of the earth and the poor, 72, 81–82; distortion of, 129–30; and the Eucharist, 99, 216–18; as transcendental precept, 118–19, 123, 124, 139; as transformed through religious conversion, 139, 163, 168, 216–18, 220

Augustine, 33, 127

authenticity: definition of, 118–19, 162–64, 233; in history, 123–24, 162–64, 169; redemption and, 137–38, 141, 177–78, 183, 208, 220–21, 230; threats to, 135

Bacon, Francis, 81, 166

Bartholomew I, 84

Basil of Caesarea, 33

Baxter, Michael, 4n16, 14–17

Benedict XVI: and common home language, 42; on the grammar of creation, 41–43, 47–48, 55, 59, 99, 200, 210, 224, 227; on human ecology, 7–8, 40–52, 59, 69; and integral approach to care for creation, 21, 40–45, 178, 194; on liturgy, 52–59, 211–12, 221, 224, 234; on *Machbarkeit*, 47, 56, 167; on the relationship between human beings and rest of creation, 45; on solidarity/relationality, 41, 43, 45, 48–50, 55, 59, 199, 224

Benedictine monasticism, 14, 52, 100, 179

Bergoglio, Jorge. See Francis

bias: dramatic, 129–30, 218; general effect of, 130, 149–50, 164, 205, 230; group, 131–32, 134, 167, 195, 196, 198; general, 5, 132–34, 136, 137, 151, 165, 175–76, 196–206; individual, 131, 134, 198; in *Laudato Si'*, 194–206, 218; and reign of sin, 135; religious conversion as healing, 139, 141–42, 170, 181–82, 185, 219; and the technocratic paradigm, 5, 174, 176, 196–206, 222, 225, 226, 232

biocentrism, 57, 58, 84, 94, 209

biodiversity loss, 22, 44, 64, 94, 193, 226n125

body of Christ, 49, 108, 142, 170, 184, 216, 217, 226

Boff, Leonardo, 67, 71

Brueggeman, Walter, 98n168, 206–7

Caritas in Veritate, 42–44, 46–48, 56–57, 59, 227n125, 233n154

Cavanaugh, William, 3n14, 16n47, 89n129, 226n124, 228n131

Centesimus Annus, 25–26, 30, 32, 34, 35, 36, 38, 42, 44, 45, 194n11

Christ: and Catholic social theory, 15n41, 17, 107, 111, 136; and the church, 89, 108, 142–43, 170–71, 183, 184, 216, 217; conversion to, 6; cosmic dimensions of, 33, 35, 37, 55, 208–9, 211–12, 216, 217, 237, 240, 241; eucharistic presence of, 35, 55, 96, 108, 181–84, 209–12, 217, 240, 241; incorporation into, 6, 49, 56, 59n151, 139–41, 169, 184–85, 209–15, 217–20; and mercy of God, 78, 96, 216; priesthood of, 33, 35, 37, 182, 186, 208–9, 211, 215, 237, 241; pro-existence of, 49; and religious conversion, 139–42, 181–84, 209–12; repentance of, 217–20; restoration of all things in, 110, 136. See also body of Christ; Law of the Cross; redemption (vector)

Christifideles Laici, 24

Christus Vivit, 77n63, 86n116

classical inquiry and laws, 114–16, 118, 119n58. See also statistical inquiry and laws

Coakley, Paul, 2

coincidental manifold, 116–17, 118, 157

273

common good, 68, 131, 165, 195, 199, 225n119, 226
common-sense knowing, 108, 123, 130, 132, 134, 150, 156. See also practical intelligence
Comte, Auguste, 75
contraception, 39, 44
conversion: ecological, 1, 6, 13n32, 27, 220, 222n109; integral, 8, 10, 22, 59, 153, 202, 204, 222n109, 233, 237; intellectual, 139n158; moral, 139n158; psychic, 163–64, 167, 168, 218; religious, 138–43, 147, 149, 150, 167–68, 180–86, 207–8, 217–18
Corpus Christi, Feast of, 95n158, 212, 241
cosmopolis, 136–37, 205
COVID-19, 12, 241
creating, 9, 149–50, 160–64, 167, 170, 176, 230–34. See also progress (vector)
creative minority, 13, 170
creatureliness: Eucharist and embracing, 212–15, 219, 222, 226–27; sin as rejection of, 47, 202
cry: of the earth, 72, 102, 193; of the poor, 71, 73, 172–74, 186; of the poor and the earth together, 72, 82, 93, 173, 192–94
culture: of care, 221–25; of encounter, 78–79, 83, 87, 97, 223
Czerny, Michael, 241

Dawson, Christopher, 126
Day, Dorothy, 205n43, 220, 235
decision (level): and choosing the good, 145–46; meaning of, 118–19; transformation of, 148, 205, 208–12
decline (vector) : Doran on, 164–68, 172, 175, 186; in *Laudato Si'*, 10, 72, 151, 156, 192–206, 217, 221; Lonergan on, 9–10, 122–23, 128–37, 150–51, 220; the longer cycle of, 132, 136, 137, 165, 175, 176. See also bias; mechanomorphism; technocratic paradigm
De Lubac, Henri, 27n29, 49n124, 65–66, 89, 90
Descartes, René, 166
description, 12, 107–8, 123, 172, 191–92. See also explanation
determinism: emergent probability as alternative to, 113, 115, 120; evolutionary, 57; redemption as surmounting, 141–42, 220–21; in the technocratic paradigm, 86, 197, 204
Deus Caritas Est, 58n148, 78n69
development: from above and below, 148–50, 208; category of, 24, 26, 42–45, 66–67, 70, 72, 92, 177–78; integral human, 44, 45, 66, 70, 92, 177, 178; problem of, 126, 128, 129, 144, 148, 167, 176

dialectic: of contraries, 161; of community, 161, 164, 165, 166n54, 174; of culture, 165–66
dialogue, 28, 49, 75, 84, 92–93, 230–34
Dies Domini, 36, 218n96
Dominum et Vivificantem, 35n65
Doran, Robert: ecclesiology of, 170, 171–78; environmental concern of, 157, 160; on Eucharist/doxology, 179–86; and *Laudato Si'*, 161, 163, 165, 166–67, 172–73, 177, 178, 187–88; in relationship to Bernard Lonergan, 156–60; and theology of history, 159–71
doxological ecclesiology, 15
doxology: Benedict XVI on, 52–59; biblical descriptions of, 32–33; in connection to the Eucharist, 10–11, 91, 182–83, 207; and the church, 15, 89–91; integral, 17; as integrating, 7, 8, 33; John Paul II on, 34–38; in *Laudato Si'*, 91–100, 212–13; and the scale of values, 9, 178–86; theological descriptions of, 33–34
dramatic artistry, 129, 163–64, 182, 210

Ecclesia de Eucharistia, 37, 39, 95n158, 221n105
Ecclesia in Oceania, 36n70
economic ecology, 226–29
Elizondo, Virgil, 67
emergent probability, 113–21, 124, 135. See also schemes of recurrence; sublation
environmental refugees, 44, 134, 193
eschatology, 49–50, 95, 142, 210n62
Eucharist: cosmic dimensions of, 35–37, 53–59, 91–100, 207–17; culture of , 221–25; definition of, 11; as integrating, 8, 37–38, 55, 58, 61, 92–96, 221–24, 234–35; in *Laudato Si'*, 91–100, 207–30; as marker of Catholic identity, 5–6; and politics, 15, 225–26; and the scale of values, 9, 178–86; and the social mission of the church, 5, 14–17, 180
Eucharistic Revival, 241
Evangelii Gaudium, 66, 67n17, 70nn32–33, 71n37, 74n54, 76n61, 77nn62–63, 77n65, 78nn69–70, 79n73, 79nn76–78, 82n96, 89, 97nn162–63, 103nn180–81, 198n22, 224n116
Evangelii Nuntiandi, 67n17, 67n20, 92n140
Evangelium Vitae, 26–27
experience (level): distortion of, 129–30; meaning of, 118–19, 123, 163; redemption of, 137, 140, 148–49, 184, 216–17; in relationship to description, 107. See also attentiveness

Fessard, Gaston, 65, 90n134
finality, 116–18, 120, 183n125, 210n62, 211

INDEX

Francis: and encounter, 78–79, 83, 87, 97; on the Eucharist, 89–91, 96–100; and idolatry, 89–90, 238; Ignatian influences on, 78, 82, 89–90; and integral ecology, 65–100; intellectual influences on, 74–76, 80; and language of care, 82–83; and liberation theology, 71–72, 174, 202; on mercy, 77–78, 82, 88; and polarity, 65–66; and polarization, 13–14, 69–71; in relationship to John Paul II and Benedict XVI, 7–8, 21, 63–64, 237; on spiritual worldliness, 89, 90, 93, 102–3, 203; on the technocratic paradigm, 80–82, 86–88, 196–206; on throwaway culture, 77, 79, 81, 200

Francis of Assisi: and cosmic doxology, 33, 34; role in *Laudato Si'* of, 63, 68, 72, 79–80, 91, 94; stigmata of, 219

Frankfurt School, 133

Fratelli Tutti, 79n74, 234n157

Gaudete et Exsultate, 77n65, 87n122, 103n182, 103n183

Genesis, Book of, 44, 53, 85, 162, 201–2, 209

Gnosticism, 77, 79

good of order, 125–27, 131, 144–47, 161, 164. *See also* dialectic; values

good of value, 125–26, 127, 132, 145, 147, 162, 167. *See also* cultural role in healing of values; dialectic

Green Party of Germany, 41, 44

Guardini, Romano, 66, 80, 86, 97, 133, 220–21

healing, 148–51, 167–68, 173–78, 185, 206–30, 232–33. *See also* redemption (vector)

Holy Spirit, 140, 168, 217

Hopkins, Gerard Manley, 99

human ecology: Benedict XVI on, 7, 21, 40–52; definition of, 26; John Paul II on, 7, 21, 25–32; *Laudato Si'* on, 64, 69, 70, 71, 73, 200, 221–25; limitations of, 7, 30–32, 38–39, 45–52; in relationship to natural ecology, 7, 27–32, 45–52, 194, 200, 206, 221–25

idolatry: Benedict XVI on, 47, 48; *Laudato Si'* and, 90, 100, 201–3, 206, 213, 229–30, 238; spiritual worldliness and, 89–90, 100

inauthenticity, 134–35, 139, 164, 184

indifference, globalization of, 76, 77, 78, 80, 81, 97, 198

Institute for Human Ecology, The, 51–52

integral ecology: liberationist background of, 67, 71; scientific background of, 67–68; as seminal locution, 65; in relationship to the Eucharist, 8, 12, 89–100, 207–42; in relationship to human and natural ecologies, 8, 65–74, 206, 221–25; role in *Laudato Si'*, 1, 6–7, 11, 64–88

integral scale of values, 161, 164, 169–70, 177, 179, 185–87, 219. *See also* scale of values

intrinsic value of creation, 29–30, 38, 81, 84, 94, 99, 103, 193

invariant structure of the common good, 145–47

Irwin, Kevin, 7n22, 12n31, 21n2, 26, 55, 61n153, 63, 65, 68n28, 70, 101n178, 214n98

Isaac the Syrian, 88n124

Isaiah, Book of, 32

John of the Cross, 33, 34

John Paul II: on cultures of life and death, 26, 28–29, 31, 97, 175n89; on the Eucharist, 35–40, 221, 234; and human ecology, 7–8, 25–27, 29–32, 38–39, 69, 193, 194, 223; and an integral approach to care for creation, 21–27, 178, 194; personalism of, 27–29, 119, 220; on the praise of creation, 34–35, 37; on the relationship between human beings and the rest of creation, 29, 45, 82; on the sacramentality of creation, 34–35

judgment (level): meaning of, 118–19, 123; redemption of, 212–15, 217

Justitia in Mundo, 157–58

labor, 29, 67, 70, 80, 100, 125, 229–30

Laborem Exercens, 29

Laudato Si': on abortion, 1, 3, 70, 73, 74, 77, 193, 200, 203, 224, 235; and Benedict XVI, 21, 61, 63, 74, 84, 94, 95, 96, 99, 237, 240; and the cries of the earth and poor, 71–73, 81–82, 86–88, 99–100, 192–94; ecclesiology of, 101–2; and the Eucharist, 1, 12, 91–104, 206–35; and human ecology, 64, 69, 70, 71, 73, 200, 221–25; and integral ecology, 6–7, 11, 64–88; and John Paul II, 21, 61, 63, 74, 85, 95, 96, 237, 240; language of care in, 82–83, 85–86; and overcoming polarization, 13–14, 70–71, 92–93, 221–35, 235; priestly anthropology in, 94–95, 98, 208–12; reception of, 1–2, 15, 88, 93, 101, 102, 104, 237–42; sabbath in, 99–100, 216–17; sacramentality in, 98–99, 103, 213–15; the technocratic paradigm in, 5, 80–83, 86–88, 196–206

Laudato Si' Communities, 238

Law of the Cross, 140–42, 149, 170–71, 182–85, 217–21, 233–34. *See also* Christ

Leo XIII, 121–22

liberation theology, 47, 67, 71, 76, 151, 171–74, 186–87

limitation, 161; in dialectic of community, 161, 165, 174, 195–96; in dialectic of culture, 162, 199, 200 in dialectic of person, 129, 163–64, 167, 174, 183, 187, 209–10. *See also* transcendence
liturgy. *See* doxology; Eucharist
lobbying, 3–4, 177
Lonergan, Bernard: and Aquinas, 121–22, 127, 149, 155, 186; and Catholic social teaching, 8, 111–13, 144, 151; ecclesiology of, 143–44, 178–79; economic work of, 112, 150, 227; emergent probability in, 9, 113–21, 135; on healing and creating, 9, 148–51, 160, 232–34; on human knowing, 109, 118–19, 127, 148; incomplete aspects of, 9, 108, 143–44, 147, 151–53; and theology of history, 4, 8, 17, 108–13; and *Laudato Si'*, 4–5, 10, 13–18, 104, 109, 113, 119, 134, 151, 152–53, 191–92, 234–35; on the liturgy, 8, 9, 13, 178–86; and modernity, 121–22, 128; open-ended character of, 152–53, 159; and overcoming polarization, 13–14, 109; on praxis, 151; on redemption, 135–44, 206–21; on the scale of values, 145–47, 160; on technocracy, 133–34, 196–202
Lonerganism, 152
Lumen Fidei, 90
Lumen Gentium, 5n18, 11n26

Marxism, 47, 71, 75–76, 110–12, 136, 150, 174–76, 202
mechanomorphism, 166–67, 187, 200, 209, 219
Methol Ferré, Alberto, 74–77, 80, 86, 88, 133
Metz, Johann Baptist, 171
Michel, Virgil, 14–15, 179
Monod, Jacques, 99
moral impotence, 135, 136, 137, 141, 167, 205
mystery, 128, 138, 142, 183–84

nature-deficit disorder, 166
neoliberalism, 75, 200, 226
Newman, John Henry, 127, 138
Newton, Isaac, 123
Nietzsche, Friedrich, 75

offertory, 214, 241
option for the earth, 10, 72, 173, 188, 192, 193, 194. *See also* cry
option for the poor, 72n47, 171–73, 187, 192, 226. *See also* cry
ora et labora, 52, 64, 100, 103, 104, 229, 240
Orientale Lumen, 35–36
Ormerod, Neil, 4, 11n27, 13nn32–33, 114n33, 122n71, 135n132, 170n69, 177n96, 180n108, 192n5, 220n100

particular goods, 124–25, 127, 131, 145, 147, 161, 164. *See also* values
Pascal, Blaise, 149
Pastores Gregis, 27
Paul VI, 66–68, 70, 77n63, 92, 177, 178
Pelagianism, 77, 79
Pieper, Josef, 213
Pius XI, 111, 136
Placuit Deo, 77n65
polarization: in the church, 3–6, 13, 16; and human ecology, 51–52, 60; and *Laudato Si'*, 3–6, 70, 92–93, 101, 223, 231, 235, 240; and spiritual worldliness, 203–4
Populorum Progressio, 66–67, 70, 92
positivism, 75, 99, 133, 165, 198, 201, 239. *See also* technocratic paradigm
practical intelligence: in dialectic of community, 125, 161; distortion of, 131, 165, 174–75, 195, 197, 203–4; redemption of, 169, 226, 228–29. *See also* common-sense knowing; dialectic: of community; spontaneous intersubjectivity
praise. *See* doxology
prayers of the faithful, 218
preparation of the gifts, 56, 211–12
priestly anthropology: in Benedict XVI, 54, 55, 57–58, 61; in *Laudato Si'*, 94–95, 98, 100, 103, 188, 208–12, 237
problem of evil, 109, 136, 138
progress (vector): Doran on, 9, 161–64; in *Laudato Si'*, 230–34; Lonergan on, 9, 123–27, 149–51. *See also* creating
Psalms, Book of, 32, 57, 93, 211

Quadragesimo Anno, 111
Querida Amazona, 12n29, 194n10, 239–40. *See also* Amazon (region); Synod of Bishops on the Amazon Region

racism, 131, 175n89, 219n99
Rahner, Karl, 171
Ratzinger, Joseph. *See* Benedict XVI
reception: of human ecology, 45, 46, 59–61; of *Laudato Si'*, 1–5, 7, 13, 15, 88, 93, 101–2, 223, 237–42
redemption (vector), 9, 135–43, 147, 149–51, 167–71, 177–86, 206–30. *See also* healing; Law of the Cross; social grace
Redemptor Hominis, 23, 28, 29n38
relativism, 40–41, 44, 76, 81, 97, 198–200
religious values, 146–47, 164, 167–71, 175–78, 185, 201–8, 233. *See also* Law of the Cross; redemption (vector); conversion: religious; scale of values; social grace

INDEX

Revelation, Book of, 32–33

sabbath, 36, 39, 53, 99–100, 208, 216
sacramentality: in Benedict XVI, 53–54, 56, 57, 59; in John Paul II, 34–36, 38; in *Laudato Si'*, 98–100, 103, 208, 212, 214–15, 217, 219, 222
Sacramentum Caritatis, 55–59, 211–12, 221n105
Sacrosanctum Concilium, 211n67
scale of values: 146–47, 161–62; Doran on, 9, 156, 160–78; and doxology, 9, 178–86; and the Eucharist, 13, 18, 178–86; and *Laudato Si'*, 4–5, 8, 10, 12, 16, 187, 192–230; Lonergan on, 9, 11, 145–47; personal values and, 146–47, 162–63. *See also* integral scale of values; values
schemes of recurrence: definition of, 115–17; as functioning in scale of values, 161, 168, 172; as natural, 116, 163, 193–94, 199, 227–28; as social, 119–21, 130, 172, 227–28
Schumacher, E. F., 227n126
scotosis, 129, 169, 198, 218, 229
self-transcendence, 118, 131, 135, 139, 141, 146–47, 158, 163, 180–82, 201, 205, 216
sin: as ecological, 29, 44, 85, 218; as original, 135n132; as personal, 44, 47, 122, 131, 134–35, 137, 139, 140, 142, 167n356, 182, 202, 217; reign of, 122, 135, 141, 142; as structural, 128, 135, 140–42, 160, 182, 202, 217. *See also* idolatry
social grace, 9, 160, 170, 171, 172, 178, 185, 218. *See also* redemption (vector); soteriological culture
Sollicitudo Rei Socialis, 24, 29n38, 91
soteriological culture, 169, 176, 178, 186, 222. *See also* values: cultural role in healing of; redemption (vector); social grace
Spe Salvi, 48n114, 49n124
Spiritual Exercises, The, 82, 90, 181n114
spontaneous intersubjectivity: in dialectic of community, 124–25, 161–62, 164; distortion of, 131, 165, 174, 195, 199; redemption of, 169, 226, 228–29. *See also* dialectic: of community; practical intelligence
statistical inquiry and laws, 114–16, 118, 119n58. *See also* classical inquiry and laws
sublation, 117, 120, 124, 137, 147–48, 161, 223–24, 232. *See also* emergent probability
suffering servant, 171, 232n150
symbol, 126, 138, 183–84, 211
Synod of Bishops on the Amazon Region, 12, 217n91, 239–40

technocratic paradigm: Doran and, 165, 167, 174, 177, 187, 196–206; ironclad logic of, 86–88, 97, 202–6, 222, 239; *Laudato Si'* on, 5, 80–83, 86–88, 196–206, 209, 219, 220–23; Lonergan and, 5, 134, 187, 196–206, 232. *See also* bias: general; positivism
teología del pueblo, 71, 75, 174, 202
theological virtues, 137–38, 142
Thérèse of Lisieux, 220, 228
throwaway culture, 77, 79, 81, 87, 134, 200, 222, 223
transcendence, 161; in dialectic of person, 118, 129, 162–63, 164, 167, 174, 183n127, 209–10; in dialectic of community, 161, 165, 195–96; in dialectic of culture, 162, 165, 166n54. *See also* limitation; self-transcendence
Trinity, 49, 83, 140n161, 159, 168, 179, 182, 184, 185, 207
Turkson, Peter, 64–65, 72n45, 82, 85n109, 91

understanding (level): meaning of, 118–19, 123, 129–30, 163; transformation of, 148–49, 181, 208, 215–17
universal willingness, 135, 137, 138, 139, 169, 183, 205

values: anthropological, 162, 166, 169; cosmological, 162, 165, 166, 169, 187, 199, 227; cultural role in healing of, 173–77; distortion of, 165, 167, 172, 174, 176, 192–206; elemental, 193–94, 195, 199, 208, 210, 223, 227; redemption of, 169, 177–78, 186, 208–21, 225–30. *See also* good of value; religious values; scale of values; soteriological culture

Vatican II, 5, 18, 101n178, 111–12, 180, 211n67
Veritatis Gaudium, 69n30
Veritatis Splendor, 32
Voegelin, Eric, 162

Weil, Simone, 216
White, Lynn, 34n58
Wojtyla, Karol. *See* John Paul II
wonder, 34, 35, 36, 38, 57, 118, 127, 148, 152, 238
World Day of Peace messages: of 1990, 24–25, 29, 30n41, 34, 38, 41; of 2007, 41–42, 43, 46; of 2008, 42, 68n28; of 2010, 44–45, 57
World Day of Prayer for the Care of Creation, 88

Zizioulas, John, 35n64, 95

www.ingramcontent.com/pod-product-compliance
Lightning Source LLC
Chambersburg PA
CBHW070249010526
44107CB00056B/2396